GREENIE'S PATH

GREENIE'S PATH

The Search for Christopher Hiltaychuk

GREENIE

iUniverse, Inc.
Bloomington

GREENIE'S PATH
THE SEARCH FOR CHRISTOPHER HILTAYCHUK

iUniverse books may be ordered through booksellers or by contacting:

iUniverse
1663 Liberty Drive
Bloomington, IN 47403
www.iuniverse.com
1-800-Authors (1-800-288-4677)

ISBN: 978-1-4620-4982-0 (sc)
ISBN: 978-1-4620-4983-7 (hc)
ISBN: 978-1-4620-4984-4 (ebk)

Library of Congress Control Number: 2011915128

Printed in the United States of America

iUniverse rev. date: 10/10/2011

TABLE OF CONTENTS

EXIT ONE

Life's Road Under Construction

Someone had once said to me, "Greenie, Why don't you write a book?" Actually, many people in my life said that to me, which made it desirable for me to do, and till now had been only a thought in the back of my mind as a possible activity for later in life. I have written all of my life's little lessons, packaging them like some psychoanalytic portfolio, for all to see just how different, odd and unique life can actually be from one individual's viewpoint. I've only been told by others after hearing some of my stories that it would be interesting enough to share with others, though I never saw it that way, and didn't believe my life to be any more interesting than the average person's.

All my source material will be mostly from memory as one person retains such events throughout the course of one's life, with all the relative events provability left to those interested enough to actually read this. Obviously, events and details will be missed, due to the effect time passing has upon one's memory, but I will attempt to capture all I can in these pages of all the paths I took, and the roads I traveled.

I will recall all my feelings, thoughts, actions and reactions at certain times, while describing some situations and people that I found interesting, unusual, or that I believe had some impact on my life, or events I shared with others that they believed were worthy of being retold. I felt the need to convey these events in the only way I know how, by writing it all down in my own personal unique style.

This story may not be remarkable, easy to follow, special or coherent, it may seem dull to some, unbelievable to others, perhaps spell binding or incredible to even more. I was adopted, and I am not rich or famous, but since no one knows where I really came from, I figured someone some day would be interested in discovering the events in the life or fate of a son, brother, uncle, or a grandson, they never knew, never met, but are genetically related to. I will also offer many of my personal opinions, sarcasm and bias, which many people may or may not agree with or like, but they're only my opinions and thus part of my personality, viewpoint, and my life. All the events taking place are within the nineteen sixties through nineteen eighty six time frame.

There is no secret to one's past, we all come from a similar place and the actions we all take and decisions we make are the changes and the turns in the road that guide and direct us towards the ultimate final unknown. How our life begins is a common factor, but once it has begun, there is no predicting, as far as we know realistically, what the course will be or where the road will lead us. Certainly, how, where or when it will end is the greatest mystery of all, and though none of us can fathom the end as part of reality, the knowledge in the back of our minds that all life does end eventually drives us to pursue the things we believe to be important to our existence, things to pass along to other generations, trying to make our knowledge we accumulate span the life time we have lived, in an effort to improve upon what we ourselves accomplished, experienced or began to accomplish.

I believe this life to be just one step towards another type of existence, and the basis or gage as to where we will wind up in that existence. Reincarnation into another life form, animal, tree, aquatic life form, micro organism or other form doesn't seem all that unlikely. Heaven or hell don't sound unrealistic, either, but I do not believe any one persons theory, belief or hypothesis to be more correct or believable than another's, the only true given is that the answer does lie within all of us and we will all find out one day, whether we want to or not.

My only goal is not to be too shocked with the answer if possible, and hope that the next path of existence is sequentially improved as my life force grows through experience, and not the other way around, to simply dissipate into non-awareness, non-existence, or sheer nothingness.

My own genetic past is, to date, the greatest mystery I've come across, just because it's mine. Somewhere in the mid-west, a man and woman mate around the time known as Thanksgiving in the year 1960, thus producing, nine months later, another of our species, procreating as instinct directs, as love intends, and as passion dictates.

All I can ascertain from the information I had access to is that a week before my birth on July 15, 1961, a girl from the Mid-west came to New York City, carrying a live package and delivering him to a nice, pre-determined, upper middle class family in New Jersey. Then this girl, named Hiltaychuk, who was nice enough to relay the message that she thought the child's name should be David, disappeared forever. I was born at 6:55 pm, and weighed eight pounds one ounce.

Here is the verbatim letter she wrote my mother the day she gave me up: "Mr. & Mrs. Green, there are a few things I'd like you to know, if I didn't mention it to you before. I want to thank you for helping me out, for if you hadn't I would had to tell my father and hurt him terribly. I know that David will have both parents, instead of only one, as it would have been if I made Gordon marry me just for David's sake, for I know it would have ended in divorce, for I'd never would have been able to trust him. When David gets older, I hope he'll understand that I wanted him to have the things I never had. For my parents are divorced and I found it very hard living with only one parent at a time. Also I think he'll find out that it is very hard for any mother to give up her child for a mother's love is the deepest kind. I pray he won't hate me. Gordon is Dutch and Irish. He's six-two and weighs two hundred forty, and David is the picture of him, so you'll have a big boy on your hands. I'm

3

Ukrainian and nothing else. You know what I look like. If you ever find cause to reach me, Dr. Milar had my address. I pray to god that I've done the right thing. God bless my son always for me. David's mother." So I knew my biological father's name was Gordon, but that's all.

Adoption is a great institution. After all, why shouldn't one have the choice of raising a child, or letting someone else do it? Our young are usually not wasted intentionally, there are many, many caring people and institutions designed to find parents for parent-less children. It's a blessing to those who want more children, and is a good thing in general, I believe. In my case, somehow pre-arranged a week or so before delivery, the inability of the adopting mother to bear anymore offspring, due to medical reasons was the reason they chose adoption. But mine is a bloodline that begins on that summer day of nineteen sixty one.

Though the history of the people who parented me could be considered relative, there is no genetic reference point for any children or grand children I may have, or any of the next generations to come besides my future wife's side for reference, thus coming from pure obscurity brings many unknown factors into the future for all my descendants, yet to be born.

The one thing I desire to know about the biological contributors to my life is what conditions and diseases they have passed so anonymously to me, so I could prepare for what I or my offspring may face. Naturally, believing I'm related to many unknown people, some of who could be significant to this world, whether it be for infamy or heroism, can be interesting, but I don't dwell upon it, nor did I base any life decisions on it consciously. I have the luxury of having a blood line genetic history and the history of the family who chose to raise me, one known, and one completely unknown.

The parents I was given were a definite blessing, as whoever reads this will discover, and as whoever previously knew them already know. My parents often thought that the fact I discovered early that I was adopted influenced or affected me negatively, but I was more pleased to be chosen from all the possible children, and felt saved from situations that could have been much worse. I believed I made out very well, once I was old enough to realize the negative possibilities.

We lived in the hills of New Jersey, along the first range of mountains from the coast line known as the Watchung Mountains, and here is where my life began its journey. I will document my past, beginning with my earliest recollections as the logical way to begin. I guess it's feasible to say I could recall my fetal state of breathing liquid and total darkness, if it were not so improbable to actually do. Through some imagination mixed with various visual assistance from media, TV and technology, it's indeed possible to think you can imagine what life in the womb was like. But in all honesty, this being a little too imaginative or fabricated sounding, I can say that I do recall a period early in life where my primary senses were not developed enough to distinguish between consciousness and sleep.

The two appeared the same, and when I felt the current situation was too scary, undesirable or stressful, in either reality, I was able to return to the other most of the time, like an escape route. I was able to choose between one world with apparently no boundaries, and nothing made sense for the most part, and another full of senses, solidness, and sensations, yet still senseless and confusing most of the time. I was told I was a happy, healthy baby and not very untypical as far as babies go, but my next memory I would have to call unique, and have never found any reference point or similar symptom in all the years of my subsequent life.

At around two or three years of age I began to have a sensation that was not that of a pleasant nature after some time. An intense tickle sensation seemed to begin around one or two inches above my left ear and as its intensity grew, it traveled from that point to begin again half way down the middle of the left side of my back. And if I did nothing about it, the sensation would continue to the back of my hip, and travel down my thigh to my leg, till I could stand it no more. The odd thing about it was that this "tickle" sensation did not appear anywhere between the point on my scalp, and my lower back, no shoulder, neck, or upper back, and I recall nothing that would have created this condition.

The occurrence of this annoying sensation only manifested itself when I was attempting to go to sleep, or if I had fallen asleep without preparing for it and a dream would seem to activate it. Initially, I would just be woken with the sensation along my whole side and head, as the result of the end of a dream where my mother just comes into my room and just reaches into my crib, nothing scary really.

From this point on and for the rest of my life so far, I literally have to position myself sleeping exactly the same way every night, or no sleep would be possible. I had to sleep on my left side, with the position of my head exactly so that no hair on this cranial "spot" was pointing in any direction but down my head, as if I were standing up, with my head leaning up against a soft wall, holding each hair in place and preventing those hairs from moving and causing the "tickle" to return.

I recall through the years many times having to literally pound this side of my head with my hand, grabbing handfuls of hair and trying to rip them off my head, or scratching at it with all possible force to no avail, like an itch on your chin after the dentist had injected you with the Novocain, which is impossible to scratch because you can't feel your chin, but you can feel the annoying itch.

When I was very young, my mother would come in because I'd be crying about this in the middle of the night, and I would feel afraid that she was going to tickle me again, not knowing if she was real or a dream character, if I was dreaming or conscious, during those first few confusing seconds after waking. Of course I could not convey this experience to her, not having the words to describe it yet, so I would only say I had a bad dream and my head tickled, or something similar, which never made sense to her.

Needless to say, this condition made bedtime less than pleasurable for all involved. I can recall my mother playing the game of round and round the ballie, where the ballie is actually the palm of your hand, which is where an index finger in a circular motion goes around the baby's palm. This is followed by the phrase: "pull the baby's hair", which is self-explanatory. Then the rhyme goes:

"one chop, two chop, tickle under there!" The one chop is a light karate type chop to the forearm, the second in the biceps area, and the "tickle" would usually be in the armpit. This makes the usual child of two or three squeal in joy, laughing hysterically at such a game, and adoring the attention it brings.

I found it equally pleasing to be done to me, until I tried to go to bed, and then the sensation would become part of a dream. In the dream the "tickle" would no longer be in my armpit, but on the usual side of my body, and as I awoke sweating, I would notice that I had rolled away from my familiar position of the fetal type, allowing that tickle to become agitated, thus having that sensation at its peak, unable to combat it by any means since I wasn't conscious. It was my mothers' image in the first dreams I recall, appearing as playful and normal as if I were not sleeping at all. As I grew and my imagination expanded, the dreams became more involved, more complex, but always with the same annoying and unbearable results.

I vividly recall one dream, where I would be in my room, and I thought that I woke up, but my mother wouldn't answer my non-urgent, low volume calls of "Mommy . . . ? Mommy . . . ?" Now, I was not a cowardly sort most of the time as a toddler, so I would get up, and go seek my mother even though it was dark, a small night light around a corner of the hall being the only illumination. I lived in a five level house, with a large furnished attic, down ten steps to the bedroom level of three bedrooms, down five more steps to the living room, front door, porch and kitchen level, down eight more steps to the den and garage level, and down eight more to the largest basement you would ever want to see. There was always plenty of space in this house for a toddler to wander endlessly without ever leaving home.

In this particular dream I would hear noise coming from the den level, and I would go to investigate if it was my mother or not, feeling nearly paralyzed by fear as I walk through the dark house for reasons I could not explain or understand. The noise would always turn out to be a scratching sound, growing as I approach the open basement door, and I remember thinking how strange it was for the door to be open, the door was usually shut.

As I would get within ten feet or so, if you can estimate length in a dream, an alligator looking person would come around the corner, not quickly, more deliberately, as though it was perched on the last top basement step awaiting my arrival. Sometimes it was a black cloaked faceless stranger, or even my mom or dad would be the image, appearing scarily with odd looks on their faces and ignoring any question I asked, being totally silent, as if they're not really my parents, and the image would come up from the basement steps every time, with me too close to the door to get a good head start on the dream-like slow motion running away.

I remember thinking to myself each time it happened, right before I would begin that futile dream type running from the image, how odd it was for the basement door to be open. Then I would get tickled before being able to wake myself. There was no image of hands actually tickling me, just a heightened sensation when a dream character got close to my proximity, at which point I would close my eyes and blink hard in an attempt to wake up. Since my eyes were closed, I wouldn't see what the character was doing at the moment, and didn't care since I knew it wasn't real; I just wanted consciousness to take over. There was no actual sense of being touched, no eerie contact of any kind.

Of course, I would awake, only to discover that the tickling had once again reached its peak, and my position on the bed had changed. I would immediately call my mother with familiar words to any parent, "mommy, I had a bad dream!" But what I did not explain, due to not knowing how to, was the factor of physical discomfort, which no fear of any monster, getting hurt or even dying could ever compare to. I was more afraid of feeling the tickle than of anything this earth could manifest.

Naturally, my mom would tell me: "nothing's going to hurt you, don't worry! Your ok, you're in bed, nothing's here but you and me!" This was confusing to me, since being hurt would be welcome relief, but all I could do was mention something about my head and back feeling funny, as I would rub my head in an effort to stop the feeling. So, this dream, along with other new and repetitive ones, continued for many years.

At about four years of age and after a year or so of dreading and analyzing these nightmares in my own mind, I found myself suddenly able to change my first memorable repetitive dream, becoming completely aware of the fact that I was dreaming while the dream was in progress. I knew what came next, finally. So instead of going down the stairs to the den and going towards the basement door on the far side of the room, I was able to remember that the basement door was only open in my dream, and I remembered that fact before actually moving towards it, and this time I decided to change my usual path.

I went right through the den out the garage door and outside before the 'thing' even turned the corner. Once the scratch got louder, as it always did right before the image would appear, I moved in the opposite direction. I would find enough satisfaction with this maneuver to look back upon my house and laugh out loud, causing me to wake up possibly the easiest and happiest I had ever woke in my short life.

While I was still within the dream, I thought to myself, standing there in the driveway laughing, out of sequence to the usual events, how unfinished and odd this is, and it felt like I was living some book. A book where the next page had been ripped out and I was in the void of open thought, traveling within my brain with familiar images, I remember how peaceful and calm the driveway was, as I looked around at neighbors' houses and into the garage.

I wondered if the image would follow me out side. It would have been much scarier if the surroundings were not so familiar, and I did debate going back in the house, but I didn't. Then I realized, after getting myself to wake up, that in this night's sleep, I hadn't moved one muscle, and I beat the tickle at last. That particular dream never returned after that night, so far.

I eventually discovered, by age five or six, that I could change any dream if it was repetitive enough for me to remember it while in progress. In one such particular dream, I'd be on a beach, and the catalyst figure would just be standing there, mere yards away from me. Since there was no way to change anything but my direction of running, I discovered that running did not need to be slow motion, if you believe you can run full speed.

I had tried going towards the water, but as soon as my foot is about to be wet, the dream stops and starts right over again from the beginning. I remember thinking at the moment this dream began, there must be a way, to change it enough to end it, and that I know I'm fast enough in reality, what's stopping my acceleration? Then I knew just by asking the question, nothing would stop it. I can only stop myself, and the next time I had the dream was the last time ever.

I had reached the point where I could out run any figure I was afraid of, and once I did that in the beach dream, it never came back. I simply started running as usual, and I felt myself moving more intensely and quicker, somewhat easier, as though I was breaking through the invisible barrier that acts like a speed governor for dreams. I attained full speed half way to the snack bar, in an effort to reach my mom who I could see; she was just sitting there at the snack bar looking at me with no expression at all.

As I glanced back when I got closer to her, I noticed the 'monster' didn't even give chase. I also noticed that when you're running in a dream the destination can appear to be moving away at the same rate as your approach, which is quite annoying. This was overcome as well in the same dream, just by disbelieving the destination to be unreachable, and knowing you're in control of your own mind, the destination was getting closer and not in normal fashion, it felt like I was gliding across the sand that wasn't even hot, and then I was there, it was over, and before my mom could say a single word, I woke up.

I became more in control of my subconscious than most adults ever achieve, out of sheer necessity, and I began to enjoy and manipulate the control I had found. Some nights I did not suffer the tickle, which was extremely rare and would occur only because I remained totally motionless and awoke in the same position I had fallen asleep in the night before. This stationary positioning becomes uncomfortable after a while to one's shoulder, legs, and other parts of the body, always using the same position, but that discomfort was well worth the effort to me.

My main goal as a toddler was to become conscious enough to control my actions in dreams since this seemed to prevent the tickle from getting very intense or occurring at all. But there were times that even if I did change the dream, the tickle came anyway, out of nowhere, regardless of my minds attempt to give image and purpose to the cause, just while standing still with no creatures in sight.

I would awake my usual way to find I had changed positions while sleeping, and no fear was present, no subconscious repetitive scenario existed that gave even a mere hint that this time the feeling would be preventable by simply changing the sequence of the dream. Though the dreams were becoming controllable, the feeling was not. It was not coinciding with the circumstance, and the tickle would begin at different points in dream time, unprovoked, it became obvious that stillness was the real key all along. Why or how controlling them had anything to do with subconscious movement, I had no idea.

A different repetitive dream that I recall and overcame was when a Dracula looking character is chasing me around a very high light tower, which I imagine came from some old horror movie I must have seen. Usually he caught up with me and the tickle would commence during the hard blink defense.

I remember the dream starting as usual. I'm standing on the light tower looking over the rocks and endless sea, and when the image appeared this time, as it usually did, by simply appearing to have been there just around the corner the whole time, I just jumped off the side of the rail and fell in that slow motion type of dream falling, landing on the rocks below as if they were pillows, looking back up the tower and seeing the image shaking its fist in anger towards me. I fixed his imaginary wagon for a change.

They say if you hit the ground while falling in a dream, you die. This dream never occurred again after that night, and I didn't die. Falling is an interesting sensation, like a whole different type of tickle, but this was easily overcome by someone with my experience in intense dream sensations, it was nowhere near as unpleasant as the main annoyance.

I began this book with the dreams of my youth because when you're young, this dreamland seems at times even more real than conscious life does. It was an extraordinarily long time before I had desire, need or time to deal with normal childhood issues, like waking up with the bed wet, where my current favorite blanket was, or where some specific bottle or toy I liked was. Those issues always took a back seat to my continuous battle against the tickle sensation. This condition was instrumental in my life as the first battle I would face and overcome, even though I really only adapted to it. Thus, my dreams had a great deal of influence on my early years, due to this issue, that began around the age of three or four.

Eventually, the tickle would just come during normal, random type dreams, with no monsters or scary images to go along with them, and I could always end them by the tried and true method of blinking my eye's extra hard to awake. I adapted. I slept as perfectly still as I could, and the less I moved, the less chance I had of being tickled.

Around eight years of age, and to this date, the tickle switched sides of my body for no particular reason I could find, thus causing me to begin my sleep laying on my right side instead of my left. A nasty trick to make me re-adapt, initiated by whatever forces there are that created or caused this, or by my own minds effort to rationalize them, possibly due to the discomfort of being on one side continually. That part was welcomed; going to the other side was comfortable for a long time, having almost never slept on it.

I guess I'd say that having consciousness about dreams made the other type, the one's without a tickle, more memorable than they'd normally be and much more entertaining. It made for some interesting ones, like the ability to fly, swim like a fish, and of course, run full speed.

One of the oddest dreams I remember is when I was around five years of age and I'm dreaming that I have to go to the bathroom. I would be dreaming that I'm outside playing and I'd come in and go to the bathroom, doing the usual things boys do, and as I begin to go, I'd wonder how I managed to piss all over my pants and leg, though I saw it go into the toilet, and I'd wake up at that moment and realize that I was really in bed the whole time and was in the process of wetting it. Hard to control the urge at night to go when you're subconscious gives you a reason to believe you're already in a bathroom.

A strange tickle affliction was only the beginning of my life and its' pitfalls. My mother recalled some events which I was too young to recall myself, thus she was a great deal of help in my compilation. The earliest one she remembered, just off the top of her head, was when I was in my crib one afternoon, supposedly asleep. She said she was sitting around the kitchen table with my Nana, Monique, who's my moms' mom, and my sister Helen, and the phone rings.

The neighbor directly across the street, Mrs. Mirren, asked my mother if she knew where her two-year-old was. The front door of my house is immediately to the right at the base of the five living room stairs coming from the bedroom level, at the far end of the sunken hallway which has two more steps down before you reach it. The kitchen door is less immediately to the left by a foot or two from the base of the bedroom stairs. The kitchen door had two fold-out louvered doors we never closed, so it was really just an open doorway. You can sit in the kitchen and look directly out the front door through the little diamond shaped window at about eye level for an adult or through the screen door when the main door was open if you were more than two feet tall.

My mother told me how she responded to the neighbors' odd statement, by saying: "of course! I know where Christopher is! He's sleeping in his crib!" she said this with much surprise in her voice. The neighbor said to her while laughing "no, I think you should check, since Chris's here eating breakfast with my family!" Naturally, my mother checked the door, which was closed, and my crib, which was empty. I left the house and closed the door behind me as well without anyone noticing or hearing me. I liked moving around silently, and just did it naturally; it was fun for some reason.

Another story I heard but was too young to remember is eating my sister Helens' invisible ink, and having my stomach pumped for the effort, but I honestly cannot recall this. Good thing, I guess, since I was told that I hated it. I was told that another time, on a trip to a zoo, the Turtle back zoo I believe, around age three, I disappeared from sight from my parents, and after alerting the whole zoo staff about their missing child, they found me sleeping under a mother cow some hours later, along with her other real children. The cow didn't mind, and no one else did either, I can only imagine if someone saw me there and thought enough about it to report this kid sleeping under a cow to a park person.

I was also told that I would kick violently anyone who tried to hold me, if my desire was not to be held at the moment, and I even hurt my mother a few times, unintentionally, of course. I hurt her because I had to wear very hard corrective shoes, and that's what I kicked with. I was apparently pigeon toed or something.

One of the first things I recall myself was the feeling of waking after many hours of sleep, in the middle of the night, and how pronounced and vivid everything appears, even in the dark or by the dim light of my nightlight. It was no longer a dim light, it was like a torch, occasionally flickering when a bulb was going bad, or the houses power flickered. The streetlight was as a flashlight in my face at times. The moon was as bright as the sun, or so it appeared. But even without those light sources, I discovered that with concentration, you could hear and see amazing things in the dark.

I could mentally focus harder with my eyes on an object, to the point where I could see some distant things clearly at night like writing on a poster, or things atop my dresser, as if I had infrared sight. Focus, then focus clearer, and the object would seem to get closer to my view, as if I had a built in telescope. Hearing worked similarly. I could separate individual sounds through concentration, and listen to each quite audibly. It was the same state of mind as when you can hear your own heart beating in your head.

Those things I had some control over, since it was all in my head, but my teeth I had little control of, even though they also were in my head. I was a dentist's dream. Twenty-six cavities in one check up was my undesirable record for cavity production, and I averaged ten per check up. The only cause offered was something the dentists called soft teeth problem. I brushed pretty well, but ate pretty poorly I was told, lots of fluffernutters.

I didn't know why I had to be punished for the combination of having teeth and loving snacks or foods containing sugar. No one would fix them permanently; they would just patch up the holes instead with some nasty tasting metal. I believed they had the dental technology to fix them enduringly then, so why not do it? Guess dentist's need to make a living too, and if they were my dentist, it was a good living.

As a child I was usually up by seven am, and if my folks let me sleep during the day at all, midnight was the best they could hope for as a bed time for me. Sleep was not my friend most of the time, not till I couldn't hold my eyes open anymore and daytime naps were rare. I was an intelligent child I was told, with extraordinary needs for activity and attention. I remember hearing conversations clearly through the houses ductwork from three levels up, each word my parents spoke sounded clear, usually it was some political based conversation, based on the events of the early sixties as shown on broadcast TV.

I could see in the dark like a cat if my eyes were closed long enough. I think all children have heightened senses, which dulls over the passage of time from lack of specific usage and from efforts to block some that aren't so pleasing. From discussing these things later on in life with my peers I discovered most children are not even aware of that fact. I could read at a very early age, seeing the repetitiveness of letters associated with sounds and I was able to decipher most printed materials by age five.

I was given information from my mother some time ago, a time line of events from my youth, which I could not recall, being too young. I was in a playpen at age three months. I drank whole milk the same month. I was in a highchair at five months, and I could pull myself to stand at seven months. Also at seven months, I got my first and second tooth, discovered my voice, and could wave my hand and say bye-bye. I could walk alone at eleven months. I was considered smart and learned things quickly, the only visible problem being an overabundance of energy.

She also told me that when we moved to our current house, I was almost one year old, and upon arriving I immediately went to the top of the five bedroom stairs and fell down them, rolling like a ball to the bottom. They thought I may have been hurt, but instead I was sitting up at the bottom of the steps laughing hysterically. Sometimes I wonder if that was the cause or beginning of the tickle issue, but who knows. The floors were not carpeted yet, but eventually had wall-to-wall carpet in nearly every room.

Another one of my earliest recollections was going through my mothers' dresser, which I used to like to do, and I remember finding many papers. Mostly stuff I couldn't care less about, like bills, forms, and things to that effect. But one day, at around five years old, I found something interesting with my name on it, my actual adoption papers.

My parents blame this discovery for most of my troubles as a youth, and I suppose they have that option, though it held no weight with me other than nominal curiosity. This is when I discovered my parents were not biological in nature, which meant very little to me, not knowing what biology was anyway. Since they gave me all anyone would need, and were always there for me, I felt that they were my mom and dad regardless of what some paper said.

All I did was bring the paper down to my mother and ask her what the word adoption meant. She told me, and that was it. No great shock, since where I came from meant so much less to me than what I could do now or next. I think they felt that I was too young to understand what adoption meant and were planning on telling me later on in my life, and since honesty was their greatest policy, I'm sure they would have.

My priority as a kid, no matter how great or fantastic a time I was having somewhere, I always wanted to know what I could do next, after this current activity or event was over. I believe this to be true for most children. To a degree that only their creative little minds can reach. Even the professionals cannot correctly or accurately measure these degrees, some of the time.

There are many common stages. Certain things occur within certain average parameters at an average age in life. We learn to walk, use a cup, talk, read at certain stages in our unique ways and time frames. But I don't recall ever hearing about the stage of how to deal with the nightly issue I had to deal with. No reference points, options, or solutions to the dilemma, other than my own.

My parents were the picture-perfect middle-class type of parents that anyone would be ecstatic to have, with enough love to cover the planet several times over, and remained so for my entire life. I truly could not have written this book without their consistent confidence in me. They faced some circumstance not all parents get to experience, and they dealt with it quite well, as far as I could tell. Not only did I have some indescribable sleeping disorder, indescribable until now that is, but the psychiatric world of the mid-sixties rated me as the third major case of hyperactivity known in the state.

Now, the analysis of this condition I will attempt to bring to light from the inside of a victim or sufferers mind. Hyperactivity is not an illness or problem in my opinion. It may be an imbalance of chemical systems according to science within the person, but it's also quite natural, and I believe this 'imbalance' to be somehow related to the evolution of the human brain.

One possible personal description of this condition could be that the learning center of the mind is powerless to slow the pace of the need for information or stimulation. If the subject is dull, the bulk of the pertinent information can be learned in minutes, and then boredom can set in while everyone else catches up, and you sit there fighting to keep your eyes open, or trying not to create too great a distraction to others while entertaining yourself.

If the subject matter is of interest, it can be studied endlessly with massive repetition, with no worry of boredom. If the pace of learning were to be followed for an afflicted child, that pace could lead to incredible results of a positive nature, and in my opinion would likely surpass some of those results obtained with children who are not hyperactive. Like a head start in the learning process, accompanied with endless energy and curiosity, a gift and curse, all in one.

Quite frustrating, listening to things over and over, when understanding is no longer your goal, but shutting out the source of the repetition becomes your objective, which is sometimes too easily done. There are obviously things that are essential to learn, and not everything we have to learn will be pleasant, and most of these essentials were easily learned and forgotten later in life, just as easily.

There are a lot of good teachers out there, who really try, over and over, but there is also an equal amount of poor teachers, who perform their job clueless as to how to deal with some children. In the infant years of recognizing this disorder or gift, the level of understanding was by far underdeveloped in the educational field, and still is as far as I know.

I would have thought, or hoped, that thirty years of further study and experience for the academic and scientific world would have yielded more than just the renaming of the "ailment" to attention deficit disorder, or ADD. If patience is justified within a hyperactive child's mind, and the results it brings seem satisfactory for the effort, then the hyperactive have unlimited patience. Sort of like if you wait long enough, you can get what you want, and if you're hyperactive, you can wait an eternity if you've exhausted every other possible avenue to obtain your desired goal. Hyperactive or not, the child will wait their turn for the roller coaster, regardless of how long the line is. Dancing and climbing and running around while waiting no doubt, but waiting.

I have noticed that when reminiscing about the past, many of the most memorable moments tend to be the largest traumas of the time, and tend to be mostly negative. I believe these moments are what make us who we are, how we dealt with them or avoided them becomes the path we choose and becomes part of our personality.

Positive events appear to be rewards for positive input into challenges that were overcome, or just plain good luck. I was, for the most part, a very happy, sensitive, caring child, who smiled almost continually. Of course what I cared about changed from moment to moment, or day to day. I recall playing with plastic soldiers, dinosaurs and such, like a normal kid, and I owned seventy-five original Peanuts comic books which were my favorite reading materials.

One activity I enjoyed was building the rock wall in our back yard with my nana, sister, mother and father. A metal plaque bearing all our names was riveted onto one of the corner stone's of the wall. This we did when I was merely two, and it's one of my earliest memories of our back yard. I don't actually remember carrying stones, I just have a vague image of struggling to move rocks way too large for me to move. The fun of that, along with throwing rocks and being told not to, remains in my head

Ages two and three are quite easily forgotten, most things we can't recall, and I would not recall as much as I did had it not been for the condition I live with. I remember falling a lot, getting hurt one way or another by various things, door jams, broken glass, the stove, stairs and such. But these incidents are within memory only because they hurt, stimulating the nervous system negatively and memorably, and they happen to all kids at some time.

EXIT TWO

The Road Shared

At another point in our life we all realize, the world is not our own, unless we're raised on an uninhabited island or desolate, isolated place somewhere. Disappointing as it undoubtedly is for some, the fact is that there are others like you in every way, or at least in most ways, and you must consider them in your decisions and learn to cohabitate and share. We begin to venture into the world we see every day and watch it pass by usually; believing initially that it may be fun to go see new things, places, and people, since its boring just being too young to do things.

Within your own home, the way you see life at an early age can seem similar to the fortress of solitude, for the most part. You can be yourself, kind, cruel, sweet, sour, and you know what the reaction will be, since the people around you are comprehendible in your own mind as predictable most of the time.

When I was four years of age, my parents decided it was time for me to learn how to swim. I recall being initially excited about the idea, I liked water, but after the first experience within the walls of the Garden State swim club, my enthusiasm turned to pure fear and that turned to hatred.

The location of the pool will forever stand in my mind as the big chimney visible from nearly anywhere along the main street in Berkeley Heights. Once I could see it, the tears would start. This instructor felt the best way to get children to learn was by simply doing. So before I could even touch the water to see how cold it was, I was pushed in by the instructor, and held out in water above my head with a pole, which would go under my chin and lift me if I started to sink.

If I tried to grab the pole, it was gone, forced from my panicky hand. And the water was very cold. He did give a speech about what he was going to do, and that we were in no danger, he said something like we'd be placed in water above our heads and fairly scared at first, but it was necessary for his type of instruction. I just sat there ignoring everything playing by the pool side. Then I think he asked the parents if they changed their minds about staying to watch, mine didn't, a few did, but my mom did leave.

Most of the parents had to leave before the lesson began, not being comfortable with the methods the guy used. But for as traumatic as it was, I can say that water is like a second home to me now, and the barbaric method with which I learned it by was very permanent in my mind, although I'm certain it was not that necessary. I guess the instructor believed the old adage that everyone can swim naturally, but he liked to speed up the learning process dramatically. In the near future I would achieve my senior life saving certificate, open water instructor certificate, and a scuba license, obtained at the minimum age allowed of fifteen for scuba diving anyway.

After this first swimming instructor made the point of treading water the hard way, the teacher eventually began kicking and breathing exercises and that made me think this part should have come first. Swimming almost always made me tired enough to nap; it was a lot of work, but eventually the lessons became fun and useful and worth the effort.

Around the same time, I started to attend pre-school. The first lesson I recall learning was just how mean and unpredictable other children could be, as well as how unhelpful and uncaring some adults are. I was initially excited to go somewhere where other kids would be, full of anticipation in meeting a new friend, learning something I hadn't known before, and it all seemed to me that it was a sign that I was now a big kid, ready to face the world and impress some people with what I already knew or understood, lessons I learned within my own fortress of solitude, and be impressed with what other kids said and knew.

What I found, though, was a group of kids who showed no real interest in viewing life with respect to others, or what they could do or learn from another adult or child, they were more interested in achieving what they wanted personally, not much of anything else. What toy they could play with, what snack they could get that no one else had, or a favorite chair seemed to have high priority, it appeared the bottom line was greed.

I certainly wanted to do what I wanted, climb a tree, find some animals or bugs, play with some toys, just like anyone else, but I was more interested in what others had to say, building conversations, expanding my boundaries with different viewpoints I couldn't obtain from my own view, sharing something I knew that seemed astounding and had to be talked about, even if it was not so astounding to whom I was telling. I was not impressed with what others had said at times, more disappointed really, it seemed that there was no way through the barrier of disparagement, negativity and mistrust.

When I began to find myself emulating and mimicking unjustified anger greed and selfishness, it was very displeasing and confusing to me. I found myself mirroring actions, which were not of my own choice really, just mimics to similar actions. I would come home nearly every day crying according to my mom, which I know many kids do for many different reasons.

My reason for crying I understood, I could not figure out why kids needed to be mean or withdrawn, it made no sense, and I couldn't figure out what I did to deserve negative treatment or to constitute ignoring me. I don't recall all of the actual events or actions aimed my direction, I mostly remember the intent and purpose, which seemed missing a cause. When I was guilty of doing things that weren't nice, or if I was being greedy and thoughtless, I knew it was an unfounded and an unnecessary action or solution to the issue I was facing, just a way around dealing with something unpleasant.

This blatant illogic, as opposed to the pain from someone physically trying or succeeding to hurt me, was the main source of my tears. Simple actions like taking the toy I was playing with or ignoring some statement I was making about some activity I could excel at were discouraging to me.

Even then I understood that feelings fear and confusion lead to sadness, which leads to anger, and both lead to tears when young. This can also lead to retaliation at times, immediate or not. I was extremely over sensitive at times, but I was also able to turn off my sensitivity like a switch, just not always at the most appropriate moments.

It wasn't long before I would not allow aggressive kids actions leaving me wondering if something was wrong with me, or that something I did warranted their action. I realized it was actually their problem. The question of: "what did I do wrong?" became "what's your problem"? I would not deny I never instigated any aggression, unconsciously or not, but when people pointed out the facts to me I tended to listen and believe them, I think. It may not have changed anything, but I would listen to anyone with a point, or so I believed that I would. I'm sure I was as closed minded as any child, egotistic possibly more often than not, but I was aware of it when told so, and I understood what any adult said.

The first time I remember some peer hitting me, an experience every child probably recalls, had to be around age four or five. I remember being very confused, since no one ever did that before, and it was upsetting, I took it quite seriously, to think kids would do that for no apparent reason or purpose, to cause part of my body to feel as though I fell on it without having done so, it didn't make sense.

I don't remember if it was even intentional or not, or even who did it, or why, though I recall it was a male peer, not a female one. I never even thought about striking back, as though I knew this reaction was not correct or the right thing to do, plus I was still shocked by the action and not very hurt. I remember questioning the kid about why he would do such a thing, trying to discuss what was wrong in his mind enough to cause this action, but that only appeared to aggravate this kid, and it appeared that he had no answer. Maybe he had one he didn't want to share with me.

He just looked at me confused and annoyed by my attempt to reason with him, and called me some offensive name. I wouldn't cease my efforts for a while to understand what his problem was, confronting him endlessly in an attempt to rectify something that probably wasn't important to him or was a minor issue from his viewpoint, and to try and make him a friend as opposed to a person I would just ignore completely. I believe I was somewhat overwhelming, very forward and intimidating, which may have been one cause of the reaction.

I never considered hitting someone as a good method of drawing their attention. If he was just playing, or if attention was all he wanted, he could have picked a better way of showing it or doing it. If the assault was accidental, it was never made clear to me that it was an accident. Eventually, after whispering with his assigned seating peers while looking in my direction, his group decided that calling me offensive names or trying to belittle me in other ways was an acceptable activity.

After some time and observing others, reacting to bad situations with peers became a matter of pride in avoiding, reacting with similar negativity or actions was unacceptable since this appeared to be the desired response. To react becomes meaningless or counterproductive, although the natural reaction is with similar actions to equalize the distribution of negativity, the child-like 'if you hit me I hit you' rationale. I began observing how kids interact and how aggressive kids pick out their victims, how some are docile, some active, and how the different ones, like ones with glasses, or a speech impediment were always chosen first, which I understood but did not like.

They weren't fair in their choice, and I felt bad for the victims who had no control over their differences that caused the negative attention. I thought that those who act should be acted upon with equal unfairness, simple justice, though I had no way of implementing it, or even following the rule myself, it was just a correct thought, in my mind, something about picking on someone seemed simply wrong, unless the victim was also tormenting someone, then it seemed even, justified.

My parents would tell me, "You're a stronger and better person for not doing what other kids do", and this postponed most confrontations for me, since the ideal is logical and I did feel stronger and proud when I didn't react sometimes. Just like 'do unto others as you would have them do unto you', another quote I believed in and liked. Negative words are nothing more than that, words.

Actions could be reacted upon differently, dependent upon the severity of the results. Deciding to tell, run, laugh, cry, ignore or just walk away can occupy a child's thoughts for many hours and is a large source of distraction for some, which tended to make 'ignoring' this poor behavior the first choice, which also seemed proper since the results can be satisfactory. I used to ponder what would happen if an immediate or violent reaction were necessary, if there was ever real danger, relying on my swift actions to be sufficient to assist my survival instincts along with an intense adrenaline increase.

Fortunately, children tend not to create life or death situations, so the need for a quick reaction was rare, but I thought about it, having enough imagination to occupy my time with pondering such nonsense. Letting frustration out on the other unfortunate peers was a temporarily acceptable solution, and is a method used by many kids I noticed. I saw that by not reacting to one kid and his group caused much frustration for them, which satisfied me enough to laugh at their efforts to irritate me. They say misery loves company, and children certainly do like company when miserable. Or more accurately, seeing others suffering more than you or along with you would tend to make light of your own suffering.

Not taking action when confronted made me feel better and stronger than they were. I also discovered how ineffective logic is when dealing with kids, even though I was only a kid myself. They could never give good reasons for attacking someone verbally or physically. I never accepted their statements of reasoning like how ugly my face was or how big my nose was as rational explanations or a truth of any kind.

I knew the reason for some of their actions, like being upset with failures, getting caught doing something wrong, and that would spark some aggressive action against another child. Being jerks never solved anything, but it didn't stop some kids from being ones. I'm also certain that if asked, many former classmates of mine would think I was the jerk, it all depends upon your prospective, and though I was certainly not completely innocent, I was no bully, and I was very rarely physically aggressive as a result of my own failure or unhappiness. I can only recall returning physical aggression, in the form of losing my temper, about four times in my whole life.

There were only three actual children I would label as bullies within my own town's school system that I remember, and the resentment I felt towards them would occasionally get redirected to others who were just innocent bystanders or on lookers. Normally I would just make a deep cruel statement about a less positive attribute of the acting bully, or just point out a failing of theirs that recently occurred, like any child might.

I tried not to indulge in torment of kids for things like wearing glasses, braces, or being overweight. Four eyes, metal mouth or fatty would become an insult, or the nose picker was called booger breath or snot finger. That was standard kid stuff for differences in appearance or actions, and just not necessary or that much fun in my opinion. I tried to avoid using those types of insults, though I'm sure I had used such dialogue at times, purposely or not, like when trying to open communications with someone I wanted to talk to, it appeared that sharing a perspective about someone else's failings or appearance would break the discomfort barrier, as long as the person agreed with your viewpoint.

The only kid I recall from descriptions of hapless childhood targets was that of the nose pickers, Antoine Romano, and he could not care less about what people said, and no one could hinder his disgusting habit, which I found admirable as far as his reaction to criticism, yet it was still repulsive.

Negative actions and statements were a hard thing to control, but I could catch myself more often than not, my main goals being not to become as the bad kids were, if and when possible, and to not react in any way close to what they expected, ever. At the same time, turning in people for cruel acts was not beyond my doing throughout my grammar school experience.

It depended upon just how bad the act was according to my own youthful morals, along with how I felt about the person doing the act at that moment. My morals apparently did not include refraining myself from biting my nails continuously to the point where picking up a coin off a flat floor became next to impossible. This habit has followed me all of my life.

Pointing out cheaters and spitball throwers was not my specialty or purpose, and usually I tried to ignore negativity directed my way, knowing sadness was the only appropriate feeling, trying to comprehend why others needed to show anger and hate, their need to feel dominance and control, but never really achieving it. I remember thinking how sad it was that they felt the need to belittle and act with cruelty towards others.

I didn't believe kids like these would enjoy much of their lives. I tried to remain neutral mostly, showing indifference in either direction, and usually I managed to do so. I tried to remain unconcerned with what fellow students did most of the time, until it was made my concern by no choice of my own. I didn't like fighting because it upset me to think about what I felt like doing to someone while angry enough to fight, so I wouldn't. I thought knew how to defend myself, but wouldn't bother to or create a situation where I would need to most of the time.

One type of cajoling I did participate in was when the smartest kids made errors, just to put them in their place, make them realize they're not perfect. I did insult or belittle myself often; I found humor in picking on myself, or being silly, since I couldn't hurt myself or anyone else by doing so. Other's found this quality very amusing, for many reasons I figured. I didn't worry about which one. An attention getter, the main reason for acting out or disrupting class, and it always worked. I could tell at times why some kids would be amused, believing these actions I displayed to be ones of little intelligence, or being strange enough to pay attention to long enough to laugh just from the sheer entertainment aspect of it.

I also remember feeling fear. Not fear of new situations or meeting other kids or the kind of fear one feels when entering any new situation involving others, but fear of having the peers in my class attempt to test my patience and temperament having never reached it, just for the sake of the fact that they couldn't get any reaction from me, and what my reaction would be if I lost control.

Tell someone that you've never lost a Chess game, and their first instinct is to test the statement, and the same applies to stating control of your temperament, someone will inevitably test you. It's what the bullies wanted from you, to see some reaction they could either respect or find amusing or weak, which seems to be their way of amusing themselves. Do it, you sort of give in. I didn't feel comfortable giving in. Losing my temper was not my way, and a very bad idea.

I would talk my way out of most confrontations with simple child diplomacy or distracting subject changes, even possibly blackmailing someone into believing they'd be in trouble if they continued, but sometimes I would have to use stupid acts of bravery or mischief if dialog failed. The actual dialog of these confrontations escapes my memory, though I believe the words were typical of most children in grammar school. I tended to be wordy and used a lot of sentences to distract people from the main point of the topic, thus avoiding negativity whenever possible.

I was honestly more afraid of seriously hurting one of the kids I went to school with more than I may have feared damaging myself in the process. At times I would just ignore some bully giving someone a hard time, unless I was directed to not convey what I witnessed to the teachers or they'd get me after school. This was done in the polite form of a statement like: "Greenie! Keep your mouth shut or you'll be eating dinner through your asshole!"

This would cause me to laugh and do the exact opposite, not fearing any retribution from the bully, challenging my bravery sufficiently to tell just because they told me not to. I would become the bullies' nemesis, without becoming one myself, or any bully-like actions I took were directed at the bullies themselves, sort of the bullies' bully, without any physical confrontation involved.

I did listen to my parents and try and communicate any negative issues to my teachers before contemplating taking my own action, being young and foolish enough to believe they could or would do something about it, or could understand or relate to my situations. From the teachers' perspective, dealing with my issues must have been minor compared to dealing with the issues affecting the majority of students, and thus not a priority.

Most of the teachers seemed to not believe most of what I was telling them, as if my goal was not to correct a wrong action but to only be a tattletale, and some would approach my statements with the attitude that I probably was the catalyst of the event, pushing my concerns aside like a bad desert they didn't want to eat, or a story they were tired of hearing. "I'm sure your exaggerating," they would tell me, or "don't be a tattle-tail" and statements like that, used to avoid actually doing anything about a negative and, to a child, an important event.

All my effort would only generate more negativity from the aggressive kids I grew up with, seeing my efforts as a weakness or telling on them was viewed as an attack somehow. Apparently their parents couldn't care less about, or refused to believe, how their children acted in school.

The attitude the principal had was that kids will be kids, and I should just avoid confrontations, bringing the matter to him if needed, which seemed logical to me. But when I did, the result again was less than adequate and only caused more resentment from any student I was discussing. I realized that I would have to deal with things on my own, in whatever way I felt necessary, as though they were forcing me to decide on what should be done, or to see how I would react, which I thought was fairly unwise.

Kids will tell adults about wrong doings they witness or are subjected to, because they feel the action is wrong, and the goal is to give the situation to adults who will be able to correct the offender with their big words, explanations and correct or punish them for the action, in hopes of ending further similar actions. Other motivation would be to become the good child in the teachers' eyes, thinking that pointing out unfairness would give the teachers reason to favor you. It may open communication with the teacher as well, believing that you're getting special attention and rapport with someone in authority, but this also was not my personal goal.

A typical day for me would start around 6 am, with breakfast cereal with a chopped banana in it, along with many scoops of sugar on top. Then my mother would bring me to school, and I'd join many other kids in waiting for the doors to open. We did normal school studying, at whichever grade level we were at, and take breaks often, like go in the playground, lunch room or auditorium for some movie or educational project, as any school does. I would avoid anyone negative or looking to cause trouble, something I could usually see before they saw me.

Fairness is a large concern and focal point for children, who may tell on someone who has committed some act that they themselves failed to get away with, such as getting away with desert at thanksgiving before feasting began, deeming it unfair for someone else to succeed where they have failed, and not necessarily because the act itself is wrong or irrelevant to adult eyes.

I usually tried to convey why an action was wrong directly to the perpetrator, but since I was only another child, my words had a completely different impact on them, and was unlikely to prevent more occurrences. I was the wise guy, the jock, the coward, the lunatic, the clown, the brain, and the one with green teeth. They were not actually green, just because my last name is Green; any object you can associate with the color green was used in reference to me. My nickname from grade one on was Greenie, and I don't recall who called me that first, but that nickname lasted a lifetime.

Through all this negativity, I do recall many positive aspects of youth, feeling proud for accomplishing tasks, completing assignments and tests flawlessly on occasion, having answers to teachers' questions before anyone else, and that was quite satisfactory. I was allowed to feel knowledgeable and proud, understanding things quickly and better than most of my peers would in some cases, and being above average at most physical challenges or games in the gymnasium or outside on the field.

I remember one kid who would continually call kids names and try to trip others on the playground, causing some pretty bad scrapes and bumps on the victims, emotionally and physically. When he tried to trip me and missed, I felt obligated to taunt his efforts, saying how slow and stupid he was for trying that trick on me, and that I saw it coming from miles away.

He was too predictable, and when I pointed that out he just tried to shove me to the ground, which also failed. I only laughed in his face, ran back to the classroom and to the protection of the teacher, and later, while he wasn't around, I ripped up and threw his workbook in the garbage, which I knew would cause him more grief that any fall on the playground would.

For this I felt no guilt, it seemed deserved, and it was a nice mystery for him and the teacher to ponder. Just because he never discovered what happened made no difference to the level of satisfaction I felt, having gotten away with it. I didn't know how to measure the degree of justice or retribution needed, since I was only a child, but I realized that hurting people was wrong, having enough sense to understand that. At least hurting someone in a way that would express its self in the form of bruises or permanent injury was a bad idea in my mind, based on a past experience.

This experience I mentioned occurred one day while playing croquet with my grandma, sister, and some of her friends. I was not always a good looser, but I was a good winner. If something is fair, I saw that two conclusions could be reached equally. That seemed reasonable.

But I was quite adamant when confronting cheaters, or players who found short cuts I had not thought of first. Upon playing, I believed I had been cheated, which I probably wasn't, and when I was confronted by a friend of my sister's and told to stop being such a baby, or some other remark similar that I don't recall exactly, with great rage I took the mallet, and using a helicopter blade motion, without aiming really, I threw the mallet across the yard towards her as hard as I could, and shattered her shinbone. Her name was Betty Walter.

I did indeed have a nasty temper when I allowed it to surface, and I usually wouldn't allow it. That was when I was around six years of age or so. I did not wish to hurt her, and when my parents took her to the emergency room, I did cry in remorse, since I realized how fragile a person could be, and it affected me sufficiently to have never since thrown an object at anyone else again, except where it's required as part of the activity or game.

I began to realize that most kids are the same, in actions and temperament, only their viewpoint and reaction to certain situations are different. While an event of any kind is occurring, if the event affects you personally, it always seems more severe than if the event affects another, just because it's happening to you. Like if a fast ball hits one kid in the head, the player on deck is not going to think it hurt so bad, since the ball didn't hit him. He may be more nervous, but at the moment still uninjured. He just hopes they change the pitcher.

I didn't feel as bad as Betty did that day. Oddly, she forgave me and baby sat for me several times, though I couldn't forgive myself, since I recall it over three decades later as the most damage I caused any person physically.

I figured if I avoid using physical violence, physical violence would stay away from my path. So I changed my temperament and reactions, victimizing mostly those who did the victimizing, and those who consistently crossed my path negatively, without becoming physically violent, or with letting those who drew my attention know their confrontation with me was not resolved.

It became a mind game of sorts, advancing as I would in a chess game, one move at a time, an immature battle of wills, determining who gives the final blow, defensive or offensive stance was irrelevant. I selected this attitude since I realized that no matter how many chances I gave some kids to be at peace with me, they would not appreciate the effort or change their aggressive or negative nature.

I had an abundance of resources for use in retribution besides words, I discovered, like household or common chemicals, cleaners, food products, and many times I found use for these things in methods not normally used. The fact they existed I always knew,

I knew what they were meant for and used them in the normal way many times as well. I actually liked helping my mom clean our home, felling proud of the neat, organized way she made the house look, with my contribution.

But time and patience gave me new insight to the destructive value of these products, it allowed me to not stress myself over the negative actions of a peer, and expanded my imagination as to the use of things around me, even if just imagining how I might use them. One good side effect of being victimized was awareness of your surroundings and the objects that were accessible, though being aware of them and using them were two different things.

When not dealing with aggressive peers, and during the timeframe of kindergarten or first grade, I began to build my own zoo. I had always enjoyed nature, from the birds and squirrels making their unique noises to the whole galaxy of life found under a rock. During my youth I had several dozen mice, a dozen guinea pigs, a collection of about thirty different species of snakes, some rats, hamsters, gerbils, turtles, frogs, and goldfish or carp.

The animals were not always within my collection at the same time, and the highest count I remember was about one hundred ten individual animals at one time. The rodents, besides the Guinea Pigs, were food for the reptiles.

The mice and rats made it to school several times, just to prove to the non-believers that I did have such things, and for show and tell, as well as for causing panic and a break in the day's routine. It was amazing to watch so many people move so fast due to, in my opinion at the time, unfounded fear. It was just as interesting watching who runs and who stays to play with the creatures, and that surprised me sometimes.

The time one female teacher came over and picked up the mouse I brought in off the floor without blinking stands out in my mind, as though she had much experience with such things. I remember she gave the mouse to the chemistry teacher, in a different part of the school, who held it for me till school was over, but not before I, along with the rest of the class, nearly died laughing when the mouse urinated on her.

The principal wasn't pleased, and my day ended earlier than usual that day. My mom only wondered how I kept the mouse from her view when she dropped me off that day. I just said I was sorry and I wouldn't do it again, but that was a lie I wasn't even aware I was telling yet, and was only beginning of many similar events. The mouse was in my jacket pocket, zipped shut so my mom couldn't see it

I had my own way of coexisting with nature. It was either my friend, coexisting as it should with respect to the eco-cycle, or my most bitter enemy, once something went wrong within the harmony, like getting bitten or stung. Animals I caught I expected to bite, but bees were hard to coexist with, since they cater to no one. I did feel as though it were just wrong to destroy nature in general, yet for some reason, it appeared at times that it was an act of dominance in the most primitive state of mind, with no repercussions I was aware of.

Possibly the same feeling bullies got from their victims reaction, or lack thereof. I was technically and physically able to conquer, so I would. It makes a small child feel much larger in the scope of things, being in control of some poor creature's destiny, the childhood version of a superiority complex. The poor ant, working hard to get food to some needy colony members or the queen, could never get by the typical magnifying glass, wielded by the most deadly of insect murderers, a child.

I only hoped I wouldn't be confronted with any animal where surviving the encounter would take all the resources I have. Like running into a rattle snake, wild dog or bear, which are the only truly dangerous animals I may see around where I live. Must feel much different, I remember thinking, the way Africans' and South Americans' have to live with so many deadly creatures on their door step, keeps them on their toes, I would imagine. Similar to places in the American mid-west or south, where Rattlesnakes, Gators and such effect how far into an unknown woods one wants to venture.

One of the mostly positive experiences in my life was admiring, observing and caring for nature in my own home zoo. I caught most of the reptiles and amphibians myself, finding snakes, turtles and frogs in every woods I went in. So the first animal I kept was probably a Garter snake, though it may have been a ribbon snake, can't recall. The first snake my parents bought and I didn't catch myself was a Sonora mountain King snake I named Sonora, for lack of a better name. He ate mealworms, and disappeared a few months later, when I was about seven years old.

Then I got Barney the Bull snake. He ate mice, and was a very calm and seemingly friendly snake. He lived about two years and when he died from pneumonia, I dissected him on the driveway with a kitchen knife. It was my feeble attempt at an autopsy, and during it I began to picture how much schooling would be necessary to understand fully what I was looking at. I thought I found all the organs; I just had no idea what else I was looking for.

My favorite snake was a six-foot yellow rat snake named yellow. I would let him wrap half of his body around my arm, and then I would suspend his head and the other three feet of his body over the aquarium that all the mice I bred were in. Then he'd just reach out and grab a mouse, kill it and eat it while still hanging on my arm.

This is an unusually domestic way to act for a snake. Yellow died when I fed him a hamster that bit me, because it bit him too, right on the neck and that caused a great big bloody mess all over the basement. I fed the same hamster to the Boa, who had no problem with it, what so ever. A much stronger constrictor, it would seem, or luckier. And naturally I had a reticulated python named Monty, but not for many years. Unfortunately, all my big constrictors died of pneumonia, even though I force-fed them medicine and food as directed by a veterinarian.

The first furry pet I ever had that was not meant as food for my reptiles was Coretta the Guinea pig, when I was five. Cory, a white albino short-haired Guinea with red eyes, lived seven years. I loved Guinea pigs, they were cute and fun to pet, mostly docile and they made interesting noises, though at night they were somewhat loud. My mother held Cory for hours at night in her lap. She fed her cabbage, carrots and apples and things while holding her.

Cory had twelve children, six in one litter, which is very odd for
Guinea pigs; the average litter is one to three. Corys' mate Martin
once bit me while I stood atop the stairs to the den, which caused
me jump in shock and pain and toss him down the stairs to his
death. He made two impressive holes in my finger, and I was very
surprised because Guinea pigs don't usually bite. Their born totally
developed, which I enjoyed, since they just look like miniature
versions of themselves, real cute.

My defense from hives of bees, which were obviously a threat
even I could not control, was a can of hair spray and a lighter. Spray
paint was also a magnificent source of torch power, with a nice
odor to go along with it. I would just aim the spray at the hive and
light the torch, and watch the bees drop from the sky and the nest
with their wings burned off, stepping on the earth bound survivors
as they try to crawl away. I would get rid of the wasp and yellow
jacket nests around my house and never got stung doing so or ever
caused an uncontained fire.

I learned about fire and water quite early in life, always awed
by the power of each, and how they extinguish and distinguished
each other as opposites. Fire evaporated water and water, of course,
puts out most fires. Though I don't remember where I got my first
one, I always carried a lighter, just for use in emergencies. I always
felt the need for having fire as a tool, even when I was only six or
seven, and if for nothing else, at least for building campfires to
roast marshmallows or hot dogs over, a use I never outgrew.

I did possess toys other than a lighter, and I recall that I
continually broke them, unless they were made of hard plastic
or other durable material, pet rock wasn't invented yet so many
windows were safe since I'm sure my pet rock would be able to fly.
I liked dropping things out my bedroom window to see what would
happen to them when they hit the driveway below, or what happens
to a toy truck when a giant meteor, which would be a rock from my
yard naturally, fell on it.

Most of my toys were either books or made of extremely
strong materials. I broke some windows, though that was usually
unintentional. I liked pulling out weeds by the roots, but since I

didn't know the difference between a weed and a flower, I pulled out many things from the ground that my mother didn't want removed, or that I shouldn't have touched, like poison ivy, which I never recognize for some reason.

I enjoyed observing what eggs did when you threw them up in the air on the street, or when you dropped rocks on them. I liked running into walls and doors, pretending I was a wrestler or I was on a ship being tossed around, but doors and walls sometimes break I discovered.

Mixing cleaners and chemicals on the driveway was also fun, like creating my own home made version of a chemistry set, till I mixed Drano and bleach, which made a cloud of gas I had to run from. I believe my dad told me mixing that combination of ingredients made cyanide gas, which was not a good thing and I shouldn't play with those things.

I liked to spend time on the roof of my house, always enjoying the view and solitude while cleaning out the gutters because they were full of leaves usually, which is why my parents didn't mind too much that I enjoyed being up there. Our roof had a flat part, roughly twelve feet by twelve feet, and I would bring a chair or blanket out to watch stars on clear nights.

I always tried to find high places, with the best views, and my roof was well made for this, since we lived on a mountain and the back yard was the slope down into the valley. I could clearly see into the houses windows behind mine, which may or may not have been acceptable to my neighbors; I never heard any feedback from them on the issue.

The backyard ground was over fifty feet down from the roof, so dropping things from there was fun for me, it was the best impact I could make and was the highest I could go without climbing a tree. I usually targeted the small concrete slab outside the storage room door, but that was way off center, and I had to throw things to the right to hit it. Eventually I found higher places like power lines, bridges and things, anywhere I could climb to get a good view, just for fun, I loved being in high places.

Driveway baseball was one activity I indulged in with other neighborhood kids; it was one of the more normal activities that I remember doing. My driveway from the doors went up four or five feet on an angle to the street, and between the doors was a three-foot wide column of brick. This was home plate, of course. It was the best driveway for the game on the block, too.

This activity became somewhat destructive, though unintentionally. Foul tipped balls had found their way through the garage door windows more than once, till my parents put in plastic ones, which just fell out instead of shattering. I was the only lefty, so neither side of the garage was safe from our game. Sometimes we left the doors up, preventing any further window damage.

During my turn at the plate, I hit the ball towards the house to the right of the house directly across the street most of the time. I was the only one of our age and group able to hit the ball over the house directly across the street, which the Mirrens' didn't seem too annoyed by. I knocked out maybe two of their windows over the years, when my fly ball fell short of clearing their gutter. They understood usually, as long as someone paid for the repair, like my parents, but the house next to it on the right was a different issue.

Mr. and Mrs. Walliman lived there, and Mr. Walliman was not a friendly man. He was old, grouchy and hated children, and everyone was afraid to get balls hit on his yard, or go near his yard for any reason, everyone, except me. He was your typical 'children should be seen not heard' type of person, believing kids to be more trouble than their worth, and he had none to carry on his name and philosophy, which I found fitting.

He was a rather big guy, around six four or so, average build, and he'd come screaming out of his door, yelling: "Green, I'll make your parents pay for that, and you'll never see anything you get near my yard again!" He'd say this after I just put a ball into his den through a window. I pulled the ball enough to reach his window, impressing myself and those around me. I never did get his large picture window, though, always managed to miss that, though I was not honestly trying to hit it.

I always laughed when he began raving, running circles around him and taunting him like the little brat he said I was, and then I'd just leave. More than once, he followed me home, ringing the bell to complain about me, and all I heard once was "if you don't control your spoiled little brat, the police can!" This really made my parents madder than I ever saw, but not at me. This anger was more directed towards Mr. Walliman due to his attitude; I was just playing a normal game that all kids play.

My mother would try to explain that I was only a kid, but I was the one who bothered him most often, and sometimes on purpose. He couldn't stand the fact that I did whatever I wanted to, and would tell me what would happen if I were his kid. It all just made me laugh more, his constant raving about how bad I was and how good he had to be growing up.

I couldn't figure what his upbringing had to do with me, but he thought it had some relevance, and I didn't. He truly hated living near me I thought, and though he couldn't prove it, his garden did not flourish sometimes, and he felt that it was usually my fault. Only once or twice was that true, but he didn't know that and I wasn't offering any information to justify or dispute his suspicions. I was not very patient with that old man, hoping I never become as cranky as he was.

I listened to my parents patronizing him, always stating that they would talk with me about whatever it was I did, and they would do just that. They wondered why I would taunt such a guy, and I'd explain that the only reason was his lack of understanding when we, the kids playing ball, happened to get the ball on his yard and he would take it.

So I saw no reason not to annoy him, since he tried so hard to annoy us. My mom would just say please don't, because then Mr. Walliman annoys her, and since he has no kids it's hard for him to understand kids in general. I would always agree, telling her what a weak and illogical reason I thought that was, but patience was her forte, and she attempted many times to enhance my understanding of the need for it. She didn't like making excuses for that guy, I could tell.

EXIT THREE

Childish Action Freeway

In my front yard there was a fairly large plum tree and I was noticing for years how horribly destroyed the tree was every spring, and how the half eaten plums and broken branches would litter the yard like some hurricane hit that tree alone. Birds and squirrels we're largely at fault.

Though I couldn't think of anything to stop the birds at that age other than rock throwing, which only worked temporarily, squirrels were a different story. I knew I could never talk my parents into buying me a BB gun, which was probably a good thing at that time, saved a lot of birds' lives. So I would get an empty aquarium from the basement, and set a trap under the plum tree. I would put the plums under it, propping the aquarium up with a stick, and I'd tie a fishing line to the bottom of the stick, and wait in the garage with the other end of the line in hand.

I always thought there were way too many squirrels in the area, and felt that no one would miss some, if they vanished. I caught two in the aquarium within minutes, and I ran over to put my weight on the top. Then I would slide the steel mesh top under the bottom of the tank and then flip it over, and get a real close look at these resident rodents, who were none too pleased.

I realized then that I never want to get bitten by one of these vicious little rodents. Their teeth were pretty big, and the noise they made while trying to chew through the metal cage top was more threatening and intimidating than any animal I had. Then I put a large rock on top of the aquarium, filled it with water from the hose, and watched them drown.

Unfortunately, I didn't have a constrictor large enough to eat these vermin, so either the garbage can was where they wound up, or on Mr. Wallimans' front porch. I had heard him once complaining about what squirrels do to his garden, so I thought of it as a small favor, thought I doubt he did. Plus, his garden's real enemy was the chipmunks; he didn't seem to know this. Those I have never managed to catch, likely since I've never tried. Our yard and rock wall were full of them too.

I guess this activity occurred around ten years of age or so, and I would do the same activity with the already captive rodents I planned to feed the snakes with, but I added my own customized bizarre little twist. When I was certain the rat or mouse was dead, by suffocation or drowning, I would use a train set generator to shock the animal back to life.

Then I'd just feed the shaking, recently resurrected creature to one of my snakes. I figured, since the rat or mouse was just food, what difference did it make? Their fate was determined long before my experiments, and disabling the rodent is safer for the reptile, as I learned from watching Yellow die. A mistake I would never make again.

I'm certain many will see this activity as quite cruel, but cruelty was learned in many ways. Not just from a few wonderful peers who fueled and inspired it usually, but breeding mice, rats, hamsters and gerbils was an interesting course in animal behavioral science. To watch a mother rodent devour her own children was incredible enough, but letting the males all co-exist in one cage to prevent over population was a sight not to be believed.

These creatures were obviously designed to be many barriers away from each other when possible, with the option of leaving the area or running away possible at all times. Of course, in my zoo, this option they did not have. I found no large difference in this attribute between mice, rats, gerbils or hamsters, but I'd say from my own observations that gerbils are the worst.

Nasty little creatures, gerbils, and the only exception were Guinea pigs, for no reason I could figure. They seemed more civil, almost like dogs or pigs, easily domesticated though I wouldn't walk one with a leash and doubt you could teach one to sit, fetch or anything else. Rabbits I had no experience with, so I couldn't say anything about them, they were too large to handle in the environment I had and too big for feeding purposes.

As another experiment I would occasionally take a bully rodent, which I watched fight and bite and abuse the weak ones constantly, and I'd drown it just enough to make it docile and not dead, in preparation for the snake's dinner. Then I would put the weakened rodent back into the cage for a while to observe.

At first the timid runts would show the normal fear of their tormenter, cowering fearfully in a corner as usual. Then they look confused as if they can't believe their toughest peer is now weak, as they slowly move about the cage with caution. Then they begin to get curious and start to move towards the dominant one slowly, getting closer each time they pass him, then they begin to take the cheap shots.

They would take a nibble or bite and run, and wait for a while. Then, eventually and inevitably, they would just attack the "old" bully once they discovered that there would be no consequences. I would have to stop them so the mouse wasn't unusable as food after a minute or so.

I found this interesting, and discovered that most rodents are not that different from people. People appear to thrive upon each other, once weakness is shown; the advantage takers begin to stalk viciously and continuously. Often, people will confuse apparent weakness with just a calm, complacent attitude and wind up biting off more than they can chew.

In school, when other kids were obnoxious, it seemed natural to become obnoxious as well simply by default. One person could cascade a mood throughout his or her peers, just by performing the simplest act or making the oddest comment out loud. I was one to always have some answer and method of setting off events, and had the most "two cents" to offer any discussion, whether people wanted to hear it or not.

I knew no child had the right or authority to tell me what to do or not do, what to say or not to say, and no one would convince me otherwise. The threats of such kids like Fred Penn, Edward McLane, Craig Barren, shut up or else, or don't dare surpass their minimum academic performance, was sufficient reason to cause me to do all within my power to do exactly that.

The opposite of what they wanted me to do usually became my goal. I lived for being at the end of the bully's sentence, from the second the negative garbage left their lips, to the moment I performed the act or made the statement that would annoy them the most, and whether it came immediately or delayed, made no difference to me. The results were the same, irritating.

I would beat them to an answer, correct their mistake, or set them up with some class-disturbing device like one of my animals. If they stuttered once I would repeat the stutter several times with mocking inflection, or whatever it took to create real hate and agitation, much as they would do for another poor victim.

I enjoyed imitating the bully who would be struggling for an answer he didn't know, attempting to make them feel as stupid and insignificant as they would do for me or someone else in another situation. Fortunately, only one of the jerks I mentioned was in my class at any one time, and only during gym, lunch and recess was I within all their sights enough to catch their combined attention.

That is, till sixth grade, when we all began using different classes for different subjects, and are forced to co-exist continuously for short time periods. These times were when the statement of: "I'll get you after school, Greenie" were heard the most. The threat was commonplace, for a while.

One time, when a bully was playing the game of "what bounces off Greenies' head" while the teacher wasn't looking, I decided not to wait for the teacher to turn their back to react spontaneously, an extremely rare event. I recall that I got hit in the head with a hard rubber eraser, and no more than two seconds after it hit me, and before I gave it any thought, I took the perpetrators workbook and ripped it up in front of their face. Then I threw it up in the air like confetti, right in front of the teacher, never losing my smile and giggling while doing it. That would be what I considered an act of bravery, and so would the peers who witnessed it as they sat there in shock.

The teacher would of course reprimand me, never noticing what was lying on the floor next to me or hearing me tell her that this kid threw something at me, or even noticing the big eraser dust mark on my head, she'd only send me to the principals' office. The bully would have to sit in shock and steam about what I did, not being brave enough to retaliate in front of authority as I did at that moment.

I would leave the class with a glance towards them signifying a thank you for getting me out of class, and have fun sitting there all day, since I don't have to now, sort of like saying: "So long, suckers"! In essence, I made it appear that the kid did me a favor, which he hated. Oddly, I don't recall which of the bad kids were in my class first or at any one time, but names are just names, we all have had similar people we grew up with and had to deal with. I cannot even recall who the specific kid was in this example.

I remember once going into my classroom early and finding, I think it was Craig, in the process of hiding all the teachers' chalk, which would make teaching difficult for her. I would have said nothing to the teacher as a rule, but I was told by the person doing it to not mention anything to the teacher, "or else". This would almost automatically cause me to tell, which I did, just because of the threat.

I liked a good prank like any kid, but hated being given ultimatums by anyone. So when the teacher came, she looked around confused for a while, long enough to have some giggling begin and whispers to fly, and then she just stated: OK, where's my chalk?" I just pointed to the kid who hid it and said: "Why don't you ask him?" Thus opening the door for more resentment, this was becoming less and less of a concern to me, and more of a form of entertainment, a negative attention reinforcement tactic. He of course would deny any wrong doing, and I had no evidence, so the teacher blamed me naturally. Since I knew where the chalk was and returned it to her, I must have been guilty, right? I got the chalk for her, muttering 'believe what you want' along the way back to my desk, finding amusement and laughing to myself at her accusation and ignorance.

After some time I found amusement in being challenged, chased and threatened, the challenge and the adventure of getting away from whomever or to get home without confrontation became my forte and became a sport or game to me eventually. I had ten or eleven different routes to get by and my mom would pick me up if I called her to sometimes, and when I ran into Craig and Edward one day by turning the corner too quickly, I didn't react at all.

I knew well I could out-run both of them, but would not change the pace of my approach, feel or show any concern or fear, and I was not changing my direction or pace for any reason. Continually, I walked up to pass them, since they had suddenly lost the will to walk with any homeward bound intent, and as I passed them they just jumped on me. I would immediately go down, right after the first or second harmless swings, moving my body parts just enough to allow no damage, and let them ground me while they hit and kicked me, oh, four or five times, I think, then I just pretended to cry. I could not generate the tears from the pain, since that was minimal, they really couldn't hit hard anyway, but I could from the anger.

I spent a good part of my school years avoiding abuse, though the verbal abuse was abundant as well, just not very aggravating, and everyone seemed to indulge in that activity, like it was a game. Everything was used from being called green teeth to several sexual positions my mother should try with a dog, and just general put-downs to try to inspire a reaction to humiliation.

Sticks and stones may break my bones, as the saying goes, and I believed in it. On this particular day, when I ran into Craig and Edward, I figured the dodge ball game I had won pissed them off, along with other events they probably didn't even remember other than the threat they made about getting me some day. So there I was, lying in the street, looking completely helpless, crying, until the pair resumed walking home laughing and left my sight. Then I would get up and laugh because there was no damage, and just walk home as usual.

Since I wasn't hurt, there was no need for extreme retribution or direct confrontation. Just testing the sharpness of my knife on one of their parents' car tires, sending a rock through their garage window, cutting one or two of their clotheslines, or dousing their books in school with vinegar or bleach sometime in the near future was enough. I don't remember which I did exactly, for this incident, probably a few things, just at different times.

I figured it made them wonder what they did to deserve such bad luck. They knew from attending gym with me that I was durable enough, having seen so for themselves, so I wondered, even while they were attacking, if they would realize how fake my helpless act was, but they didn't. The thought I had for not feeling the need to fight back at that moment, along with no desire to waste so much energy was just that I didn't care. They simply weren't worth it, and I knew they would suffer some consequence, delivered by me or not.

They both seemed surprised the next day when they saw no change in my attitude, along with no evidence of their attack. I called them the 'two on one wimpy pussies', and ignored their offers for one on one challenges. I would walk away just going "boo hoo hoo!" sarcastically and laughing the whole time, imitating their words of doom like a parrot in a high, squeaky tone, as annoying as possible, "squawk! Let's kill Greenie, squawk!" as I walked away undaunted, laughing.

On a positive line of thought, I enjoyed thoroughly the sports played in gym, mostly because I was good at them, and even if the team captain hated my guts at the moment, (which was usually the case, since most bullies excel in sports too), he'd have to pick me if winning was his goal, which it was. Kickball, dodge ball, football, soccer and baseball were very natural to me.

Even that stupid little cart game, where you sit on a board with four wheels, propelling yourself like an upside-down spider or crab, and try to kick or hit a ball around, without getting off the board was an easy challenge. I was one of the few, lefties or righties, able to reach school roofs with hits and kicks of various balls in various games. I did make outs and errors, and looked stupid or clumsy sometimes, just like anyone else, just not very often. My grades in gym were usually very good, so I believed I was good and sports came naturally to me.

I loved hearing the kids on the other team say: "back up, Greenie's up!" which was nearly every time I stepped to the plate against people who had played with me before, and that did wonders for my confidence, nearly as much as when I played with kids who didn't know me and were surprised by my performance.

Hearing the expletive's they would shout while chasing a ball I hit or kicked clear over their heads was very satisfying to my ego, combined with the cheering shouts from my team mates as I rounded the bases. Everyone on my team was pleased to have me there, cheering if I made the winning hit or kick or winning defensive play, and I wondered why my personality could only be overlooked during these moments, and not other situations.

One of the main reasons I didn't attempt to join little league was because I didn't like the precarious way pitchers threw the ball at you, and they usually threw it at me, since they knew where the ball was going if they didn't. Fear of a fastball kept me from pursuing that sporting career, along with no external support from any guidance counselor or coach, and the fact that no one in my family would or could tempt me into confronting this fear. My parents were supportive to a fault; just not for things they had no knowledge of, like baseball, or skiing.

I had no way of knowing I would out grow it or overcome it, which may be the only regret I have in my whole life. I was that good at it I was told, and few people I saw matched my out fielding ability or intensity. When I was in the field, everyone tried hitting the ball away from me, and I wound up usually standing around doing nothing in the field the whole game. I always wondered, while standing there in any field waiting for some action, what it would be like, standing in center field at Yankee Stadium like Bobbie Mercer, thinking it would be most likely the same as now, keep the ball away from Greenie or loose.

What I disliked about scholastic sports was the locker room where any bully would get the chance to cause grief to someone, and that was usually me, since I would be the cause of their defeat sometimes, or since they couldn't catch me as promised after school. I would go about my business of getting dressed unheeded, even while one or two of the idiots would stand around me taking cheap shots, believing accurately that I wouldn't react with any type of temper loss, but also getting frustrated by my grin they could not erase.

So I would avoid that sometimes by either getting dressed before anyone else or after everyone else, and this worked most of the time. I would just laugh at their attempts to bother or harass me, and their usual after school threats were also becoming quite boring and monotonous after a while, perhaps as annoying as a pesky fly or gnat.

Like anyone else, I would ignore some situations that didn't involve me, letting the bullies have their way without recourse or concern from me, just because I felt no need to interact at that moment, or felt like simply observing how others reacted to the aggressions of the bullies and vice versa, or just because I felt a little lazy at the moment. Non-aggressive students who were actually normal and pleasant seemed to not appreciate my attitude, since I was quite obnoxious at times, so they also had reasons for disliking me.

I guess I appeared just too happy and care free, and everything was a joke to me, I was never very serious in school. I also projected the "know it all" attitude sometimes, only when I believed I actually knew something about what was being discussed. I shared this attitude with the smarter kids, who seemed to have that quality built in to their personality most of the time.

I have had my share of normal, uneventful days, where everything worked fine and no incidents took place, which are not as memorable as when things went awry or equally impressive in a good way. I recall at times suffering the school hours with slow torment, using peripheral vision to coordinate what the teacher's saying with the minute hand of the rooms' clock by staring between them and concentrating.

Watching what others are doing, with perfect discreteness, seeing if any events could or would unfold. Looking at the chalkboard, trying to determine what's needed to crack it, puncture it, or render it unusable, without intending to find the time or opportunity to actually do so.

Finding the prettiest girls face in the room and admiring its features just for their sheer beauty, and wondering how it is that I never tire from looking at them. Wondering what other students around me must be thinking of, from each of their perspectives, about what's going on in class. What path I feel like walking home on today and when I thought I may leave for the day. These thoughts occupied my times of boredom, when the lesson became too repetitive.

As a person, I believed that I had the ability to be very kind, and although some of my actions would give evidence that this was false at times, I was sensitive enough to save fallen baby birds, release trapped animals, become teary eyed when saddened by a movie or sad event, like when my snake Barney died.

I remember using my mother's yellow rubber dish gloves to bring a fallen bird back to its nest, knowing my scent would cause the mother bird to possibly disown its offspring. Another time a mother raccoon made our chimney its nest, and she brought some annoying hitchhikers, fleas. I recall hearing odd noises for a few nights, which seemed to come from the living room, and I knew every sound our house might make at all times. This sound was not one of the normal ones, and I couldn't determine why there were fleas in our house, till I examined the fireplace closely.

I personally took the baby raccoon's out, using ski gloves I had for such things as handling animals with large teeth or claws, and I put them in a box in the back yard, for their mother to retrieve. Then I used some wire to prevent the mother from getting into the chimney again. My dad was no roof climber, and I liked to be on the roof, so I did the wiring. I remember how cool the baby raccoon's were, and I wanted to keep one for a pet, but not with fleas. Of course, my parents wanted nothing to do with that with or without the fleas. The mother did come back and get them I think, since the box was empty just a few hours later. The fleas stayed a while, till my parents bombed the house.

I also thought I was a good person because I had the ability and habit of finding kind words about people's positive attributes regardless of the negative circumstances they were temporarily subjected to. I would distract bullies from other less fortunate or female peers when I could, weather I liked the targeted person or not, simply by calling their negative actions cowardly with a comment like: "how big a pussy do you have to be to pick on someone like Lou? Duh, I dunno!" said with sarcasm aimed towards the intimidating person or just spoken towards the floor, which always worked.

I would help other students with advice on how to comprehend a subject they have been having trouble with, just by giving a different perspective or way of approaching things. I liked putting myself in others shoes, and seeing how I would feel if I were them in a negative situation, and admiring their feelings of accomplishment in positive ones with envy. The time frame was around second through fifth grade, where interacting with my peers was becoming much more interesting.

I was concerned more about how someone else would feel than how I did, which seemed natural and more understandable than my own feelings, and I could view situations more objectively and impartially when I wasn't involved. I understood why a few kids were always telling on someone, why some were always whining and complaining about the work, and why some were targets for bullies more than others.

Those individuals were normally the same three or four kids most of the time, like Barney Colon, Pete Billows, Louie Negron and a few more I can't recall the names of, along with some of the over sized, overweight or poor skin condition, acne challenged girls, which it seemed to affect the most. Girls seemed so sensitive to everything, which I could appreciate, becoming over emotional was simple but expressed differently by boys.

EXIT FOUR

The Academic Special Education Drive

Academically I suffered because homework was not my priority, and some teachers claimed that homework represented forty percent of our grade, and though A's or B's were my usual marks in testing situations, it almost never matched my overall grade. I was no genius, either, or at least I never felt like one anyway.

There's sometimes a feeling of guilt when a student knows they're intelligent, but doesn't apply or use that intelligence, and I suppose I felt guilty of that perhaps half the time. I attributed that to probable laziness, which may or may not be wrong, but it doesn't accomplish much, like stagnation. I had the nerve, the brains and the heart, but I was no wizard. I was not one to burn myself out with constant effort, as most people I paced what I did as I felt necessary to accomplish the goal set before me, doing things "as best as I could" for the specific task.

There were a few subjects that didn't easily fall into place for me, but those I would study either in other classes, recess, lunch or one of my many wandering moments where I could be alone without distractions. I even went on the school's roof many times to find peace, and to watch others, some looking for me, going about their business below. Unfortunately, the roof was visible from the first hill in the back, which rose higher than the school's roof, so avoiding detection by anyone was a fun challenge.

I was confused and even felt a little insulted when any teacher said: "try harder, put more effort into it", because there really was no such thing according to me, and I knew it was their job, essentially. What may be possible is to decrease distraction from the immediate task, which appears to increase effort, but it only increases the percent of your mind that's working on the main issue, by ignoring other issues, the issues that are sometimes more relevant to the individual than the subject being studied.

This doesn't mean I wasn't trying, it just means I had other things on my mind and had no way of distinguishing which issue was more important, as measured by my own mind. I always tried my best, as far as I could tell, and no teacher would convince me I needed to assert more effort into any subject, since the issues were mine, and I knew additional effort was not a realistic solution or even a possibility at times.

I would attempt any task many times if I had to, if it were a prerequisite to reach the next level or grade. Not harder thinking, just different due to circumstance, same level of focus, trying the same task again. So that's what I did, I focused then reasserted myself and that sufficed their needs and expectations enough to pass all grades.

I did understand the importance of repetition, but only to the point where it became imbedded in my mind, and that usually didn't require much time with subjects I liked. I discovered that if I studied something too frequently, it became less memorable than if I just studied it once or twice, like over repetitiveness could be deterring my efforts.

No one puts one hundred percent effort into everything they do one hundred percent of the time, and if they claim to, they're lying. Practice makes perfect as they say, but not every time, and I believe it is possible to over practice or have no natural talent for some tasks. For instance, I knew I'd never be a great painter; I don't and never did enjoy painting, so why practice painting? Tone-deaf people are unlikely to become musicians or musical critics, colorblind people cannot become pilots at night, and a lifeguard that can't swim is unlikely to be hired. Can a two hundred pound person ever be a jockey? Not if the horse has any say.

My father always said you can do anything you want, and though in a broad sense this is true, most people only seek what they want to seek, attempt to make a difference in this world in their own way, and not spread themselves too thin by trying to do too many things at the same time but focus on what they feel is important to them individually, have their uniqueness viewed as an accomplishment in the eyes of others and excel beyond what average efforts could accomplish in the same field of interest. His other favorite saying was: "you can be a bum, as long as you're an honest bum", an interesting thought in its self.

History was my main academic nemesis. I couldn't care less about what was, and I figured since it's said that history repeats itself, why not forget it so there's a chance it may not, or use the information to ensure repeats are not possible? I knew the point was to learn from what occurred, not so much forgetting about what path was traveled, but realizing the road could lead elsewhere, with different results, if enough effort is made to make it so.

That didn't help much, it was dull, and supposedly it repeats anyway, no matter what we think we learned. The only other subject I had a tough time in and had to actually study for was higher Math, and I knew then even though it was difficult, I had to know it, unlike what I believed of history. Math was the only subject I allowed my parents to help me with, because my dad was so advanced in it. How important could knowing the date of the end of the civil war be to my life? I still passed all my courses, and never needed that tidbit of information, along with countless other facts that are long since forgotten.

If I could not finish my work in school, it was unlikely it was coming home with me, as I didn't like carrying things around, besides a lighter or animal collection container perhaps, especially while outwitting the peers who were stalking me. I also didn't want to have to spend time doing school work at home, when I could be out doing things I liked.

I knew the material at hand, usually very un-interesting, but manageable as a tool used to get the next level of school completed. It was rare for me not to finish work during the school day; I believed in getting things done quickly but without rushing, while the material was still fresh in my head and I could complete the assignment more accurately, and then go do what I wanted to do.

My main goal was the completion of work, then my main interest was to befriend any person who showed any common interest or thought pattern that matched my own. It didn't take long to realize that one common factor or even two were insufficient to bond a real friendship, and unfortunately I seemed to have more in common with troublemakers than normal, average kids.

My sports ability, irritating wit and humor, and my defiance for authority were all attributes more readily shared with the degenerate set of students, and that was somewhat frustrating and confusing. I was searching for people who were open and willing to go deep into conversation and theory, and besides a male peer or two, most of the peers with these attributes were the girls.

Girls didn't possess interest in wildlife much, as I did usually, and they never showed interest at this age in befriending boys, any more than boys would want to befriend girls. I found girls much easier to get along with in general, though it seemed that they were thinking and speaking from a different planet at times, a much different thought process it appeared, not totally compatible or understandable without their desire or effort to make it that way.

I firmly believed that anyone, in any given situation, could be anyone's friend. Determining the individuals' need or desire to continue to advance cooperation or communication is the only factor preventing everyone from being everyone's friend, which simply can't be, there are not enough hours in the day, when considering a friendship that consists of participation for hours as a daily routine. So we don't, for the most part, we just accept most people as acquaintances, friendly or suspect.

We base this on intuition, the only tool available really. We try, in our early years, to make our friends based on geographical location and visibility, we see someone we have seen before a few or many times, eventually we talk to each other and occasionally we get along enough during the conversation to seek activities to do together, or share an interest in something together, like butterfly collecting.

There's no way for a child to realize how we appear to others with any useful insight for many years. The only logical approach is to obtain feedback from others you think are competent enough to give fair insight, perhaps because they showed you their competence once, and then to believe what you're told. Until a higher age, we allow emotion to guide us, so feelings of apprehension seem to hinder the desire to converse with a person, or fear that we won't be understood correctly or sound awkward to someone.

The opposite would be reckless forwardness, or confidence, not caring in the least about what someone may think about you enough to stop you from speaking to them and trying to connect. I felt both ways many times, from one extreme to the other, and I found that openness as opposed to paranoid passiveness seemed like a favorable quality with better results usually.

Understanding discontent others may show is not simple, especially for the people who think and whole heartily believe that they are good people, not bad. I think all kids believe they are good, for the most part, but have little clue as to how others view them. I know I've been caught off guard. I lived off guard usually, believing everyone and everything till I saw evidence to the contrary.

I often contemplated what others saw when looking at me, knowing how incorrect I'd likely be, but still trying to find a common opening, where minds would meet on a different plane, one of just theories that happen to match, ways of observing things uniquely, yet similarly. For most boys, this would take shape in the form of physical activities, sports, running around and playing tag, kick the can, basic children's games.

While attending school I believed I should be allowed to come and go as I saw fit, never belittling the need to attend, but thinking I have the freedom to just go if the need swarmed over me. I remember that I spent a lot of my grades four through six either going to the nurse, the office, the bathroom, the principals' office, wandering the halls peaking in at people I liked from the classroom doors window, or just leaving and going home or to a nearby stream to catch something alive.

Feigning sickness to get out of school was one of my favorite methods of dismissal. I would leave a classroom with a ninety-eight point six degree temperature, and just by concentrating it would be almost one hundred one by the time I reached the nurse. She would, of course, call my mother and send me right home. Then, by the time I walk out of her office and got to the car my fever would magically disappear.

My mother would pick me up and bring me home, naturally. I would no sooner get home than I would be looking to go outside to play or hunt in the woods, which made my mother wonder just how sick I really was. She would prevent me from doing that, saying "if you feel good enough to go out, you can go back to school too"! So I'd be trapped at home for the day, but still happier than if I had been in class.

I actually enjoyed being sick for real, except for the weak shivering lethargic part of it, having a fever seemed to make me more relaxed and focused, and the feeling of warmth from my blankets felt overly satisfactory, as though I hadn't been warm ever in my life. Knowing I had to do nothing but recover and rest was a very peaceful state of mind, as though the rest of the world had been put on hold during my recovery.

Even the great tickle couldn't transgress a fever, which was very pleasing and appreciated, as if whatever virus I had was doing me a favor unconsciously. My mother would always make me lightly buttered jelly toast, with warm milk or ice water, dependent upon what I felt like having. I believe all kids like to be catered to, when they can feel the most sorry for themselves, like during illness or injury.

So watching television became the activity of the day when I was actually sick, and since I felt like doing nothing else, that was fine. The best feeling while being sick was after a trip to the bathroom, when I'd leave the secure warmth of my blanket and go shivering into the bathroom, then upon returning to bed, getting under my pre-warmed blankets and soaking in the heat like a tree absorbing light from the sun.

A very comfortable, peaceful sense of relief, like when you get to the beach too soon and it's cold, and then the sun comes up, and melts your goose bumps away. I knew photosynthesis was how trees absorbed light energy, having nothing to do with heat, and though I knew my skin was no leaf, I occasionally believed I could photosynthesize, through my skin or my eyes, so I would stare at the sun sometimes, believing this would strengthen my eyes.

Luckily, I never was damaged from this odd practice somehow, even when I looked at a total eclipse once, wondering why everyone kept telling me I'd go blind if I did. I never looked too long though, even at an eclipse, I would observe for a small length of time, believing more could be too much of a good thing, like studying, and too much indulgence would have adverse effects.

When I did go outside during the course of a normal weekend day or after school, I would go animal hunting in the woods. Different species of salamanders were always great fun to find, and they were usually seen first when lifting any rock in the area. I marveled at the different characteristics of such a creature and its environment, very quick, and slimy, a simple life form perfect in design. Made good fish bait, though I didn't like fishing much.

I had my Popeil pocket fisherman, which broke soon after I got it, but I found fishing very boring, unless it was necessary for survival, and it never was in my case. Dropping a line into water and waiting for something to happen seems dull to me, pointless, and a waste of time. I found more sights of interest in a stream, swamp, or under a rock than in half of my classes.

I found many insects, along with turtles and snakes, and I never got bored looking around the woods. Searching places no one went always gave me the feeling I might find something that no one else ever had, diamonds, fossils, alien space stuff, gold, I always thought to myself as I searched: "you never know what you'll find". I only found a fossil once in my life. Still seeking the other things I mentioned to date, and so far, unsuccessfully.

In school or anywhere else, I never enjoyed watching boys picking on girls, this was totally wrong to me, and it bothered me more that seeing other boys get abused for some reason, it was more irritating to watch, possibly since I felt it unnecessary to bother with girls in this manner, they posed no threat, or perhaps due to primitive survival of the species instincts, knowing one would become my life's partner some day, it just seemed wrong to hurt them in any way.

There were girls that could be bigger jerks at times, and even larger in size than most guys, but they never directly bothered with me. Nikki Brach and Vera Litvane were my primary female friends, both at different times, neither were the quick growing type as I described before, in fact, they were quite short and thin, frail, and I found them interesting and pleasing to be around.

By friends I mean they would agree with my point of view, seeing my side of any conflict, and work with me on projects, and talk to me fairly uninhibited. I noticed early that girls were not interested in competing with boys or each other in the way boys do, and conversation was their specialty and interest. They made good communicators and philosophers, as well as study partners.

I loved to philosophize about everything, and most boys of the age I was wouldn't hear of it. If some sport or contest wasn't involved, there was little or no interest shown by my male peers. They didn't care much about why people exist, where we all came from, how we got here, if the chicken or the egg came first, or anything they had no immediate answer for or that they deemed irrelevant. Discussion of attitude relative to actions or reactions was simply above their comprehension, thus not a possible subject for discussion.

I would wonder about things like, what point could there be to life? Thinking that I had already lived two life spans of experience, then one millisecond of thought later found it insufficient was common. I knew one person's lifetime was a tiny span or event compared to the scope of the galaxy, even before seeing this fact displayed at Hayden planetarium, which only supplied me with perspective. I contemplated the equalization of the right and left side of the brain, once I knew they existed, finding the medium between calculation and speculation, emotion and thought, total feeling and total numb paralysis, creativity and fact, imagination and reality. Since they all come from the same place, there has to be a medium.

These topics were more interesting to my female peers, thought not many girls could handle it for long either. If a tree falls in the woods, does it make a sound, if no one is there to hear it? I think that whether or not someone is there to witness it is irrelevant. The resident deer or squirrel is there to hear it, along with countless bugs and microbes, though they'll never tell. If no one sees a lightning strike, and a fire ensues, did the lightning strike, though no one saw it? Ask the firefighter who's engaging the resulting fire now. I went to the zoo one time, just an average trip with my parents to Turtleback zoo, and I recall thinking that if you put a basketball hoop in a monkeys' cage, and put a court right next to the cage, thus allowing the monkey to watch people play, would the monkey also learn to play? Would a Gorilla?

If all religions are correct, and they vary immensely in some ways, and are believed by millions, does this make them all right? Or all wrong? I believe they are all correct for the one who does the believing, but incorrect in ways not fathomable by our species yet, maybe one day we will understand it all, and we all do understand the whole picture once this life is over, at least I hope, or believe. It's as though this life is the infancy step to a greater existence, not bound by physical parameters as we understand them, just the beginning, death is only the next step to rebirth within a different reality.

I believed the girls loved talking to me, I always seemed interested in what they said, and was mostly, and I also think they kind of felt sorry for me at times, watching bullies get their way sometimes didn't seem logical to them, not realizing what did or didn't really bother me. The cheap shots, the name-calling, were events that occurred on a daily basis usually.

The girls cheered when the bullies didn't get their way or were made fools of by me, laughed when I entertained the class by making ridiculous or funny comments out loud, and I think they were drawn to me because they couldn't figure me out. I wouldn't bother directly fighting back, answering violence with violence seemed useless, and they seemed to like that, not ever acknowledging or realizing how vengeful I could become.

Or perhaps it was because I always smiled and laughed, after I was insensitive to the effects of negativity, regardless of the seriousness of a situation. Maybe they liked my bully distraction methods, the way that whenever someone had something negative to say about someone specific, no matter whom it was they were speaking about, I always interjected and found a positive attribute about the person, while disrespecting the perpetrator, and inevitably I would redirect the negative attention to myself.

I remember once Craig attacking Nikki verbally, with things obviously relating to her name, he'd sing: Nikki Bock, the girl with a cock, what a shock" over and over, till she appeared affected by it. I would call to Craig in mid chorus and say: "yea, you wish you had one, huh, pigmy brain"? This would cause him to forget about Nikki, and make him confront me, trying to get me to wince at his fake punches, which I did without losing my smile.

I didn't care if he could get me to blink, that's what eyelids are for. But the main point was to cause him to forget about harassing Nikki, which he did. Then the usual threats about what he'll do to me when teachers aren't around or after school would pour out of his mouth, as they had so many times. This was not unexpected, but it mattered very little, my goal was already accomplished, which he never even knew.

Even though I could never condone boys who picked on girls, I had said my share of hurtful things once in a while, like calling the fat girl fat, the exact phrase I used was 'penisless pachyderm', though I knew she was really ok as a person. Hillary Mirren was one of the girls' names, and I remember her mainly because she lived directly across the street from me, and though she mostly ignored me, she knew I would not usually intentionally or continuously cause her anguish.

The one time I remember being mean and saying something about her size, I remember the hurt look in her eyes, wondering what she did to invoke such a comment, and I realized it was not needed, what I said, and that feeling of inner satisfaction you feel when someone is hurting more than you disappeared. She was mad enough to never really associate with me, she held a grudge well, and we had nothing in common anyway except for our street address.

I would see her crying in anger nearly every day as she got home, slamming the doors, knowing someone did or said something to her. I would only smile towards her when I saw her, letting her know I would cause no grief and I was no enemy. She was always seeing me do bad things. Like when I siphoned my mom's cars gas tank and lit it, she called my parents to tell them there was a fire in the garage.

It was actually on the driveway, I wasn't that stupid, but the flames were a good ten feet high, so it may have looked as if the fire was in the garage from her viewpoint. Or when I threw rocks at the birds in the plum tree, broke something made of glass in the street; anything I did that she observed would be shared information with my mom.

Once I ran across the street to Hillary's' house, and tried stopping my forward momentum with my hand on one of those small, rectangular windows that sometimes surround a front door, very thick, not the see through type, but my hand when right through it, cutting me pretty deeply on the hand.

I didn't get any stitches, but it bled for about twenty minutes. The crying continued beyond the point when I realized that it didn't hurt, just the site of this trauma caused enough fear to cry about. This girl I'm certain would have a whole novel of events she found me involved in, but she generally ignored me, and I did the same, which was a kind of peace treaty between us.

For the most part, physical differences I viewed as uniqueness, not weaknesses or handicaps to be preyed upon, though I would occasionally take advantage of them as any kid would, simply because it was easy to do, and I remember feeling guilt when I allowed myself to be so shallow, cruel or superficial. I never attempted seeking revenge on a girl in my life, or gave much thought to it, since they were so different I just wrote off any negativity from a girl as just a 'girl' thing, incomprehensible to a boy's viewpoint. This was rare, thought, girls liked picking on other girls, about things that would have no effect on a boy, like making fun of clothes, hair or nails, stuff like that.

EXIT FIVE

Friends, Animals and the Crooked Ramp to Psychology

There was only one black child in the whole town of New Providence when I grew up there, and he was somewhat handicapped, being restricted intellectually to the point where there were some things that he simply couldn't learn. He was the first real best friend I had, which lasted for many years, and I think we met in third grade. The first time we met, we fought till I pinned him down and forced him to stop fighting.

He was one of the few people I ever actually hit as a kid, but only after he hit me a few times, naturally. There was no discussing my way around confronting him, he was too simple minded to listen to reason, he had nothing I could damage and was always in trouble just like me, so my normal retribution was useless. He started the fight because some idiot peer of ours was claiming I had said something negative or derogatory about him apparently, which I didn't, but he wasn't smart enough to be suspicious of kids lying to him. After he told me what someone claimed I said, though I cannot recall the exact words, I assured him it was a lie and we became friends.

Peter R. Hollimond was every bit as hyper as I was, and found interest in some of the same things I did. We would stand in the schools' field and throw a baseball around for hours at a time, throwing and catching as many pop ups as we could. When we wrestled, either for gym or for fun, neither of us could pin the other, even though I did pin him the first time we met.

We were matched pretty closely, physically. I think I was a better bowler, pool player, or golfer, but he didn't really play those much. I can imagine now hearing his fake southern accent voice, calling me from where ever: "Hey, Greenie! What's up Stymie?" I called him 'Wheezer' or 'Stymebob' back, and he'd say something like let's play ball. I used the name Styme or Stymie frequently later on, but usually I pronounced it as Shtymie or Shtyme with the silent 'e', which sounded more normal for some reason. Wheezer I got from the little rascals, which we both liked.

I was fairly certain this boy would never become a rocket scientist, no matter how much effort he put into it. We would go for hours to a place I loved going, the Great Swamp, which we had to be driven to, and we'd collect anything live, and bring the creatures' home to our weary guardians. We'd walk to the Watchung reservation, since that was much closer than the swamp, and catch water snakes or frogs, and bring them home too. We were usually covered with mud or completely soaking wet upon arriving home from either the swamp or the reservation.

Peter was usually the subject of many insults, and the only kid who was insulted racially, an easy target for the bullies because he didn't understand most of the time that he was being insulted. I thought it was tough to be the only black person around, and the only other person as isolated as he had been was me, which made us our own group. I didn't mind so much when others made fun of him because he was slow, he was, not by his own choosing, but I hated it when his color was the point of an insult, since I didn't see any point in isolating him for that, seemed pretty pointless and wrong, and quite annoying.

Peter lived with his grandma, who was one of the nicest people I can recall. She made some old home style southern dishes, pigs' feet, chitlans, fried chicken, as if she knew that the best and only way to control her grandson was through his pallet. They lived in the only apartments in New Providence that there were at that time.

These apartments were very red and made of brick, close together, scenic, and rather expensive for its day.

Through the woods at the end of my street towards Peter's apartment you had to cross over Livingston path to get to his house. This path ran from the top of a high elevation road in the area to the beginning of Livingston Avenue, a short road in the town. The path was about a quarter mile long, ten feet wide, and was the best sledding area around, since no cars are allowed on it.

In the summer, it's where all the wildflowers grow, on the sides of the path, and the bees and butterflies are everywhere. This is where all the kids went to sled, so it was a little crowded and dangerous, but no one seemed to worry about it much. I never cared, and I would go later or at night just for the pleasure of being alone and having all the space myself, me and my Flexible Flyer. The only other place I remember sledding besides here and Bear Mountain was at Sleepy Hollow, the place George Washington made a fort in, back in civil war days, around Morristown New Jersey. That was great, and deer were often wandering around while people were sledding, which was amazing to me.

There were pretty steep hills on both ends of my street. It was basically a mountain, which isn't saying much in New Jersey. The mountains of New Jersey were enough for me, having never been to the Rockies, Sierra Nevada's, or the Great Smoky Mountains yet. These mountains were mine. I knew every inch, tree, rock, path and hideout there was. I built many tree houses in these woods through the late sixties and early seventies, also some lean-tos', places I could go when I felt like disappearing or to play fort with others.

The property was township owned so when employees discovered my forts, they destroyed them; my guess was that they had nothing better to do. I rebuilt many times, each better than before, and a couple of times I would stay in them overnight, leaving my parents panicking about where I was. I was about ten the first time I stayed out all night. I would just walk back into my house the next morning, walk in like I was just coming home from school and nothing was wrong and I'd simply say: "hi mom!"

My mother, in tears, would come running to me, saying how worried she was that I might have been killed, kidnapped or something. She was always happier to see me than angry enough to try punishing me for being out all night. She'd have to call the police to tell them to stop looking for me, which I think they did anyway themselves.

This would only happen on Friday or Saturday, or during the summer, since I had school other days, and for as much as I wanted to skip those days, I wouldn't. While I was young, mostly animals, toys and food would be brought to the fort, and later on, Playboy or Penthouse magazines would replace the toys, though food would still be part of the experience. I would build small fires, for heat, cooking or light, at every age.

In the tree house, fires would be a little difficult to build, so I took a concrete stirring troth from the construction site two houses away from mine, wedged it into floorboards in the fort and cooked in that. I had many good times in forts, never being hindered by anyone or anything, I felt like a pioneer, out on the trail, which was ironic because the town's schools team name was the Pioneers. I thought it was odd, since no one there seemed to be looking for anything, except me. The non-pioneering pioneers.

From there forts I would catch many animals, as I always enjoyed doing, using my hands mostly and sometimes small traps made of household items, laundry baskets, salt bags or silverware trays. I began to notice that this animal catching practice made my hands very quick, since I caught most things by hand, and if anyone thinks that's easy, try it at a swamp one day. Frogs and water snakes can be very fast, and all snakes might bite. I felt like I could run through woods like a gazelle, bouncing off rocks and fallen tree parts, like slam dancing off nature's landscapes, and it felt like I was almost flying.

I chased down and caught a baby rabbit once, behind my friend Roy's house, which I can't even think about doing now. The bigger you get, the more apparent obstacles become, like tree branches. Plus, it's easier to run quietly when you weigh one hundred pounds as opposed to two hundred twenty, not to mention ankles grow older and more fragile over time. Baby rabbit's only run fast in short spurts, so the challenge was predicting the direction of the next spurt, which I did one time by the sheerest of luck.

One day, possibly the same day only later on, one of the neighborhood kids, Roy Hangert and I went behind his house into the woods. He lived across the street and down five or so houses, and his backyard was also the woods. Roy was a friend of mine at times but really more of an acquaintance, a real jock with the basketball hoop on his garage, and enough sporting equipment to last a lifetime.

His main game was golf with his dad, he practiced a lot in his yard, and though my dad played too, I didn't practice nearly as much as he did. He usually beat me in basketball since I made no serious effort most of the time, but I did win occasionally, making the effort just to be competitive and show him I was not bad at the game, or because I was weary of his bragging. This had an odd effect on his attitude, he'd become very displeased, which I thought was strange, since he usually won anyway. I guess you could say he was a poor looser.

This day, he decided to play my game, which if it wasn't Star Trek or dinosaurs, it was hunting in the woods for things, animals, rocks, butterflies, or whatever. As we went in, we heard a loud hum before we got thirty feet in, and by the time I looked at Roy, there were two hornets the size of small birds on his head. He screamed, I screamed, and we ran out of the woods as if a fire had been set to our clothes.

He got stung a few times, I did not; I only wondered why I had not seen this nest when I was around the same place earlier. He wound up with giant welts on his head and one on his shoulder; I discovered where not to go behind his house, unless I'm armed for hornet attack. Roy was never too willing to go back into the woods again with me. He was also the only person I knew who had Spiral Meningitis. That didn't look fun, and it kept him from school for what seemed to be months. I never had the child diseases, no measles, mumps, pox, or anything, except one time.

When I was about six years of age I got a disease resident to Cape Cod exclusively, and ran about a 105 fever. It was like a pox, small itchy spots all over like a rash, but according to doctors it wasn't chicken-pox or roseola. That was the sickest I've ever been, nearly to date. That's where my parents liked to go in the summer.

The jersey shore came later; I went there with my sister more than with my parents. At the beach, if I was not in the water, which I usually was thanks to my overzealous instructor, I was digging giant pits to bury stuff in, or hunting for cool shells or those sand crabs to play with. I got sunburned nearly every time I went, since I wouldn't sit still long enough to let anyone put sunscreen on me.

I always thought, while watching my sister bake in the sun, that sun bathing was a big waste of time and completely useless, and I still do. If you're going to the beach, you should swim or look for items not found anywhere else, perhaps with a metal detector, not sit under the sun to tan, because that can be done anywhere. The only good reason I could think of was to dry off after swimming, and get warmth at the same time, otherwise, I liked shade.

We also went to Bear Mountain in New York often, where I would immediately climb to the top of the mountain upon arriving. Very pretty place, remote, serene and pleasing to the eye, it made the reservation look tiny, noting but massive mountains and woods as far as I could see. Pretty high, too, I'm not certain how many feet, but it's a long walk to the top. I would leave my family in the dust upon arriving, making my dad become very fit while trying to follow me around the mountain as best he could. I would usually loose him and meet the family back at the lodge, where they would be sitting around wondering where I was, and I'd just appear, asking what's for lunch, dinner or whatever, as though I was never missing.

I got the usual lecture about the dangers of being alone once I came back. My family didn't ski, so we usually went there during the summer for the hiking, swimming and so on. I do remember going in winter once, the sledding was spectacular, and I was half frozen and suffering from hypothermia by the time my parents convinced me to come back to the lodge for some hot chocolate. I recall that it was a long drive there, and that's the only complaint I had about it. The ride home was forgettable, since I was usually asleep, having expelled all my energy on the mountain temporarily.

I found that swimming would also exhaust all my energy, without causing one drop of sweat, and you never realized it till you stopped. Sleeping after swimming was ok, but at night I dreamed about swimming often, it was the floating feeling I loved so much and I had many good swimming related ones, which created a dilemma. My mother told me some years ago that I was not potty trained till very late, six or seven, and the dreams were the cause of this as I remember.

When people go to pools, there are signs everywhere to please not urinate in a pool; "welcome to our ool, notice there's no "P" in it, please keep it that way", and other clever signs, which I obeyed mostly, but never while in my dreams unless I realized that I was dreaming at the time. So while swimming around in my dream, feeling quite peaceful and relaxed, I would at times feel the urge to go, which I would, and this would cause me to wake, and realize, I just wet the bed. This was very irritating, as anyone could imagine, but more so because I didn't realize I was dreaming and I usually was conscious of dreams, most of the time. What was odd was that no memory of the usual tickle occurred during dream swimming, though I am not sure why.

When I was about eight years old my parents decided to send me to my first summer camp, Camp Riverbend, around the corner from my house sort of, four or five miles away, but still on the same road. I assumed my parents needed to get me out of their site for a while, letting the camp deal with my insatiable appetite for adventure, with no more than their phone number to save the camp staff from me.

I believe it was the second week, or the beginning of the third, right after singing the song; "and the green grass grows all around, all around, and the green grass grows all around", which occurred every day, that I became intolerant of the sing along and circumstance and just left the camp and walked home disgusted. My sense of direction was uncanny, and I knew exactly how to get home, from here or anywhere else.

I'm not sure what my mother thought, but the shock of finding me home when I was supposed to be at camp was apparent. She blamed the camp for loosing me, though I knew there was nothing they could do about it and probably didn't realize I was gone for a long time. An arts and crafts class with many sing-alongs was not going to spark any interest for me. That camp didn't last very long, just up to that day.

To cope with my need for adventure, or to slow me down some, my parents tried every diet possible, including no sugar, salt, MSG, food color, and such. I also remember taking a few pills every day, for a long time from around age six or so, like Ritalin, vitamins, and that era's version of Thorazine and Stellazine. I didn't think any of them worked on me anyway, and they had no effect on the tickle at all.

What did keep my attention was having female friends to talk with, or subjects and activities I actually enjoyed. I have always liked having female friends, more so than any male friend I remember growing up with. Cooties were just some stupid word for boys to use who were afraid to socialize with girls, and I couldn't care less about their supposedly having them. When very young, little boys indulge in activities like using each other as tackling dummies, or punching bags, or garbage disposals, backboards, and the like. Little girls, I observed, use each other and boys for entirely different reasons. Knowledge being one of those reasons, the other appeared to be a power struggle between other girls, a position battle to be closest to the guy they liked.

They also like to hear opinions about themselves, what looks good, bad, or what I think about this person or if I thought the person liked them, just normal insecurity issues. They like those things along with simulating life as a married person, or having kids, which is why I figured they like dolls. Sort of like playing mommy, having someone to care for, while boys like playing army and only care for themselves.

No, I wouldn't play with dolls, except to maybe melt them or shoot them towards space, but I was open to discussion on any topic they had. I realized early that a good, truthful and unselfish mate would be preferable to just good looks through time, and analyzing potential and attitude for a prospective mate became natural, even when I didn't realize what mating was all about. I only knew that the girl I marry would have to be my best friend, and thus befriending girls seemed logical and natural.

I saw myself shuffling actions and reactions around my own mind and emulating or being able to emulate them for my own expression. I had a tendency to give back any attitude directed towards me, sometimes sarcastically enough to annoy others, especially teachers, who always claimed that they were not being as sarcastic as I was. But how others spoke to me was how my reply would be generated, with the same inflection and attitude, whether they liked it or not.

I tried to adapt the level of communication to suit whoever I'm talking to, in an attempt to minimize misunderstanding, and reach people on their level. Or I simply expressed their attitude or inflection back to them, in an attempt to give illustration of how they are communicating with me, allowing them a chance to contemplate either a response, or discontinue the mood or tone of dialog they started with. But I could also be unconcerned about how people talked to me, each other, and so on.

As individuals, we soak our heads from the inside with this galaxy of information called life. We can only give what's received. From age three to five, or two to five, all we see remains forever in our minds, or so it is said, by professionals. I think I learned much from little girls, about relationships, just through conversation. I saw the physical distinctions. I have played "you show me I'll show you" with possibly two girls in my life, the only one I recall was Louanne Brea.

I was around six or seven years of age, and obviously we never felt as though we were being perverse, it was just simple curiosity on both our parts, she was as curious as I was. We did things like that, and it was interesting, but mostly we did other activities, like cooking, playing board games, bike riding, and looking at nature of course. She moved while we were very young, but I never forgot her. I remember thinking how impossible it looked for a girl to have a whole baby come from such a tiny hole, and that I was very glad I wouldn't have to experience that myself, being a boy. How painful that must be, I couldn't imagine, nor would I want to. I felt sorry for girls, knowing they would want the experience eventually, no matter how painful it would be, and how odd that desire was.

I asked my own mother one day, just prior (or after, possibly) to the show and tell I described above, in my most innocent little boy voice, "what's that between your legs?" She then described to me what a vagina was, quite deliberately. All very calm and collective, which my parents specialized in, she gave me the whole process, which made me a genius among little men.

I understood, kind of already figured, and said thanks, and then I went to sleep. This, the making of life, at that time left no impression upon me, other than the fact that I liked biology as a subject. I couldn't quite picture the procedure, and I was in no rush to find out. There were better things to do. I understood and believed one day I would have my own family, and it wouldn't be for many years. It added to good reasons for liking girls in general.

I just figured eventually a girl like Barbara Eden would just magically appear before me, the proverbial "Jeannie with the light brown hair", we'd have perfect children, the perfect house, and we would be happy. I also hoped we would be rich, as well, or at least as well off as my parents were. I could only day dream that finding this perfect girl would happen, that issue never appeared in my nights dreams, no place for the tickle to interfere I suppose. The subject wasn't traumatic enough; the feeling of peace and understanding, deep trust and contentment were all I could imagine.

I never worried about succeeding monetarily in life, I just figured I would get by fine, as I always had, never realizing the cold hard facts of adulthood that would spring upon me one day when I least expected it. I never had an allowance, and didn't need one since I needed nothing that cost money that I knew of.

My parents provided all my necessities, and there was no need for extra cash. If I wanted to go to a movie, my mother would give me a ride and the cash needed, and most of the time all I wanted to do was to hunt for snakes and other animals, which costs nothing to do. I was not a consumer in any normal respect; I did not buy anything related to things I liked, baseball caps, posters, and memorabilia from any sport or activity, as I found these things useless.

The only time I had things like baseball or football cards or franchise specific clothes was when relatives and friends gave them to me, and usually I'd give them away to someone just for fun and to have them believe me to be generous. Pet care supplies were all I needed, and I managed to keep a good supply without trouble.

When I was around ten or eleven years of age, I recall a specific adventure in the Great Swamp, on the Chatham side of the swamp, with Peter, which we labeled with our own language as a strangeoddity, a cross between strange and odd, and it sounded cool to say.

My mom, which is what Peter called her as well, drove us there most of the time. The road into the swamp was about ten foot wide, and a half-mile long, and the gate across it was open all the time except during July or August. It was the best life form collection dish of the state, in my small opinion at that time. Surrounded by nature, with nets, gloves, containers or pillow cases, we made our way off the side of the road, picking a spot for my mom to stop before we'd be seen going into the woods from the park rangers view, right under the sign stating: "area off limits".

About a hundred feet into the swamp, the edge was awaiting with life galore. Snakes were our main goal, and water snakes could put up quite a fight. We never saw or thought about snappers, moccasins, or rattlers; I had never seen any there so we never worried we would have a dangerous encounter. I never told Peter that these creatures were native to the swamp, either, so he wouldn't worry.

Wading two or three feet into the depths of the swamp is a strange thing. It just engulfs your legs completely, and causes incredible suction on your legs as you attempt to walk, like your legs weigh hundreds of pounds each or you're walking on Jupiter. I'm absolutely certain there are individual sneakers I used to own embedded somewhere in the depths of the mud in the bottom of the swamp. I lost at least two pair before getting the right boots to wear. My foot came up, the sneaker didn't, and I would have to go all the way home with only one sneaker and one extremely dirty sock.

The swamp water has trees, dead and live, growing and fallen dead in all directions like some oversized version of the game pickup sticks. There are also large, round clumps of grass and sticks that I suspected were beaver nests, but I never dissected one to find out. My guess would be these clumps were 3 to about 6 feet across, and a few feet high, and there were many of them.

As soon as we began our hunt by becoming silent and listening for signs of life, one of those clumps decided to start moving towards us. It was about twenty feet away, and we both noticed that it was getting closer to us, and not very slowly, either. We decided we would run and scream, or scream and run, but we ran fast enough to catch my mother before she left the swamp driveway.

I have never before or since seen those move, even when I had been hip-deep next to one holding it for balance, which occurred often, but one decided to move today. That was Peter's last trip there, it scared him that badly. I noticed that the chill up my spine didn't begin till I began running and I thought that maybe we didn't really have to bother running away.

With that plan temporarily gone, we went home and started a little fire in the woods, just off Livingston path next to one of my forts, a controlled, contained, marshmallow and hot dog cooking fire. Though I never got burned from any camp fire, I did singe all the hair on my arm and half my head once, when I turned our Kitchen's gas oven on without lighting it, waited till I smelled the gas, then opened the oven door and lit a lighter in front of it. The fireball was impressive, but it didn't start another fire in the kitchen, or cause any damage. Just the smell of burnt hair was left throughout the house, and since we had an attic fan, I was able to get rid of the odor quickly, before my parents smelled it.

When I went to the swamp alone, it was usually during June and July, and I would ride my bike there once I was a little older, maybe eleven or twelve. There was an astounding number of deer fly in the swamp during those times, which is why I went alone. I would bring a butterfly net with me, and drape it over my head. Then I'd let all the flies, numbering at least fifty at a time, land on my head, then I'd invert the net catching most of them, and crush them all with my foot while catching snakes, turtles, frogs or whatever simultaneously.

By the time I was done with the first wave of flies, another wave would attack, like the Chinese during Vietnam. I had almost no time to put the net back over my head before I was covered by the flies again. I did this all day, even though the swamp was closed because of this fact during those months. I would never bring anyone with me during fly days, knowing how unpleasant it is to be there. I also could not let my mother drive me, since I knew she wouldn't leave me there while the place was closed for the season.

I never concerned myself about the weather when going to the swamp, it could be blazing hot or thunder and lightning, it didn't matter. When it rained, I would go eagerly because all the wild life would be out everywhere, not just in the swampy portion that was too deep in some places to wander into without boots or a boat.

I was there once during a large storm, and I was looking around one of my favorite spots when I heard this huge thunder clap. I looked around as I heard the large oak tree about twenty feet away from me crack and I realized that lightning had just hit it, seeing some smoke rising from the base behind the tree.

As I saw the dirt on the far side of the tree begin to lift out of the ground, with seemingly slow motion movement, I began to run away from it on an angle, towards the clearing right next to where I was and away from the path of the falling tree. I heard it coming down right behind me as I just made it far enough to be a few feet away from the trees' main trunk, which was now lying right in back of me in a giant heap across the entire clearing.

Had it fell towards the other trees more in towards the swamp, it probably wouldn't have come down completely, and I would have had no reason to run. Somehow I managed to be between two large branches that were now on my left and right, five feet difference in either direction would have pinned me under one of them.

I went back to the trees original standing point by jumping up on the trunk and walking down to the base, which was now just a great big hole in the ground, with the roots and dirt making a ten foot wall where it used to stand. There I found three snakes and a badger, who were all still too shocked by the tree's fall to move, along with many bugs and worms all displaced from their usual cover. Naturally, I caught two of the snakes, both ribbon snakes, and I still don't know why they didn't leave, they seemed frozen with fear but once I started reaching for them, then they moved, pretty rapidly, enough for one to get away.

Badgers are not friendly animals, and this one just lost its home, which made it look quite pissed off if one can imagine a disgruntled badger. They make this sound when they're mad, like no sound I ever heard before or want to again. The Badger was on the other side of the pit, about 20 feet away from the snakes and me. I was surprised that it just turned from me and walked away, never appearing like it needed to run because I don't think badgers fear anything. I think the Badger fell out of the tree as it fell, it seemed stunned somewhat, and didn't appear to have any desire to attack me. Maybe he knew I had nothing to do with the loss of his home.

The event left no impression on me, and within the next few days, I decided to bring a mouse into school and I let it go in the teachers' lounge, mainly because it was the first door I saw. Then I stood by the door waiting to hear some reaction, I got to hear a few screams that day. I was a little upset when I learned that a teacher crushed it with a shoe, but only because I wanted it for snake food, and I thought, what a waste, to die as an insect does with no purpose.

The principal's office was like my second classroom it seemed, where I specialized in attending. Though most adults seemed to be honestly attempting to help me, I couldn't let them be bothered with me, school helpers, teachers, guidance counselors, and all these people wasting their time trying to figure out what my problem was. They would never address the real issues anyway, which was not me mostly, but the occasionally aggressive peers I had, along with the boring and repetitive curriculum that seemed to never end or move on.

It wasn't that important, and I dealt with those situations my own way by now. I had their answers academically, I did the work assigned, and I even allowed them to force me to write right-handed, even though I was a natural lefty. When psychological aid was recommended for me at age five or six, my parents agreed that it might be helpful somehow.

I was just considered a "problem" to be solved through some other educational means, like placement in a specialized class. But since that resolution wouldn't come about for many years, the adults in my life all figured that to begin helping me, analysis would be the most productive course of action. They, of course, did not ask me what I thought was needed, and they probably wouldn't have listened anyway, since I had told them all my issues many times to no avail long ago.

So off we go, to the land of analysis, where the main topics discussed were philosophy, and chess game moves. For sixty bucks an hour, that's a very expensive philosophical chess game. Most of my sessions were chess games, literally and figuratively, since I believe Chess to be a mirror to real life in many ways, and I found the doctors obvious redirection of topic to my concerns and thoughts quite amusing.

My parents just said that someone wanted to talk to me, as a friend, but I knew the real story and I couldn't understand why they thought paying someone to hear about the same problems I had told everyone about already for free would be worthwhile. I knew that there are three basic things that affect a person thought their life, their parents, environment, and friends. I knew a doctor would not change any of those factors, nor could they.

The first doctor's name was Douglas I think, and all his questions seemed pretty standard. How do you feel, what's bothering you, why do you disrupt class, how do you feel about homework and peers, why do you continually bite your nails, these were normal questions, and I tried to give the answers that he was looking for, but this wasn't the point, according to him.

The answers I gave were honest, though he didn't appear to believe them. Responses like I felt fine, nothing's bothering me, I like to entertain myself and others, some kids are assholes but I can handle it, why do unnecessary work, and who needs nail clippers when teeth work so well, were all unacceptable responses. Like something was wrong or insincere about these answers. He called it over rationalization, which was odd since the only other response I thought would be considered irrational, and that didn't seem logical.

This first doctor swore in writing to my parents that if I were not entered into military school, I'd be a lot of trouble or have to be declared incorrigible. He may have been correct for the most part, but teaching me to use and maintain weapons didn't strike my parents or me as a necessity or even as a good idea. I have never felt the need for owning or having a gun, and I think no one needs one with the possible exception of needing them for survival, like hunting for food, self-defense, or during a war where the opposition also has them.

The cops in England don't need them, and they get by fine without them whether the opposition has them or not. We're the only creatures on earth with enough wisdom to kill each other, and ourselves, one by one, or to create devices able to wipe out millions at a time, or one by one just by pulling a trigger. What an intelligent, talented, superior and gifted species we are! Too bad we can't cure the common cold or solve the homeless and poverty issues of our planet, though at least my dad was trying to solve the world's waste problems.

I attempted to communicate what I saw as the perfect world to these doctors, where everyone has everything they need and want, working ten or so months of the year and having no need for money, everything free, problem is who would want to be a garbage man, if no one had to be?

I felt this was a schooling issue, determining potential and talent and building on it for the perfect career, I suppose a month out of a year would have to be reserved for needed tasks, such as garbage collection, construction, and maintenance oriented jobs that simply have to be done, and should be by anyone able to do so for enough time as to balance the flow of necessities and desires. This way, during the six to eight weeks off, people can do anything they wish, having real vacations with no worries.

Too greedy a species are we, where most feel a need to be 'ahead of' or 'better' than others, leave competition to the athletes and appreciate those feats, play those games for the real reason, till they cannot continue due to age or health and only for fun, feel no remorse for the jobs we do to assist society's continued growth and care, they are as important as any.

I could see a star trek type world without the aliens yet, which I found truly inspirational and possible, perhaps our planets future destiny created out of necessity. How many people would strive to be a doctor or lawyer, if this gave them no advantage over common working people? There would still be a need for lawyers, only with different priorities.

I also found far too many conflicting philosophies, in each individual opinion, and while they all make sense, none truly do completely including mine, and all appear sheer human speculation at what is not actually fathomable till one is at the end of their road, in other words, in death we'll find out, theoretically. All topics have unlimited possible view points, for each statement there are counter statements, no definitive single answer to most, just general human understanding of what may be a good or bad thing, varying greatly from individual to individual and topic to topic. Over rationalization of the species, I suppose. Math seems to be the only true real constant with actual solid conclusions, in basics anyway.

The doctors were not impressed with my thoughts, I was too easily distracted and single minded was their determination, which appeared to be conflicting I thought. How can one be distracted while one is single minded about what ever topic interests them? Or was it the idea that I was distracted from things that were, by them, thought of as necessities in society and thus the educational and pediatric psychology field believed I would not cope or contribute to society if I could not pay attention to matters they deemed important?

They could only determine that I needed Ritalin, the miracle-calming drug with completely unknown long term effects, but that was fine by me. It was made especially for the hyperactive, but I never noticed a change in my interest levels in anything but what I already had interest in, during the years I took it. It appeared to me as though I was able to wait longer, in hopes of learning information that was useful, not just repetitious. I was feeling more determined in my searches for various animals, snakes, turtles, and things. But schoolwork was still boring and just as intolerable as it always was, with or without Ritalin. The suggestions of special schooling or military school, my folks decided, were overemphasized, and not needed.

One time I gave my neighbor, Walter, a dose of my Ritalin, and I often wondered if it was only a placebo each time I took it, not believing it to be very strong, so this appeared to be the perfect test to determine this. He thought it would make him sleepy, and I didn't share my thoughts of his guinea pig like act and all the possible effects this may have, but we discovered that on supposedly "normal" children, Ritalin reacts the completely opposite way or at least for Walter. Walter could not stop racing around, he acted like someone gave him ten cups of coffee.

He kept singing, running and jumping everywhere, climbing trees, hopping fences, non-stop for hours. He wound up with a big head ache and completely lethargic after a few hours. While he laid flat on his back in the middle of the yard looking at clouds and appearing half asleep, I asked him if he felt like he was dying and he just said: "nah! I'm just tired". We never told anyone and I know I never tried that on anyone again; it was funny, but scary. This also made me wonder why adults thought this stuff would calm me down, and what other effect it would have on me in the future.

The doctor I was seeing at this time thought very little of my nightly tickle problem, claiming it to be a condition in my head and completely psychosomatic, and he said he had never heard of anything like it before. He said it should go away as I got older. He couldn't even give me an answer to the only real problem I had in my life or even pretend to think of ways that we could investigate it with, and the only issue I would discuss with him openly first because I did want an answer, but the responses made me realize how futile these people were to discuss it with.

No doctor ever came up with the answer to that issue; all of them just said the same thing. After a few months of this analysis, and with every 'new' doctor I would see, I was starting to win the chess games, which was the whole idea I thought. Unknown if they were letting me win. I knew they were trying to get to the bottom of some large, horrible hidden reason for my attitude, and they couldn't accept that there was no great secret or mystery; it was just my way of dealing with this environment, which they could not change.

I remember having this particular chess set of very large plastic figures of English monarchy that I used through several different doctors from when I was five, till about twelve. The last doctor, Dr. Louie Donotel, kept it forever, because we forgot to take it home, and you know how poor psychiatrists are, he must have really needed it. The reason these doctors played chess with me was in hopes of making patients comfortable, since I expressed interest in the game, and they wasted no time utilizing the game in an effort to relate to me and to analyze some deeper issue, too bad there wasn't any they could solve. It was entertaining, playing chess with them, but that's only a game and I wouldn't have much to say while planning subsequent moves during it, too deep in thought.

It was interesting being called or referred to as a 'patient' without actually being or feeling sick, like someone just found some label under your bed saying 'occupant sick' so you must be cause the sick label never lies. You can't copy it and make it say: "occupant does not need to go to school" though, that'd be too easy. You don't go to school when you're sick, strange explaining to your peers about being sick when you're not, only conclusion drawn was adults are strange, or I was. I only hoped it got me out of other things, like home work or something, but it didn't. I got to spend more free time going to hospitals and clinics.

I had been tested endlessly, and one of the more memorable ones was the Glucose tolerance test, which were six blood tests over four hours after drinking a big glass of the nastiest sugar water you could imagine. I was put on test diets reducing MSG, salt, sugar and caffeine intake, I was given vitamin supplementation, reading comprehension tests, intelligence tests, attitude tests, and it all appeared to solve and prove nothing. In fact, the tests only showed above average intelligence and comprehension.

One of the doctors even tried hypnotism, which failed since I would not allow my mind to be that defenseless, relaxed or open to suggestion. I didn't believe they could do it, so they couldn't. Simple mind over matter, I didn't mind that they didn't matter. I often felt while watching these doctors supposedly 'working' with me, or while working on chess moves to get out of the strategic predicament I had them in, that they were not content with themselves, as if having all the answers to human questions made life even more difficult and unfathomable for them. If they weren't paid so well, I might have felt sorry for them.

My physical condition was perfectly normal, I recall having excellent hearing ability, I could hear most conversations clearly, even when not in the room, or many rooms away. From the doctors waiting room I could hear my parents talking about me, and though I don't recall any specific conversations, some of my written text here related to what they said, without them even knowing I had heard it, or my remembering when, where or who I heard it from.

From my bed through the heat ducts, I could hear my parents in the den, three levels away. Being their dilemma was not my intent but usually I was the subject of their conversations. I heard many discussions on how to deal with me, from special schools to state or military ones, to juvenile shock schools, none of which appealed to me. I heard all the conclusions the doctors drew from analyzing me, and what my parents thought of them. I was basically dealt with mistakenly at first as a handicapped or retarded person, or a social misfit. I guess what upset me most about these talks were hearing my parents trying to blame one another, it was so out of character for either one and neither were at fault really.

My hometown was structured as such; kindergarten through fifth grade all took place within one classroom, besides gym, lunch and recess, of course. Grade six thought eight were like high school, one classroom for each subject, still the same building just a different end of it, and high school was ninth through twelve grades. I had friends, all neighborhood kids, who would invite me to birthdays up until around age seven, when the hosts' parents could no longer handle me. I would accidentally break things while rough housing, take things from their house, and go exploring through their bedrooms, attics, and garages.

After a while, no parent really wanted me over. At this age I felt that if I wanted something, it was ok to just take it usually. When confronted about the things that would appear in my room, I was always honest about it, never trying to hide anything, and never fearing the truth.

I was not attempting to be deceitful or immoral, I just wanted things, of no real value, just to have for use in some odd experiment I thought I could conduct, like magnifying glasses, chemicals I never heard of, small or unique tools, stupid stuff. I had the courage to return things to the people I took them from, apologizing quite sincerely.

I thought so little about it that I don't recall any specific item I had taken; I only know they had very little monetary value. I was also continually giving things I owned away to others, just because I didn't hold much sentimental value to any possession I had, which was probably why I thought taking things was ok, since I gave away things just as readily.

I gave away baseball cards, my book covers that my mom made, shells, rocks and butterflies from my collections, and generally anything that someone wanted they could have, no strings attached. I was generous to a fault sometimes, giving away things belonging to my parents or sister as well, which never made them happy. I also loved to take the tools at the dentists' office, the little tweezers, mirrors, picks and things, just to have things most kids don't. They leave you sitting alone for so long, I could think of nothing else to do than to go through the drawers and get some unique things to bring home.

EXIT SIX

Personal Insight Lane, Foul Language Ahead

I rarely cursed as a rule, and never in front of adults. My parents cursed at me around fifteen years of age, and I still never cursed back. Never though it necessary, when other words could describe so well any point I felt like describing, my vocabulary was quite adequate. Around age seven or eight is when I got to hear such wonderful explicative's as: Fuck, Shit, Cunt, Bitch, Cock, Prick, Dick, Snatch, Scrotum, Asshole, Pussy, Booger, Butt, Anus, Retard, Fart, and more vulgarities I may repeat later. Only as time went by did I learn what they all meant anyway.

If someone directed curses towards me, I would normally just play the mimic game, repeating what they say word for word with sarcastic inflection, till they were annoyed enough to stop or bring the insult to another level. Eventually, I would ignore their ramblings, becoming bored with such useless commentary enough to have them believe they won some great contest of bad words. And the winner of the pointless nothing contest is . . . the brainless bad-mouthed moron over there!

I enjoyed calling people other things, more descriptive to their nature. Just words of profanity weren't always enough to describe some people at times. I used words usually associated with body parts, even if I didn't understand their full meaning. I used phrases like Llama labia and Puma penis, Gofer gonads, refried Afghani lesbian nipple cheese, invisible stank puff, smegma and placenta breath, or Amoebas' anus. I would invent words to describe people's mothers, usually beginning with a species of dog or bird their family resembled. It's amazing how people do resemble certain species of dogs and birds at times, and that amused me to no end. I would be first to insult my own family or myself before retaliating against someone with my own insult, just to show how unimportant degrading comments were.

I remember a kid saying once: "your momma's a great big dyke" and my reply was: "yea, but your momma sits on her face all day while your dad and sister watch and masturbate each other". Don't even recall who that was exactly, but they didn't think my reply was as funny as I did. It made him rather mad, and then the curses just spewed from his mouth, in an attempt to better his position in front of whoever was listening. It would have been funny if a teacher was listening, but there wasn't. The rhetoric was less than important to me, it did not matter to me whatever upper hand they thought they had in the insult contest and most of the time I wouldn't bother responding. It all still made no sense.

As far as what I looked like, I was the blondest kid you could find, pure toe head with a big nose and large Spock like ears. Only five foot three a hundred twenty pounds till age fifteen or sixteen, then six foot three, two hundred twenty pounds. The girls hated and loved my hair, since it was blonder than most of theirs. I was average size. My eyes change color from green to blue and shades between, when the lights right. I've never worn or needed glasses or braces in my life. I attribute my balance and quickness to the size nine and a half feet I have.

As for a description of my street, it looked like this: when you leave the driveway of my house and turn left, there's a small hill till the front of the next house, then it goes down a steeper hill to a corner. At one o'clock at this corner is another equally steep hundred-foot hill leading down to the main road. Turning left at that same corner, at the position of nine o'clock, is a level road, which goes down another hill after you pass the next street behind mine.

Turning left onto the road behind mine, it's fairly level and you can see the back of my house from this street easily. About two hundred feet beyond the house directly behind mine the road begins a right, forty-five degree angle curve, which goes immediately down a steep hill, and about half way down you can turn left. Upon turning left, there are about three houses on that block before you reach another intersection, and turning left comes back up a hill towards my street again.

At the top of this hill, the road curves slightly down and left sharply, and if you turned right, you'd be in the woods after about fifty feet of road, which only has one house's driveway on it. After the sharp left curve, it curves right and goes by one more house on the right, the only two houses on that whole part of the street. Then it stops, and if you turn right, there's the other dead-end leading into the woods again, about one hundred feet from that point, with two driveways on both sides of it.

If you turn left, you'd go up a hill, and then five houses later from the top on the left would be my house. So I was basically on a hill, with both sides of my street being pretty steep hills, which made winter travel interesting. You could get within a hundred feet of my house, but without proper tires or the right car, and with very bad winter conditions like ice, it could be very tough to reach. My parents have had their car stranded down the hill, and they had to walk home and retrieve the car the next day, at least a couple of times as I recall during the years my family lived there. Looking at the block from above would make my block appear like the shape of a gun.

So back to some more school memories. Once during a gym dodge ball game, I found myself left with only one opponent, the worst bully at that time, Fred. I usually was one of the last kids left during this game, just not always. Fred was one to always threaten this and that type of bodily injury, if events didn't go his way. This must have been around my sixth grade timeframe or so.

This time Fred stated: "Greenie, if you don't let this hit you, I'll pull your eyeballs out and skull fuck you!" What he meant, of course, was he would join his fellow bullies in the futile "chase Greenie after school" marathon. He was almost fast enough. Everyone knows this type of kid, we all had at least one in our class growing up, the one who wanted to fight with anyone continually or always tried to anger others enough to fight with him. My solution for him was to never allow him the satisfaction of fighting with me, no matter how badly he wanted to, which worked very well for me and frustrated him endlessly.

Even thought I would allow intrusions into my space usually, simply because I didn't really care, I felt the need to re-establish superiority in this case, partially because of his statement, but mainly because I loved the game and I would never lose a game intentionally for anyone. As he suspected, after we both eliminated most of the opposing team, with some help from our peers, we were the only ones left and he had the ball.

I let his first throw just pass by my ear, listening to the swish as it went by, and before Fred could even walk back towards the middle of his side, I caught the rebound off the wall, and with my left hand side arm I whipped the ball as hard as I could, unfortunately right at his head. Fred turned, not realizing I had launched the ball already, and it smacked him dead in the face. The ball was one of those inflatable rubber balls that our gym teacher liked kept solid.

As his nose bled, while lying prone on his back on the floor, he screamed: "fucking Greenie! Your soooooo dead after school!" I went over to explain, apologize, since it was truly accidental. All I got was a shot to the back of the head, while I was walking away. I almost lost it then, my temper, but it didn't faze me quite enough. I knocked him down and made him bleed, the tough guy, and it didn't matter his revenge, since I knew he would probably never catch me. He was none too pleased to hear everyone laughing at him, either, and that brought some satisfaction to me. I lost that game on a disqualification, hitting in the head was not allowed.

There were other memorable children I grew up with, like Barney Colon, who was consistently annoying and obnoxious to the bullies and everyone else, simply because he was smart and disabled, and spent much of his day telling the teachers and the principal what he had witnessed others doing wrong and praising himself for his academic accomplishments. Somehow, just by coincidence I assumed, and I'm sure not so coincidental on occasion, he'd be the one observing me doing various things, always around the corner or just happening by, so often that it was bordering eerie.

I would not confront him, and my only competitiveness with him was academically, which seemed equally satisfying but he was quite smart so it was challenging. Once I put out a fire in the woods by the school by using the hose from a house next to it, Barney was walking by during this and saw me hosing the fire out, and then he claimed I lit it to begin with, but I didn't. I never cared if he said anything or not, mostly. He had bigger, more permanent issues, ones I wouldn't trade anything for.

His heart wasn't good he claimed, and he could just drop dead anytime, with too much stress, anger, physical activity or a well placed punch. He had open heart surgery, which then, around year 1970 or so, was very serious and dangerous, left a big scar too. His sister was also disabled, being somewhat Mongoloid, suffering from Down's syndrome I believe. I enjoyed competing with Barney intellectually sometimes, he was every bit as smart as I, smarter in some subjects, not in others, but usually he was just a whiny complainer about everything, with little sense of humor.

Blatantly obnoxious with a 'know it all' attitude, had answers for everything, and got special privileges from school officials, like always being excused from gym's physical activities. He was the most self-pitying person I remember, and he used his disability like a security blanket, making bullies afraid to torment him, with statements like: "I could die and you'll go to prison" as his weapon, which worked on some bullies, much to my amazement.

He was always projecting his resentment towards his condition, never understanding why he was afflicted with it and no one else was, which I understood. Like the child who's born with only one arm, wondering why they were given a handicap that very few others had, pretty frustrating, I would think.

He would rat out anyone if things didn't go his way or if he thought someone did something wrong, even if he wasn't sure. He wasn't fast, and his only advantage besides his over protective sister was the fact that his house was the first one directly behind the school, so getting home quickly was easy for him. Outperforming him academically was rare but satisfying, since it made him so upset and there was nothing he could do about it, he would nearly cry if he lost a competition to me, such as spelling, or if my test grade was higher than his, he'd claim I cheated somehow, which I never would, watching him stew after losing was entertainment at its best. He didn't like when anyone did better than he did.

Once, he did his usual ratting, on Edward, for putting glue on his chair or hitting him or something, which he was suspended for. Edward was not the forgiving type, and didn't seem to care about his condition. I knew he'd be waiting, right up the walk in the back, a fifty foot hill at the top of which was Barney's house. That made it easy for Barney to be as arrogant as he pleased, especially with his psychopathic retarded sister who chased away anyone who came near him or their yard.

Edward was not afraid of Barney's sister any more than I was. He had already beaten her up once, but she never learned from past errors in judgment. Anyway, there he was, sitting atop the fence at the top of the hill, and on this day I decided to yell to him: "hey Idiot! Your mother's vagina smells like your dog's left nut!" and then I ran back into the hallway leading to the gym, where after school activities were under way and teachers were hanging around.

Edward would naturally come running in angrily, wearing his little sarcastically evil grin he wore often, just in time to see me running out the opposing door in the gym, and he would get back out side just in time to see Barney walk in his slow pathetic hobble safely into his back yard. Thus, all anger at Barney found its new home, and the game of "let's get Greenie" had begun again. I had come around the building and went across the field by then; Edward didn't see me creep by on all fours at the slope at the far end of the ball field.

I was able to see him clearly over the grassy horizon, he could not see me. Then I went home by the creek in the woods, past the strange house with a pool in the woods, over their fences and out to the street a full block away from the school's walkway, where Barneys' house was. At this strange house, I have actually caught frogs in the pool; they never used it as a pool or cleaned it. It belonged to a famous movie director's daughter or someone famous like that I believe.

My grammar school was set on and against a hill, with a fifty-foot grass carpeted slope about thirty foot high the whole length of the back and large fields on its left, which ended at woods with a stream running into the brush towards my home, and the Passaic river in the other direction. It was a path home I took occasionally, like the day I just mentioned. I thought it was very scenic, wild, natural, and undeveloped. Towards the right of my school was the hard playground, with the continuance of the hill from the back, only getting less pitched as it reached the road in front of the school. In the back at the base of the hill about twenty feet from the school began the individual younger classes' recess area or blacktop; the pavement went right to the doors, which lined the whole back of the school with perfect symmetry.

I wanted no thanks from Barney, which I knew he wouldn't offer anyway since he didn't see Edward waiting, he might have thought my comments were directed to him, and I didn't really care, I was only doing it to antagonize Edward, or for fun. Edward didn't forget about Barney, and was able to pick on him another time when we had recess, but he wasn't as angry as he initially was on the day I distracted him, thus his torment of Barney wasn't as severe as it could have been. Of course, he was in trouble for it anyway, sent home for the day, I think he just tripped Barney this time, the old knee scab trick.

I noticed that positive and negative actions usually even themselves out, whether you personally cause the equalization or not makes no difference. My father always said: "Honesty is the best policy". He was so righteous in that belief that I eventually had to agree, especially when he told me one story about honesty he had experienced. His wallet fell out of his pocket one day, in a New York City taxicab, and when it was found and returned, it had nothing missing from it. This, he believed, was due to the fact that he had never stolen anything in his life, and by just being honest, he was rewarded with this exceptionally unusual and rare event. I also believed in his saying that two wrongs don't make a right, even though there are times that it appears it would, and I acted as though it would occasionally.

Thoughts of retaliation became a daily daydream activity for me, though my plots didn't always get acted out literally and were quite over-exaggerated usually, they killed time at least. Unrealistic thoughts of vengeance, like destroying some bad kids' house many different ways or pouring bleach or pen ink over some bullies head, just came and went without the actual implementation, as entertaining as a movie, written off as imaginary fiction. Fun, but the consequences far outweighed the temporary satisfaction it may bring. I eventually dealt with situations or conflicts with indirect, thoughtful calculated retaliation that would cause no physical damage, and this too, is not always the best way to handle negativity, but seemed acceptable for now and always worked.

Deciphering between the two evils of direct violence and revenge is persuaded by the belief in that what anyone does to you will be returned, which has allowed many trying situations to pass unanswered before me, throughout my entire life. I often found myself in the wrong place at the wrong time with the wrong person, but it was never as bad as it could have been.

There was a good amount of satisfaction watching some bully get into trouble for nothing related to me, as though that was his punishment without any action of my own for something he did to me. It felt about the same as when, for instance, you're driving, and someone cuts you off and there's no way to get even with them, then you see someone else cutting off the same person who cut you off further down the road. The person who cut off the same guy who just cut you off had no connection with you, they didn't know that person did the same thing to someone else, but it's just as satisfactory as getting to cut off the original driver yourself. They got theirs, it doesn't matter how.

My father always told me things could be difficult if you let them be, just do your best to deal with or avoid them, and always try to make any situation into a positive experience. My father was a brilliant man, an inventor, a chemical engineer, and when he went to college at Cooper Union, all he had to pay for were his books.

He was born in nineteen fourteen, which to me was almost unimaginable. He was a runner for Wall Street, and was one of the people giving all the use-to-be millionaires the great news that they no longer have money worries, or money, either. With three sisters, my father helped support the whole family through the depression and go to school at night, just to live his American dream. He was deemed too important to society to be wasted in war, and thus stricken from the draft list, due to international interests in his work.

His goal was way ahead of his time, to clean the whole world's waste products before they became too environmentally dangerous to us, and reuse them as fuel, feed, or whatever was needed most. Carl Green was his name, born May twenty ninth recorded May thirtieth, celebrated the thirty first. He entered the world named Greenfeld, lived his life as Carl Green. Record keepers of the era were less than proficient.

One of my dad's first jobs or projects was in Canada working on the refining of cod liver oil, a very useful material for some reason; there are pictures of him using a horse drawn sled as transport, to and from his work through the relentless Canadian climate. My mother and he corresponded through the mail, they were a perfect couple. My mother was equally intelligent, graduating Hunter University about the same time Bella Abzug did, I think she may have been her classmate.

Being bi-lingual, she was useful to our government as the interpreter of letters written in French, looking for some code that a foreign power might use to spy on our country. She was doing this job the only time a plane hit the Empire state building, and was witness to this. Another good cause my mom contributed to was UNICEF. My Aunt and she would be constantly involved, believing the cause to be a just one. She truly looked for any positive input she could contribute to any situation and was optimistic to a fault; never a kinder person existed to my knowledge. I almost never acknowledged just how great my parents were, I was extremely blessed or lucky to have had them as my mom and dad.

They lived in Brooklyn when they grew up. When I would visit my Grandma there, I would love to ride the elevator all day, or eat chopped chicken liver on Ritz crackers, have the best matzo ball soup ever made, or just watch TV. I would also ask for money and go to a movie or bagel store, or wander around looking for things I shouldn't see, like Playboy or Penthouse magazines, various pocket knives or fireworks. Brooklyn has the best bagels on earth, there on Kings Highway. While at my grandmas, I would become repetitively annoying, beckoning for my freedom without end, till everyone's opinion was in my favor, and they let me go out.

I know my aunts, uncles and cousins would never really believe my parents to be lacking, but it's hard to explain how to deal with a child who's so self-centered and has the energy level of three individual kids. I would hear my relatives asking my parents: "what can we do for Christopher? How can we help? How can you deal with it?" They didn't have an answer for them. My parents would only say things like, he's not that bad really, the doctor says indulge and reaffirm, he's just curious, and similar phrases on different occasions.

On cold days, I would go in my grandma's bedroom and watch TV, until the door closed. Then I would listen to conversations, or search the room for things of interest, and make believe I was sleeping when the door opened for some reason. I never found that much, pictures, clothes, jewelry, ornaments. Grandma's room was boring for exploring.

Wandering and exploring was my tendency, entertainment and calling. I never got lost, always made it home fine, and worried many people for different reasons. Locking me in my room would be difficult, since one of my bedroom windows was two feet off the roof of the garage, and jumping ten feet down to the ground was a simple feat. This I would do just for fun and I knew that my parents would never nail a window shut, or build a prison by barring the window. My parents didn't believe in spanking either, and I think it would have done more damage than good, in my case, but who knows. Endless patience and care have their rewards, or so my parents at least had hoped.

In an effort to occupy my time, such as camp Riverbend did one summer, I believe in the year 1968 or so they sent me to a camp named Camp Dolphin, where they deal with mostly Down's or autistic children as their campers. I remember getting out of the car and seeing some handicapped people standing around, and I wondered what exactly I was here for. It was a nice camp, plenty of woods and fields, nice facilities and good food, but I couldn't figure why I was here in the first place.

I didn't see any kids my age, or any with equal intelligence, and the staff just kept looking at me strangely, like I was some alien being or something. I recall one staff member asking me what I was going to do here, and I had no answer, and he seemed confused by my mere presence. Then he told me to go help out some other staff person with the activities and sports. That made sense, I was sent here to be a counselor I guessed.

I remember trying to play baseball with them, I was the only one who could run all four bases in the right order, or even come close to hitting the ball. It was Chris against the other ten or twelve kids standing around making noises, drooling, singing or picking their noses and crotches, quite unfair. This made me begin to wonder who they thought I was, and if they were just testing me to see if I was capable of any responsibility or leadership. That only lasted a week.

A whole week for them to figure out I had nothing in common with mentally handicapped kids. I entertained myself as best as I could, and everyone thought I was a junior counselor, including the handicapped kid's parents. I'd catch animals and show them to everyone, just to keep myself busy and to feel useful. I figured I was just put here to learn to work with handicapped, and I wondered why they thought I may have any interest in doing that type of work. I did enjoy the fact that what I knew or could do with animals was impressive to these campers, giving them their possibly first encounter with a multitude of wildlife.

I endured that, along with camp Riverbend, and made it through the grades I was supposed to somehow. Principal Roden and I were very familiar with each other, but not by his choice. I believe Principal's remember students that are the most incorrigible and challenging, and the most brilliant. I was fortunate enough to make both lists, occasionally.

He had his job to do, and I allowed him to believe I understood his cause, though I would seldom show it. He had a difficult job. I wound up using more of his time than most students do, and I'm certain that even forty or fifty years from the time I left, he would recall me. I'd go in his office, he'd start talking to me with a big sigh while running his hands back through his thinning hair, and he'd always start with: "Chris, Chris, Chris, what will I do with you?" My usual response to that was something like: "Let me go home?" which made him chuckle sometimes, but not always, it was my typical response.

He truly believed and understood that I was capable of a lot, and was frustrated by his staff's failure to get me motivated, or any hint of interest, which was not always a controllable factor for them. He was a good man, using logic and simple psychology quite well, "we're all looking out for your future", he'd say.

Nice guy, but he didn't understand how I thought; he only knew I was intelligent enough to know better in some cases. His confusion was not unfounded, since he wasn't a child in my position and had nothing he could compare what I did or what I endured, in his own experience. He was a safety zone for me, a team Greenie player, with the standard "my best interest" factor being his main point of discussion. He had to deal with me for nine years.

On to the topic of my interests as a youth, I was first a Yankee fan and Packers fan. But I was a bigger fan of cartoons like the pink panther, courageous cat and minute mouse, or Scooby Doo and Bugs Bunny. I enjoyed Star Trek, from the sixties to the nineties, so all my references to Star Trek will be from any given decade involving all spin offs to date.

Wrestling I've always liked, not the mat or Olympic kind, more the kind starting back when Mil Mascaras ruled the 'sport'. Some other shows I liked, such as I dream of Jeannie, Bewitched, F Troop, Monty Pythons flying circus, Get Smart, Honeymooners, the Munsters, Gilligans' island, and a lot of others from the sixties and early seventies. My favorite movie was Laurel and Hardy's March of the Wooden Soldiers, and it still is at times, having seen it more than any other movie in my life, including wizard of oz. The Yankees were quite inspirational during their moments, and I always thought of myself as an avid player and fan, but watching wasn't usually enough. Didn't really enjoy watching sports that much, but what I saw had its moments.

I was only a Packers fan because Roy was, who always tried to imitate Bart Starr, and after that tiresome following wore off, I was a Giants fan, due, again, to one of my friends being one. I was always a Yankee fan, and Bobby Mercer was my favorite player at the time. I loved playing the field, especially center field and he did this so well.

So about wrestling, watching these guys was like watching art in motion, and adding women for balance was a great, predictable and eye pleasing idea. It just had to be that way, to include the likes of the fabulous Mula, sensational Sherry Martel and many others. I always believed in the danger, and risk, and I understood they had to know what was going to happen before it did to survive in one piece.

Good stories can't be too tough to come by in that field, since their intelligence was never in question no matter how hard they tried to express their lack of it, such as in George "The Animal" Steel's case. Though he sounded and acted stupid and retarded, I knew somehow that he wasn't before this fact was published anywhere, his being a college professor in reality.

I had an issue about breaking bones, I felt that it was something to avoid doing, especially my own, and that career can and will break many things, so for as much as I liked bouncing around rooms and floors or people, I would not follow that path. It was indeed enough fun just to watch. Like roman gladiators without swords, where if the pain and blood was intentional, real or not, it didn't matter. You could get seriously hurt or killed, like Billy White Wolf did when he received the swinging neck breaker from Ken Patera or as Owen Hart did many years later, in a tragic accident during his entrance of one performance

Watching wrestling is not unlike why people stop to watch other people fighting, just the confrontational aspect for some reason interests people enough to watch, the raw emotion and aggression fueling the interest. Fake or not, doesn't really matter. It reminded me of why there was always a crowd gathering, awaiting my arrival after some bully claimed to be getting me after school, just waiting to witness some violence.

Too bad they were always disappointed to learn I was an expert at avoiding such useless, unproductive scenes and they never had a chance to watch any bloodshed. Watching the professionals was always preferable to having me possibly be injured or injuring someone. I knew the outcomes were fake for as long as I watched it, but that made no difference, it looked like it hurt, and I always thought it was the most dangerous thing people could do, just man against man.

Star Trek was another of my favorite shows and imagination outlets at the time, since I was into philosophy. I was always imitating in a limited way a Vulcan like Spock. He was the best. There was no other Captain Kirk, either. I'm sure they'll bring him back, when the nexus comes around to the location of Kirk's body eventually, just like they did for Spock and the Genesis planet in the Wrath of Kahn movie.

More recently I wondered if the dominion were the next evolutionary step for the rock creatures Captain Kirk found, where he fights with Abraham Lincoln by his side. I'd like to see a final countdown movie for all, the Dominion, Borg, Trelane, species eight four seven two, or some other impressive characters like Nomad, Gorns, Plato's step children, Apollo, the Gamesters of Triskellion, five centuries after, they meet, get drunk on Klingon blood wine, served by Guynan, Neelix and Qwark, that kind of thing. The Trek series really epitomizes humanities efforts to understand the future as a dream of peace between multiple species to be made into a reality.

Creating the Q species was a slightly erratic thing to do, not leaving any room for advancement with a race that uses super novas as weapons of civil war. They were just too omnipotent to be anything less than biblical gods, like the entire universe revolved around what they wanted to do. They gave ultimate power a name, and thus have nothing to go beyond that for any philosophical advancement.

The Q could end any situation or problem with just a thought, and no species could have more power than them, which hardly seems fair. Perhaps they evolved from the species that stopped the Klingon versus Star Fleet war in the episode where the inhabitants looked like sheepherders but were really pure energy, or the Gary Seven humans or even Trelane's parents, for those who really know their trek trivia.

I think the only failing of the next generation was in not showing more of the beings Kirk found, evolved and different than when Kirk met them. They must still exist, so where were they? What happened to captain Pike eventually, and the aliens on Tarsus four that saved him? Much more could have been done in that respect, I think. They tried, like in the wrath of Kahn, but fell short in my opinion, although that was a great movie. So what became of the being Voyager became when it collected all there is to know in the galaxy and merged with the guy through the bald girl at the end of the first Trek movie?

I envied their monetary system, as I said before. I thought it should be that way, where all who contribute to society reap the rewards of freedom to do anything, and by doing your job consistently is how it would be obtained, having the barrier of different income levels or "classes" of people based on income removed.

Then I heard about their "credits" system, and even though this could be just a tool for dealing with other cultures, it still seemed to reek of greed. Creating the Ferengi was pretty well suited as explanation for the lack of currency in the Trek world, using gold plated Latinum as currency, like another form of Platinum. I didn't really care for the Ferengi, too predictable.

Computers will obviously show us the path. Somehow I always knew that computers would become a reality, a tool of the future that Star Trek understated. Only a few things can occur, through all this technology. We destroy ourselves with it as depicted in a sci-fi movie like Terminator, or we evolve with it to a level that equals or surpasses what Gene Roddenberry imagined.

I always could imagine a world with no need for money, disease, and unpredictable natural disasters like quakes, volcanoes, tornadoes and such. The show gives hope for us to do the things we must to survive as a species, and I do believe we are not the only life in the universe. It's just not statistically reasonable to assume we are. I would enjoy writing science fiction I think, even possibly horror, or combination of both, and I may yet one day.

So, captain Kirk, often portrayed by Roy, with Peter being a Klingon, and I was usually Spock, go to the planet where all you wish for suddenly appears. There were always aliens attempting to abduct Spock, or Kirk, and we were always in "their power" somehow. I liked Spock's continual logic, and I always thought of myself as being very logical, so I tried to be as close to his character as I could be when debating things realistically. Too bad his Vulcan neck pinch was only an attribute of his character; it would have come in handy a few times in my life. My apologies to those who have no clue what my Star Trek references are about.

There were other things I played with, like army men figures and dinosaurs. They fly when thrown, melt under a magnifying glass, disappear, and that's about it. I used to enjoy attaching a figure, an insect or a mouse to one of those water-propelled rockets they made those days and send it up a few hundred feet. The mice survived a fall that would certainly kill a person, giving me evidence of just how durable they can be. I also played chess with my dad since age four, when I exhorted enough patience to play the game, and I played golf since about age ten.

Here's a poem I once wrote, one of many that filled my head: "Like a moth who attracts to the light, I shall never give in to my plight, my purpose is almost clear, but at times unattended, to those of you I know and revere, the one's I've befriended, we aim our goals high, then sit back and sigh, when it all unfolds in front of us, there are very few we can trust, but believe we will in people's possible kindness, their help and support, their interest and blindness, to all we are and all we do, it's my greatest path, my life, and it leads me forever to you".

Once I thought of a movie that I shared with a doctor for fun, where the plot is based on a murderer who discovers that the people in his dreams are really his deceased victims, and they tell him so, and the dream people are showing him the horrible fate that awaits him every night once he dies. I thought this was an interesting thing for the doctor to hear, to let him debate that for a while. I don't think he did, though, since the only reaction he had was no reaction, very boring. It was a common reaction to any discussion I found interesting, and I couldn't figure why, it seemed valid to me.

The other idea I had was what would happen if our continent broke from the structure lowest to the center of the worlds' core and turned sideways? Now that I've written it, likely it will become a movie one day, believed to have been thought of by someone else. I had this thought in the sixties, once I discovered what percentage of our planet is mostly water, and I realized this would not be a good thing. I think the idea came partially from a movie called "crack in the world", but taken a step further, without the extra moon creation from that movie.

Many ideas come and go; sometimes we're lucky enough to see some come true, preferably the pleasant ones. One favorite fantasy of mine was the indestructible kid, no powers like the kid in Twilight Zone had, able to use my mind to kill anyone, but nothing could harm me or effect me, just like superman but impervious to Kryptonite as well. A common desire or daydream for kids, I figured.

I also believe dreams can be much more than most realize, mostly a misunderstood or under rated science. They found out about the human brains' Alpha and Beta waves, electricity, and neurological systems, but they can't figure out where it goes when the body can no longer sustain? Up to date, no one would say electrical energy is destructible as far as we know. It can only change forms or disperse, and the dispersion is what would create the dilemma in the topic of what occurs once it leaves the body when you die.

Perhaps if the learning experience isn't quite complete on this planet, we return to lower life forms, spreading our energy over masses of other lower life forms, or a single one, a step back in the evolutionary path, some might call hell, or starting over as an Amoeba or other microscopic creature, or groups of them, and then as we die, we return escalated back up the path to higher life forms till were a person again, given another chance to reach the highest plateau, which some call heaven.

Discussing things like this drove my doctors wild. It wasn't much fun for my male peers, either. The doctors could not overcome their preconceptions of religion, death and the universe, which was all I wanted to discuss when they refused to discuss my only other issue. Answers they didn't have to questions not relative to my case or reality in their opinion. I thought these things were quite normal to ponder, and since I did often, I figured everyone did.

Every week, the doctors had nothing new to add, what do you feel, do you hate your mother or father, are you mad because you're adopted, stop biting your nails, the standard approach. Get paid for nothing, and a lot of pay at that. So why should they be philosophical with me? They still get paid and live as they want if they provide answers or solutions or not.

I do recall some accounts of conversation, mainly aimed at the doctor's never ceasing point of my apparent issue of being adopted, which I would never substantiate, but I would tell them what I thought about it. The only negative aspect of adoption I saw was the fact that there will be the need for mankind to find a solution to planetary over population within some amount of years, and find the way to, perhaps even mathematically, determine how many people can exist within any given time based on the resources available to support them all equally, or increase all resources through science to maintain everyone, then conquer space for extra needed space.

I never could stop thinking about what possibly may have been different in this world had I not existed, which any child would think about if they had seen the classic movies based on that story line as many times as I did, like 'It's a Wonderful Life' or one Trek episode I remember, 'City on the Edge of Forever" I believe it was. At the same time, restricting people's right to procreate would be equally poorly met by most, but even at age eight or nine I questioned, just how much room could there be on the world its self?

Had to be a tangible number, how much could it have mattered if I didn't come to be? I tried endlessly to explain that my life would likely be mostly normal, that I would have children, a wife, and if I made no other impact upon this world, my mate and offspring would. They saw no sense or relevance to my line of thought, instead they showed more concerned about what actions I would take to accomplish what I wanted, even though most children, including myself, have no clue as to what they really want, or even think too often about it.

Eventually, my parents came over to my viewpoint and agreed that they were wasting a lot of time and money. What these doctors thought they could do about my life from sitting behind their desks miles away from my house and school, I had no idea. Were they going to call the parents of assholes I knew and have them change? Or call my teachers to make them aware of their own failing in discipline? I didn't think so, since it wasn't part of their job description and I was the only problem in their mind. The only difference was my parents actually cared enough to try to help me, no one else's did I figured. I loved my parents a lot, though not being good at showing it was normal for me, but I could always talk with them about anything, knowing honesty is one of their greatest assets and I would always hear the truth from them, even if I didn't always offer it back.

My parents decided that I could use some interaction with the community and had me enrolled into Cub Scouts, which I wasn't really interested in but went along with the idea anyway, just for a change of pace and to please them. I think I was around nine years of age, and besides my exact age I remember it quite clearly.

Two blocks away from my school on the same street, the Fellsway, I went every Tuesday or Thursday night for meetings. Meetings were in a scout leaders basement, don't even recall the name of the owners right now, but I was sitting on the edge of the bench, at a table like you'd find at a picnic area, and the bench was pretty well occupied so I just sat on the end.

Someone pushed the line on the bench in an attempt to sit down; the kid sitting next to me got pushed into me till here was no room left for me to sit. For some reason, my feet were looped around the leg of the table, and I fell right, completely off the bench and smacked my head on the sewer drain cover most basements have. I would cry when hurt usually, if it hurt enough, like most kids, but this time I didn't actually cry. I just got up and spewed out some curses, repeatedly, holding the spot that hurt and rubbing it as my eyes watered from the pain. I had to go home and see a doctor, and I did get a big bump on my head from that.

Then, at the same house only a week later, the sun was at twilight, and it was more dark than light. The kids, including myself, were playing a miniature version of dodge ball, since it was only a driveway and not a gym. I ran out into the street to get the ball, and even though I was quite adept at using my peripheral vision, I never saw this car coming.

It was a dark car, with no lights, and it hit me with its left front fender, bouncing me about twenty feet back down the driveway onto my butt. The car didn't even stop, which surprised me and everyone watching. Roy and Edward, Curtis, Walter, Phillip, and Herb all were just stunned possibly more than I was.

I just got up, brushed off, looked at all of them, and started walking home, with no expression on my face at all. I said as I tried to leave something about what I thought of scouting, and since I could light a fire with one match, survive in woods better than anyone I knew, I didn't really need to be here.

The kids' father who owned the house wasn't going to let me go that easily. My parents were called to get me while the guy was reprimanding me for being in the street, saying things about not paying attention, you must be blind to not see that car, real encouraging words. Naturally, that was the end of my scouting career. I broke nothing. Just scrapes and bruises were all I got. The whole experience in my mind was avoidable if I had not tried to "fit" in. They never found the car that did, and I have no idea how hard they looked for it.

I didn't care that much for group activity. I usually enjoyed just one on one activity, animal collecting, and deep, personal interaction. But alone was even more desirable. No opinion or view to consider other than my own. No pressure, either, to abide the interest of another person. I did go many places with my parents in their attempt at providing me with culture. I got to see you're a good man, Charlie Brown, at the Lincoln center once in New York City which was great. I collected all seventy-five Peanuts books there were at that time by Charles Schultz.

I also saw Carmen at the center, and it was impressive, in an artistic sort of sense, like Beethoven. Loved the fifth, and a lot of the rest, but music didn't impress me really. My parents listened to classical which seemed to make great background sound, soothing, complex, but not necessary really. I also saw Monty Python live there, which was fantastic, if you could decipher the heavy British accent they all had.

We visited New York's Hayden Planetarium and Museum of Natural History frequently. Usually, I would disappear from my parents and find them many hours later panicking by the security station and looking for me. Eventually they would become bored with worrying I think, realizing I'd find them if need be no matter what, since I never got lost.

Coney Island was often visited, being my first real amusement park around the corner from my grandmas', since Great Adventure didn't exist yet. I always had the front seat of the Cyclone, or close to it. One time when I was about eight years of age my mother brought me, and I remember going on the ride they call Hell Hole.

Hell Hole is the little round room that spins so fast that the centrifugal force pins you against the wall and they drop the floor out a few feet from under you and you just stay suspended against the wall. Great Adventure calls it the Rotor. I thought I was clever because I found a way to get on the ride free, thinking no one could see me going in. After going on this about six times, I realized that the guy running the ride did know, but apparently didn't care because he knew how sick it could make someone, to repeatedly go on this ride.

I wound up throwing up next to my mom's car, and have never again been able to stomach high speed spinning on any ride after that. The guy knew this, thought he'd teach me a lesson I guess or was just being a natural asshole, so the next time we went to Coney Island, the Hell Hole was put out of service because someone had thrown a piece of broken bottle into the crank area, and broke the ride indefinitely.

So we went to the Aquarium instead, since the Cyclone was also broken and it was the only ride I really liked, seemed that it was often out of service for one reason or another. In all the years I went there, the great parachute ride that you can see for miles around was never in operation, so I never got to experience it.

The Aquarium was impressive, but fish usually bored me, except perhaps carnivorous ones while feeding. Those are interesting to watch. But all this was only temporary, all weekends end and we return to the mundane world of the week, be it work or school, the time off seems too short, even summer goes quicker than a normal two month span during a school year it seemed.

EXIT SEVEN

Path to Discovery and Destruction

A lot of my school day was spent avoiding confrontation with the aggressive kids of the class, as I mentioned too often before. They couldn't stand to not get a reaction from me, even though they did in such an indirect manner that their limited intelligence couldn't conceive the fact that I did react, and got satisfaction with interest. At one point I decided that some of the abuse needed to end, and I would make an example of the next perpetrator that crossed my path.

This would be when Craig decided to hit me with the softball bat in the head, which hurt for a while. I would like to believe that it was accidental, he had been swinging the bat awaiting his turn at bat and I got just too close, but I think he saw me and over-extended his back swing to reach me. Then he laughed right in my face and said don't be such a pussy, or he'll do it again, which made me think about just how accidental it was. I felt like beating his butt right then, but decided not to bother expelling the energy, besides I now had a massive headache and only felt like taking some aspirin and having a nap. I did manage to bat my turn anyway though it was an unmemorable result

We lived on a block set against a mountain, or as much of a mountain as you'll get in New Jersey, the shape of the block was that of a pistol as mentioned before, and I think it's called the butt, the two notches in the back, were dead ends into woods, extending several blocks to the next main street after Livingston path.

I was out my door or window without a peep, my parents not usually catching me. The woods across the street behind the neighbors' houses were the adjoining woods to the end of the street. It was quite simple to not be seen for many miles. So off I'd go, headed for some interesting places. Craig's was one place to see, don't recall the setting of the house, but I remember a rock sitting next to his parents car in the driveway, nice ones, both the car and rock. I introduced them to each other with emphasis.

So, fun was had by all (or at least by me) the next day with hearing about someone busting Craig's parents' car window. No one had any idea who could have done such a thing. I just told Craig in gym later that day in a very matter of fact way that his story about the car sounded almost as bad as someone hitting you in the head with a bat or something, of course without the possibility of permanently damaging someone.

Craig's face went pale, his mouth dropped open, and he threatened all kinds of bodily harm while cursing, while I was laughing, but he knew no one could prove I did anything and it was simple to live with denial. He especially hated when I laughed in his face after he missed hitting me with some cheap shots. I thought this was funny because his actions are what caused the reaction to begin with, and I would let the stupidity circle continue as long as he wanted to test my patience and ingenuity.

Revenge for an act of revenge seemed useless, appearing as a misdirected form of entertainment in a continual sitcom. I took the attitude that what was done to me would be miniscule compared to what I would do back, or what natural equalization would bring without any action on my part would be sufficient, and though it may be, I didn't always wait for that to happen, waiting long enough to give destiny its chance.

This can be a temporary cure for stupidity, but some kids' heads are thicker than others. I showed kindness by truly feeling sorry for Craig and trying to rectify the relationship later, but that didn't take well and only made him a bigger nuisance, with more impending doom on the horizon.

I tried to point out how wrong his actions and mine were, but he was too stupid to understand that he was as much at fault as I was. I once had to climb a tree, to get away from him. But that was more for fun than from fear. Once on a limb, with your feet you can keep most anything away from you coming from below. Knock them right out of the tree, which I did till he gave up and left, scratched and frustrated, cursing up a storm at me, claiming he'll get me later. I eventually told Craig I'd leave him alone, if he left me alone, and that apparently worked, since he never bothered me to that degree again, I could see some slight fear in his eyes occasionally. This blackmail method didn't work with everyone though.

Eventually, since I couldn't fall asleep normally anyway, I would spend many nights of mischief within the mile or so around my house, without my parents even knowing I was outside. From busting windows to gluing car doors shut, or gas covers closed, or attempting to halt construction on one of my favorite vacant lots by completely draining the oil tank left there to fuel the construction vehicles, which, of course, didn't work. The vacant lot was one house over from mine, and it was one of my favorite collection areas for butterflies, praying mantis, beetles, and moths, along with anything else that lived around the wild flowers there.

I delayed the building of a new construction site elsewhere by the same means, adding the excitement of tipping over all the portable bathrooms there. I believed it to be environmentally conscious of me to do this at the time. Save the greenhouses that were there first and fertilize the land. I would also put different substances where they didn't belong like condiments, Windex or bleach into cars gas tanks, amongst other places. I cut clothes and phone lines and tied up objects with them, like people's front doors, tying them shut or open depending on if they opened in or out, or their car doors together.

I also added many common household chemicals to peoples' back yards and driveways, Clorox their porch or their outside furniture, pop tires on their cars, use bolt cutters on their water lines, or shove onions up car's exhausts. Once I put some people's hose through their basement window or garage and turned it on to create their own indoor pool, and then another day just cut a hose into nice even segments, I believe that was Fred's house.

Egg throwing was also something I considered fun, just at houses and cars generally. Other times I would get one of my rodents and tie its tail to a string, then tie the other end in front of someone's door on the light or other fixture, so the rodent would be hanging right in the face of the next person to come out the door. I did play a lot of ding-dong ditch it.

These acts didn't occur too randomly and were aimed mostly at the kids who disliked me for no apparent reason. I figured that giving them good reasons to dislike me was the logical reaction, since I would not fight with them about anything, because that's what they wanted. If they wanted to be my enemy, they shouldn't be surprised when I react offensively or destructively as though they are.

Although they usually never knew I was the cause of anything odd that occurred around their house, I had hinted to them that their actions may have had something to do with these strange occurrences, directly or not, and I know I was not the only delinquent in the town or the only person who disliked these kids either.

I once took some roses for my mother from one of my friends' mothers' garden, the Wilmens, who lived at the end of the street. Curtis was a friend of mine for years, until then. Apparently, his mom saw me take the roses, she called my mom, who made me return them, and the next night I went back and trampled all the foliage this time, crushing all the vegetables and flowers there were.

Curtis came over the next day and said he never wanted to see me around his house again, trying to sound as angry and threatening as he could, and I laughed in his face and slammed the door. I figured if he wanted to end his association with me because of some garden, then he was useless as a friend. That was the last time I saw him, they moved some months later back to the south where they came from. My mother was pretty disappointed about where I got her gift, she told me. I agreed not to do that again for anyone.

Though it's true there were many nights spent in destructive ways, I would have to say that about fifty percent of the time I would just go out to look around, not damaging anything, just to peak in windows and look for larger moths around people's spotlights, and be generally nosey, overly curious.

I liked to crush coins on the local train tracks, like so many kids do. I also liked to climb power line towers, since they were the highest things around, and I would just climb up and sit and watch the people below, enjoying the feeling of being on top of the world with a great view, out of site to most people below me, wishing I had the ability to fly.

I liked to go to the community pool in town, climb over or under the fence and swim for hours at night. The pool was much more peaceful and pleasant after hours, largely due to the lack of the crowd and the night sky with all its starry vastness. Going off the high dive around midnight was always fun, but I couldn't get anyone to go with me, fearing legal repercussion.

It would take the whole police force to surround the pool to capture me, which I knew would not be their priority since they never came, thus I never got caught going there. It was very relaxing to do; even the one time I did get Peter to go with me, who only whined about not having any girls to go skinny dipping with. Floating on my back under the stars was so relaxing, placing perspective on distance and existence, realizing how small we are compared to the view above, just a sub-atomic particle circling a nucleus in some expansive object somewhere, truly tiny, how insignificant our world really is in the scope of the universe.

Mischief night, the ceremonial night before Halloween, was one of the few nights I didn't go out, I would just sit on my roof with the garden hose and a couple dozen eggs waiting for retribution, but none came my way except once, the time I wasn't ready of course. Halloween for me was six to eight hours of collecting, from the minute school ended till I could barely walk anymore, mainly at Peter's apartment complex, since doors were so close together.

Trick or Treat for UNICEF was the standard phrase for us then, though I usually split the money evenly before giving it to my parents. My aunt did a lot of work for UNICEF and it seemed to be a good cause. I always filled a pillowcase at least, and ran around like a maniac from the sugar I would consume that night and the days to follow. Sugar gave me additional quick energy, and it lasted longer for me than it would for most kids, along with no down time once gone from my system.

My costume selections were less that original, I went out as the color blue once, covering myself from head to toe with blue food dye. Or I'd just rip my shirt and pants and go as a bum, nothing that took too much effort as I recall. I just wanted candy, without going through the theatrics. If I did actually ever have a costume, like a ghost or vampire, I don't recall it, but maybe my sister would from when I was younger.

I remember stories of bigger kids stealing other kids' bags once they were full, but I never saw this happen myself. These were the days before some sick people tried poisoning kids or injuring them with hidden substances or razor blades in the candy, no one worried about this yet, it was safe enough except for the candy thieves. I doubt anyone could catch me anyway, with all the sugar energy I had. It was one of the very few times of the year my parents would allow me to eat sugary treats. Halloween was a happy event for me; no one bothered trying to chase me those nights.

Pursuing me did become futile to the select few kids who tried, or to everyone but Barney's sister, the mental disaster waiting to happen. She was one of the few people I really did not like as a person, handicapped or not. Possibly the rocks, chairs, branches, snowballs, cats, books or driveway chunks she continuously tried to hit me with influenced my opinion of her. Damn good thing I was good at dodge ball, because I could see that in her feeble mind permanently damaging someone meant nothing, and she apparently had no morals I could identify.

Any object within her reach became a projectile if she saw me, which accompanied an ear piercing, lunatic scream that she'd unleash simultaneously, she was quite maniacal and forgave no one who bothered her or her brother ever. I assumed that since she never was able to actually perpetrate any revenge on me, she would try continually.

One of my shortest and normal paths home was right by her house, and I would take that at times, especially if I told someone earlier I'd be taking another path. A few kids would be waiting for me in the woods on that path I'm not taking for their chance at revenge, and never getting any. There was a white fence atop the hill, with paths on each corner on the dead end street leading to each end of the schools back yard.

The first house on the right was Barney's as one leaves the school. His sister would run after me for thinking I was teasing or bugging Barney, which in reality I didn't do often, or for making some unapproved facial expression while looking at her, or for no reason at all, which made that path all the more challenging to take. She liked to spin her arms like a helicopter, screaming wildly and cursing while running at me, which I would block with a stick or my arms if I didn't feel like running, laughing the whole time, and that really irked her.

I also used my feet for defense if she was lucky enough to have snuck up and tackled me, which only happened once, I would lay on my back, and bicycle kick wildly towards all parts of her, knocking her over making it possible to regain my footing and impossible for her to damage me. She didn't go to her brothers and my school, and she was like twenty or something but with the mind of a four year old.

She was one dangerous person. She got Barney one day, with a broken bottle or mirror, and he wore a scar for many years. I would generally leave her alone, since I knew it would take considerable damage to stop her, and I didn't like the idea of needing that drastic a measure. Barney used her like a deadly insane bodyguard, saying that his sister would kill someone if he told her to, in an attempt to dissuade people from picking on him. Pretty low, I thought, using her in that manner when his disability alone failed to stop others from tormenting him.

She was the only girl who I even considered perpetrating vengeance upon in my life, since she could get away with anything, and I just let that brick build without actual intent to throw it, I saved it for a rainy day. Normal revenge tactics were futile with that one; I would need much more imagination to deal with her. I still felt saddened by her condition, through all the fears of having to deal with her just because I walked home in that direction most of the time.

On a different family topic, my father traveled a lot, since he was an inventor with worldwide implications, and he can be found in the book of Who's Who in the east for his pollution processes. This left my mother, sister, and till I was eight my nana, which was my mom's mom, to watch over me.

My sister didn't know what to do with me, ever since I was three years old and I ate her disappearing ink, and had to have my stomach pumped. Nine and a half years older than me, a teenager in the sixties, she was not the average teen, not into drugs, bra burning, rebellion, or doing anything wrong, she was an intelligent and good sister, who actually seemed to want something good for her life.

She is a terrific person with hardly a selfish bone in her body, just like our parents. She didn't know what my problem was, and she was likely relieved to know I wasn't her blood brother at times, though she never treated me as if I wasn't. It must have been interesting, getting a little brother and not seeing your mother go through the process of getting all fat and uncomfortable, much like a pet, I would guess, sudden and unconventional.

Helen was the one who planned all my birthday parties, usually in our porch since it was always the middle of the summer, but I cannot recall any real details of those for some reason, I think I made it disappointing to the crowd somehow. I enjoyed having my birthday in the middle of the summer, this was convenient since no school kids could share the wonderful formal procedure of "birthday shots" with me and thus I avoided all the abuse.

The shots were punches, and you got one for each year of life and one for good luck, and I had seen this occur constantly to kids with school time birthdays, relieved that I could never be the victim of this practice. I never took part in it, either, when other kids were the targets, I found this to be a stupid practice and took little or no advantage of the fact that I could never go through it.

My mom tried finding ways of occupying my time with programs like big brother. The one they picked, don't recall his name, took me to McDonalds once, played some basketball with me, but couldn't handle hours upon hours in the Great Swamp, which is where I always wanted to go. He lasted maybe a week.

I couldn't understand why he wanted to hang out with me to just play games or watch TV like a common baby sitter, really just a misguided teen, with the painfully incorrect belief that understanding or controlling me would be a simple task. My parents were disappointed by the guy's lack of effort. I would go to his house, and he would be busy with some girl, car, or something, and I knew when I wasn't wanted. After he would ignore me for a while, I would return home shortly after leaving, which made my mother ask what happened. I would tell her the guy was too busy to do anything with me, and ask her what the point of going there was which she eventually had no answer for and thus she stopped sending me.

After that, somehow a guy named Claude Kramer was introduced to me, he lived a block or so away, and his birthday was the same day as mine, sixty years earlier. He taught me a card game called Sanba, which is sort of like Canasta, which included three decks, and a lot of time. He also taught me to count in Japanese, and speak some too, and was a very nice guy overall.

I went to his house often, playing cards or chess, and hearing about the wars he was in. Strange, his interest in me, there seemed to be no reason other than his own boredom for playing with kids. I was not the only one. My parents believed he was not a deviate, and they let me go there whenever I wanted.

This was when I was around eight to ten years of age, and those two years was all it took before I violated his trust by stealing something, and he requested I never come over again, after I gave him whatever it was I took at his front door when he answered my ring. This didn't have much impact on me, he was just some old man with no wife or kids, who wound up dead a few years later anyway, and he didn't ever want to go to the woods or swamp with me. But he kept me occupied, which my parents needed, and they were not happy.

Then they decided to let me play basketball in the PAL league. Unfortunately, the coach of the team was the father of one of the kids, and he'd let his kid play more than anyone else. I was an average player over all, but the coach would just let me sit on the sideline, never really giving me a chance to participate. I was around ten years of age then. This coaches' trait I discovered was not uncommon, and to sum up the point, it's simply a very unfair practice, the best players don't always get to show their talent and if the coach doesn't like you, there's little chance of playing no matter how good you are.

So I would go with my dad on weekends to the YMCA in Summit, where I could do multiple things and usually remained very busy. This YMCA is where I got my senior life saving certificate at age thirteen, open water instructor at age fourteen, and Scuba license at age fifteen, which is the youngest you can be. At the YMCA I got one of the worst injuries and scares of my life as well, when I was about nine years of age. If you've ever played gym volleyball, you know that there is sometimes a crank on the posts, that makes the net rise and tighten, and that crank has very sharp teeth it grips to pull the cable up onto the spool with.

In the gym of this YMCA, they had activities like basketball, wiffle ball, volleyball and kickball, and one day we were playing kickball there. My dad was running on the track above the gym floor, and I was playing with some people, and I kicked it lamely, which is rare, so I had to run quick to first base, which was the volleyball post. I was safe, but I also ran head long into the crank-wheel, missing my right eye by one quarter of an inch, requiring three stitches in the corner of my eye socket. Blood was everywhere, and my dad was not pleased to see me sitting in a puddle of my blood crying and bleeding all over the gym floor. He felt the staff was to blame for leaving the cover off the post, and I never saw those employees again after that.

The Y was also a place that emphasized fitness and exercise, and I liked pull-ups and weights to some degree, but preferred swimming endlessly in the pool, till my dad was blue in the face yelling, trying to get me out. This is where I discovered an interesting sensation accidentally, still only about nine or ten years old, and a sensation unknown to me at the time, one all humanity relies upon to continue its existence, its purpose, one that most literature and art are based upon, the most basic of all life's functions, of course this was an orgasm.

I discovered that while doing pull-ups one day in such a way as to hang from my arms and pull my legs up to my chest, holding them in place as long as I could until they began to drop some and shake, and just open and close my legs quickly in an effort to stay at the same height, during this shaky last effort at staying at a stable leg height, a great feeling came over me, giving me a boost of adrenaline making it possible to hold position easily, energy I simply could not believe I had.

This feeling built and built upon its self, as no feeling had ever built before, then it just paralyzed me for a few seconds, with such an intensely good feeling I thought I had went to heaven, hoping it never ends, and then stops suddenly, with my arms feeling like spaghetti and my stomach muscles on fire, but I was still happy and contented with the effort, as though it were completely worth it, quite amazing. It felt like some great reward for achieving an optimal physical feat and the sensation seemed localized to my upper legs and groin area. Immediately after, I noticed my energy was reduced significantly, making each next attempt much harder.

But from then on, whenever possible, trips to the bathroom would include the activity of literally hanging around on the frame of the stalls, achieving orgasmic peaks five to six times every day or two. My limit before complete exhaustion was three orgasms per visit in five to ten minute trips to the bathroom. Of course, no fluid was produced at this age, so there was no way of knowing the cause of the sensation and it never felt sexual to me at all.

This caused my arms and stomach to get strong, being able to lift myself indefinitely from any perch and hold it for a long time, which made climbing even easier. I tried to explain the experience to peers of mine once, and wound up creating a sort of literal "hanging out in the bathroom" scene one day. Just picture five or six nine and ten year olds all hanging from their arms in the bathroom, trying to get orgasms without even knowing what one was or that this was the actual goal.

I just told them that if you hung around long enough, holding your legs just so, an interesting thing would happen. No one who tried it succeeded, or could hang on as long as I did, but it was fun exercise for me anyway. They all told me I was just crazy, and now their arms hurt for nothing, which made me laugh and pissed them off. It was quite a shock two or three years later when I discovered that a sticky fluid would emerge along with the feeling, suddenly for no reason, as though I had broken something in my groin, and how uncomfortable and embarrassed it was to have this stuff all over my underwear for the whole school day.

I had to dismiss myself early that day, and I couldn't really explain why I had to leave, so I just left, much to the teachers' dismay. It does explain some of my calm nature during fourth through sixth grade, though. And my parents just believed that the Ritalin was working. They never knew, and I've never mentioned it till now to anyone except the peers who didn't believe me at the time when I told them, I have no recollection of who the peers were though.

This activity also made all my teachers wonder why I always came back from the boys room flustered, sweating and out of breath, also very relaxed. I had been asked by some, "did you run all the way?" never had a good answer for that. I just would say yea, I ran since I had to go so badly. I think the teachers also thought I had some sort of urinary tract or bowel disease, since I would request a bathroom pass much more often than anyone else. They would ask me if I was all right sometimes, or ask me if I needed a pass to see the nurse too. Very addicting, orgasms, especially when you don't know you had one or even know what one is.

There was no need for the average almighty "wet" dream, and though I had a few erotic dreams, none resulted in discharge. Odd thing, the wet dream, since women have to be told about their uterus shedding every month and that bleeding for days is normal, who tells little boys that one day they will awake with sticky stuff all over their bed and sweating? I think in this respect men have a distinct advantage, blood is blood and that would freak me out.

If one were naïve enough, you'd think you sprang a leak of some sort or something turned your piss white, or you contracted some strange disease. That was the extent of my exercise during those years other than gym class, which was my favorite subject, and probably is for most children, maybe not for the same reason. So I found the ultimate stress relief purely by accident. My attitude reflected it, being even more complacent and mellow, and I was able to communicate on a deeper level, especially with girls. This relaxed my whole attitude and I didn't even realize this till much later, I found peace and focus.

Also around nine years of age, my parents decided to start sending me to sleep away summer camp, for usually two week sessions or more. Not the mentally handicapped sort anymore, just plain camp, to give them a break and peak my interest with a change of scenery. The first camp I went to was called camp Tohony, somewhere in the Poconos. They play lots of soccer, capture the flag and knock hockey at these camps, which I liked, but the kids were the same as in school, most didn't like me, for no apparent reason.

I was overwhelmingly anxious to make friends and other times too shy to even speak. There was no in-between for me. My forwardness and over abundance of energy was a little overwhelming for most kids, I think, and I may have been slightly too competitive at times as well.

My name was sewn into every piece of clothes I brought, including my underwear, and though the camp said you're supposed to, I was one of few whose mother actually did it. It was a laundry issue, as I understood, and my stuff always came back to me, other kids weren't so lucky all the time.

Camp always began the same way, with orientation and introductions, meeting all the counselors, aids and staff, and activity choosing work sheets we filled out to decide what we enjoyed doing amongst what they offered us to do. Naturally, my first activity from the first second was a foot tour of the entire grounds, within visibility but as far as it would go, the beach of the lake, various cabins of various sizes for various purposes, scattered randomly, ho pattern at all, very serene and quite pleasing, like real pioneers, only with cars and trucks, and other modern conveniences.

The counselors and camp owners appeared to like me, or pretended to do in an effort to control me. One day another camper in my cabin decided it would be funny to throw a five gallon bucket of water out the window of our cabin on to my head. Guess he was mad since I won the capture the flag game against his team earlier that day. The bucket hit the side of my head, and it barely got me wet, and that just made me sad and angry, like it usually did when there was no reason for doing something like that, so I cried, but not from the pain.

Later, when he found his sleeping bag and bunk on fire out in front of the cabin with me roasting marshmallows over it, I believe he though it may not have been such a good idea, or even that funny. I thought my reaction was pretty funny, too bad he didn't. They moved me to the counselors' cabin for some reason, of course calling my parents at the same time.

The owner initially called my parents to come get me but then agreed to keep me there till the weekend. I was no longer obligated to attend normal camp activities, and I was allowed to just wander around the camp myself, because imprisonment was not a legal thing to do to a kid, or they just didn't have enough help to watch one camper all the time. They also wanted to keep me separated from the camper whose sleeping bag and bunk I destroyed. Probably a good idea, though I felt the issue was closed, I still wound up worse off I thought, with a bruise on my head that took a long time to go away.

The next day, I went across the soccer field to look for a stream, or some wildlife, or interesting things, and I realized I had to go to the bathroom rather badly, I didn't mind having to piss in the woods, but this wasn't the case this time. I saw no toilets, so I just pulled my pants down and let loose in the woods. What I didn't realize is that I was relieving myself right on a yellow jackets nest, and they did not appreciate me crapping on their doorstep, which they showed by attacking me with my pants down.

I ran screaming out of the woods, trying to pull up my pants while feeling the squish of the left over feces I had no time to wipe spread all over my rear end, while getting stung about six or seven times in unusual places on my body, luckily they missed important parts of me completely. Good thing I'm not allergic to bees. I recovered from that and the poison ivy I sat in that surrounded the bee's nest as well that day, and continued my isolated existence, except when soccer was the activity and they needed an extra body to complete the team.

The one time they did that I was on the team opposing the jerks team, and I got satisfaction again by causing our team to win. I was on defense and every time that same kid came to my end, I was in his face kicking the ball away from him. I did that no matter who had the ball. I remember the kid trying to kick me out of frustration, and that made me laugh in his face, even though he did kick my legs a few times. I was sufficiently satisfied not to need further retaliation, since he got in trouble for doing that too, and I tended to kick back as well, but didn't get caught.

If arts and crafts were presented as the activity, I would leave and roam the area to do what I wanted, since they couldn't allocate anyone to spend the day assigned to just me. I would go in search of animals, or a tree branch to hang from and do my thing. I was the only camper to just go swimming myself, since I could swim so well I guess they didn't worry, but no one said much about it or watched as I recall. I also could canoe myself, picked that up quite easily and was allowed to go myself after a few instructional rides. I liked archery, rifle range and camp zoology. Then came the day my parents came to get me, three days after the bee incident.

The camps owner had a motorcycle, which he gave me rides on occasionally. I never saw anyone else in camp ride with him. He was a nice guy, forced to hang around with me because I was the only loner or problem in camp. This day, I was wearing dress shoes for some reason, and as I was sitting behind him on the bike, I noticed a hot sensation on my ankle, and before I could say a word, the heel of my shoe was wedged in the spokes of the motorcycle, which would have ripped my whole heel off if I wasn't wearing hard shoes.

I screamed, the owner stopped and looked in shock, and I realized that the pain was gone, but my heel was bleeding so profusely, that it made tears come from my eyes out of fear and shock. He pulled me off the bike, and ran me down to the nurse, anxiously babbling: "oh my God, oh, my God" under his breath the whole time he was running. She had to put fourteen stitches in my heel. Then my parents finally arrived, and got to hear about this incident. With my foot all wrapped up, they took me home in time for my birthday, which is July fifteenth. I didn't do much else that summer except for recovering from my wound.

Camping wasn't that bad except for Tohony, though I was always sounding sad and saying it was terrible to my parents, who would only tell me to try and make the best of it. I would write letters or call home saying how much I hated being here, but my sister would always just send me her home made chocolate chip cookies, which were my favorite. Other kids would always try to take them, though unsuccessfully. They were quite good. My mother would also send marshmallow Fluff, which was another favorite of mine, and bread with peanut butter would complete the package for making Fluffernutters. The bread and peanut butter I got from the camp.

This would usually give me enough satisfaction to remain and try to have fun, getting to eat homemade cookies with sandwiches whenever I wanted. During any meal, my saying was: "worst comes first, best comes next" when contemplating eating food I didn't like, such as vegetables. I always ate what I disliked the most first, leaving the food I liked to finish my meal with, thus giving me a good taste in my mouth upon completion. Made sense, and I did hate vegetables like most kids do I noticed.

While at camp I had to get replacement clothes often, since I always destroyed what I wore by doing my usual things. Climbing trees, wading through swamps, using clothes as ropes or catapults for rocks, or just taking them off and losing them someplace in the woods. I liked to find remote places in the woods where nobody was or would be, and I would strip down to just sneakers and streak around the woods.

I felt like I was the early Indians, who had no use for clothes during the summer, and it felt quite natural and peaceful, besides having to make sure no one found this little naked kid running around in the woods. Hiding was fairly exciting, but besides the protection of my feet, I felt like I was as any other animal in the woods, no clothes, just my own natural skin feeling the cool breeze from the mountain passes on hot summer days, almost an erotic feeling, if I knew what erotic even was at that age.

This also aided in my unusual practice of hanging around, causing the orgasmic sensation to take far less time to achieve, having been aroused by the natural setting of the woods, the solitude, and the lack of clothes. It beat the hell out of the school bathroom, where the only excitement was the much higher possibility of being seen or caught by someone. That wasn't all that exciting either, since everyone liked to climb around the bathroom, just not for the same reason I did.

Only in the first two summer camps did I indulge in this back to nature activity, as well as at the swamp, if I went alone. And my mother thought the bag I brought to the swamp was just for animals I found; not knowing it was really intended for holding my clothes while streaking. Of course, when I was done running around, the bag would be full of wildlife eventually. I never did get spotted or seen, and just like any phase, it soon ended, or re-directed to a different level later in life.

I loved to be home. When we left the house, I would always say "good bye, house!" which was probably cute when you're five or six years of age. I had a playroom like no one else, my basement. It was ten feet high and twenty six feet long by twenty two feet wide, with a two inch concrete ledge running three quarters of the way around it about six feet off the ground.

Most adventures while indoors took place there. I would walk the ledge all the way around, like I was mountain climbing sideways, and I never fell off. I had a Ping-Pong table, which I destroyed after a year or so by using it for things other than what it was made for, and a pool table. The pool table was placed so that if you took a cue, holding it out against the edge of the table with the tip against it, you could go around ninety-five percent of it without hitting anything. The only obstacles were the two lolly columns holding up the main support beam, about four feet away from the table. They never made much of a difference to my game, or were too much of an obstacle to play around. It was the perfect room for pool.

I became what I believe to be a pretty good pool player after some years of practice, to the point where later on I even got to play against Lana Janes in her own pool hall in Orange Knowl, where I did beat her a couple of times in eight ball. Of course, she beat me usually, but just winning at all was a thrill, even though I am not completely certain it was her, just a girl named Lana, that's what I recall.

I had to run the whole table to win, because she rarely missed, and this was still awhile before she became famous I think, late seventies, she was a great player. Anyway, I had this table about five years, from age eleven to sixteen, and I used to dream about playing it. One time, or perhaps more but one specific time I know of, I woke up in the middle of the night, and found myself standing in the basement, with all the pool balls exactly where I dreamed them to be, playing with no one.

I know it was a dream, because in it, I was playing against someone and there were a lot of people around. I realized that I sleepwalked to the real table from three flights up, and everyone was gone when I woke, except my mother who asked me what I was doing down here in the middle of the night. I never sleepwalked before or after to this day that I know of. The tickle never occurred in these dreams for some reason, like it was on vacation while I would shoot pool, I found that odd.

I would rarely sleep alone down there, since my dream alligator nightmare days made me leery of being down there alone in the dark, but I would camp out there if a friend of mine was staying over, usually in a tent created with sheets, cardboard or blankets draped over chairs or poles with sleeping bags inside. Besides the dream, which wasn't real anyway, I only had two bad experiences in that basement. Once when I was ten, I threw a baseball strait up, and the six-foot fluorescent light bulb fell and exploded on my head, but left no cuts at all somehow. I was smart enough to close my eyes and not get the gas in them, but the mess was impressive, glass everywhere possible. There were two sets of lights, both six foot fluorescent types, on each side of the room.

The other time was when my parents hired someone other than Roy's sister as a baby sitter. I had to be nine or ten years of age or so. It was difficult to find me a sitter, and usually Roy's older sisters, Hillary, Norma, Vera, and Celine and my sisters' friends were recruited, because if I liked them as a person, I wasn't too difficult.

This was some girl who had never been to my house before, and never would be again. I kept most of my animals in the basement and had ten or eleven aquariums full of animals, mostly mice and guinea pigs. I thought it would be fun to share my animals with this sitter, who decided to have friends over my house while my parents were out.

I knew they weren't supposed to be there but didn't care much, just more people to entertain. Unfortunately no one was impressed with the animals I tried to show off with, I started off small with just a mouse or two, so when I complained and went back down to return the mice to the cage, one of the guys she invited over just cursed at me, and pushed the door closed to the basement as I was coming back up to get a snake from my room.

I tried to come out, but the door was locked from the den side. I shouted to let me out, but only heard laughter, which really pissed me off. So I took a chair, came back up the stairs, and smashed a hole through the door to get their attention. That worked fine. Turned out some asshole had their foot against the door. They started calling me things like crazy, stupid, insane, mostly what I found complementary, since I was far from done and I figured they'd have more to talk about later, beyond their derogatory statements.

So here I was, a ten year old standing nearly in tears from anger in the middle of the den yelling at teens to get out of my house, before I really got mad or before I tell my parents about the party. It wasn't enough to vacate the premises, but it did make them laugh and continue their poor attitude towards me. They tried to lock me into my room after that, and within seconds I was outside through my bedroom window and off the roof, with a can of hair spray and lighter.

I stood in my driveway and yelled," Get out of my house, or else!" There was no response, just a bunch of teenagers looking confused by this odd kid, not really believing in the gall this kid had, kind of giggling and laughing at the idea. They were also wondering how I got to the driveway, but I gave no information about that.

So I lit the torch, aimed it at the gas cap of one of the kids' cars in the driveway, and shut it off. I wasn't sure what would happen, but I just put ten teenagers into shock, because they were standing right next to the car by this time as well, having come out of the house through the garage to see what the commotion was about. That was sufficient enough to make most of them leave, cursing and complaining about the burn on the cars paint and what a lunatic I was as I ran by them back inside and hid till my parents came home.

The sitter and her boyfriend looked for me for a few hours, couldn't find me, not where I hide. Once I heard my parents' car, I appeared, right in front of the confused sitter, who was still wondering how to tell my parents she lost me. That girl never came back or got paid for her hours or the fire damage to her boyfriends' car. When my sitters did get paid, it was five bucks an hour, and this was in the sixties when two bucks an hour was considered high pay. Many of the destructive nights I described earlier were directed at the kids' houses that were there that day, along with the usual bullies' dwellings, and on occasion innocent neighbors' houses, just to even the distribution out and avoid suspicion.

I had another way of dealing with sitters, less cruel, sort of, the disappearing act is what adults called it and I just described one time when I did use it. Now I have to describe in detail some of the inside of my house, so anyone can picture just how interesting this hiding place was.

As you walk up the five front steps and enter, you're standing in a two-foot deep four-foot wide sunken entrance, about twelve feet long with an iron rail along the whole right side, behind which is the living room. Directly in front of you would be two angled carpeted stairs up to the space of carpet between the kitchen entrance, and the top of the second step, about five feet.

On the left are the five carpeted stairs leading up to the bedrooms. The two stairs are on such an angle that they become one double high stair on the left corner, meeting the corner of the wall that begins the other stairs to the bedroom, so they go from the end of the iron rail on a ten o'clock angle into one step.

There is also a sliding door closet in the sunken hall, which takes up about half the wall on the left as you enter. As you go up the five steps towards the bedrooms, the ceiling just shoots up on a ninety degree angle about four feet and there begin the ceiling for the bedroom level.

The corner that hovers over the stairs is directly over the bottom stairs lip, lining up perfectly with the wall in the living room. I used to pile pillows at the bottom between the step and the kitchen entrance, and I'd run down the bedroom hallway and leap down the stairs about ten or fifteen feet through the air and land on the pillows, never getting hurt. Well, except once when I was older and taller, and my head hit the wall lip and landed me flat on my back on the living room floor.

So, as your standing atop the fifth step on the bedroom level, actually in the hallway, you see two doors about ten feet away, another door immediately on your left, which is a closet, and a space of around two feet wide on the left of the left most visible door, right after the closet, and there is the third bedroom door facing out the front of the house, Helen's room.

My room was the middle door, which also faced front. Also from standing at this point, turning immediately right would give you a view of a bathroom, about six feet away, and if you begin walking towards it, you find another nine steps on your right immediately after a wall, leading up to the attic bedroom, with walls on both sides of the staircase. When you go up those stairs, go in and close the door and stand facing the same door, there are big closets on both the right and left sides of the staircase.

If you look immediately left against that wall, you'll see another smaller, four-foot high door, made to fit the pitch of the roof at that point, about five feet away, which is one storage area. Going into this door leads you into a normal attic; where the ceiling pitches down to make it get shorter and shorter as you walk in. About four feet from the door as you walk in and face right, there's a crude wall, with a small opening, about three feet high by two feet wide, right at the end of the wall on your right, which ends at the back wall of the two closets I described.

The rest of the wall, about two foot high, continues left towards the front pitch of the house, with just insulation lining the side above and below it, but the space is what's of interest here. As you look into the space you can see, about thirty feet away, the entire attic fan and its large opening to outside. As you climb into this space, there are some boards to walk on, which lead you into the unfinished side of the attic, quite large and open, but unimpressive and dirty, with no other way of getting into it.

Then I discovered something interesting under one of the boards when you first enter through the hole. There was a space about three feet on the right immediately as you enter the area. The space was about six or seven feet deep, and three foot wide by three foot long. My guess is that there was some extra space next to the front door's hallway closet, and they just didn't use it.

I could hear anyone in the house from any room they were in, and I was completely undetectable in this space, and I brought pillows to line it with, and flashlights and candles to see with, I even kept food there sometimes. I would replace the wood board over it while I was in it, and never told anyone it was there, so even if you look in the attic or even stick your head into that whole to look around, you wouldn't find me. Of course I had to be completely quiet, which was easy for me when I wanted to be.

There were many other places to hide around the house, some dozen closets, beds, couches, and the basement, but I only used those for playing hide and seek with friends. I rarely resorted to my favorite place, unless I didn't want to be found or to prove a point. If I did hide there, eventually I would just appear in the bedroom hallway after I heard panic setting into a nice sitter's voice, not wanting to get into trouble with my parents.

They would always accuse me of going outside, therefore cheating, but I never gave up my secret and I let them think whatever they wanted to. I once even hid from my parents there, not wanting to go on some trip with them, and they'd have to leave before finding me, which they did, and that gave me full run of the house. They locked the door, figuring I must be out somewhere, and were puzzled about how I got back in without breaking anything.

I believe I was around ten when I did that. I got to build a fire in the fireplace and roast marshmallows and hot dogs. I also could play owner of the house, running around it free as I wanted to be, and I did odd things, like sweeping the garage or basement, doing dishes, playing the piano in the living room, vacuuming, some gutter maintenance, like it was my house and needed taking care of.

My favorite sitter, Kat Segal, knew how to deal with and entertain me. She was the daughter of my parents' friends. We'd go on the roof and watch falling stars, or build a fire for hot dogs and marshmallows in the fireplace. She liked the fact that I would clean the fireplace so well that my parents' wouldn't even know that we used it, till she told them so. She was one of the few people I would let help me with my homework, if I decided to bring it home one day and she was there.

She also understood my philosophy, where by our brains are our religions, since eighty percent of it isn't used or understood, what else could it be, room for improvement or evolution? I believed, and still do, that whatever you believe in your mind is likely very close to what actually happens after you die, with the exception of those who were truly bad people, or one's who took others lives for any reason. Those who believe in the pearly gates will most certainly see them when they die, provided they didn't kill anyone or commit true sin, as their religion dictates.

Those who believe themselves hell worthy could certainly have their conscience put there, their "spirit" pushed off the earth and drawn into the sun, or the reverse, to the Earth's core, the only places hot enough I can think of that matches when people describe "hell" as a hot place. Since the body runs on electricity and electricity as far as we know cannot be destroyed, our "soul" goes wherever we want it to or believe it to go. God is in your head, existing as part of your conscious and subconscious, every step of the day. Since the main belief of most religions is the fact that God is everywhere, this statement must be partially correct.

Another theory I mused with her and others about was the theory of reincarnation, where by the energy of your soul either spreads out to many new life forms, or a single form of an about to be born person if you energy was cohesive enough. Strength of the soul would determine that, the weaker one's being spread out, the stronger one's either guided to the light, which could be the sun, or to another individual chemically bioelectric attracting unborn person.

Like having a nine month dream, which would naturally seem much shorter, and waking to find yourself empty of knowledge and completely ignorant of the surroundings, and once again an infant. Of course, since there is no nervous system any longer, trips to the sun couldn't be painful, and the sun may just be a bioelectric magnet for strong or "faithful" souls. The weaker one's could experience hell on earth and be reborn as several life forms with no true conscious, like microscopic life forms, or blades of grass that get decapitated every time someone mows the lawn, or a tree that can't run away from a forest fire, chain saw or insects.

Still others could be transient, wandering the earth in the form of pure energy, not desiring either re-birth or dispersion, looking for another answer to what is happening to them, better known as ghosts. The true outer body experience, like a never-ending dream you cannot wake from. With what some people experience in life, it's easy to imagine that hell is really just our life on this earth, in this overly fragile form. I figured since there are many forms of electricity, what you do and where you go after death depended upon which form of energy you take, bio electric, electromagnetic, static, or just which electrical property our conscious takes, that would decide if our soul is omnipotent or doomed, both or neither.

I understood these things and discussed them at an early age. Kat was at least seven years older than I was, and she seemed to enjoy these discussions. She was the only person I would listen to, or respond to even if I didn't want to. Had a normal crush on her, she was quite sexy in my eyes which may be partially the reason for my attitude. But I could get past that, and accepted her as a friend of mine, and a pleasing vision to admire. I would find myself wanting her to like me, and wouldn't try doing some things that may change her attitude towards me or cause her to dislike me for any reason. She liked all animals, too, which made sitting me much easier, having no fear of any of my pets.

My parents let me celebrate both Christmas and Chanukah, and I had never been baptized or Bar Mitzvah'ed never worrying about whatever force watches over me or consequences this might have. My mother was raised Catholic and my dad Jewish, since they were French and Polish, respectively. I am actually descended from a woman, who was Ukrainian, and my father was half Dutch and half Irish, she was pregnant and engaged, he cheated on her before the wedding and she decided not to marry him and give me up, but that's all I know about that. I did prove to myself later in life that we are cared for and monitored, and what we see before our eyes is not the whole story really. There is so much more to this galaxy and mere existence.

It's the only explanation for merely surviving this long, and also for what occurred when Peter was sleeping in my room one night, but it wouldn't happen for many years from this point in time. This was when I was about seventeen years of age; Peter was actually living in my room, because his Grandma moved back to Georgia. I was thinking to myself, while he snored, very quietly around three a.m. just thinking about life's big picture having been woke by the tickle at that point, so I thought to myself if there really is a God, let him fill the room with light now. At that moment, Peter stopped snoring, sat up and opened the shade, the room filled with the street light, and he looked out, lain back down, and was snoring ten seconds later. Guess I should have asked to have the tickle disappear forever, which would have been nice.

I just thought to myself, in my own mind, thanks, and if I was going the wrong direction in life, show me another sign, which didn't happen. Possibly pure coincidence was my conclusion at the time. I would still believe that what lies ahead is not known due to the capacity of our mind, incomprehensible, by human standards. Star Trek aided that thought process philosophically, and what Gene Roddenberry conceived appeared quite feasible.

It could be as simple as our life energy getting re-disbursed, into many hundreds or just a few other life forms. This sounds very logical, but kind of depressing, since living as most other creatures is not a pleasant looking proposition from the human standpoint. Could that be true hell? Maybe heaven, if you're a Peregrine falcon. I'll use the phrase Leonard Nimoy portraying a Vulcan delivered so well, "interesting". Too bad the whole event besides Peter's part came from my head. Still believe that I'm blessed, in many ways, though I took that for granted when I was young and still do sometimes.

As I grew up, I had two Uncle Aarons. Aaron Milar was my moms' gynecologist, and delivered Helen and I. His wife, my aunt Faith was a big part of UNICEF and had the job of getting dignitaries of the world visiting the United Nations their schedule of events or itineraries. Very nice, well off, Park Avenue people, who's home I went to with my parents every New Years eve, because my parents didn't really like leaving me home alone or with Helen.

These people were not related to me, they were just lifelong friends of my parents. The other Uncle Aaron was actually related to us. The wife of that uncle was my Aunt Dee, and Uncle Aaron was one of the founders of Abraham and Strauss. This Aaron was my mothers' cousin, and I remember them for giving me only books for any occasion, which I despised since I hated reading. They lived in a mansion in King of Prussia Pennsylvania, and had a big outdoor pool, which was one of the main reasons I loved to visit them. I had an Uncle Pat, or Patrick Celin, his wife Felice and sister Linny, don't know what that was short for, nothing according to my mom, and their children and my cousins Deidra and Jenny were regulars for Thanksgiving. They lived in Long Island, and when we'd go there for Passover I would spend the day collecting toads in their yard.

Then there was my Aunt Elvira and Uncle Pete Werner, who had my cousins Mary and Nina. I had an Aunt Stemmie and Uncle Sidney Frake, who had my cousin Ralph as their only child. My cousins were all at least seven years older than I, most over a decade older. I was always the youngest and therefore in charge of the question reading at Passover, which I loathed. They were all regulars to family functions. The whole family was pretty upper middle class, usually listening in horror to stories my parents would share about what I had done recently. They all played with me, various games, and were always nice to me as I remember, the little blonde black sheep of the family.

I was not a physically affectionate child, I hated when relatives would try to kiss my face with their big, wet, lipstick-covered lips. I usually wanted no contact with anyone, never feeling that it was necessary to be kissed, at least till I wanted to reciprocate myself. Even to this date I make most people feel uncomfortable with hello or good-bye kisses, not caring either way if they would kiss me or not. I never saw the point, never feeling more or less loved or cared about whether I was kissed or not. Save the mushy stuff for your mate, is how I felt and still do usually. Don't throw your lips my way, it means very little to me, I know how you feel without making my face wet.

My family was very good at discussing things, well read intelligent college types who articulated everything quite well, and I really never fought about anything with them, they made me realize that words were true power, being able to string together complex sentences with meaning and purpose was much more fun than just abusing our language with emotional outbursts of explicative's and having a point was deemed important. Unfortunately, this was not a practice anyone I went to school with was very adept at, guess since they were closer to my age, or just didn't have the benefit of a good family.

Besides with Peter, I only had two other fights in school from grade one to twelve, and one of them wasn't even in my school. One was with Edward, who finally irritated me to the point of action, but it took him years and the right circumstance and mind set for me to even consider, I think it was the same day as a bad dental visit or tooth ache or something. I didn't fight him till I was about twelve.

As I recall I was standing in front of my locker and I heard Edward coming down the hall saying; "Hey Greendick! Your momma licks cow scum off dead rats!" He would laugh between each third word, and he continued; "Hey Greenfuck! You eat your momma! Ha, ha, ha, ha. Look out Greenie!" At that moment as I turned my head to see what the warning was about, something bounced off my head and skidded down the hallway. I felt the anger build, holding the tears from anger back and rubbing my head as I saw what the object was, an old portable radio lying broken on the ground.

Edward just walked away laughing as if everything in his world was perfect. I attacked him a few minutes later, never letting him completely out of my sight or letting my anger diminish, jumping him in the gym with a flurry of quick rabbit punches, then tackling him and cursing while I continued the assault on his head with very quick fists. I gained enough respect from him to leave me and my work alone from that day on, but he still wouldn't associate with me. My actions surprised and shocked him enough to make him not even try to fight back, which was very odd for him. I guess I caught him completely off guard, and all he did was fall to the floor and cover, my old trick, and wait for an authority to break us up.

The three teachers' it took to remove me from Edward's chest were equally shocked, never having seen my temper displayed before. I was pretty shocked as well, never before feeling enough rage to let it out that way besides the one time with Betty, and though it felt somewhat good and satisfying, I still didn't like it. I broke free from the teachers' easily and went home.

The teachers knew that Edward was the catalyst, since a witness to the event told them so, thus I was in no trouble this time, especially since I never did anything like that before. Edward never bothered me the same again after that, but he finally got the reaction he was looking for, just not expecting it this time, so I kind of lost that battle. This fact I resented, and it proved to me such violence is not the remedy to a situation, even though it temporarily resolved mine this time, there would be no fights with him anymore.

I did take pride in the fact that I usually got A's in tests, but refused to do homework, thus my grades reflected that. Most of the time my partner in any school project was a girl, Nikki and Vera favored my company because they knew they would get a passing grade working with me. Vera always enjoyed my company and my odd way of looking at things, and she also liked to make fun of Phillip Dinkle. Yes, I said Dinkle, right, tinkle wrinkle, pinkle, stinkle, winkle, and put nearly any consonant there. I took it easy on him most of the time, because he was a nice kid really. The only other person with an odd name I ever knew was Edith Hymen. No, she didn't have a brother named Buster or a papa either. I convinced Vera to make fun of people if she had to while they aren't present, so as not to create hard feelings for them, and it's still just as funny as ever, even better sometimes.

When in sixth grade, about eleven years of age, I had a senior college reading and comprehension level according to tests, even though I disliked reading, so my intelligence was never in question. It was never in question until I let loose five mice in the school hallway, more than I ever had before. That had to be in nineteen seventy-two or so. Teachers were not too happy, and it was a mad struggle to capture them all back, one was never found again.

I never denied doing this, which got me into some trouble with Mr. Roden. I was told to leave my entire critter collection home from now on, and I did just that. They used the argument of how unsanitary these creatures were, and I had to agree, knowing this fact already from the odor in my basement between cage cleanings. It was also considered disruptive and distractive, which I knew and thought would be a nice change of pace, some excitement, oh well.

Biology and chemistry were my favorite subjects. What I did once in chemistry, before class began or possibly when I wasn't even having class, was to light the sources of gas for the Bunsen burners, without the burners attached, causing streams of fire to shoot out both sides of the sink fixture they were attached to, on all ten sinks there were, simultaneously.

The professor wasn't too happy to come in and see me roasting marshmallows on the fires I made in his classroom, using pipettes and other school utensils as the sticks, wasting away whatever source of propane they had to nothing, and heating up the room to the level of a sauna. I think it was because of me they began to lock those rooms when not in use, though they may have done that before anyway and I just never noticed. But I loved the subjects, knowing the whole periodic table quite well and enjoying working with chemicals, a microscope and dissecting things, and the teachers were much more tolerant of me, since I usually did very well and was not too distractive, and highly participative.

I also loved taking Spanish simply because the teacher was so attractive, a fact I didn't know before signing up for it. My parents spoke two languages, my mother spoke French, and my dad spoke German, so I picked a different one just so I could talk and they wouldn't understand me, like when they spoke their languages and I couldn't understand them.

I never heard my Dad speak German, was only told he could do so. Should have figured that they would have made excellent tutors for one of their languages, and it would have been very helpful, but I had to be different. I got straight A's in that class for three years, but I realized that if you don't use your language skills continuously, you do forget how to speak the language after a while. I sometimes wondered why my parents didn't speak German and French to me continually, so I'd assimilate the languages and have a head start on my peers.

When I was eleven, my dad took me on a business trip to Washington, D.C., with his Japanese associates. We drove down, over the Chesapeake Bay Bridge Tunnel, where we stopped and took pictures and marveled at this view of engineering genius. We stayed in a hotel once we reached DC though I couldn't tell you the hotels' name, but as soon as we were walking in, I was gone. It took so long to get there; I just couldn't wait to check it out.

My dad, of course, made his apologies and made his way to find me. I saw every monument, every store, every foot of the whole nation's capital, all by myself. I didn't have anyone around to explain what I saw, so I wasn't really certain of what significance I was seeing, but it was impressive from an art like and historical perspective, people seemed really focused on the various monuments and things, like they knew the whole unknown relevance about them.

Around five or six p.m., my father found me, waiting for him on the steps of the hotel. He decided to send me home by plane the next day, by myself. That was also an interesting experience, with all the stewardesses paying close attention to me, giving me distracting material items to try and occupy my time, playing cards, puzzles and things, and that was my first flight ever.

I spent ninety nine percent of the flight glued to the window, it was awesome. The Japanese business associates understood the situation, and were always very nice about things, with a basic 'boys will be boys' attitude about it all. They gave me some great gifts through the years and always liked me, for some reason. I remember one of their names being Mister Nagamatzu but don't recall the other ones name. They were very nice polite people, but distant, as if from another world.

Their culture must be just so different, I found nothing I could relate to usually but they enjoyed the level of energy I had, as though this was a good thing and if sent down the right path, the energy would create much and find purpose and goals. Very happy people, and they loved looking at anything I had to show them, they found great interest in anything I appeared to put effort into, such as my animal collection.

Along with my large collection of animals, I had a large butterfly and moth collection, Great Spangled Flitteraries, American Painted, and an Atlas moth, the moth I had to have my parents buy since they're very rare. I had a Tiger Swallowtail, Viceroy, Monarch, and twenty other species, too. I felt like a scientist the way I sedated the butterflies with Chloroform, and carefully spread their wings flat and placed them on the cotton of the collection box, then covering them with the glass top for display, quite detailed and entertaining.

This hobby did not have many followers around me, only a couple of guys had shown any interest in this portrait of natural wonder, amazing as it was, girls liked them just because of color, which I had to agree with, impressive display of such a small part of the ecosystem, such a seemingly useless insect showing such amazing diversity.

EXIT EIGHT

Bumpy Road Ahead, Requires Action

Some of my favorite activities with or without company were riding my bike, climbing anything, and swimming. Once, I climbed up and slid down a telephone pole, a real bad idea. Still have a splinter from that day in my hand, because my grandma said it would work its way out naturally, it didn't. Decided to stick to climbing trees, which I climbed regularly like a cat, and I never fell out of one, got a splinter or got stuck. I did have a few neighbors to play with that lived on my block, till around age thirteen or so, mostly the same kids as I went to Cub Scouts with.

We used to play a game called shmeer the queer. This involved football, where who ever had the ball would be tackled by everyone else. There was no goal, no touchdowns or points, just random chasing of each other to get the ball by tackling whoever had it. I was very hard to tackle mostly, and I could carry several people on my back and drag a few as well before I would fall.

I also played basketball and soccer. In basketball, it was always annoying to play against me, because my hands were quick, and getting by me was difficult, as Roy learned. I always hit the ball no matter what move you made, usually pissing off the opponent or making them yell foul. I wasn't tall, so I had to be quick. Very irritating for those with no sportsmanship, every time the ball got near me I'd knock it away. I was not the greatest shooter, but defensively I was not often matched. Soccer was the same, except I was a good offensive player in soccer.

Among my other normal activities within my youth, like playing chess with my dad since I was five, I played baseball or shmeer the queer with friends, and going to McDonalds with my sister who always gave me McDonald gift certificates for any holiday. I loved to cook, and have pictures somewhere of myself as a little kid in an apron. I liked to make brownies and eggs and always was very organized and neat, but not always clean. At around nine or ten years of age, fourth and fifth grade, a few of my friends and I would do some other, what some may consider not normal activities, like streaking around my house.

Herb Wilson and Vera Kline were my usual friends for this activity, and they helped to begin my fetish for this activity as I described doing in camps already. Just males were no fun, we had the same body parts, which I didn't care to see, and so it had to include females, or be completely alone.

My house had a porch off to the right, and behind the house was a door made of three quarter inch plywood that led under the porch, and that's where weird little naked kids liked to run to and hide. Never did like clothes. It was all relatively harmless, till Vera told her mom what she was doing with her afternoons. She was never allowed in my company again. My mother told me that is was not appropriate to ask little girls to take clothes off, even if they offered first, which as I recall, she did.

I understood, of course, to the degree of how she saw the situation, and how Vera's mom would see it, still didn't know what the panic was about. Herb, on the other hand, after some time began to get a little too happy with the idea and thought that any touching from whoever was doing it was ok by him and something that needed to be explored. I thought streaking was about feeling natural, not touching, and I did not feel the same as he did about it. Though contact can be pleasant, I also knew that in the chapter of my life where sex and girls began, that it was just that, sex and girls. Herb was a definite candidate for the closet I thought.

Never found anything interesting about a penis, except my own, only because it's there, and didn't really feel comfortable with how Herb over reacted to simple nudity. Thus, I never suggested it to him again and only went solo, or with a female when the opportunity struck again, which it didn't for many years and by then, it was sexual. Herb would continually suggest the storage room for naked binges, perhaps with another neighborhood girl, besides his sister Dale, but I knew where he was leading.

He no longer wanted to do other things, like find animals, or play games. I didn't disagree with the basic philosophy that if it feels good, do it, I just understood that there were two sexes placed upon this earth for a reason, and unless you're an earthworm, or any organism that can mate with itself, the need to venture past natural instinct could never be too important or natural I figured. A woman is a work of art, unmatched by anything in this world from a male's point of view, and though a man can be appealing to another man, and a woman to a woman, something just doesn't seem right with that, instinctually, perhaps only for me, but that's the way I always felt.

I believed that the sensation was so intense during the act of procreation, that it was like getting a reward for continuing the species, and since the penis could feel so good, I figured that the woman should experience some reward or intense feeling, like the miniature version of the male counterpart, without which no woman would feel the motivation to experience pleasure in the sexual way, it would just be some other natural bodily function, like waste disposal. How dull that would be, for a girl to have sex feel no better than pooping, and having birth be so incredibly painful, didn't seem fair.

It's like the invisible "force" from Star Wars, which could be manipulated but never destroyed, used for evil as well as good, but it's a feeling that surrounds you, aiming in the direction of the future, and sex does have a profound effect upon the path we will travel at some, or even many points in life. The path to happiness in life is to find the way to be who you are, and I never could do anything less. Pleasure could be self-manifested, within private surroundings or hanging around literally, but ultimately the truth would be that only a woman could fill any space I may have in my life, and it would be many years before any space would open or need filling in that respect.

Naturally, I found nothing truly wrong with a woman's desire for another woman, something I could relate to, but that is only because I am a man, thus given to such stereotypical reactions, one way offended me, another did not. If this was right or wrong I would say is irrelevant, since I cannot speak from the viewpoint of any woman, and can only take the word of certain girl's who told me how they feel about the issue.

The girls I asked said roughly the same thing in reverse, accepting sexual relationships between two men as opposed to two women was easier and less offensive, which seems normal. Just that they were willing to share this information with me was interesting; at least it was good conversation, and it had to be Vera who shared her insight. Our conversational flow had no boundaries or weaknesses, all topics felt comfortable and normal.

I think one weakness of mine though, in school, was when I shared my academic knowledge with other students who were less intelligent. Sometimes on tests I would give some kids answers, even if they were bullies because I was very forgiving and figured we all need more than one chance.

I hoped it may also change their attitude, but it didn't and it was never appreciated. They probably figured I was protecting myself, giving them answers in fear of their threats, which was not the case at any time, since I wouldn't share anything with them if threatened. I only felt sorry for them when they were obviously struggling, and I liked to help anyone I could. If threats were involved, the usual cajoling would be my first reaction. I also thought that by sharing with the others they would at least be in acceptance of me and my knowledge on subjects.

If either Barney or Louie discovered I was cheating or helping someone cheat, they would immediately rat me out. Barney didn't want people to get good grades without earning them, and no one could do anything to him due to his heart condition without drastic

141

Greenie

consequences. Louie was an acquaintance of mine, who really did nothing to bother anyone, and played some ball with me on occasion, but for a reason I cannot remember, I took his violin when he was walking home one day, and smashed it on the street. I didn't hit or push him; I just snatched the case from him. Cost my parents a thousand dollars to replace. I agreed with them that it wasn't a viable solution to the problem, but I was also sure that Louie would stay out of my business for a while, and he did, pretty much permanently.

Another downfall I brought upon myself was the first and only time I was caught shoplifting. I had stolen so much from the local Quick Chek, usually soda, a lighter or candy, that I decided to brag to other kids about what I can get for nothing. The next time they were ready and waiting for me, on a day I chose to invite some kids to watch my great trick and talent. They snagged me right as I left the place, and arrested me, police car and everything.

The kids watching were impressed, some laughing, some in shock, seeing me get loaded into the cop car, but they didn't really say anything about it after that day. Then I had to go in front of the Town Council to let them decide what to do with me. I just appeared very regretful, mainly because I was dumb enough not to see it coming. I also agreed with them that it was not a good action, since that's what they wanted to hear, and I got probation for three months which meant nothing to me at the time. I was more annoyed with the fact that these adults had enough influence that I had to listen to their righteous rambling. Like getting caught showing off wasn't unpleasant enough.

Punishing me was a difficult task. I didn't really have much I cared about, and the things I did have were alive, and my parents were never cruel to animals. Locking me in my room wouldn't work, because I would just go out the window. Spanking was an option my mother disagreed with, since she was spanked and she thought it was adverse to a productive resolution.

Grounding me to stay home was more like punishment for them, not me, so they rarely did that. Plus, my bedroom door opened in, and there was a wall three feet behind the door equally as wide as the doors opening, so if I slid my dresser into that space, there was no way to get into my room without smashing the door in and climbing over the dresser. My dad was not that type.

His mind was elsewhere, thinking about how to save this planet through waste management, which he had many patents on, worldwide. I always thought he would create an engine designed to run on human waste, since it's the only substance I'm certain we'll have enough of forever. Just break it down to the methane, and utilize it more proficiently. Unfortunately, I don't know what the byproduct of burning Methane would be, but it can't be as bad as some other byproducts. All garbage can be used for something, and I always knew from listening to my dad that our world was in danger from the over abundance of waste.

My dad didn't play or care for baseball or football, but he did play golf, so at twelve years of age I was playing Florham Park country club's course with him. I had only a three wood, five iron, a pitching wedge and a putter, and only added a driver and a one iron later, never needed any more clubs. I'm also a lefty, and own the only left-handed one iron I've ever seen. Tough to hit, but a good club for those line drive shots, and if you happen to hit it right, it seems to go forever.

I have played many courses in my life, Pebble Beach and Lincoln in California, a few in Florida, Fox Hollow in New Jersey along with ten different courses in the state. I snuck onto Baltusrol once, but they caught me after only two holes, just as I was lining up a shot to the green, I saw the little cart coming, so I hit the ball well and started walking with my bag like I belonged there. These two guys came over to me and asked me what I was doing, as I'm walking along there with my hand cart of clubs in tow, walking towards a ball I hit, so I told them, I was fishing.

They were not amused, and brought me and my clubs to the gate, whining about how bad me being there was and trespassing is serious, I had to hold back laughing. Great sport, but I generated no interesting stories from playing it, except regarding the wild life I found in abundance on golf courses, and stories about how annoyed other people I played with would become. At least I can play this game for the rest of my life, for as long as I have my health anyway. I've never gotten a hole in one, and I shoot around the ninety's. And I get to see Geese, turkeys, deer, snakes, frogs, raccoons, fish, dogs, cats, turtles, possums and nearly a species of every animal that inhabits New Jersey.

Chess with my dad was fun, it was hard to cheat since you could see what every piece could do, that was the point, and he usually caught my efforts at repositioning a piece and normally he won. It took a long time to be able to win once in a while, but this was a game he knew, and had played for a long time. I became bored of the game after a while; saw no point in playing except for the deep thought involved to play

Through many years in school, it was like chess games between Barney and I without the board or pieces, a conscious and subconscious battle of who was actually more intelligent or who could be more obnoxious, or cause the most grief, and he had told me once, only once in all the years I knew him: "I hate you, Greenie! I hope your mother dies tomorrow, and you break your fucking neck, you fucking scum bag!" increasing his volume on each word till he was screaming hysterically with tears pouring out his eyes. He also mentioned what he'd "do" if he could, which is when I felt like laughing the most, because he lowered himself to that level, and I knew he could do nothing to me.

This was the only time he became brave enough to get in my face and bump his chest off me in an attempt at intimidation and aggressiveness, which also made me chuckle. Barney didn't say this till we were twelve years of age. He said this because the day before I took the chemistry labs three percent sulfuric acid home to play with, and squirted his white pet rabbit with it along the way, causing it to turn reddish yellow on one side and go blind in one eye.

The blindness part was an accident, the rabbit jumped into the acid stream itself, not part of my plan. I don't recall exactly what he or his sister did to me to make me feel the need for such un-planned drastic retribution, but I knew how to hurt someone in the most effective way, without physically damaging them or coming even close to touching them, and this battle would finally end, on that day, with a whole community watching, no final score.

My original intent was to bring home some of the acid to experiment with, which I did anyway, but the cage was on my way home and I thought of the idea pretty spontaneously, thought it would be funny to have a multi-colored rabbit I guess, plus I knew how mad it would make Barney and his sister. I believe it was just the accumulation of what Barney and his sister did that I couldn't retaliate against that gave me the motive, the final, ultimate, most effective payback.

No one else thought it was too funny, with the possible exception of Peter, who didn't care one way or the other. Barney had even tried to hit me several times the next day, once he was done yelling, which he never did to anyone, so I knew how intensely I had angered him, and I was amazed he didn't have a heart attack and die that day. His little pussy punches had no affect on me other than to make me laugh even more in his face. Even his usually aggressive sister couldn't react at all, I finally left her action less and speechless, which I thought was a moral win as well, but I didn't believe she understood that in any way.

I had at first uncharacteristically denied it, but I never could deny truth for long, and even if it would cause additional recourse, I always spoke the truth. This next day, the day Barney first accused me of the act, the class I was in saw my yellow hands, which is commonplace when using acid, and they were divided nearly evenly over the fact if I had done it or not. I was confused as to why the issue stood so greatly in their minds, this was unexpected. One Spanish class was arguing like a forum as soon as I walked in, "Greenie did it!" one side would say, and the girls who liked me the most for who I was, along with my peers that had no problems with me would shout back "no he didn't!" This went on till I was sent out to guess whose office and a detective met me there and gave me a ride home, where I told him about it.

I explained I meant not to hurt it, although it died about a year later of natural causes, but how it looked is what the problem was. They sometimes used this rabbit for exhibition for small kids, which I was unaware of, and they couldn't anymore since it was disfigured. Officials couldn't charge me with any crime besides removing school property from the premises, since I was only a kid and it was just a rabbit.

It felt as though they were investigating some big international crime or something, I couldn't figure what all the fuss was about, it was just a rabbit after all, no capital offense, it wasn't as if I hurt a person, but you'd think I disfigured the President or stole from Fort Knox, listening to them go on about it. My parents didn't know what to say, wondering what would go through my mind enough to do this, everyone seemed to over react I thought and I didn't know what they could do about it but was about to find out.

One day right after the rabbit incident, I came out of my house, walked to Roy's where I noticed he was playing basketball in his driveway, so I walked right up to him, as though nothing was different or out of place, I could smell the tension as I crossed the lawn and felt the tightening of muscles in preparation for anything, and said: "hey Roy! Wanna lose a game?" He just ignored me as I walked towards him, all the way till I was standing under his hoop.

Then he said: "get out of here, rabbit killer! I don't play with assholes!" And his dad came out of the garage at the same time saying" Yeah Greenie, you're not welcome anymore, get off my property!" I reacted with "yea, bite me, I only turned it yellow, big whoop". "Yea, and blinded it, too!" said Roy, as he just continued to shoot baskets. I said, "That was an accident, ya know". "No, you're an accident you little jerk off, get out of here!" His father said, with threatening motions being made with his fists. "I knew that, already!" I yelled back and gave them the finger as I walked away. This of course sent him running after me, but he could never catch me anyway, and I knew this while running back to my garage. I just had to laugh.

Next stop, Herb's house, because even though he had enormous gay tendencies, he still was a guy who used to like things like baseball, hiking, and things of that nature. He wouldn't even come to his door, and his big brother Gus came and tried to hit me, but missed and hurt his hand instead. "Greenie," he said, "I hope I never see your face outside again!" I just took off, not really afraid of the situation, even though Gus was a big wrestling icon, and was very fast and older, but he never could pin me when we wrestled for fun.

I never held anything against him, plus he was more logical than average, and could be talked out of a situation if need be. There were kids older than I on the block; Gus was one of the nicer ones. I only knew him from hanging around Herb. We did activities together, with both Gus and Herb, even their little sister Dale, before the rabbit event happened. We played Monopoly, chess and checkers, and typical stuff, but I always managed to get others mischievous sides to show up. Torture the cat, make experiments with household products by mixing them, torture the cat again, teach them the squirrel catching trick, and of course, torture the cat some more. I really began to wonder about Herb after watching him jerk off their dog one day, pretty disgusting to see. Thus, no further would these kids follow me down my path, veering off to their own destinies, and more power to 'em, I figured.

Going back to school those few days after the event was interesting, no response from any normal kids, tears from some girls, death threats from the usual bullies, but even they would no longer come near me or think about acting, knowing now how capable I was of ruining their lives if they do, not remembering or knowing I had done so already long ago. They just didn't know it was me then, and now they had fear. Fear of me was something I never thought I'd like or need, but I did for a while, it gave me some power over them, and the endless battle with them was over.

This is around the age things got more interesting socially, twelve or thirteen years of age, when my life certainly changed paths. My friends' parents wouldn't let their kids play with me anymore, not that they wanted to anyway, and normal schooling was out since so many people were angry with me. As punishment they sent me as a day student to Bonnie Bull farm, a reform school and farm directly across the street from the VA hospital in Elmoville, New Jersey.

I was bussed in every day, with Louie Hudnod of Berkeley Heights, and went to school with every incorrigible boy in the state, most of who had to live on campus. That's how I spent the remainder of eighth grade and all of ninth. The attitude I generated because of kids like these, they were now going to subject me to, permanently, to punish or help me? Were they going to test the strength of my attitude? I thought that was pretty stupid, and I refused to allow it to affect my overall attitude and view of how to live my life. Of course, I still refused to do homework usually, which they interpreted as part of my problem instead of part of my personality and normal for me.

This place was like bully heaven, every bully and troublemaker was there from all around the state, and it was a field day for them to have someone to pick on without any known recourse. Couldn't harm their families' possessions, since they all lived there, and I still refused to fight, since it wasn't my nature. Abuse was abundant. From getting smashed in the head with the classrooms globe, to being pushed into the pond by a few inmates, or punched and hit from all angles at different times, but this didn't hurt me, no one hit hard and I was good at blocking.

I would always tell the teachers about these things, but they acted as though they couldn't care less and gave off the attitude that it was probably deserved and too bad for me, and I should have thought about that before I did the action that brought me here. I didn't care much, I could go home and they couldn't, and I still got A's usually in every test. That was justice enough for me. The classes appeared to be all lower level, which insulted my intelligence but made things easy for me, academically.

During my time here, many of these misfits had the habit of breaching all barriers into my personal space, Dave Drough was one of the primary offenders, a big, deep voiced, ugly scumbag with massive acne from who knows where. Very large and doofy, and very unhappy that I broke his record for sit-ups in one minute, which was sixty, and was sixty-one when I left. I'm sure if you search all prisons' inmates' records, you'll find him on one, if he's still alive. I can still remember his voice, deep and unintelligent, sounding like how a Walrus would talk if it could, saying things like; "hey, Green, is your mother as fucking ugly as you are, or did your dad just fuck a pigmy?" and other remarks that I would ignore. Every time a teacher would leave the room, I'd hear some stupidity from him, like I was the only one left in the room.

On the paths to the gym or cafeteria, he'd be right there, trying to get cheap shots in, most of which I was able to dodge, of course. He was pretty slow, in speech and physically, and dumber than dirt. My last name appeared to be his favorite word to speak usually, and I understood why he was here, normal society could have no reason to tolerate such a moronic waste of life. I guess calling him "Davey dead dick Droughnut" once in a while didn't help, but it was fun.

The school had an interesting property. Mostly cornfields with a large pond in the back where I caught my first giant snapper turtle, about two feet long. I accidentally caught and killed by hand a ground hog one day. I caught him in the cornfield from behind the neck, and as I looked at the two-inch teeth sticking out of his mouth, I became too afraid to let go or loosen my grip. I hoped he would just wake up, as some creatures do when they appear dead, like a moth. I wanted to show a teacher what I caught, but never got the chance, since hours later the groundhog was still where I left it, obviously dead now. As the bus left, I could see the crows and even a vulture in a cluster around the spot I left the thing, having their dinner no doubt.

The gym teacher here was an ex baseball player, and for some reason he picked me to go out in the field occasionally, where he'd hit a hard ball to the clouds, and I'd run around and catch every hit every time. He told me I should go into little league, but in my town that was impossible. I excelled in all their sports, which I always did, but these kids were less than impressed by that kind of achievement.

Why we were put here was the main topic of interest, and my story appeared miniscule compared to other's reasons for being here, like statutory rape, assault, arson, burglary or grand theft. Blinding some rabbit was a laughable reason to this group of deviates, all they'd say is that I was a pussy for doing it and I should have beaten the kid to death instead, or at least killed the rabbit, which is what they would have done supposedly, or so said Louie on one of our bus rides. My ventures in destruction proved more valuable here, they were somewhat impressed.

Here, I met another kid named Gary Trent. He was a nice guy who would stop the idiots from picking on me when he thought it was enough, including Dave, who he was not intimidated by, even though I didn't care or need help. I went with him early that summer to his boathouse along the bay at Long Beach Island. I had never driven a boat before, and it was a rear engine boat, which works in reverse of steering wheels.

Gary let me take the boat out myself, and I was going about thirty miles an hour, I tried to turn away from the bridge pylon, but I pulled instead of pushed the steering handle, and hit the pylon head on. I sailed across all three seats in the boat, stopping myself from hitting the pylon with my body by aiming my foot at the last seat, stopping on it and spraining my foot.

That kept me on the couch for the rest of the weekend, writhing in pain all night, and just sitting all day while Gary went out fishing, girl chasing, crabbing, or whatever without me. I didn't break anything, but that hurt for weeks. Once I left Bonnie Bull, I never saw Gary again, and I didn't have to pay for the damage to his boat since it was his own fault for letting me drive. He was a very busy guy, and lost touch easily. He had to live there, along with seventy or so other kids, but was allowed to go home in the summer. The one's who weren't would do farm work all summer. They all did farm work on weekends, since it was a farm. Like the little house on the prairie turning criminal, or green acres gone immoral.

I was a target for one other kid in particular as well, besides Dave, a small, very insecure kid whose name I don't remember because he was that insignificant to the end result, only some of his actions were memorable. He liked to hit others at any opportunity he could, but since he hit like a little girl, it didn't bother me. He was the one who smashed the classroom's globe over my head, which didn't hurt and made me laugh, but it made the teacher mad about the destruction of school property. Of course I told the teacher who did it, which the kid vowed revenge for of course. He also hated the fact that I was usually laughing or smiling, for some reason, probably because nothing he or anyone else could do would wipe the grin off my face, including dropping a globe on me.

This guy had an insult for all mothers and he always began with a curse of some kind, like: "Your fuckin' mother is a great big lesbian crotch eater", or any answer to any question was: "your mother!" "So, how was your day?" was answered by: "any fuckin' day your mother dies is a good one" or something like that, were standard replies from him. He was a real treasure trove of polite conversation. So I created a song for him, to the tune of "The Nobel Duke of York", and it went like this: "Your momma is a slut, she fucked ten thousand men, and I don't really give two shits, unless I was one of them, cause then I'd get some disease, which makes you itch and pee, so I hope I never get to fuck her, that would fill me full of glee". No one thought that wasn't funny, except him. Same old adage, the person who dishes crap out usually can't take it themselves, and he was no exception.

Since targeting their homes at this place was impossible, and mocking them academically was not effective, I decided that hitting them where they live would be just as good, and nothing would work better than that hornet's nest Roy and I ran into some years back. I caught some residence' of the nest with a large butterfly net, managed to get twenty or so into a jar with holes, without getting stung, and then I rode my bike in the middle of the night to the school. There, I knew which cottage the real assholes were in, and I tossed the jar through the open window after unscrewing the top enough so it would open upon impact, and bolted down the street as fast as I could back home. It was the weekend so I had no worries of the next day, or that they would catch me at all.

Many of the kids got stung, including Dave and the other instigator, and they just blamed the other residences, that started an intra cottage war as I recall. After all, it was a reform school full of troublemakers. No one thought a day student would bother coming here when he didn't have to. Laughing at them the whole next week was quite satisfying, asking if their mothers butt was as sharp as a hornet, never cluing them in on who may have done it.

Laughing at them was great fun, mostly due to the lack of knowledge they had about things, like the handicapped class and the drug addicted class mixed. True scum of the earth, most of these kids, I thought. Probably their parents fault, in some way. I enjoyed watching the accusations fly, and I let them with nothing but my usual large smile to give any indication that I knew what happened, but I did that all the time anyway. I never told them the truth, since they never asked.

I never told them who managed to give all the cottages where they live fleas, either, or bother explaining how the school building was immune for a while. I recall where I got them from, one neighbors' dog I remembered had fleas, and catching those was no easy feat, I figured I'd need at least twenty or so a jar, with one jar for each cottage, and I believe there were three dorm type cottages.

Every time I'd open a jar to put one in, three would try escaping, and usually did, so it took a while to get all I needed, and I decided to just use one small jar, they would spread fast enough. Then, during one of my invisible detour tricks on our regular walk to lunch, I'd walk by the closest cottage and toss the jar, with the top still sealed, against a rock under the stairs of the front porch, this would break the glass, but fleas are quite tough, they'd all survive, and I knew it wouldn't be long before they would be everywhere.

I also didn't tell them where the tools were from the shop class that I tossed into the pond. I found my own file in the office, while it was unoccupied and unlocked for some reason, and all it talked about was how unpredictable I was along with how I refused to fight back other students, and they made that sound like an issue. But then I realized they were testing my attitude, to see how they could get around it and mess with me or change my attitude, which apparently needed an "adjustment", but that wasn't going to happen, I left the file exactly as I found it, took the cool letter opener off some secretaries desk, and went to lunch as normal. I didn't mention loosening every screw in the boys' bathroom one day, that was fun since the little asshole was the one who discovered it first, and didn't have fun doing so. Wish I could have seen that, but I didn't. I only lit two or three garbage can fires here, nothing too radical.

My day's highpoint was to point and laugh at them from the bus window, while my bus was leaving, indicating how pleased I was that I could leave and they couldn't. This was the new escape route, getting into my bus before any of them could get near me, like the race I ran so often in regular school, just to get home. Louie would only say: "You've' got some balls, man. Don't you know we'll be back tomorrow?" I would just say while laughing: "who gives a shit?" because I really didn't care what these idiots thought or felt

I thought about who would save them if I ever did discover where they lived, when not living here. Lou and I were very cool, both from the same type of town and family, neither of us were very bad, I can't remember what he did and doubt he'd remember me. We talked about everything, and since we shared consequences of our social failure we really had nothing to hide. He and Gary were good people, I often wonder what became of them, as we went through the path of our lives separately, branded incorrigible, trouble or dangerous. We all spent our time wondering how we became so outcast in this phase of life, where the path had turned for the worst, yet we believed our fate to be unjust.

That summer, when I was done boating with Gary, and after my foot healed, my parents sent me for two weeks to camp Greylock, again in the Pocono Mountains. Things were pretty normal here, it was a very nice camp set on a lake, which on the other side of this lake was the girls camp, about a mile away. The story I heard the first day here was no one ever swam across to the girls' camp, being supposedly too far and dangerous. That was all I needed to hear. An hour later, my counselor discovered I was missing, and the lifeguard grabbed a boat and found me half way to the girls' camp already. They weren't happy I went out with no help or warning, but they stayed right beside me as I refused to get in the boat, and I swam on to the girls' camp. I only did it because I knew I could, and it took two hours to do it using the breaststroke. The adults weren't pleased, but they had to acknowledge the fact that I was the first to accomplish this feat.

The rest of the camp weeks went well. No incidents, just soccer, horseback riding, hiking, some streaking, knock-hockey, archery, capture the flag, rifle range and such. The other campers were sufficiently impressed with my swimming and athletic ability to not become annoying or annoyed by my obnoxious "do what I want" attitude.

For the first time I didn't even want to go home, and no one appeared to dislike me here, they would ignore me at times which seemed normal, everyone does that on occasion. My parents were shocked, when I told them I actually was having fun. This was also a camp where I first remember hearing scary stories around the campfire, and the Green hand story was likely to add another character to my visions of a tickle monster.

All my camps had stories around the fire, but this story I remember most vividly. The Green hand was severed, but lived by crawling up to sleeping people and removing various body parts, eyes, and ears, whatever. And it always cut the throat of its victims with its long nails. The Scratching by the bed three times and tugging on the covers were sure signs of impending doom. Strangely enough, it never became a nightmare of mine, as I thought it would.

I collected many snakes there, as usual, along with other creatures, which was still my favorite activity. Here, we also walked the Appalachian Trail for about fifty miles or so, spending a few nights there on the trail. I found it awesome, the fact that this trail wouldn't end till you reach Georgia, or back the other direction to Maine, and I would love to hike the whole thing one time, just so I can say I did.

That camping venture went so well that I had nothing else occur the whole time I was there, and I went home literally a "happy camper" for a change. Interestingly enough, I don't recall a single person from there, camper or councilor, not one friend that would keep in touch with me, and I never gave that a second thought. I remember this camp trying to teach us how to use a compass, which I understood completely, and was able to do, but I had to explain to them that there was really no need for it, I could tell directions with such ease that I would never get lost, with a compass or without.

This attitude was not too appreciated, but they had to accept it when I proved it. I did this by letting them blind-fold me, take me into the woods, and letting me find my way back myself, which I did.

Another favorite activity of mine at camp or home was dead tree smashing. Anywhere there were woods, I found great exercise and stress relief by knocking down dead trees that hadn't fallen on their own yet. I would climb one and use my body weight to bend and break the tree, sometimes pausing for the little orgasm while hanging there, at least before that became a messy thing to do. This was a little dangerous too, like if the tree broke too high, I could impale myself on its sharp stump. I felt that this was reasonably safe and normal, just speeding up progress of the inevitable, dead trees fall, sooner or later, and it was fun.

I guess I could tell of some interesting dreams, for a change of pace, but getting those in age order is difficult, yet there are probably five or ten distinguished ones, so I shall now recall a few choice ones. I'll begin where I left off. I was a faller, when I dreamed. I fell everywhere and anywhere I could, and for the most part, intentionally. I had this reoccurring one every so often, where great cavernous mountains are the landscape. It roughly resembled Yellowstone National Park.

I always find it through woods that resemble the Grand Canyon's woods, thin and spaced freely. I'd be walking the rim of this great space, and then I would notice that there's water at the bottom and I began to believe that falling couldn't hurt, but was still nervous about falling. There were times I realized that I was dreaming, which made this one especially fun. But mostly, I got a deep odd feeling, the sort of, "how could this strange place be real" feeling, with its scarily over emphasized proportions, but no one I saw in my dream usually answered questions rationally, or at all sometimes, if I was able to speak to them.

I do, of course, end up too close to the edge to come back, and fall, which is said to be a sexual sensation according to doctors in the field. I can understand that, it's just as intense as sex, and you have to be conscious of the dream to realize you can't get hurt, or you simply wake up. Having consciousness can take some of the chill right out of the experience. Plus, I actually did reach the water at times, and swim under it, breathing fine, like a fish.

That brings me to recall this dream of an actual tangible place, where I was riding my bike, a five-speed banana seat Huffy incidentally, and I was riding over the Verrazano Bridge, on the outer edge of the walkway, and there was no fence to keep someone from falling into the Hudson River however many feet below. The odd thing was how the bridge turned left going west, which is what it does in the other direction in reality when heading from Brooklyn to Staten Island.

I was coming up on the turn, I slipped and hurled immediately off the bridge, and while falling I kicked my bike from under me, hit the water and went under, came to the surface while still dreaming, and looked up at the bridge, closed my eyes, then found myself back on the same approach to the curve again on my bike. I began to realize I was in charge of this episode.

So this time I turned with the traffic, and went to the tollbooth, and as I entered the lanes concrete beginning and closed my eyes again, where those yellow cones or posts are, I wound up at the beginning again, still on my bike,. The third time around, I would jump. I did the fall roughly three times, going for the safe route the same amount of times. I actually enjoyed that dream; I can remember the New York skyline quite vividly. It was a bit overemphasized, like in an animated movie. I must have seen this movie before the dream some time in my past, but don't recall. The skyline I had seen many times throughout my life, very clearly, so memory of the view was planted permanently in my head.

It was around the time of this dream's occurrences when I discovered how to run full speed in my dream. It's like a prelude to flight. Once you're conscious is aware of this, there is no end to the possibilities. You can't help but believe these subconscious worlds play a part in the path, direction and finality of life, since we spend a third of our lives in that state for no reason we can comprehend. When I was able to run full speed and beyond, I was ecstatic, as though released from any detrimental boundaries. Fear was no longer a part of the dream experience usually, except for the usual tickle sensation. I could outrun most imagined entities. So then I began altering repetitive dreams, to eliminate them.

A good dream I had sometimes was similar to the Mr. Limpet story, but I wasn't a fish. I just knew I could breathe in the pool under water, and everyone was in the pool, like any normal pool day. The female lifeguards were naked, of course. But this wasn't a sexual dream, though the lifeguards had perfect bodies, I just enjoyed swimming through everyone's legs, and since I knew I was dreaming, I just had fun.

I would dive off the high dive, which naturally appeared hundreds of feet high, going under water and hanging out sitting Indian style at the bottom of the deep end, watching everyone dive in, while I sit there breathing normally. That was pretty entertaining, for the few real time minutes the dream occupied. I remember thinking how strange time works in dreams, some dreams seem very long and you've only slept a few minutes, others seem very short and the whole night had passed. Dreams must have very little to do with the actual passing of conscious time.

Once, I dreamed of going to bed. I was so tired; I could just feel the bed under me, like on my side, as I walk up the hills to my house. Every detail was perfectly accurate. It was just getting light, and I was at the door, silently getting to my room, yawning the whole time just dying for some sleep, climbing into my bed after throwing my clothes on the chair.

As I get the blanket just right, and the pillow in perfect position to stop the tickle, I turn to set the alarm irritated that I forgot to do it, and then turn over to sleep. As I think of how to stop thinking, the second I think it feels so good to be in bed and cozy, and I felt like I'm just about to fall asleep, the alarm rings, and I wake up. I was in my bed the whole time. Went to bed around twelve and felt like I didn't sleep at all. This would fit my description of a real nightmare.

That reminded me of another dream, where I was talking on the phone, and my mother was trying to wake me, and I told my mother to stop talking to me because I was on the phone, and then the phone would disappear from my hand, and the reality of a new day would stare me in the face and my mother would say: "What are you talking about, being on the phone?" This caused much laughter between both of us for a while.

I would dream of being in the playground, and I was in the schoolyard. It appeared as my playground did exactly, yet everyone was moving very slowly and looking very confused. It was my turn to kick the sphere, which I did with such confidence and power that all my covers must have flown off the bed. As the ball left sight towards the clouds, I became fully aware that I was dreaming.

I ran by third base and noticed that home wasn't there and I was really running away from all my classmates, who had all changed into grayish green creatures with large yellow stripes running circularly around their bodies like barber poles. So in slow motion, I began to run and confront these creatures, and realized I could fly if I wanted to, since I was dreaming. Now I was in control and I began to rise up from the ground and into the sky, like a pelican taking off from the water, and I watched the playground figures look up at me in amazement as I disappeared from sight.

Then an uneasy feeling came over me, like when you forget a friend's birthday, and I went back and landed in the cafeteria, because the windows were gone for some reason. There were all my deformed peers, all looking up at me in shock, like some poorly drawn cartoon characters. I said: "Here I am, what is it you pigments of my figmentation want with me?" of course I meant to say figments of my imagination, but that's how it came out, and the meaning was still understood, since these characters were created from my own imagination.

I figured they could read my mind to some degree, since my mind was their home. But all that happened is what I expected; I woke to the sound of my mother's voice asking me what I was talking about. The dream figures never gave me an answer in time for me to hear it, no matter how hard I tried to imagine them giving me one. My mother asked me what a figvacation was, and why I wanted thin mints. All my covers were on the other side of the room, of course.

One type of dream I disliked was when my parents were involved, because I knew they weren't really my parents. They always had this really scary grin on their face, and didn't answer questions in any normal fashion. I would be lying in bed, thinking I'm awake, then I would go down stairs to the den, where both my parents would be sitting, they would look up at me, get up and start walking towards me just like the kids in the playground.

I would go running out the front door, just as they reach the bottom of the staircase, fearing the literally ticklish consequences of getting too close to them. Before I run, just before they take one step up the first step, I would ask them: "why are you chasing me?" They would stop momentarily and say odd things like the moon is in the garage, hamburgers make great sleds without pickles, or rocks and toenails are good for digestion. They would also say once, as I recall vividly, that they're not chasing me, just trying to help me, and come here.

That's how I knew I was dreaming, and the next time I was aware of that fact, I would go past them to the garage without even glancing at them and bolt down the street. Never had that particular dream again after the alteration I made. I believe that consciously altering any repetitive dream will end them. I have seen no exception to this rule yet, besides the next one which is really just different aspects of the same subject, water.

A more obscure dream involved multiple swimming pools, sometimes set on the scenery of a park, others around a big mansion that resembled one my uncle had. The one with the mansion was strange, it had three pools, one wading type about four feet deep and huge, another very deep long one with an unusual diving board around the base, like a bugs bunny cartoon, the endless ladder that had perches every so often but no top in site, and one narrow, deep black pool, about the size of an average bathtub but so deep I never have reached the bottom.

This pool even has the feel of walls closing in or being deep enough to have the walls collapse if one stays too deep for too long, and oddly, I never realize I'm dreaming as this dream happens. There is no apparent point or meaning to this one, just random choices as

159

to which pool I feel like swimming in, and I chose differently each time, different order, different depth, and it comes back still, like a subconscious amusement park.

In the pools that have the park for a background, I always seem to be saving others who have fell in and cannot swim, and these pools have walls between them, which move, along with waves that appear to be ocean born, but there is no ocean. I manage to move people out of the path of large waves, and I play in them as I would at the beach, and I wonder how such great waves could be indoors. That's a strange one, but fun so I found no reason to change it, since it was enjoyable, so I never tried. Some dreams I changed that I meant not to, but just altering them slightly, like asking a question when I hadn't before, was enough to lose some dreams forever.

The most interesting part of some running dreams I had after discovering how to run full speed were ones with no particular plot. Just running was the basic point, and I learned that if you use the same concentration on running while running, that you would begin to become airborne, like a glider on wheels. At first, just lifting off the ground feels as if you are walking on the moon, with over exaggerated steps as if gravity had failed.

Then, after a few experiences I would be able to lift myself higher and higher, to the point where coming back down became the "falling" feeling. After a few of those superman leaps, I noticed I could suspend myself in the air and actually fly like a bird or helicopter, till something distracted me enough to break my concentration and cause me to plummet back down and wake me up. Even landing became more smooth and glider like after some time. I guess some would call that an "out of body" experience. As I got older I noticed that this talent grew dormant from lack of use, and achieving the consciousness of realizing that I'm dreaming while dreaming was more difficult and much rarer.

EXIT NINE

━ ━ ━ ━ ━ ━ ━ ━ ━ ━ ━ ━ ━

The Wicked Fork Through Derf Land

Back in the world of reality, my parents decided some more summer camp would be good, since the last time went so well, and to get me out of the still hostile environment, into one where no one knew anything about me. So just before my fourteenth birthday, in nineteen seventy-five, I would go to camp Wawayanda somewhere in New York State, better known as Frost Valley, which was a YMCA camp. I would leave for two weeks, to where my life path would forever change, as would some other peoples.

By now, I was an experienced camper, who knew most of what was expected from me, whether or not I complied was a different story. So Frost valley became my sixth camp, Riverbend, Dolphin, Greylock, Tahone, and Spears were the other five. Camp Spears I hardly remember except that I only stayed there a few days. I wound up making my parents come get me because it was so boring. I refused to participate in any activities they had, and all I did was drive everyone crazy by disappearing constantly, going into the woods for some animal hunting and streaking, which was the only fun I had there.

They wanted me to do things like egg tosses and coloring, crochet, basket weaving and finger painting, make birdhouses and things that were extremely lame in my mind. They were as anxious to get rid of me as I was anxious to leave. I did find the most beautiful natural fresh water stream there, and drank a lot of water from it, thinking this is where bottled water must come from. The taste of that water I may never forget, unlike the camp itself.

Frost Valley would be where I meet someone who altered our lives paths permanently, Fred Feldstein. He appeared to be around thirty years old, thick beard, big head with a receding hair line already, thirteen years old, and the closest personality matching mine that I knew of to that date. Upon arriving and being gathered in the mess hall, some kid decided to sneak up behind me and hit me in the back of the head.

This was the first time I ever saw things go black for a split second in my life, but I did not lose my balance, or fall. So I turn around, holding the back of my head, waited the second it took for the lights to return, and said, "why did you do that?" very slowly and precisely, and the answer was how ugly my head looked, and someone had to hit it. I said, with serious inflection, "I would never try doing that again, if I were you". Go fuck yourself was all this brainiac could muster as a reply as he turned and left, leaving through a door right where Fred was standing and watching for a few minutes.

I wasn't embarrassed all that much, more annoyed about how camp started that day, and that now I had to destroy this kid's idea of fun at camp somehow. I just avoid most of whom I consider an idiot, but there are a lot of exceptions making it hard to do sometimes. I did notice that Fred witnessed the event, so I figured he would be an issue at some point, or just a friend of the kid who I haven't met yet.

As the guy passed Fred on his way out, he whacked the kid right in the head, I think in the same place where I got hit, and thus, the path changed. The kid knew Fred, and had no reaction except for crying as he got up to run away. Fred and I immediately became a pair, the kind to avoid at all costs. He called me Greenie, since that's what I told him I was called. I had asked him why he did that to the kid, he told me the kid was an asshole that always came here, this was his second year with him, and his head needed to be hit, as it usually did. I said thanks; I always enjoyed indirect revenge or justice. A topic we understood, as I found out.

We were immediately assigned the same cabin by complete chance, and knew we'd be hanging around together for the duration of our stay at least. We always teamed up for capture the flag, and Fred was the only person I met who could come close to my pace for running through woods, or bothered trying to. We would usually win, if a girl or an animal collecting or mischief opportunity on the way to the opponents' flag didn't distract us. We would use each other as a distraction to the defender and whoever they went after left one of us free to win the game. Girls seemed to flock to him, probably because he looked so mature.

I loved looking at women too, of course, though I wasn't looking to just get laid really, but he was. I was saving that moment for the right conditions and if I met those conditions with a girl at that camp, I would have pursued her. It just wasn't a priority of mine at the time, and it's all Fred thought about beyond our activities and the pandemonium we caused together.

I would be in the same room while he would start indulging with his latest girl friend and just watch till he'd say: "Greenie, go somewhere." I'd say: "yea, later fem bot!", and I'd go somewhere. He wouldn't wait till I was gone of course; he'd be on second base before I would be out of sight. I found many things to do without anyone anytime, anywhere, especially at camp, and live porno of people I knew personally wasn't an interest of mine, though a glimpse of the girl's naked body would be nice.

While at camp we became very close, Fred thinking my nose too unique to be ignored, and he liked commenting about it frequently, and he had the ability to actually understand some of my rambling philosophies. We would sit up at night and discuss the camp and all things possible, and we'd leave the cabin after everyone else was sleeping. We'd walk around the camp, and one night we decided to go to the rifle range. Here, we would shoot near misses at each other, at night, after breaking into the storage room to get whatever we needed.

We would go to opposite ends of the range and just aim at near misses around each other's position. I was an expert marksman, and when we did rifle range during the normal day's activity, I was the one always knocking down all the other targets by shooting the clothespin holding the targets up and the wire that held them all, making the counselor yell at me. Fred thought this was pretty funny, as did I. Our conversations were deeply philosophical, based on what we seemed to agree on, which was much. Yet other times conversation was mere nonsense, with no points or insight, similar to any kids our age.

Fred thought, until he met me, that besides getting laid, camp was corny and useless, and his parents only sent him here to get away from him, which is what I thought motivated my parents as well. I would usually call him Derf, his name backwards, which I found endlessly amusing even if he didn't. He was adopted too, born five months after me, and his sister was of an age difference similar to Helen and me.

Our Japanese counselor Yoshi had no idea what to do with us, and referred to us as the crazy shit pair. He would always curse at us in Japanese, asking us why we did "crazy as shit" things, and he was only eighteen or nineteen himself. Bakaboota cheekso was something he would say, I forget what it meant, or how to spell it, but I spelled it the way it sounded for this example. Our only answer for him was that we were having fun and had nothing else to do at the time.

We also knew a kid there named Lefline, which entertained us endlessly, simply due to the oddness of the name, much to the poor kids' dismay. But we mostly used the name when something clumsy or odd occurred, like a squirrel falling out of a tree, we'd both look at it, break out in hysterical laughter and proclaim simultaneously: "What a Lefline!" In reference to the squirrel being Lefline-ish, of course. We turned his name into a verb or adjective for our own amusement.

While here we had fun making skunk and raccoon traps, and we had all night hikes nowhere or around the girls' cabins, and took canoes out for midnight cruises by breaking into the supply shack. These things Yoshi found odd, if he was lucky enough to catch us in the act, which he rarely did. We would just tell him we had done these things anyway, if they didn't involve destruction of camp property.

He didn't like us roaming about at night, claiming it to be dangerous with bears and skunks and things, along with jeopardizing his job security, but we would laugh about that while trying to seem concerned at the same time. Since we were the only one's wandering around at night besides counselors, he likely knew who broke into the mess hall, rifle range, office, mess hall and canoe building, though he never asked us.

We did the normal types of summer camp mischief, like covering someone's things or bodies while their sleeping with sugar or honey to attract every ant or fly in the woods, putting a bucket full of bug juice or water above a slightly opened door, so whoever opened it would get soaked. We used shaving cream cans, which only Fred and counselors used, to spray onto sleeping campers' hands and then tickling their nose until they wipe the cream on their face, spreading it all over their pillows, which they enjoyed so little.

We also built a huge arsenal of water balloons and eggs, for any occasion we may need them for. The water balloons, for some reason, never were used, except on each other. Neither of us cared how wet we got. The eggs we would launch from the cafeteria's roof top onto a sidewalk or path where people were walking, and though we never hit anyone we did make a mess of the area.

Fred was the type of kid who just liked to hit someone as a bonding method, and in me he saw someone who could take abuse at high levels. He was like a bully in many ways, but he claimed that he never hit me as hard as he could, and he apparently enjoyed my company, laughing at much of the same things I did. He didn't complain when I hit him back or got the better of him either, and apparently, I was the only one able to better him at that camp, in things like chess, pool, swimming, and rifle range.

I was not the only person he would hit either, like the looser kid on that first day, who he would hit whenever possible, and much harder than he would hit me. He would tolerate and participate with most of my ideas for fun, like tree smashing, bow practice around two a.m. and he was as creative at causing destruction as I, and I guess that was what kept us friends for so long. He also was one of the very few who could relate to me; we were always on the same wavelength and would finish sentences for each other. Like we always knew what the other was thinking, and we'd react the same way we expected to react in most situations individually.

I told him that in ten years he and I would probably be walking through prison together. He didn't believe me at that point, and neither did I really, though I had dreamed about it before. It wasn't a clear dream, only the point I told him about stood solidly clear out of the fogginess of that dream, knowing that we were both incarcerated. That dream was weird and too specific for me, almost eerie, and it occurred only days after meeting him.

He had already been at the camp for a week when I got there, he was leaving the next week, and I was staying, with the original asshole I met the day I got there, for another week. Thus, we decided that the kids' demise was apparently needed. We lured a skunk into the middle of the tent of the kid around three A.M. by throwing food into the tent, and then we'd toss in firecrackers once the animal was well near the middle of the tent. Very effective, never got caught, caused a very smelly situation for a few innocent bystanders. Another fun activity was tossing in powdered sugar to attract bugs, which was really messy. No one was injured or hurt by anything done, but no fun was had by them either.

I discovered Fred also liked Snakes, Butterflies, and despised and enjoyed torturing cats, just like me. I only started really disliking cats when I became so violently allergic to them that I thought I would die. Just suddenly, without any warning at all, one day not allergic, the next, highly allergic, what a strange thing to happen, I thought. It was at Betty Walter's house, a few years after I broke her shin, and I think I was around nine or ten years old. I used to feed them for her she actually gave me the key. I was surrounded by about five of them one day, which was not unusual, and I suddenly couldn't breathe too well, I could not stop sneezing and coughing, my eyes and ears itched so intensely, that no amount of scratching could stop it.

This happened very suddenly and thus, I never played with or was nice to cats again. Before I was born my sister was resting her head on a chair, on the arm, and her cat jumped on the arm and almost blinded her, we never again had a pet cat. We never had a pet dog either, because my parents were older and didn't want to have to take care of it, and didn't believe I would.

They were right about that. I liked taking care of cage-able animals, where the environment was controlled by me. Still don't care if I ever have a dog, or a cat, and in my opinion a cat is just a large smelly pillow you have to feed and clean up after. This story caused Fred to crack up hysterically, jump on my back and yell: "hoy, vey, you're SUCH a Greenie!" Fred agreed with that description of cats, but dogs he thought were OK and I agreed.

Fred introduced me to Pink Floyd dark side of the moon, the bestselling album in the history of music I believe, and a favorite of mine to date, along with all other Floyd albums. It was the only music that really made sense to me, sounded right, inspired and entertained many thoughts, and was the only musical influence in my life really, just a perfectly engineered use of sound.

I couldn't understand why Fred seemed to think Pink Floyd had something to do with drugs but he said it did, called it burnout music. I didn't think much of it at that time though, wasn't impressed yet. Fred also liked drugs, I didn't and at this point I believed I never would, probably due to my experience with Ritalin. Didn't care if he did them, and even though he could lift one hundred fifty pounds over his head with one hand like it was nothing, he couldn't get me to try many things drug related, no matter what he did. He also smoked cigarettes, which I thought was useless.

Fred was an intelligent guy, and usually he liked to show this by always trying to outdo everyone or know more, and he usually did. He was able, like me, to see multiple sides of any situation, and logically deduce solutions and answers for both directions of conflict, see various outcomes to present situations, or create conflict for entertainment, like between his girl friends or other campers.

I discovered, eventually, how much he liked electronics, music, and mechanics. Even though we were both somewhat intelligent, we referred to each other as left nostril hair, Lefline, right twat lip, divided anal plate and just anal plate, and many hundreds of more variations of anatomy along with random names like Styme-Bob or fembot, as taken from one of our favorite seventies shows, the six million dollar man.

Fag was another favorite of many names we used often to refer to each other, not certain why it was funny unless just the knowledge of our own heterosexuality made this statement such a falsehood that it was funny, like when I called him a one legged Lepidoptera.

I spent some time being his lookout over at sequoia, the oldest girls' dorm, and Molly Songi was one of Fred's main girlfriends it appeared. I would hang out with the other girls there, and just attempt some intellectual connection. Philosophy is what I called it, and my main concern was watching for the counselors coming who wouldn't approve of where Fred and I were.

Fred found my nativity when it came to women a great point of humor and amusement, but he was not like most thirteen year olds, and I was not as naive as he thought I was. Nice girls, in that camp, it was interesting too, not knowing any of them and being able to talk with and establish communication with them without the air of uncomfortable insecurity. I never had any conversations with girls in camp, and was surprised that they showed enough interest or boredom to talk to me.

Fred was the catalyst for this discovery, since I'd never approach girls on my own, but the circumstance he created put me right in their faces, and that was good I thought. I would discuss anything with them, such as why girls found it gross to rip legs off bugs and why guys didn't, the usual 'boys have no heart' type responses were expected, but I always brought things to another level, finding the path to what possibly could be another answer, like finding girls who thought it was funny too, or just not gross, perhaps cruel, which I could understand.

What makes kids interested or not in what happens to bugs once we hurt them? Perhaps to find similar responses if we ourselves suffer from pain at some time, knowing we can cause pain as well as receive it, usually with unequal measures. Most of them got lost once I began being philosophical, so I tried keeping subjects simple, like mostly camp related or girl and boyfriend discussions, what boys think, or what we think girls think, how bad the food was here sometimes, what counselors sucked or were cool, typical stuff.

Sneaking was already my specialty for years, and I discovered it was also Fred's, and we would get into the kitchen late at night and cook some real food for us and some of the girls brave enough to join us. I met Madeline Hall here at this camp, she and I discussed many things about life in general, and she was good looking and very open to conversation. She could comprehend my discussions better than most, which was fun.

I remember hoping one day she'd be mine, feeling as though our lives were beginning to merge through conversation, I was even able to envision what that would be like, and she gave me her phone number, but sadly, that would not be the case. She would eventually leave my years of some minor false hope lying dead in the dust like so many insect carcasses in a ceiling light fixture. I always figured on many broken hearts and hopes throughout my life, so I didn't expect too much usually, knowing reality can be disappointing at times, she was simply another pretty face to remember. Possibly I could re-establish our rapport at some point in time down the road, but I wasn't going to hold my breath waiting.

The piano in the mess hall was where Fred and I learned by ear the Pink Panther theme, and it's still one of the only songs I know, along with Green sleeves. He also sang songs like: itenditenlittleditenotendotenlittledotenitspitlyotendotenbo boskedeetendatenwadatnchw. If that was a long rock music line I never knew it. Fred never said, either, and wouldn't teach me that one, claiming it would take too long. We spent many hours at the piano in the mess hall, ignoring all other activities taking place and entertaining a few girls who would come and listen to us play on occasion. We almost never participated in the camp's planned activities, always opting for doing things we wanted to, and that's what we did, much to Yoshi's dismay.

One night on our way to dinner, I took out a bullet I got from the range that I had in my pocket, and I put it on a rock as we walked, casually as though I was just bending over to tie a shoe or something, then smashed it with another rock making a loud noise that caused everyone to jump. I wound up getting a piece of it stuck in my hand forever. Fred thought that was pretty stupid and funny of me to do, as he watched and laughed hysterically, saying "You're such a Greenie!" He appeared pretty pissed too, since he was standing not so far from the point of impact and could have been killed, even while laughing he could seem mad, giving me a look of disapproval as we continued our walk, just shaking his head in disbelief. He did jump when the bullet went off like everyone else who was nearby, which is why I think he wasn't overly entertained by this, possibly wondering why he hung out with me for those few moments. He called me a Lefline.

We had many key words that meant things only we knew, we referred to females as femmels, and if Fred thought he had the opportunity to get laid he'd sing the song or state: "needle fem", which simply meant he needed a female to screw. Needle fem, needle fem, needle needle needle fem, was sort of how that went, accompanying whatever tune fit the words, in this case, that lollypop song was the tune. We changed tunes all the time to fit our version.

We also liked to sing the tune "Candy man", but with our unique twist, using elbow macaroni, which we thought of as a another part of female anatomy, and as the main word for the song, making the tune go; "elbow macaroni, dip it in some dew, cover it with semen and a miracle or three, the elbow man, the elbow man can, the elbow man can cause he mixes it with scum and makes the world taste shitty, the elbow man makes, everything he makes, start to taste like diarrhea, go to your local pizzeria, they will give you gonorrhea". Of course, order of words and context were not usually the same twice, but it was always quite silly and amusing, very immature.

Bunseedsesameaononionspicklescheeselettucesauce specialpattiesbeefalltwo was another favorite song of ours, with daanaanaanaanaa in between each verse. Fred would hit my shoulder between each verse, till I started dodging him, he seemed to think I made a good drum, but I was good at dodging as he discovered. His other favorite song to sing was a verse from a song called "Hocus Pocus" from the band Focus, which has no words; it sounds like someone yodeling for the chorus and has a silly sounding babble in one part, which he used continuously. I never realized, till I heard the song myself, how accurately he mimicked the song for his use. I just thought he was creating some more nonsense language, I never imagined he got this babbling from a real song.

Fred was my partner in analysis of the people and things in this world, their causes, reactions, consequences, to the point where we discovered rationalization for all the things we did, justifying our acts no matter how negative or positive they were. We knew there was a greater or larger reason for things, beyond what the obvious factors were, and we spent many years philosophizing and experimenting with things, usually for no greater reason than the fact that we had nothing else to do.

I remember thinking, with Fred concurring with me on most possible theories including this one, which we were just part of some great omnipotent beings dream and didn't really exist at all. It was a theory that seemed reasonable, yet too simple. Too bad that the fact of our senses existence makes that conclusion improbable, at least to the conscious naked eye.

One day Fred and I were out looking for animals as usual, I caught a Garter snake, and when it bit me as expected, it hurt to the point where I actually said "ouch", which was very strange. A little two foot thing, and I've caught and been bitten by six foot common water snakes, and they didn't hurt as much. We kept pondering the story we heard of Garters and Rattlers cross breeding, but we couldn't recall where this was heard, and I didn't get sick. Fred thought it was hysterical, but wasn't about to find out himself by catching the snake again, since I let it go once I determined it had no fangs.

I called him a pussy and a blemish for that, but he just laughed maniacally, bouncing up and down like a hyperactive jelly bean, which he did often while stutter babbling like porky pig, and he said something weird back like: "ohhh, niggars, niggarettes" while trying to punch my arm. I found it funny, even though I knew how prejudice those particular words sounded, but I didn't care if he was prejudice or not, since I wasn't. So the story of the Garter that hurt remained a topic of our conversations forever.

One evening, we were walking to the main hall to watch a movie, and there were some skunks on the side of the path. They ran further from the path, but I followed slowly and quietly, and they never reared their tails, just keeping about their business. As I got three feet from one, Fred tossed a rock at it, the thing spun around with tail aimed, I heard a noise that sounded like someone spraying air freshener, and I dove back towards the path. I didn't get hit, but the area smelled for days. I had no idea what I was going to do once I was close to the Skunk, but I called Fred a few names anyway, stupid Lefline.

We also managed to find a place where we could see into the girls' shower, and spent many hours there, watching all the girls we could. Fred kept trying to cover my eyes when Molly went in, but he wasn't always there so he couldn't prevent me every time. It was in the attic of the large bathroom they all shared, which we had to climb into very quietly to not be discovered. Needless to say, it was the best part of either of our camping experiences, to that point. And even though Fred got laid many times by then, he still was first to suggest going there almost every night, and I had no complaints about that activity. There were many nicely shaped femmels here camping with us, pleasing to any normal teenager's eye.

As I said before, Fred had been at camp a week before I got there, and was leaving a week before me. I endured the time he wasn't around by doing actual activities, like seeing it's a Mad, mad, mad, mad world for the fifth time, horseback ride, archery, boating and bug juice, campfires, grits and winning capture the flag games, along with going solo to the attic.

In this camp I had no chances to streak, and didn't even feel like doing so, since I was occupied with people I met through Fred, mostly girls, and I was actually somewhat sociably accepted this time. The asshole kid was still there, but gave me no problems during the week Fred wasn't there, though I don't know why. Molly was also there, and all she would do is talk about Fred, while we did the activities I mentioned. I gave her my usual philosophy on relationships, but never attempted to distract her enough to have her feel amorous towards me, so I thought I made a friend.

I was not a pushy or perverted guy. A woman would have to practically jump on me before I would get the message. I was great at explaining how everyone else felt, and how to avoid undesirable feelings, since I could see situations from every angle possible, but if the feeling or desire was directed towards me, I could not recognize it.

Molly and I would hang out and talk to Fred by phone, Fred telling me to watch her, so she wouldn't cheat. She began to see how I knew people, and liked the viewpoint I gave her on things, and she began trusting me to the point where nothing was beyond discussion with me.

Molly couldn't quite follow my deeper philosophy though and usually she would only say what Fred did, "you're such a Greenie", most of the time. But she enjoyed my company, and that's always a start. She was fairly sexy, which made being around for whatever reason quite pleasing, picturing her as I've seen her, naked in the shower, so many times, just the shape of her body all wet was enough to make me sweat.

I believe she did make some moves towards me, which I only realized looking back on the situation later, or so it appeared. I never felt comfortable getting too close to her, since she was Fred's girl, and I would never manipulate any person to my direction from anyone else, that wouldn't feel right. I was better at bringing them together.

She would go canoeing with me and would be wearing the tightest possible shorts ripped nearly to her labia, and not sitting with her legs closed. I did understand why Fred wanted her watched, not very loyal and over voyeuristic, this girl was. Loyalty should rank high for relationships if you wish to keep them, I believed then that it was important and I still do. I can honestly state that I have never cheated on my woman, or at least not without telling her before the fact that I was not going to be loyal. That holds true even to this day.

Fred was not loyal in any way, and cheated on his women every chance he got. He was more the type of person who would visit some ones house, use the bathroom, and while in the bathroom take the people's toothbrush and brush his pubic hair with the bristles. He also liked to blow his nose on someone else's clothes, like on the guy who hit me that day, but he never got me with that trick.

When talking to girls Fred knew, I was actually dually motivated, trying to discover what women saw of interest about Fred, when the fact was he was uglier than sin with a bad temper. Molly had some answers, confidence, strength, and attitude all meant a lot to her, appearance didn't, which I found strange since appearance is highly important for guys when looking at girls.

She went back to her home town of Clark, knowing she would see me again, and it made camp very different than it ever had been, because no one I ever went to camp with remained in contact with me afterwards, or would even say goodbye to me. It was the first camp I ever had any contact with girls in, even though I did not build any lasting deep relationships for myself with them. I was in the crowd with Fred now, and all that entails would become apparent soon after camp ended.

The rest of that summer was spent biking or getting rides back and forth to Kevin Road in Scotch Plains, about seven miles one way, where Fred and I discovered what happens when you burry a cat four feet in the ground, after tying it to a rock. It bites its way off the rope, climbs out, finds you and tries to be your friend again, like nothing happened.

No matter what we did this cat would not stop coming to Fred's house and look for some attention from us. Even when we threw it over the rail of an overpass right on top of a moving train, two days later it would come back, meowing, with its back bent in half, looking for our attention again. We were the first kids I knew of to think of this idea, tie two cats together by the tails, throw them over a telephone pole wire, and watch them claw each other to death, but we never got the chance to try it since we only knew one cat.

This cat would completely heal from whatever we did to it. "Throw him in the pond", as Monty Python actors would say. We tried it, didn't work. Cats may hate water, but they can swim. Eventually, we just ignored it and then it stopped coming around, which if we had known before all we had done to it; the cat would have been saved from some traumas.

Monty Python's Flying Circus was one of the greatest shows of all time, according to us. We'd sing the "Spam" song often, just because it was so funny. I still never have seen anything quite like it to date. We also both liked the Pink Panther movies a great deal and walked around quoting Peter Sellers in many situations, with that great foreign accent, or other characters in those movies who said things like, "My dug duz not bite, that is not my dug!" or "There's a minki in the rim with the telepyone and it's rrringing without the proper liceounce" as inspector Cleuseau had said, each word in individual and unrelated sentences, with that definitive accent. We enjoyed mixing words and scripts to be more creative, interesting or silly.

Fred also liked to have me carry him piggyback everywhere as well. Said it was exercise for me. I knew that, and it does work, even though it wasn't that necessary. On occasion, I'd drop my head between my knees while he was on my back, making him go tumbling over me onto his back, just for fun, and this pissed him off since no one else could get him off their backs.

Our average conversation would begin like this: "look here, asparagus apparatus, you're a great big leaping labia licking long nosed, Louisiana lesbian with an anal plate". The reply was often: "no, no, no, no, a divided anal plate"! Or Fred would say back something like "your momma was the amoeba upon my mommas' left vagina hair crab's right testicle hair, besides, your nose is far larger". I would just reply, "True, true". Extremely intelligent conversations, I assure you.

This is another example of how we spoke to each other: "Now looketh here, Stymebob! What the fucks going on?" He would say. My reply was usually "nothing, you fag!" and he would instantly reply "no,no,no,no, you're a fag" and he'd punch me and say, "how can you be such a faggot?!" I would move quickly away from him after hitting him back, saying the same or FEh, FEh, FEh, or iron, iron, and blocking additional shots. "Don't be such a Lefline" would be other responses, along with "get off me you fucking fag wad" I'd say, since Fred liked to climb people and by this time he had jumped on my back usually.

FE, the chemical sign for iron, along with zinc deficiencies were largely used phrases or exclamations, which seemed better and more original than standard curses. Looketh, hereth, and other various semi-British or old English type words were also frequently used. Looketh upon My hairy assholeth, nictitating membrane face!" "Thouest quite a fag, hermaphrodite".

That summer, during one of many sleep over's at my house, we decided to go out around midnight. We siphoned off several gallons of gas from a neighbor's car into a garbage can, walked the can down to the woods, poured it out in a huge circle, and lit it. It would have been a great idea if we weren't in the circle at the time. We just looked at each other, and started laughing. He started yelling while laughing: "what the fuck is wrong with you Greenie?" Which I thought strange since he also didn't notice the circle we created, so I just called him a fag.

We had to dive through the flames and run, which we did without getting burned at all. It was about one A.M. in the morning by then, and we stank of smoke, so instead of going back to my house we headed for the Watchung Reservation. I knew the place like the back of my hand; don't know how Fred knew it but he claimed to know these mountains well too. It was my kind of hiking.

I never pondered what my parents would think, finding us gone when they woke, and getting called by me from Fred's the next morning when they thought the sleep over was at my house. At least I did call them, early enough so that they were unaware that we were gone till I called. I remember my mother's confusion, asking if we had slept at Fred's or here, thinking the sleep over was planned for Fred's anyway, but she was barely awake at six a.m. when I called and wasn't too sure either way.

Fred just wondered what he was doing there, when he could be screwing some bitch, getting surrounded by fire and nearly being burnt to death with me. We went through the pipeline, the six-foot tall sewer that is near the reservation, about a mile long where it reaches a room, with all the smaller pipes funneling in from all directions, the junction room, I suppose.

The other end was behind a McDonald's and led into the large creek next to Blue Star shopping center, the halfway point to Fred's house in Watchung. We entered into a sewer at the room end, which was closest to the reservation, coming out at McDonalds. From there we just walked to Fred's the back way down the power lines, I went to sleep in the guestroom next to Fred's, and an hour later Molly was at the door, waiting on him.

I could have listened to the conversation, but was much too tired to even bother. We both still smelled smoke, even though we were through swamp like terrain and sewers on the way to his house. Molly was apparently complaining about where Fred had been that night, from what I could tell. Fred's parents were quite surprised to find us there, since we weren't supposed to be.

A few weeks later, we were pretending to sleep at my house again, we went out around midnight as usual and went to the barn. This barn was in the middle of the woods between my house and Fred's in the reservation. They had horses and antiques of all kinds in there. Fred thought it was fun to break into places, like the kitchen at camp, and decided to get in by using me as a ladder and going through the open loft door above the main one. We hung out, looking at how cool everything was, the old stuff rich people gather, going up and down the loft, carefully observing the main house a hundred feet from the barn for knowledge of our activity. Fred smoked, I didn't. He had matches, but I always carried a lighter, just for the sheer need of fire occasionally.

One favorite trick of his was putting a match against the striker, holding it there with his thumb, holding the book firm with his other hand, and shooting the lit match by flicking it off the striker thus igniting it and sending it many yards, depending upon the wind. Usually he'd flick them at someone, like me. Once he jammed a cigarette out on my cheek, a real friendly kind of thing to do, of course I hit him and called him names for that, but he only laughed. The match he flicked this day missed me, as it often did, and landed in the hay, which ignited immediately, thus starting a fifteen-foot blaze right there in front of us within seconds, even larger than the one with the gas. We both yelled: "oh, shit", and ran to the door, which I had to smash open with my body. Then I let the horses free of their pen, without getting kicked, and we watched all the fire trucks as they came to help, staying just out of sight from anyone. We were back in my bedroom sleeping before anyone knew what happened.

Another night, perhaps a week after the last one, we decided that we weren't pleased with construction taking place in some woods by Fred's' house, it was disrupting wildlife we figured, so we let the fuel out of the fuel tank on site and lit it, then we ran and listened for the explosion that never came, it just emptied out and burned away instead, into an empty muddy ditch, no trees caught and the fire never spread. Turned out they were building a church here, which we didn't know, and may explain why nothing else was burned.

Fred was very picky about noise while he slept, and if I snored while sleeping near Fred's vicinity, he would either hold my nose till I woke up, or punch my arm or face, depending on what was easiest to reach. He stopped hitting me while I was sleeping when I woke once and nearly knocked him out kicking him in the head thinking he was just part of that particular nightmare. He had done the same thing to a few campers in our tent, if they were too loud. He would dump water or some other liquid on them, or just slap them and dive back in his bunk, pretending to be asleep; never getting caught, but I saw him.

I was fourteen, he was thirteen, he looked twenty-five, and I looked nine. He got a lot of money at his bar mitzvah; I refused to study Hebrew so I didn't have one, and only got a few hundred bucks, which was gone quickly. That was stupid, according to him. Did I mention the fact that Fred was adopted too? Well to do Jewish family, Jewish for the most part. Religion is not that binding in the choosing of a mate these days. But both our parents were married in the nineteen-forties and at that time inter religious marriages were frowned upon, so they were likely considered rebellious. Thelma and Henny were his parents' names, which I had fun with at times.

The more I associated with Fred, the deeper in trouble we both were. One night we went dancing down a street by his house with baseball bats. The bats were for smashing car windows by the row, singing the same songs as in camp, and always getting away before anyone saw us. The summer ended, I went back to Bonnie Bull and Fred to Scotch Plains Fanwood high, and our parents decided separation was needed.

But the phone could always keep us in touch, and I found myself on Saturday and/or Sunday hanging out in Scotch Plains anyway, watching Fred and his friends' work on cars, drink, smoke, get high, and bring girls inside to have sex with. I would not participate in drug use till many years and much circumstance later and never did go for the "in" things people around me were doing. All my mother would think, as I walked out the door on any given weekend day, was that I went to the woods, which would be true; I went to the woods, just to go through them on my way to Fred's.

One last note on Bonnie Bull, in the closing comments and moments of that experience, when I left the place permanently at the end of the school year, I typed a little letter, and left copies of it spread all over the main driveway. As the bus was leaving, I tossed the stack of them out the window several at a time the whole length of the driveway. This is what I wrote: "Your mommas all suck cow scum, and I think a lobotomy is in store for all you losers, so stop sucking the furry Egrets asshole and come down from the cotton pony you fucking scum bucket asshole mother licking smegma pods from a different universal brainless society! You endless gaps of uterus flow that seeped from the vulva of an oversized orangutan, why don't you crawl back into the primordial ooze that gave birth to your grandmother yesterday, and tell her to climb out from under that pony and take it like the real perverted camel rectum that she is! Go drown in fly urine, placenta breaths! May you all die slowly and painfully from weenis cancer! Have your dad make us some warthog vulva sandwiches, like the kind he shoved up your momma's canal in hopes of aborting you! Eat camel smegma from the bottom of your momma's nipples! Get a ladder; it's time for you all to lick the rhinoceros rectums and giraffe's scrotums you call mom and dad! Your momma eats the maggots from your grandpa's dead liver! Your grandmother's vulva could house fifty gerbils and seat twenty midgets! You bunch of divided anal plate faced piss holes! Go choke on a moose's bowel movement, scrotum breath! May you all inhale a dog's diarrhea while you're dreaming about chocolate pudding and choke to death! Tell your dads atomic reactor butt to stop sending cloud signals to Australia, they don't understand fart language! The world's spittoon is your momma's snatch, and every homeless loser that spits should have it land in her! You were all originally conjoined twins joined at the asshole, but your momma separated you with her teeth so you could have different birthdays, and so she could have a little snack! The sight of your faces is sufficient to cause massive tremors throughout the continent due to the fact that upon viewing you, one has to run as far as possible, and making so many people pound their feet simultaneously just to avoid dying from ugliness shock causes earthquakes! You all look like old uterus that simply won't shed! Was that a fart, or did eight pit bulls climb up your anus and die from suffocation? Your faces resemble the slime left by slugs as they try to escape your mothers' vagina! The one thing I hate about you all is the fact that up until now, I thought you might have been bred from pure breed ass wipes, but since you're uglier that sin, I can only conclude that it was pre-destine that you walk the earth as the perfect examples for the many reasons for abortion and birth control! Thus, you should all be cast into the Arthur Kill, naked, with a wire tied to your nuts, and leeches gnawing on the veins of your scrotums, in the hopes of never recreating the genetic coding that formed your useless existences! Thank you all, buffalo bile brains, for showing me life forms lower than the amoeba's asshole and sharing your infinite lack of wisdom with me for the year I had to suffer knowing all you scumbags! Go fuck yourselves up the ass with two by fours, since I know you would all like that, you bizarre collection of psychopathic latent homosexual hermaphrodites!" I didn't get a reply from that, never heard about it again, but it was fun to write at the time.

Anyway, now back to the section where I would hang out with Fred, and yes, he did his monkey spin backwards while laughing hysterically while reading a copy of the letter, then he suggested a more fun way of returning my unpleasant experience to the residence of the farm, better than the bees. But I didn't care if they lived, doing the garbage can of gas routine around their cottages wasn't necessary, though I appreciated the thought. I don't believe I ever hurt anyone seriously in my life, never wanted to in any way, after that crochet game. Any other time would only be an accident, or so I hoped.

I would ride my bike over to Fred's, and he'd be sitting in his driveway eating Frosted Flakes, and listening to some rock or playing his guitar, or mulling over a coffee can full of oil, with some motor parts soaking in it. His mom came out once and saw me sitting there, said something to this effect: "Chris! What are you doing here, you know you're not supposed to be here, now go home!" She'd say this in the most drawn out, Jewish accent, and we'd have to laugh.

I would get up and walk away, claiming to be on my way home and I came here because I had to bring Fred back something of his he left at my house. Then I'd go through his woods in the back, till I could see the driveway but no one there could see me, waited till she left, then just come back as though I never left. Fred knew this as well, and he'd just sit there and have a yelling match with his mom, and while he did, he'd look over to where he knew I'd be watching, and smile, almost laugh out loud in my direction, when he knew his mom wasn't watching him directly.

Once, his friend Reggie Arnolds came over, and he became another friend of mine pretty quickly. He was a self-proclaimed maniac who had the same birthday as I did, two years earlier. Reggie had a sixty-nine Chevelle sitting in Fred's driveway, which seemed to sit there eternally, in pieces and mounted on cinder blocks. Fred had me stand on the engine mounts, while strapping a sheet on my back that was tied to a rope going under the engine and transmission, and lift both, with my back and legs, so he could fix some stupid part he couldn't reach himself.

I did it, and honestly thought of dropping it on his sorry face, but too many women hung out with this guy, and I figured eventually one would take notice of me and how different from Fred I truly was. No matter how similar people can be, the differences are what count to those around you in the long run. Most strive to be different or unique; I strove to be whatever suited the situation at the moment, while being myself at the same time. People also crave company, and seem to conflict about it constantly as a part of their personality, the war between solitude and tolerance of others waging endlessly.

So I followed Fred and he followed me, even though the only reason I think Fred followed me is because I was the most durable person he knew. He enjoyed hitting things like walls and trees, windows and cats, also people, using short knuckle punches, spider bites, a type of pinch more painful than most. Of course, I would start hitting back after a while when I learned of his habits back at camp, and that always made Fred start laughing.

He could take it, too, my strikes having no effect other than to cause laughter, and he claimed I couldn't hit hard enough to really hurt him anyway. He said that he never really hit me hard, even when he hit me with a two by four and broke it across my back once, which I could believe since I saw him once punch through a plywood wall with nearly no effort, and lift my whole weight set over his head with one arm.

He was the kid who always walked around on his hands, just for fun, which I could never do. He had adult strength as a kid, a scrawny body, yet very strong, and I eventually caught up with, and passed him, in that department. He didn't grow at all since I met him, only lost his hair perpetually throughout his life, as I watched his forehead just get bigger and bigger. He also hated anything with egg in it, because his parents forced him to eat raw eggs when he was young, so he claimed.

We were always thinking alike, as I said before, and as an example of this, once a guy named Barney told us there was a lot of money on a tall dresser in a house on the corner of Raritan road and Lambertsmill road. I think we were about sixteen years old during this story. We went there; hitch hiked to that corner, Fred broke the doors window with his hand, which was in a vestibule type porch that was unlocked anyway.

I ran in quick and found nothing in the spot I believed Barney mentioned, and ran back out. A younger neighbor kid who was going by the same location saw me coming out of the house at the last second, and ran home. We went to the curb and sat, disappointed that nothing was there. We didn't speak about what to say or really think anything about the kid who saw us, but when the police appeared a few minutes later they arrested us and brought us to separate rooms for interrogation. Fred said I went to use the bathroom, I said the same, and we had no theft charges pressed against us, since nothing was missing, just breaking and entering. Our parents had to pay for the breaking part.

Then I remember another trip, going to Molly's house in Clark on a Yamaha sixty, a very small motorcycle, in the ice and snow, which was exciting, till he crashed doing about thirty into a fence while sliding out of control across a grammar school's yard near his house. That didn't hurt us or stop us from going to Clark.

Molly lived near another friend of Fred's, Elton Scarducci, and one of her ex-boyfriends Jacob Rasputer, who each will travel many paths with me throughout my life. Jake, as he liked to be called, was a six foot two, two hundred fifty pound obnoxious Greek, who was just like Fred when it came to women, but at least he didn't try to deceive them.

He was Elton's best friend since middle school, and he became my best friend for much of my life. Jake could never figure why Fred was my friend and he couldn't stand him. Possibly because Fred stole things from everyone he knew, and I was the only one I knew that Fred didn't steal something from. I actually met Jake earlier than Fred since his sister lived in the same complex as Peter did. I didn't really meet Jake then, just saw him around, so he looked familiar when I saw him again around Elton and Molly. I would hang out in Molly's garage with Elton while he screwed her in the house, and just look for anything cool to snag, there was nothing.

Sometimes we'd hitchhike, walk, bike, or whatever it took to get to his women. Hitchhiking was something new to me, made sense, stick out your thumb and wait for some stranger to stop and give you a ride, odd I didn't think of this before. Fred didn't care if I got any women, though he always wanted me to come along anyway. Possibly so he wouldn't have to travel back home alone later. What I found really strange was the fact that he had four and five women at one time, just drifting between them randomly, based on the needs the current one could fulfill for him in his current position, like rides places, money, cigs, drugs or food, or multiples of each, along with any number of combinations, sex included.

We did have fun while wreaking destruction on the land, but we also did normal things like using his CB radio or other electronics, doing yard work for both our parents, and going to movies, like the Pink Panther series, or the Gumball Rally. After seeing the Gumball Rally, any time a destructive notion crossed our minds, we'd just whisper, or yell "Gumball"! It fit many occasions, like when we were knocking down power lines by getting a propane torch, bending the nozzle back into the canister of propane, lighting it and tossing it into the high grass around the tower, and running away. I'll never forget the subtle, muffled "BOOM" we heard after walking and running about half a mile. It was still loud. We figured no one would get hurt, considering where it was, and no one did. Power for the town of Fanwood did go out, though. This town may experience some relief in knowing that Fred and I were responsible for unplugging the town's Christmas tree by the train station for several years, usually just a few days before Christmas, or on Fred's birthday, which is the day after.

One winter event of that time was when Fred came to my house and we decided to walk around the road at the top of Livingston path. This road has almost nothing but mansions on it, a very exclusive high-income area. We liked throwing snowballs at cars, so we crossed the road at the top of the path to the other side, hid behind large rocks in one mansions' front yard, and waited for some cars to go by. It didn't take long.

I threw my snowball and hit a car right in the face of the driver, Fred's snowball hit the front right tire, and the car's rear went air-born when the driver slammed the breaks and skidded on his front tire about five feet and dropped to a stop. The guy came out of the car, began running after us cursing, but we just circled around a few houses and got back to the path, never letting the guy see us again. I had never seen a car do that before, neither had Fred, so it was comical to us for a long time.

I guess that since Fred used ice and rocks for his snowball that the cars tire was wedged enough to make it jump up from the back. Fred and I were hysterical naturally, convinced we'd never get caught for real trouble, just petty stuff, this was petty, and this time we did get away with it. Winter ended, summer came, and with our parents being annoyed about our time together, mine decided to separate us and broaden my horizons in a major way.

EXIT TEN

Detour through the Great United States

I will be forever grateful for the fact that my parents chose to separate Fred and I, because that summer they decided to send me on a six-week camping trip across the country with the YMCA. Something I wasn't sure at first if I really wanted to do, yet I was ecstatic about the chance to do so. We left, I think around July second or third, and I've waited long for the opportunity to write this experience down. It was one of the greatest adventures I had in my life, and being the natural exploring type, fit me perfectly, and could fill an entire book in its self, if I could remember more about it.

There were about fifty or sixty kids, on two big greyhound busses. We left from Nyack, N.Y. out west route ninety. First stop, Niagara Falls. Niagara Falls was unbelievable. I never heard such loud water, and the cooling mist gave you a bath of fresh rain, which felt nice because it was hot that day. We only stayed at the falls for lunch, and headed to Ohio to camp for the night. Most of the time we stayed at K.O.A. campgrounds, which stood for King of America, and there's a lot of them out there. This was nineteen seventy-six, and I was fourteen going on fifteen.

In the buses storage areas were mass quantities of camping equipment. We worked like the army, setting up camp every night in various places, quickly and efficiently. Going to do our laundry together was less military like, but kind of fun for kids. We were all between twelve and fifteen, equal male/female ratio. We all helped pitch tents, empty the busses, Get water, fire wood, and the food.

They always had the evening campfire, where a girl named Lucy Green would sing Stairway to Heaven, among other songs standard to campfires. We all had a lot of travelers' checks, camping stuff, and duffel bags. They gave us a limit per week decided by our parents while signing us up, and it turned out to be insufficient for me every week, of course.

Souvenirs were plenty, at every place we stopped. I didn't want most of them, thinking them cheap, overpriced, and useless, for the most part. I wound up with fireworks, a jacket, a money belt, bullwhips, clothes, bug repellant, knives that I collect still, and family member specific knick-knacks. My sister was fond of candles, so she got that, my mom was fond of nothing specific, so I just got what I thought she may need, and my dad wasn't into wasting money on non essential things, so I didn't get him anything.

The first night was orientation with the plans, the people's names, where we're going and what we'll do. We were always assigned the same bus, but not the same seat. Eric Bratfeld was the name of the first kid I sat by, and we instantly had a rapport much like Fred and I had, but without any abusive tendencies either way. We both enjoyed making fun of our Jewish heritage, eating and looking at women.

He was only twelve going on thirteen soon, and later on I'll go to his Bar mitzvah and actually sing bad, bad Leroy Brown there, while everyone watches, most of whom I won't know. Eric liked wrestling as much as I, the ring kind, not the mat kind. We talked about Mil Mascaras, Mick Foley or cactus Jack, Mankind, or whomever else he was known by. Practiced some minor moves, and mostly gossiped about which girl on the trip liked whom and vice versa, and what we could talk to them about, never finding that answer for him or myself, perhaps other than the spectacular scenery we all could see.

We both agreed that some of the bodies of these girls were quite fine and nice to look at, which we did whenever we could. Eric was too nervous to converse with girls, and I knew I couldn't solve that issue for him; he was just too young and got over excited about simple things, like seeing the girls' underwear at the Laundromat, which was a big deal for him. Eric looked a little like another friend of mine, Elton, they were both large, over-weight, clumsy, happy, friendly, paranoid, and of course, completely girl crazed. He was from Wayne, New Jersey. We referred to each other as Stymie, which he seemed to think was amusing, and it caught on quickly for both of us.

During the course of the trip, we loved to try to get peeks in the girls tents, but never could get far, and hadn't the guts to approach one in earnest ourselves, I felt that I didn't know any of them well enough to be comfortable yet. They did approach me, though. Can't even remember their names, but I was usually busy with fireworks, wild life, or hiking somewhere and couldn't be bothered with small talk that wouldn't lead anywhere at that age anyway. At the falls we were all able to get good looks at everyone along for this adventure, and there wasn't a real bad influence in the bunch, besides me and another kid, that is. I caused some problems, like performing my disappearing act my parents were so used to, but I was having too much fun to go overboard and wreck it by getting sent home.

One kid was sent home early, got hurt following me down the side of the mule path at the Grand Canyon. The path zigzags back and fourth down the side, never just falling steeply, and the paths were about a hundred feet apart, you could see the next turn as you approached it, as well as the roads below you before you reached them. So when we approached the last turn near the bottom of the canyon, I decided to jump off my mule and slide down the steep gravel portion of canyon between the paths, and wait for everyone else to catch up.

I slid down on the heels of my feet and butt, with the heels of my hands guiding the back. Didn't realize how steep it was till I went over the side. But a guy followed me, and towards the bottom about ten feet up or so he tumbled forward. That I did not do, and it took a lot of effort to not tip forward. I scraped my hands good, and the other guy had to be brought back up the trail and get medical attention. They almost sent me home for that.

My jeans were ripped almost off, as well. I had a few pairs, and I liked shopping for things, so replacing my jeans seemed the obvious thing to do. I enjoyed shopping for myself, as did Eric. I found being looked up to pleasing yet discerning, flattered to have known someone who though I was intelligent and interesting enough to lead them and guide them to some great point of understanding or entertainment, concerned that I would lead anyone, and get them into as deep shit as I was usually in.

Eric and I would simulate some wrestlers, and become very loud and obnoxious, saying things like: "OK Animal, I'm going to kick your ass all the way to Plutarski!" Plutarski was our own word for a fictitious place we created for use in phrases. I would reply: "Yea Putski? Well, I'll knock you into next week!" as we simulated George the animal Steele and Ivan Putski, big wrestlers of that era. I would always just put him in a Greenie head lock, my favorite move where I put my arm around his neck from behind, put my hip behind his back and hold him there so his back is bent backwards over my back, as opposed to a usual head lock. One would have to back-flip over me to get out of that hold. I wouldn't do it to the point where it may hurt him, because I was not sadistic like Fred.

It became clear after a while that only Eric was willing to adventure the way I did, once the planned activities were done and the only thing left to do was explore. The word Plutarski was used for many years, Fred and Peter thinking it was as weird and funny as I did. I imagined that it had to be someone's name somewhere, but I've never seen it.

The only other individual boys' name I can recall is Chris Fish. We would sing: "we wish you a merry Chris Fish, we wish you a merry Chris Fish," and the rest of the song, till it appeared to me like he wasn't pleased by the cajoling. He was a nice guy, so I helped him address his sensitivity to people making fun of his name, simply by pointing out how unimportant the people teasing him were, at which point Eric walks up, and starts saying: "hey Green teeth! What are we going to do now, Stymie"? Words spoken should not affect him, only being words, as in the live example Eric presented us. I was the instant mediator, seeking the good out of the bad the others showed, and insuring peaceful coexistence. I was always able to put down my own mother before redirecting insults at others.

I even stopped one fight, between Chris and another guy, I don't remember his name but he took a swing at Chris that I blocked, since I happened to be standing right there, and when he swung at me in retaliation, I just side stepped it and swept his legs out, landing him on his butt. This was impressive to Eric and the few others standing around watching, and I never had to intervene like that any further along the trip. I surprised myself that the move I did actually worked, didn't have a clue how.

When you sit next to kids on a bus for many hours, and try to battle for position to sit next to the females, and have no idea where you are, seeing places you never had before, things can get interesting. Naturally, I wasn't battling, I never cared where I sat or with who, and Eric always wanted to sit by me anyway, which was fine. For the girls, I imagined it was like living the ultimate romance novel of the American heartland.

At that age the excitement takes a different form for boys and girls. The guys just want peaks at the girls, and maybe to talk to them, trying to feel out the factors needed for some close encounters while viewing the scenery of America, and to get under their clothes. The girls just look around, some seeming depressed by the selection of guys they have to share this magnificent scenery and experience with, pining perhaps for a boy friend they left home, or someone they know to share it with, or just enjoying it themselves for what it was, in silent awe, with home sick thoughts fading as the sun behind the mountains of great landscapes.

Along this trip I caught about two dozen snakes, which no counselor liked since some could be dangerous, and they were afraid of them, too. They only saw a few, I usually let them go before bringing them back to camp, so only Eric saw nearly all of them. I think, including the drivers, that there were four adults on this trip, and the only name I can remember is Jack.

I was the animal expert of the pack, always finding the best creatures to be marveled at by my peers and the adults. Within the first week I caught a common king snake and brought it into the camp, which separated the wimps from the real campers. I was always and still am amused to hear people scream for no reason, like at a harmless reptile or roaming mice.

The counselors weren't amused and made me let it go before I wanted to. The girls were impressed by my knowledge of nature, Eric was sort of too, but he didn't care for snakes either and was pretty squeamish about them. I remember when I saw the King snake, don't recall which national park it was in, but my eyes lit up and my adrenaline soared, finally seeing and catching a creature I never could have in the swamps and woods of New Jersey, overjoyed by the prospects that awaited my animal catching instincts.

I'm not certain of which city along Lake Erie we went to next, but we all canoed and boated all over the place. Huge place, and I did take pictures of everything, but I destroyed them later on in life, for some peculiar reason. I remember it being impressive, but that's about it. We then trekked through Iowa and Chicago Illinois, up to Greenfield Wisconsin, where we ate at the strangest restaurant I ever saw. I don't even remember the name, but it was like part castle, dungeon, and caves all together. There were streams running through it, and paths through doors to other environments, moss on trees inside, animals on display in Aquariums, and it was huge. The food was great, or at least the steak I had was.

Next stop was Jellystone Park in Bagley Wisconsin. I remember Yogi and Boo Boo, but not much else. Nice place for small kids, lots of paddleboats, canoes, and swimming, but not that memorable otherwise. We spent hours there, camping later at some K.O.A. headed for Iowa, Minnesota, and the black hills of South Dakota. We went through Bad Lands National Park on the way, where I caught a Bull snake, and some lizards.

Just tons of space, which I had never seen besides on TV, seemed to be barren, for the most part. I liked the lack of population, the endless miles of space, I remember wishing I could live somewhere like this, unpopulated and open, with wildlife everywhere. How natural that would feel, yet scary, with no options for retreat, you're there, in the middle of nowhere, no help for many miles, should you need it.

From there, we went into Cody Wyoming, the Turquoise and Sterling Sliver capital of the country, according to them. I bought a lot of things here, souvenirs for family, bullwhips, fireworks, and some native Jewelry. I was also still an occasional shoplifter, and got some silver for the trip, which I would sell in Reno, or Vegas. I knew either city would have many places to do some pawning, being the money oriented places they were, I thought it'd be easier possibly than even Manhattan, where anything sells and I was right.

But we weren't near there yet, and Cody was very western and exciting, gunshots everywhere, Stagecoaches with horses and cowboys, very interesting place. This was the first place I ever saw a rodeo, which seemed to be the area's most common past time. The only uninviting quality I can remember is how the whole town, and possibly the whole state, smelled like sulfur. I like that smell normally, like when a match lights, but this was extremely overwhelming, as though a trillion matches were lit at the same time.

Then we headed south through the canyons. Here it really started to get scenic. It was becoming landscape that I could associate with the moon, or another planet, with very few signs of civilization. We went to all the National Parks time made possible, we had snowball fights in July atop the Grand Teton Mountains, twelve thousand feet plus in altitude. What I remember vividly about the driving part of our trip was that while looking out the window in the front of the bus, I saw clouds along the horizon. They looked very dark and weren't moving it seemed.

As we came closer to them, and I noticed that they weren't moving at all, I discovered another odd thing. These clouds were not clouds, they were mountains. I had never seen cloud-high mountains, and the first reaction would be excitement, awe, and even a little fear, all bundled together. Then you realize you'll see them closer, and get to climb them, so I did many hours of rock climbing, that summer. Grand Tetons in Wyoming were the best opportunity for climbing thus far, but I didn't do any climbing there.

Both busses unloaded into the snow, all wild and crazy, the kids launching snow in all directions, at everyone, I just watched and marveled at the warmth combine with snow. Gives perspective of how different environments can exist, and New Jersey is as unique as any. Just not as impressive, on the size scale. Unfortunately, I also knew the reptiles would not be in sight, being just too cold. So I stepped out for a few minutes, just to breathe some incredibly fresh air and throw some snow, then I got back on the bus since I didn't feel like putting on my jacket, took some pictures from the window, and talked to Lucy about the present experience.

I thought she was quite sexy. She didn't go snow crazy, either, she wasn't feeling well this day, and so she stayed on the bus. She was the one who sang at most of the campfires. We just talked for a while, her not being receptive to actual deep conversation, just small talk, but watching her was enough to occupy my time. She had the eyes you could just stare at, deep and soft, with a body of pure art form, the type only nature could create.

Then we left and headed towards Yellowstone. This park just overwhelms with space and height, as I noticed as we parked next to great big stone walls going straight up for hundreds of feet, with the avalanche warning signs covering the area. Old Faithful was that, faithful, and the sulfur smell penetrated your head no matter what you did, but you get used to it, like in most of Wyoming. The hot springs and lava bubbles were very interesting, and as I stood contemplating it all, I suddenly realized we were standing in an active volcano, kind of.

Signs everywhere said no loud noise allowed. But it was very spectacular, and wandering around it was very discerning. I had a fantastic sense of direction, and this place would put it to the test. I walked around for miles, with Eric along just whining about how lost we were, and saying: "were gonna die! Were gonna die out here, and my parents will be pissed!" but I never was lost. I wouldn't share that information, though. Waited till he was nearly crying, which he was by the time he realized we were back at camp, from the other side. But along the way we saw many deer, bear, squirrel and raccoon, and other residence. It was worth it, and obviously, we didn't die. Eric was still kind of shaken I think, even after we were safe again, I could see him sweating.

Then we camped, and set our sights on Utah the next day. There, we started in Salt Lake City, where it appeared very calm, serene, and uncrowded, with the mountains surrounding two thirds of the place, which was awesome. We came from the east, from the top of an endless mountain road that just went up for what felt like hours, coming down with an overview of the city was incredible.

We didn't interact with the residence much, anyone I spoke to made me feel as though I was talking to a saint or priest, overly friendly and so proper you could puke, these people seemed to be in a world of their own, and all quite nice, but appeared distant to those who didn't live there, thought this may have been just towards the fifty teenagers that invaded them on this day.

The Great Salt Lake was odd, and massive, no matter how far you walked, it never seemed to deepen. But the flies were everywhere, a kind I've never seen before, and they bit pretty hard. That was the only down side, along with the salt coating you have covering your body when you get out. It was pretty salty, and appeared lifeless, like this is where all the unused salt goes when no one needs it. What impressed me here was the sheer size of the lake, you couldn't see the other shore of the place, and it never seemed to end, an endless vastness.

I walked into the water and before I knew it, I was half a mile from the spot where I entered. It's also quite hot in the summer, and I sweat profusely. So my tee shirts were always drenched anywhere we went, with my giant salt stain looping down my shirt like an ugly necklace. But here, the stain gave new meaning to disgusting, the whole shirt, when I wore it, was totally covered with salt.

From here, we continued on to some incredible examples of what whether can do to the earth, if one form of it, namely wind, were to fail to cease over the course of thousands of years, combined with water along the way from time to time, these magnificent spectacles created by mother earth herself were called Zion National Park and Bryce canyon. One of those I believe has the rock formation known as the "Chessmen". That picture, wherever it is, is etched in my memory for its sheer natural beauty and complexity.

Most of the time I was able to envision all these places, canyons, and valleys as full bodies of water at one time. I kept expecting it to become one again while visiting them, just for fun, and to scare Eric some, made him hope for no rainy days. We were told to stay in pairs at least, which didn't matter to me one bit since Eric kept following me around anyway, literally followed me around the whole country. Groups of three or four were what they really wanted, and a couple of kids did join us on some adventures, I don't remember who, but I remember it wasn't often. We also were told to stay close by and don't wander too far, but all this was just too awesome to not be wandered around in, we saw so much so fast, it didn't seem fair to restrict where we'd go, as long as we came back, and were in one piece.

All along the trip, we were allowed to experience the taste of interesting and different food, like grilled rattlesnake, which tasted much like chicken. We ate a variety of foods, from snapper turtle to moose burgers, venison, duck and goose, cactus juice and catfish, along with possibly cat or dog or something in Tijuana that they called pork, but no one knew for certain what it was.

It was pretty good anyway, as were all the so called delicacies from the regions we were in. Every meal was an experience; the variety was endless, the way it was served, always different. We did eat at many McDonald's and other fast food places, diners and truck stops too, just out of necessity but I think budget had more influence than any adult would admit. I always loaded my bag up with gum, candy and chocolate, Fritos and Bugles, my favorite snacks, and lucky me, they were Eric's too. Watching his sugar initiated hyper fit was always amusing, he'd run around aimlessly, as though given a shot of pure adrenaline, usually babbling about how hot some girl looked and how he was about to burst, or attempting a wrestling hold on me and getting tossed around.

There was a place called Checkerboard Mesa, and I did get to play both chess and checkers while there, as a nighttime camping activity. The natural formation was, of course, most interesting and impressive, rocks shaped by wind, water and time into the shape of one end of a chessboard's pieces, hard to imagine how this occurred. We camped out in tents here I think.

I'd guess half the nights on the whole trip were spent in various lodges, on floors in our sleeping bags, or in auditorium type rooms, so we always had light enough to do things on those nights, like playing cards, or wandering around the building. The other nights were spent in the tents, with only flash lights for use as light sources, or my lighter. Waking up all over the country surrounded by such beauty and fresh air is an experience I'd like to share with anyone, and although the rest of the world has many incredible wonders, this country has enough beauty and scenery to last a lot more than a lifetime. I plan on taking my kids one day to see much of it; the difference would be to spend more time in each place, which was my only complaint about this trip. We never stayed very long in one place, too much to cover in too little time, so we spent enough time to have some culture shock, and then we were off to the next destination quickly.

I thought initially that we'd be bored a lot, and though driving for hours was tiresome, it was well worth it. We headed off for northern Nevada next, and since we all were minors the gambling aspect of this state was not the main attraction. We went to Lake Tahoe, where I tried water skiing for the first time, but I couldn't stand up for more than a few seconds and needed more than the three tries we were each given to do it. It was still very nice there, but most of Nevada seemed barren and desert like, and we didn't stay there long at all.

Couldn't imagine settlers staying here, with nothing but tumbleweeds and cactus for scenery in the desert area and not having any modern conveniences to survive with or be entertained by. Lake Tahoe was unbelievably beautiful, and it was strange to discover gambling was legal there, on the Nevada side, and not on the California side. The water was higher quality that I had known in New Jersey, as if the sheer size had some impact on the clearness and freshness of it, like the great lakes we had seen already.

Northern central California was next, starting with Sequoia National Forest, and these redwood trees that were too big to climb and appeared to reach to the clouds, I felt like a Lilliputian standing next to them. Their roots in the ground looked more like the size trees I was used to seeing, laying down. We went through a tree that the road was built through, there are no trees in the world I can imagine or picture more massive than these I thought.

Even I could not climb any, due to their size, but I did try, the problem was no branches to hold for maybe a hundred feet. We only spent a few hours there, Eric and I walking around, looking up for some opening in any tree that would allow us, or me, to reach the ultimate height in tree climbing, but I only managed twenty or thirty feet, clinging to the bark. It was strangely obvious, that of all tree life, it would be so apparent which are the kings of the tree world. Why the difference had to be so massive, I couldn't figure. So since we couldn't climb one, we concentrated on the life living beneath them. Caught some snakes, as usual.

I think Yosemite was next, Eric was fun to hang with there, always so panicky on all matters, like when we saw bears, and I launched bottle rockets at them. He went running through the park screaming: "What are you nuts, Stimy?" "Listen Styme", I replied, "they're more scared of us than we are of them" as I ran alongside him laughing. "Just scared him off, that's all. The worst that would do is start an avalanche, but did you see that thing run?". "You're a fuckin nut, man." He said. I replied: "Nah, and it's a good thing I chased him away, because if it started chasing us, no way would you out run it Styme, I don't think I even could!"

He just went on, saying stuff like: "Oh, my God "! Over and over, and: "I can't believe you did that, you're crazy man, just don't get me killed, my parent's would be pissed"! When I asked why he would care, since he would be dead and his parents being pissed could not affect him because of that, he just said he didn't want to die before getting laid, plain and simple, which I agreed with. We sang songs while hiking, when Eric wasn't fearing for his life, like: "if I could save Styme in a bottle, the first girl that I'd like to screw . . . ." our variation of the first line on the great song 'Time in a bottle'.

Created many others as well, all with disgusting or nonsensical variations of words, which I believed was just a pass along tradition that Fred and I began. The translation from Fred to Eric was quite different, I was the centerpiece of the group here, but that was not the whole reason and the obvious difference, like me being years older than him, wasn't a factor, the wording was just different. Eric's uniqueness was one difference, he was basically Fred's opposite, except for his desire for females, the one thing we all had in common.

Eric idolized me, but I didn't idolize Fred. Fred didn't follow me, we were equal in the direction of the path we chose unless I was following Fred for lack of anything better to do, and Eric waited for my decisions and followed me everywhere he could. Also we weren't looking for trouble often, unlike Fred and me. There was enough to see without causing problems. We wouldn't cause trouble and get sent home, that would be a waste, and we'd miss out on everything.

We left Yosemite and headed towards San Francisco, where I met with my sister, who moved there a few months or so before I got there with her boy friend Henry Martel. They took me to Great America amusement park, which was lots of fun, and we also went to many beaches in those two or three days, and I remember how different the Pacific Ocean was compared to the Atlantic.

I remember diving under waves, one of my favorite things to do, and these waves were much larger than the east coast's. I went diving under this rather large wave, and when I re-surfaced, I was half a mile north of where I dove in. Very strong currents, with waves that made New Jerseys look like a wading pool, and every time I tried swimming, the tide pulled me north; I had to keep readjusting my position to where I recognized the beach by swimming hard to the south. I couldn't surf, had no board, but I loved the challenge of this mighty tide force, and stayed in the water for many hours, just body surfing and swimming, south the whole way, letting the tide make it feel like I was swimming in place.

I don't know what the rest of the gang on the trip were doing, I think Eric told me they went to San Quentin, but we met them somewhere around Fisherman's Wharf, just before they went towards Los Angeles and Tijuana Mexico, I wondered, just for fun, if they'd leave without me. The drive through southern California was awesome, stopping in some places that were unbelievably scenic, and towns with names you've heard of, mainly for the movies and news about them, and golf courses in them, Pebble Beach, for one. The west coast towns seemed familiar compared to the Jersey shore towns, only larger in area with huge mountains for backgrounds, along with endless woods, rocks and space, but same arrangement of little stores, with their unique names, wares and sporadic shoppers.

The cities were just that, cities, looking more or less the same, just different structures, landscapes and architecture, with the same nameless faceless people busily rushing around, and others hanging around doing nothing. The only activities in the cities for our group were meals and laundry, perhaps a museum or other site of interest, so we never stayed in cities for long, and always went to the nearest camp site somewhere just outside the city. So all I can recall about Los Angeles or San Diego is that they were big cities.

In Tijuana I had the opportunity to barter, getting some nice marble horse bookends for my mother, and the food and water didn't make me sick, though we were told not to eat or drink anything. For the most part, it was just dirty and confusing because most people there did not speak English, and it smelled bad. There were interesting fireworks and crafts, sombrero's and clothes, all kinds of food stands with unrecognizable delicacies I wouldn't try till I was hungry enough. The border looked like a plain tollbooth, with no fuss being made about our busses by the authorities.

Walking around with Eric, standing in Mexico with these other kids, was just so odd, unrealistic, and amazing all at once. None of us knew what to do or where to go, just walking through shops while keeping a bearing on where the bus happened to be at the time, I kept telling Eric they're gonna leave without us. I think he was fairly disgusted with it, but the culture exchange wouldn't last long, I think we stayed only a few hours.

A few people did get sick there, but nothing serious. Eric refused to eat anything, calling me a crazy ass Styme bob for eating a taco and drinking a bottle of Coke. But I had to, knowing somehow I would not see this place again, even possibly ever. It seemed surreal, not actually how any people could live, yet they did, seemingly entranced with endless complainant stares in their eyes, a salesman smile with purpose in their grin.

After this we drove through the biggest wasted space I ever saw in my life, called Death Valley. Nothing but miles and miles of nothing, and very hot, it felt like you were standing in a frying pan if you stayed in the sun. Impressive in its openness and un-ending desert terrain. We stopped at a rest stop along the road to stretch, Eric and I went wandering about, I caught a rattler with a stick, and Eric ran away about twenty feet or so, till I let it go.

Didn't get to see the Gila monster or skink, just found some other lizard, I think it was a Chameleon. As we looked around, I thought about the many people who must have died here, wouldn't take long if you're stranded without supplies, it would be one nasty way to go. You'd melt away, dehydrate within hours. Eric was getting nervous, since we were out of site of the group, who all stood around in the shade of the busses or the little building with bathrooms in it. As we walked around he kept saying: "shut up! Stymie! We gotta get back!" I laughed and kept talking nonsense, while walking in the circle I plotted to get back to the area where everyone was, continuing my rambling about how death must love this place that were gonna get lost in soon, how vultures were gonna steal Eric's eyeballs, he was so paranoid.

The space was so vast, so undisturbed for what could be thousands of years, vacant, giving the one viewing it true sense of mortality, emptiness. If the drivers drove away, leaving all of us behind but off the road by miles, I don't think we'd all return. Like lord of the flies without the island, I certainly would live. The roads were so long and barren, sudden turns or obstacles can be easily missed. As far as the drivers and counselors go, they were good drivers I think, really didn't pay much attention to them, nice enough to be forgotten easily. I knew they wouldn't leave but had to tell Eric about that fantasy to get him paranoid.

Then we made our way to Las Vegas and Circus Circus. Vegas was unimaginable, I had never seen such waste of power with such grace in wasting it, with spectacular arrangements of every possible use of neon, fluorescent, and regular bulbs that resembled multisized Christmas lights. It was daylight at all times, visible from many miles from all directions, with patches of dark areas between massive casino hotels where normal lighting made the night apparent.

Circus Circus was incredible, having a whole circus in the hotel, and it seemed the only place minors were allowed anywhere in the city. The performers were very good, just as one would expect. The whole kid's section was like a boardwalk on the beach only indoors, with the usual impossible games of skill where you could win stuffed animals and things, but no money. Throw a ring onto a bottle that's barely narrow enough to fit the ring, shoot a basketball into a hoop almost too small to even fit it, things like that, was all we could do there, a real waste of money.

I happened to have some nickels, and asked some guy to put them in a real slot machine for me, which stood only ten or so feet from the entrance threshold I could not cross. He agreed, and the slot hit for about four hundred dollars, and money just poured out of it. Takes a lot of nickels to make that much, but I didn't even get the five I gave the guy back. Once he heard me cheer some and begin to get excited, he had security escort me out by yelling: "hey! There's a kid in the casino!"

I was not pleased, and I just watched while the guy collected all my money and cashed it in, from an entrance where he could not see me. I watched him long enough to see him go to his car, but he wasn't wise enough to leave in it, just getting something or putting something in it, I figured now that he had money he'd continue to gamble, and he did. He appeared to be one of those chronic gamblers you always hear about.

I remembered my new knife was folded in my pocket, and once he went back into a casino, I got my money's worth back by making him need four new tires on his car. Everyone in the city seemed preoccupied with the gambling, which I found interesting yet sick, overwhelming. All the cities in Nevada and the airports have some form of slot machine, or other gambling apparatus, even in the KOA's.

A teacher of mine later would say there's no crime there, since everything is legal including prostitution, which resided sixty miles west of Vegas. We never had reason to go there, the drivers may have wanted to, but Eric wanted to badly. I didn't see how that could be, no crime, people are just people, and this place certainly had good odds of having a full complement of bad people, statistically speaking.

There was no camp ground right in Vegas, so we drove towards Arizona and stayed outside somewhere. During the whole trip through California and Nevada I looked for gold everywhere since I had read somewhere there was some, a thought that followed me through the western states. I never found any, but Eric always seemed hopeful, he liked the idea and never gave up looking for the "pot of gold".

Hoover Dam and Lake Mead were very interesting, but all I wanted to do was throw things off the side, which would only cause trouble. I pictured my dad creating something like this, such economical power generation, having water supply electricity just by being in motion, the power of forced water. I kept wondering what will happen when the dam breaks, since no dam built by man can last forever, mother nature will see to that. The tour was short and boring, but there was nothing else to do. We did some boating on the lake, swam around and stuff. It made me wonder why we hadn't invented ways of using the sun or wind for power, of course we had, but no amount enough to make the concepts economical at the time, no way to have your car run just by moving and creating wind energy, perhaps they should line busy highways with wind catchers, enough to make cities light, crowded highways generate a lot of wind, except during traffic jams naturally. Eric thought that was awesome for some reason. But the best was yet to come.

The Grand Canyon awaited, truly mountains lying down. This place is the biggest adventure zone I ever found, and I couldn't stop wanting to go roaming all over it. For as many pictures as I've seen of the canyon, there was nothing quite like standing next to it or in it for real. After the incident of getting down to the bottom I mentioned before, we rafted and canoed in the resident river, the Colorado. We stayed there for days, at the bottom and every campsite around it too.

Just Massive, so much so it gives perspective on how small we all really are on this rock. Watching the Indians was interesting, with all the ceremonious outfits and things, their connection with environment and wildlife, very honest and natural, I understood it. We spent a few days here, since there is that much to see and more. One Indian adult told me he saw me creating incredible and wonderful things one day, and kept calling me "Wandering Eagle" I think it was. I guessed that he noticed how I wondered around his land with joy and ease, never getting lost while enjoying the wild life everywhere.

As we set up camp, it reminded me of the Brady Bunch episode when they went there, except we didn't run into any ghost towns or prospectors, and I never met Jim Backus. I remember hiking with Eric around the whole place, and even a few girls and other guys went with us one time, dropping back one by one as we went further and further, or picking their own direction, Eric staying with me the whole time, and complaining as usual. Two kids from the trip actually got lost and had to have the local Indians track them down. They started out with me, but picked their own path, I thought they just went back to the camp when they left us, not thinking they could get lost. I was also listed as lost at one point, along with Eric, but I got us back before the Indians could find us, and we were never really lost.

Eric and I disappeared after breakfast, returned before dark from the opposite side of the camp, and we brought food, snacks and water with us. Eric was whining about what a bad idea it was to leave the camp, and we hadn't even walked fifty feet away yet, but we got to see more of the bottom of that canyon than anyone else did, went places that appeared to be never stepped upon by humans, we were truly on the moon, as far as we knew. We saw snakes, lizards, birds, tons of interesting rocks, but none were gold.

We were reprimanded for that, their point being our parents wouldn't be please if the counselors didn't return with who they left with. Their precious head count was all they worried about. I remember clearly Eric continually saying: "I'm scared, how are we gonna get back? It's gonna get dark and we'll die!" He must have said that fifty times on that and every other hike we took, along with things like worrying about the fact if he dies without getting laid, he'd be very unhappy, and who would screw an invalid if he fell down a mountain and was disabled? His other main goal was not to hurt his weener before he got to use it. At least he didn't worry about me pushing him off a mountain, though sometimes it was tempting. I told him to stop being such a weenis, which had him laughing for hours.

We left there and went on to Colorado, and the Rocky Mountains. It was extremely scenic and overwhelming, but the whole first few weeks of the trip were, and it was beginning to look similar in appearance, just wave after wave of awesome mountains, valleys, and spacious wonders of nature and man. It's certain to change the prospective of anyone who lived in New Jersey all their life and never saw these places, the sheer size being so different, immense.

Colorado was where the jackets we brought became a necessity, since it was quite cold up there at night. I remember thinking I would hate to live here only because I'd never know if I needed a jacket or coat, and that having to bring one everywhere I went would be annoying. For the most part, this was near the end of the voyage, with nothing but sprawling farmland and long road trips back towards the east, which was sad but inevitable. We would stop at some restaurants on the way home, but nothing that spectacular. Eric would remain friends with me for a while, and when we got back, we talked by phone about the trip in general, and the girls on it.

I was never one for long goodbyes, and no one really got close to me on this trip besides Eric, so I just left with my parents, not acknowledging anyone on the trip except him. My parents asked me why I didn't say goodbye to any one and if everything went OK, but I was not concerned about kids I would likely never see again, who shared an experience we would never have again, and I did say bye to Eric, who I knew I would see again.

Everyone else went to some after trip dinner, which I was invited to, but I would rather be home, not caring one way or the other. I loved home, and did miss it. All I said to Eric was: "Later Styme!" Then I had to explain to my parents that Styme was not his real name. I also had many things I wanted to show and give them from the trip, and I didn't want to wait long for that. It was the best trip I've ever been on and I wanted to share it as soon as possible.

EXIT ELEVEN

The Toll Charge for Teenage Wisdom

My parents were glad to see me as usual, even thought I called them collect about twenty times during the trip and had them wire me money at a few points since I ran out. But I brought lots of trinkets, pictures and stuff that made telling about it interesting. When I came back Bonnie Bull was over, and New Providence high school awaited me, with about one third of the students having fond memories of me to share with all the new people we had to go to school with from the other middle schools. Fred had another new girlfriend, and I could tell he was pretty jealous of me for possibly the first time ever because of the trip.

All he wanted to hear about was the girls we had on the way, and did I get to lose my virginity or not. Not, was of course the answer to that question, but I didn't care since it was so much fun, there simply wasn't time to even bother with chasing girls, watching them on occasion was sufficient. Peter, of course, was the same, not too concerned with people's opinions or even knowing what the fuss was all about, everyone ignoring me in school or showing anger and fear with stares or expressions. He would hang out with me, and almost no one would hang around us.

The only person who would associate with us was a gay kid named Troy. Troy was a self-proclaimed homosexual who at every opportunity would grab a guys' ass, invite guys over to his house, or just make gay faces at people, like kissing or tongue motions.

One day, he decided to come over to my locker and put his arm around me, suggesting I go down somewhere, and I tried to ignore him, but he was persistent this day. So as I got to my class, he tried following me, and I grabbed him by the hair while he was trying to grab my ass and slammed the door on his neck, knocking him out. He never bugged me again, but he hung around Peter a lot, which made me wonder about him, since I knew he wasn't too bright, and I wouldn't put anything past him.

I once asked Troy what his problem was, tried to discuss his "abnormal" feelings, and after I got through his usual comments like "shut up and suck my dick", he told me that he liked dick, and it isn't abnormal. He liked having one, playing with them, and thought it was natural to get pleasure from anyone, male or female, but women scared him, they do too much bitching. He never had a woman he said, and when I pointed out to him that he wouldn't even exist if it weren't for his mother and father being normal at least one time, he became quite depressed and reclusive, and I was able to determine that his dad wasn't that normal.

I think he sexually abused him, but have no evidence on that issue. I have discovered that there usually seems to be a reason for most homosexuality, aside from chemical imbalances or birth defects, having discussed it with several people that are. Their parents abused them, a girl gave them a bad experience that affected them deeply, or they were too shy or scared to attempt a normal relationship and were taken advantage of because of that fact.

I was shy that way too, but never felt the urge to find that kind of outlet, just thinking about it made my stomach turn. I knew eventually the right woman would come into my life, and never doubted it. For a lesbian, I can understand the attraction to another woman, since a woman's body is so beautiful and art like in form, where as a guy is just a tool. Plus, it's easier to comprehend that a bad experience would occur for a woman that would prevent her from seeking a man, like rape.

A woman cannot rape another woman under normal circumstance, and even if one found a way to do so, no pregnancy would be possible. I am not against people doing things the way they want, couldn't care less as long as they don't try to preach their style to include me or question my opinion as though it's wrong. I have known quite a few gay people, who were all pretty nice and good people, except for a few like Troy, who overemphasized his point.

At the beginning of the summer of seventy six, I was scheduled to return to normal school as a tenth grader in the fall, which I did. But somehow just before school began I began talking on the phone to one of my former female classmates, Vera. One day she just called me out of the blue, claiming to be curious about what reform school was like, and to tell me of events in her life, and what I've missed being out of the public system for so long. She forgave me for the rabbit, after discussing it with me in depth, realizing it wasn't the animal I had wanted to make suffer but the owner. In all honesty, I cannot remember the exact way I met her again, what class we took or how we began talking, but we just met and had instant connection, unlike anything I had experienced yet with a girl. She would began asking me about schoolwork, believing for some reason that I was pretty good at it, and then the gossip would start amongst her friends about how nice and helpful Greenie really could be, and that I wasn't really just some reform school inmate, with a thing for rabbits. I actually like rabbits; they are very cute animals, silent and quick.

I was a very open conversationalist on the phone; it was an interesting way to communicate with someone when you can't see him or her. I would talk for hours with Vera, almost every night. Vera thought it odd that Peter and I would be good friends, since he was not altogether there in the brains department. Peter was slightly retarded, and as it was explained to me at the time by his grandmother, there were some things he could not learn, there was an actual limit to his ability, what he could learn took much effort, time and patience to accomplish.

He was a pain in girls' butts, because he liked girls. He liked to lift their dresses and get peaks at any cost, and this can be confusing for some people, especially those victimized. He didn't hurt anyone, but he scared quite a few girls with his impulsiveness. I often figured one day he be jailed for his way of dealing with girls, so I always tried to dissuade him from being a pervert, or at least not such an obvious one.

Vera was one of the girls, who he frightened, and I discussed this with her, in fact I discussed most personal things with her, since she seemed to be the only one interested or the only one with any positive input. Her middle name was Samantha, and only I was allowed to call her that. I don't know what Pete did to her exactly, it may have been when he looked up her skirt, but I explained that Peter was not that big of an asshole, simply because it's a natural thing for boys to do, including me, and committing any act held consequences Peter did not or could not realize.

I eventually convinced Vera to take this as a compliment, not a threat, and I told her that I was just as curious about her under her clothes, which is natural, but I wouldn't do anything like that as a thrill. I told her that if she told Peter to leave her alone, he probably would. Of course, I knew that was a lie, but I also knew I could deter Peter's actions in her case by telling him to not do it, since he listened to me usually, and he never tried bothering Vera again.

Peter's only pertinent thought was about girls. How can we get some girls, when we can play strip poker or truth or dare with them, how you get your dick in them, when the opening looks so small and things like that? All guys favorite common topic of discussion is female sex organs and body parts, and I am no exception, always admiring and desiring the women's bodies found in magazines to the fullest extent, which is why they sell so well. That's what guys like to discuss, but Peter never stopped, to the point of his conversation becoming redundant.

I was able to distract him, with sports, hikes, and mischief or vandalism. Peter took to these things very easily, didn't require much thought on his part. It was part of what made him my best friend for longer than anyone at that time. Though he was the giggly, hyper, non-stop action kind of kid, so was I. I didn't giggle about everything quite the same way he did, but I could see similarities in our personalities, and we both were basically loners our whole life to that point and beyond.

I understood the usefulness of solitude; you can get a lot done. You can create whatever you want without worrying about how someone will react to it. The way you came into the world is the same as you go out, alone. When someone thinks of loneliness, they usually think only of being alone, without companionship, unlike when a man, alone, sets out to reach a peak where the sunset is of unsurpassed beauty, or dives deep into the sea to see creatures and landscapes most people don't. Solitude can be very rich in experience and beauty, usually only if the act is voluntary, where as loneliness is almost never beautiful, whether it's voluntarily achieved or not, the only point of dissimilarity either way is in the mind of the person experiencing them. These were some of the topics of conversations with Vera, we'd go on endlessly.

When Fred and I weren't together, by choice or because our parents decided we shouldn't be, I would hang out with Peter. Just before I turned fifteen, the next May or June, Peter and I decided to visit his new girl friend, Madeline Hall. I gave him her phone number, since she gave it to me, and I was too shy to ever call. I just held onto the number, like some status quo, saying yes, I can get girls numbers if I want them. I let Peter call instead, figuring she wouldn't find him attractive for long. We had to hitchhike to Somerville to get to the hospital she was in. She got sick, but I never found out what the problem was.

At this point in my life I was short, from age twelve to fifteen, barely five foot three, and I wore Peter's' six inch platform shoes this day, black and very uncomfortable. So we went and saw her, she liked Peter a lot, but didn't click with me as she did at camp. We had some good conversations then, and I thought she was deep, now reality set in. It's different when your sixty miles from home, with no one to know who you are. She was much less fictional when she was at camp. She was pretty good looking, as well, and I had always thought that if you can look at someone long enough to see the full picture beneath their first layer, you can determine if you can handle the view for the rest of your life. Her full picture was looking more and more like a badly made B movie, which was sad.

Now here we were, hitching back home from Somerville around ten at night, thumbs out, and very tired, I liked to keep moving while hitching, at least making some progress. Pete didn't and always stopped to rest every mile or so, and we'd sit, our thumbs still out towards a unconcerned anonymous row of cars, waiting for one to stop, wondering at times if one would just end our trip and hit us, just to keep our minds busy.

At the corner of route twenty-two and the road to the hospital, there was a Pontiac car dealership. The demo car was sitting alone at the rear corner, keys in it, and Peter saw that from the street somehow, in the dark. He said, "Let's go! Man! Free wheels! Free car!" He kept jumping up and down shouting like he won jeopardy or something. After telling him to shut up before someone comes out, I debated in my mind for a second how much trouble this would cause, and figured if the place wanted their demo car safe, they shouldn't have left the keys in it, and we were in bad need of a ride, so we went with it and whatever destiny it brought.

Pete drove first, a nightmare from hell type of death ride with no specific pattern or control in all possible directions, and it didn't take long before I took over. I couldn't believe he actually listened to me when I told him to pull over and let me drive, I guess he thought his life was worth enough to listen to me this time, he definitely was not comfortable driving. He apparently couldn't figure out how to stay in lanes, accelerate or decelerate when needed, and reading signs for him was tough, never mind the fact no other driver was willing to be patient while he learned how to drive, especially truck drivers. Now that I think about it, it's probably the closest to death I've ever been to at that point possibly. We were honked at dozens of times, and if any car that passed us happened to be a cop, we would not have had a very long ride.

So I took over driving, and for me, it felt pretty natural and insane at the same time, as though I were meant to be here even if I wasn't supposed to be. The traffic laws were usually clear enough, but everyone drove differently. I was having a blast, since this was the first car I ever drove. We kept the car for four days, leaving it at a dead end next to the woods at the end of my street, on Peter's side of the woods, and that made it almost exactly half the distance to his house.

I kept the keys, Peter didn't mind. We rode around, picked up hitchhikers, went through drive through service places, and got stuck one time in a storm in the mud on the side of the road, where a tow truck pulled us out without question. We never got pulled over, since I never drove badly. It was a nineteen seventy-five brand new Pontiac Sunbird, a nice car.

Eventually, the town police called me, saying they knew we had the car, and asked me where it was now. They said no charges would be pressed if no damage occurred, which it didn't, and they told me the owner was at fault for leaving keys in it. So I told him, and the keys were in it by the time they got there. I always figured Peter ratted us out, and I discovered later that he did. Luckily, my parents and his grandma never learned about that incident right away, and I'm not sure they ever knew.

Since nineteen seventy-five I always kept a copy of my parents car keys, in case of emergency, or if my parents went out and I was bored. They did not know, of course, since I took the spare keys when they were out one day and rode my bike downtown, copied them, and had them back before anyone knew they were gone. I would get to drive my dad's nineteen seventy-five Olds Cutlass years before I had a license to do so. The first few times driving my dad's car were after the Sunbird experience, around the block, down to town, always making certain the car and house looked exactly as my parents left it. I had a habit of cleanliness, and I didn't like disorganization.

At fifteen in the summer just before turning sixteen, I drove my dad's seventy-five Cutlass up to Eric's house anytime my parents let me stay home myself and only if they wouldn't be home till very late or the next day. I drove all the way to Wayne, roughly thirty miles. We would drive around the mall, town, slide around on ice, and we just had fun. Never did crash this car till many years later, and that wasn't my doing. I remember my mother driving me to his house for a sleep over, in the same car, wondering if I should tell her I already drove up here and ask her to let me drive some, but I knew the answer already.

I can still hear Eric calling me a crazy fucker, the first time I showed up at his house. I had just parked the car down the street by a school and walked over to his house and knocked, when he opened the door I thought he'd crap himself, bouncing around telling me he couldn't believe I was at his door, asking how the hell I got there, and stuff like that. He had quite a fit when I told him how, started laughing and yelling, getting as wild as ever with his brother, who just looked at him like he was nuts.

When his parents asked me where my mom was, I just told them that she was shopping and would get me later, and she dropped me off, and then we'd walk to the school where the car was parked. I told Eric about being in normal school now, he said they weren't ready for me; I agreed and called him a FE. Cruising around was like some long awaited dream life to him, I was fairly amused too. But I didn't like the way he kept yelling out the window at girls, calling attention to us without me having any license or legal method of operating a car there, I definitely didn't want to be caught and had to be home before my parents were, stopping for gas as well. He shut up after a while, once I explained the consequences of being caught doing what we were doing.

Upon returning to real high school, I realized that I was viewing life from the prospective of having traveled to and through many places, sort of worldly yet without leaving the country, the traveler who was allowed to see this country's greatest natural wonders, but I was not viewed in that way at school, so my attitude must have seemed confusing, unwarranted.

I also noticed how different some of the girls I knew looked to me, especially since I wasn't in any classes with them for over a year. They became women, and watching them became much more interesting and enjoyable. I would watch the prettier ones whenever I could, admire their new shapes and curves and existing in awe of how deeply desirable they became to me, how perfectly art like in form and shape they were.

I was still much too insecure to approach them, and along with knowing what they may have been told about me by other former classmates I figured any relationship was improbable. So I admired them from a distance, like living works of art, and I knew one day one of them would be mine to keep forever as a missing part of my existence and purpose, or so I expected. Only the right one could be the inspiration I needed to be whatever it is that I was meant to be in this life, to accomplish what I would accomplish, if anything, with my female counterpart, my true soul mate. Looking at beautiful women would be something I would never get tired of, I realized.

I lived a lot further away from High school than grammar school, about a mile, and Peter always went the same direction as I if I were to make a strait L shaped path to school, because he lived in the apartments that you reach going through the woods at the end of my street, after crossing the next main street. I would walk sometimes, through the woods and past the train station, where Peter would be walking usually or I would go to his house to get him sometimes.

Most of the time I got a ride to school, my mother believing there was too slim a chance of me actually going to school if she let me walk and this could be true. Even if she did drop me off, nothing would prevent me from just waiting till she drove off, then walking away towards where ever I felt like going, but that was not too often really. Never on the day of a test or other activity that I would enjoy, and I knew I had to pass my classes.

My mother usually picked me up after school, with a full complement of activities to do, things like teach the handicapped people to plant things, using a dibble, seeding, and watering. I did this a few times a week; since my parents thought it would be a good activity to keep me out of trouble and away from Fred. I found it entertaining; to a degree, usually frustrating, but the dibble part of the experience was just too funny. It's just a four or so inch cylinder, which comes to a blunt point at the end like an oversized magic marker, for making holes in soil to put seeds in, but just the word its self seemed extremely comical to me, and to anyone I shared it with, after taking some home for display and as a topic of conversation. There were many conversations about what the hell a dibble is, and where it possibly came from. Thus, many songs about dibble dops arose, the expressions dibble dick and dibble wad came to be, and much fun was had by all about an odd word.

Both Fred and Peter thought the word admirably strange and quite usable. When Fred saw it, he discovered that the top end of it comes off, and decided it would be useful for the stash of whatever he happened to have. He kept poking me with it, too. But I had my own, and was able to fend off most attacks with the threat of equal retaliation.

Teaching mentally disabled adults to use one was the epitome of ridiculousness from my viewpoint. Just make a hole and put the seed in, why create an entire tool just for this? Okay it could hold the seeds, but it really didn't seem like a necessity. It's like something to turn a doorknob for you, or flick the light switch for you, how needed could it be? Those things appear more desirable now with technology allowing you the pleasure, like the clap on, clap off device, which seems like the ultimate device of laziness.

These unfortunate people were very friendly, but couldn't hold a thought for more than a few seconds, which seemed sad to me, in a lot of ways. But they didn't mind, living each moment as it came like a puppy, with no regrets or shame, just permanent children, whose main focus was fun and minor accomplishments that normally intelligent people take for granted. I could relate to that, but even I had limits. Fortunately, none of them were like Barney's sister, she didn't go to this school, which I found interesting but good for obvious reasons.

Then they let me meet Ernest. When I was about sixteen years of age, they introduced me to an autistic man named Ernest and they told me to teach him how to swim, knowing how well I swam myself. So I spent the next few months on various nights teaching someone with no personality or reaction to anything how to swim. The only words out of Ernest's mouth were imitations of any words he heard spoken to him, like a big parrot.

I was also the only normal male at the YWCA, and thus had to get all the mentally handicapped men dressed and undressed, along with Ernest, because the women in charge were not allowed in the men's dressing room. Watching thirty-year-old mentally challenge men sit naked continually playing with their almost non-existent penises, passing gas and picking their noses while staring at me and giggling, was not what I thought being a teenager should be about. Pete made these people seem intelligent by contrast.

I figured I was proving a point, that I was able to help others, plus I loved swimming for any reason. I actually got Ernest to jump off the diving board, something no one else could accomplish. Too bad one can't think of these people as friends in any normal context of the word, and most appear to be on the five or six year old level of intelligence, higher communication was not to be had, and it was mighty disgusting, as well. Between the odor and the blatant way they control and disperse their bodily fluids, I could not last all that long, and asked if I could work at my dad's pilot plant instead. Dangerous, volatile chemicals seemed less nasty compared to some of the things the handicapped people do. Plus in a lab I might learn something more useful to me for later in life.

During the first year back in high school, I was immediately put in the troublemaker and a handicapped class, before I even got through the door, which was attributed to the level of education I received in reform school. I had always assumed the curriculum was the same. I had a homeroom, and took regular gym, but for main subjects like math, English, and history I was only in one class. I was not retarded, a drug addict, or even that much trouble anymore, at least in school, but still treated as such. I never forgot the poster in that room saying, "If a man does not keep pace with his companions, perhaps it is because he hears a different drummer. Let him step to the music which he hears, however measured or far away". Henry David Thoreau had a great point. The assumption was my education was lacking due to the environment I came from, I was behind the rest of the students of my age because of Bonnie Bull, supposedly.

Actually, I was ahead of most, with the exception of trigonometry or calculus. I assumed the student body didn't want to tolerate who I was, and thus I was ostracized into the remedial or supplemental world of uninspired education. I did have people threaten me, like saying the rabbit killer getting his, but no one ever made good on it, or even tried, and I was never worried, since surviving the "punishment" made me feel braver and slightly indestructible, and idol threats were nothing new to me. And now, I heard the fear in their voices as threats were made, something completely new to me.

I was indeed going to step to my own drummer, and that was all. In subjects I enjoyed, like chemistry and science, they could not keep my pace, so I would become bored. I did take drum lessons and piano, played the part of a baseball player from the play "Our Town" in a school production, and maintained exactly enough credits to graduate. Only my name appears in the yearbook, I didn't let them take my picture for school at any time.

I played the gym class sports, had never been pinned wrestling, held the unconfirmed furthest ball hit record, and acted pretty much like a normal student. The faculty didn't have a clue as to what to do with me or how to classify the group I was part of; I was just a problem due to the existing student body's attitude towards me. So I would leave, a lot, and just go to Scotch Plains to visit the people who knew me for things other than the great rabbit incident two years ago.

I did tell Fred about that, and he thought I should have just killed the rabbit when I had the chance. This, coming from a guy who fed baby birds in a nest in his yard, because he killed the mother accidentally, seemed not that strange, believe it or not. The birds didn't live too long, but one did survive we think. Fred's school was more fun since I didn't have to attend any classes, and only did for fun, which I thought strange, to enjoy a different school just because it's different, and I didn't like school in general to begin with. I guess no obligation or responsibilities helped make it fun overall, nothing I had to do, just hang out and socialize with no pressure.

That first year back in high school was surreal, walking down the halls and seeing the kids I didn't know, most of which were basically expressionless. One's who remembered me gave the look of fear, disapproval or resentment which didn't bother me; it was just strange to be in hallways in a real school again, as if the two year expulsion was really a vacation. I remember distinctly when I would go to lunch in the cafeteria, wherever I chose to sit, the people already at the table would immediately leave and go to another table, even if most didn't know me, the class I was in was spread evenly enough to have at least one former classmate at every table, and the words spread fast like a flu.

I could sit completely alone in a room of two hundred students, which was not unpleasant, it was like having real power, whether it was negative or not, and I enjoyed the peacefulness with no fear of any person there to interrupt my meal. It amused me to see such unfounded fear, and it was a fun tool to manipulate them with, though I thought I never had to consciously. The most anyone would do is call me names under their breath, or whisper to a friend or two, which meant nothing, and by now seemed perfectly normal, irrelevant.

Only Peter or Vera would sit with me, Vera only if she wasn't out with her boyfriend already, which is usually where she went. Gay Troy would sit with me too, even though I didn't exactly want him to, since he was only attempting to annoy me and trying to get some reaction from me. He never could, and all he did get was psychoanalyzed to the point where he'd have to leave before he would start crying. The one and only attribute Troy and I shared was that no one would sit with him either.

The only fun I had that year in the form of a school wide prank, and the last one I ever did was when I dumped castor oil into the coffee pot in the teachers' lounge, causing many to need several bathroom breaks throughout the day, except my teacher who didn't drink any of course. That was the end of school and peer related mischief, no one bothered with me anymore so no further action was needed, an era was over, the path went elsewhere.

Now I was too busy either studying, or figuring out ways to get out and go down to Fred's school to hang out. I did study, but only once for any specific test or subject, the first time was always the best one, and if I was going to remember it, that was how I'd do it. Just as in grammar school, too much studying was adverse to my resulting grade for the test or class, so I wouldn't over study.

I will now reprint my grades as given in a transcript, going from ninth grade in Bonnie Bull up to twelfth grade. Both systems used numbers instead of A's and B's, making an A to equal a one, a B equaled a two, C for three, and etcetera. In ninth grade I took general math, English, physical education, science and U. S. history, and my grades were, respectively, three, three, three, two and P for passed. So C's were most common, as usual, since I wouldn't do homework, and was distracted frequently by extracurricular activity constructive or otherwise, but I still got all twenty-five credits. Then in tenth grade, for Physical Education, Supplemental English, math, science, Regular biology, and personal typing, I got a two, two, two point five, one point five, one point five and a four point five. So one point five equals an A minus, and four point five equaled a D minus, but still enough to get the two and a half credits, and I totaled twenty-seven and a half for that year. The Supplemental were the courses I took with the troublemaker class, but in Biology I was so proficient they had to put me in a regular course, since the supplemental class was so far behind me in that subject.

Onto eleventh grade, where I took Physical Ed, Supplemental English, social studies, and history, regular Algebra, biology, biology lab, ecology, and consumer science, and received a one point seven, three, two point seven, two point seven, two point seven, two point seven, three point five, four, and three point two, respectively. I wasn't present in much of that year, thus my grades reflected that. I earned my thirty-five credits, though.

In twelfth grade, my least attended year, I took Physical Ed, supplemental English, social studies, regular geometry and photography, where I received a three point three, three point three, failed social studies with a W, which meant I never showed up, failed geometry with a five for the same reason, and four point five for photography, and earned twelve and a half credits. This gave me a total of one hundred credits, exactly enough to graduate ranked about one hundred sixty third out of two hundred ninety-four students, with a final rank of two hundred nineteen. My SAT scores were three hundred seventy on V, and four hundred on M, whatever those meant I wasn't sure and I never worried about it myself. Those are the actual statistics for grades, which also meant not much to me, since school always took a back seat to my social life at that point.

Although neither of our parents approved, Fred and I got together at his house again once in a while or somewhere in between more often. At his house, his neighbor had a pond in his back yard and I decided to go look closer at, trying to find snakes as usual, near the rim of the pond where I knew they would be if any were there. Fred's whole back yard was woods, so it was fun to explore, even though Fred said it had nothing, he had done it all already.

The pond had a couple of ducks living there, didn't find any other things larger than salamanders, no turtles, frogs, just the ducks, which I decided would make good moving targets for throwing rocks at, Fred agreed. I just missed one duck and the two of them flew away together, then suddenly the neighbor kid who's pond it was, a bit older than both Fred and I, came running out screaming to leave the ducks alone. Fred just laughed and I just stood there, he proceeded with a lecture about wildlife and rocks, but wouldn't direct any of it towards Fred, I think he was afraid of him. After some interesting cursing, Fred gave him some of his own, stating the fact that they were just ducks and who really cares, then we went back to Fred's driveway so Fred could play around with an engine he was fixing, building, or whatever, also to get some food and drinks from his mom, and call some girls.

Then we decided to walk to town, down power lines through Fanwood, and back. We went to the park where the swings were, since Fred liked to swing very high and jump off the swing and land on my back, his idea of fun, the Chinese acrobat. It was never as graceful, but he couldn't knock me over. Then, he showed me how to make free phone calls from a payphone, by connecting the metal inside the screw on speaking end of the hand set with the phones coin box, using a Pepsi pull tab lid, which gives the phone dial tone.

If this could not be done because the rotary dial was locked somehow, he could click the hook switch fast enough to imitate the pulse that makes digits register, thus dialing a number, but that was hard to do and he usually got a wrong number. We would crank call everywhere on the phones we could access, different ends of the country; I would use my Jacque Cleauseu accent and ask people about monkeys in rooms without a proper license. He had some type of speaker he was able to wire into the ear part of the handset to make a speakerphone with so we both could laugh at the people we reached.

It was dark on the way back to Fred's one night, and Fred decided to toss a rock through some guy's window because he said the guy did him some wrong one time, and he was an asshole. Seconds after Fred threw it, the guy came bolting out of the house, saw Fred and I standing there, Fred took off, so I did too, and the guy chased me instead of Fred. I stopped by a large rock a few hundred feet away, and he ran at me and went airborne with his foot coming toward my head, so I just stepped aside and watched him hit the rock with his knee as he tried to stop. I told him I did nothing, but he just kept calling me little scum bag, a fucking deviate, little bastard, and the like, I guess because he was in pain from hitting his knee.

He got up and started hitting me, tried to give the low shot knee a few times, failed to do any damage and I just fell to the ground after a couple swings he meant to do damage with, and pretended it hurt some. I didn't really want to hurt him, either. I was able to move the parts of my body that he couldn't hurt in front of every swing, and felt much like a turtle.

I kept telling him two guys going the other way did it, and were just out of sight when he came out. So once he discovered he wasn't getting anywhere hitting, he stopped, and asked me where the other guy was. I asked him which other guy, the one I was with or the other two, but he just tried to hit me again when I said that. I should have had him arrested for assault, but he hit like a little kid and didn't faze me. Fred was home. My parents had to come get me, because the police were called.

When I got home, Fred called and said he told the police he saw two other guys going the other way do the throwing, but he just ran scared. The guy apparently recognized Fred, and told the police about him as well. Maybe Fred's parents believed he would be scared of something, being naive enough. We had the same story when we weren't even discussing the issue, and we always knew what the other person would say. The whole world was ours to wreak havoc upon, with the usual teen blindness to consequences leading the way, a continuation of our roaming path to adventure as it was in camp, and as it would be intermittently over the next two decades. Fred was not without any compassion though.

We had run into several situations where we actually helped people out of bad situations, like fixing a broken down car for some old lady once, he usually would try helping with car issues since he believed he knew how, or doing gardening and home maintenance for an elderly guy named Mr. Tuzo, along with helping police to get a child porn seeking store owner off the street. We met the police so often we knew them by name, I guess they figured since were so good at causing them grief, we could help them too.

The porn guy owned a store in Fanwood, and Fred was very into electronics and gadgets, we both had citizens band radio names, he was Turtle I was Snake, my call letters were KAC-five-one-o-three-two, don't recall his. We went to the store and hung around often, watching the guy Chris do various things with cameras and CB's, pictures and frequencies, and Fred would help, he was actually a nice guy I thought. What we didn't know at the time, till we found some pictures laying around his back room and decided to peak in a window once after hours was that a few of the thirteen or fourteen year old girls we knew would go there to drink at night after the store was closed. The only names I recall right now were Lilly Longe, Tonya Rhuky, and Betsy Black, but Fred never really said what he saw. Chris supplied all the booze, and would take pictures of them scantily clad, as we saw in the pictures. They became uninhibited due to the alcohol and though

Chris never got physical with them or molested them, just modeled them as far as we knew; we didn't think this was right, so we let Scotch Plains authorities gain knowledge of our findings.

If it were not for Fred, my life would not be as it is, and vice versa. Chains of events led me many places with him, Vera and Peter also had impact on some events that would occur as well. There was no doubt that destiny had unfolded, the path was changing rapidly at nearly every turn, I was allowing others to choose the path to take, never worried about what glory or consequence would be waiting along the way or at the end of certain directions, not feeling like I had to choose a path myself, if I didn't want to do something, I wouldn't.

It was a point of life where I was unconcerned about what lies ahead, riding the wind of life as a leaf, always believing somewhere in my head that it all would work out with positive results, regardless of obstacles or setbacks, and also with or without whomever I was traveling with at the time, or based on their ultimate destiny that may not include me, but may have been influenced by me. An attitude greatly influenced by my parents I figured.

The next event I can recall was the teaching of handicapped, as mentioned before, just before working in my dad's lab. And although the experience with handicapped hardened me enough to live through my own child's formula vomit, it did give me an understanding of true patience. It also saddened me, to think that any force in the universe would allow such anonymous suffering, and I kept thinking how anonymous could it really be? What they must have done at some point in their life, or another, which seems possible, must have been pretty unforgivable, or perhaps payment in exchange for having all the fruits of life given to them, locked within them now or from past existence.

I believe that if there is a hell, it may possibly be reincarnation, as bugs, worms, or amoebas, possibly. But if you think about it logically from what's learned in chemistry and biology, the energy needed to sustain life cannot disappear as far as we know; it must take another form, or spread into other existing states, whether it's an Eagle, Dolphin, or some other creature. Become a tree if you're a stubborn person, or a Peregrine Falcon, if you're very lucky.

Could someone like Timothy McVey become the about to be murdered or still born infants all over the world, and get to be born again and killed repeatedly for every soul he dispersed? Along with being pitied each and every time as one of God's nasty little equalizing tricks? Kind of makes it sound hopeful or justified yet morbid, and I'm sure there is equal justice for such people, all people, whether we understand it or not. Hostile people become a moth, endlessly banging their heads into a hot bulb, or a sea turtle offspring, living longer than any creature should live, or become the life at the bottom of the sea with no known senses as we understand them, it was all theoretical anyway, not yet provable one way or the other. Those kinds of things fueled my thoughts often, the purpose of it all, where we all came from and where we'll go in the end, nothing relative to events currently in progress.

Fred couldn't dispel my philosophies, and had some interesting theories of his own, and his thing was the philosophy of the moment. What does each moment mean, and usually it was there because of a dibble or a Lefline from planet Plutarski. We had our own language, symbols of what we knew already, and we baffled most people around us with conversations about apparently nothing, except Fred and I understood each other completely. We agreed on most things. Gumball.

This was around nineteen seventy-six, and one of my favorite forms of entertainment was watching Fred manipulate others into things they wouldn't consider doing had he not intervened. We loved debating religion with the Jehovah's, watching them leave confused was fun. I explained to them once the purpose of rosary prayers, simple repetition so that in the moment you die, these words you'll recall first, and this is the point somehow that asking to be safe in the next form of life is all about spiritual understanding and consciousness. Two people die in a car, one's last thoughts are "Oh, shit, I'm fuckin dead!" the other persons is "Oh my God, help me!" Who's gonna be happier? Guess everyone finds out eventually.

For a change of topic, I'll list all the cars I recall owning and some I drove, just so I can keep track of the vehicles that carried me along my path. The first car I owned myself was a nineteen seventy-nine red Plymouth Horizon, four speed, four door. My parents bought the Horizon for me, knowing I would need some way to get to work. I eventually totaled it on ice on route twenty-two with a girl named Shelly inside, and a future girlfriend of mine, Cheyanne, and there we no injuries.

I drove my parent's seventy three-dodge Coronet, wrecked it twice on ice, on the way to school, and with Peter in front of Scotch Plains High School, but I never owned it. Peter thought for years that I aimed his side of the car at the tree. Just blind luck, really. I never had an accident that was my fault or not caused by snow and ice, also considered no fault. After that is when I owned my dad's Cutlass, till someone hit me, which I'll describe later.

Then I had a seventy-eight ford LTD, which had one brown door and was white. I drove that across the country and back, seeing more places than I had seen with any other vehicle. Then, I got a seventy-three Plymouth Fury, owned by a combustion engineer friend of my dads, and in perfect condition. It eventually didn't need a key to start, had no second gear, couldn't be locked, and the seats began falling apart. The speedometer also didn't work, which cost me two speeding tickets and six points, because I had to pace myself with other cars.

I usually drove in the fast lane, and twice my pace car was speeding on route seventy-eight with me right behind them, but the police stopped me instead of them for some reason. This car was slowly disintegrating, and it needed a lot of expensive work after a while, like transmission and head gasket work, so my parents decided a new eighty-five Cutlass supreme would be the answer, the dealer claiming the trade-in car totaled, so we got nothing for it.

This car I traded in for my nineteen ninety five Chevy Astro van bought in Florida, nine years later. During the time I had the Cutlass, I also had my parents nineteen eighty Oldsmobile Starfire, making this time period the first one in which I owned two cars, but this car gave me no trade in value, and I got rid of that car before going to Florida. Then was the two thousand three GMC Safari van, a two thousand three Kia Rio a two thousand three Dodge Caravan, a nineteen ninety-five Olds Cutlass Ciera, and a two thousand eight Chevy Trailblazer. That is all for cars in my history, besides other peoples I've driven, or were stolen by Fred then driven by me. I also drove a school bus for many years, but those were not mine of course.

Back to 1976, or the time period in which I obtained my Scuba license, in the middle of the winter before turning sixteen. It was a ten-week course, and we practiced in the YMCA pool first, then for our test we went to the Hamburg Quarry somewhere in North Jersey. The instructor Lex drove his own car off a cliff into the place some years ago, and it sat about one hundred feet down on the bottom of the quarry.

We wore wet suits, and we had to cut a hole in the ice to get into the water, and that cold shot is one I'll never forget. Once your suit is full of water, you warm up, especially if you urinate in it. As part of the test your supposed to take off all your gear while ninety feet down, with the instructor watching. I simply refused to remove my mask, due to the cold, but he passed me anyway since that was only a small percentage of the field test score, and I did everything else very well. I never had to pee to warm myself, but I did think about it when we first hit the water, almost every time.

I went to class at night, a couple times a week, and I always got to swim in the pool as well, before, during and after class. The Y was fun; my dad always had a tough time getting me to leave the pool, mainly because the air was colder than the water. I felt very comfortable in water, swimming was one of the greatest things there were, according to me, the abusive method in which I learned it seemed to pay off. I didn't care that I had to shower around a bunch of strange old guys, who seemed to exist for no other reason than to be here, and to watch young people bathe. I knew this building quite well, and could hide from anyone if I chose to; there were a lot of places to go. Only my dad suffered that game, the Y was fun to hide in, and I never let him wait too long, plus I usually was in the pool anyway, not too hard to find.

Music at this point was mainly pop, greatest hits type stuff, and much too boring and non-influential to contemplate writing about usually, like Kung Fu fighting, disco and such, the genre of the time, not my interest. My father liked Beethoven and other classical music, and they were impressive, but I wasn't the type to sit and listen to music for long. None of it played any part in my choice of paths, or inspired me in any great way at this point in my life.

I also owned the Star Wars movie sound track, and a Monty Python album, which wasn't musical in any sense of the word. For those who noticed while reading, I make almost no mention of news events during my life, because I never really worried about news, don't know why, I just never cared about what the media has to say, even when I was in the news myself. It all seems too one sided, and to get the full story I believe you need to see it for yourself anyway.

Besides, the events of the sixties, seventies and eighties are well documented and known enough by most people, and had no direct impact upon my road through life as far as I knew, thus, why reminisce about it? My parents worried about the news enough to cover me; they were very into current events, always trying to get me into the realism and politics of it. How important it all was, how it may affect your life, what can be done about it, all high level topics of their conversations.

My dad was a very scientific man, when he gave advice it was always quite calculated, very direct, with no inflection or purpose other than to educate and make a point. He usually was working on papers with a scientific calculator, imbedded deep within the thoughts of making his dream and ideas a reality, and definitely self controlled from the logic center of his mind. I knew he loved my mother, I had walked in on them in embarrassing moments, and I could only hope that my marriage relationship could be as solid as theirs seemed to be, as lasting and permanent, forever knowing only one woman for all of my life, as much a partner as my parents were partners in their life's' quest. The most arguing I heard was mainly about me, since I defied logic, or so my dad said. But even so their patience was astounding, something I knew I could count on for my entire life, and more solid than anyone I ever met, unlimited, it appeared.

Around this time my family went to California for my sister's wedding, I believe April 15th 1977 was the date. We flew, and there were two ceremonies, one Hebrew and one Catholic. Church for the Catholic ceremony, a hotel room for the Hebrew, and the Rabbi wore sneakers I recall vividly. During our time there I took some cash from my dad, the keys to the rental car, and went for a cruise through San Francisco.

They have weird roads, all set across the mountain, with odd grades of slopes and bumps. Liked the famous Lombard Street, so steep it had to be paved in the shape of an S, descending and ascending in a zigzag fashion. I was a very safe driver, and just got lectured to when I came back without incident. Had to give my dad the money I didn't spend at Fisherman's Wharf back. Very gay town, literally, and scenic, western, historic and impressive, but I've seen it before.

Helen was married in one of the oldest houses in the city, she knew the people who owned it. I got to eat some really good food, play golf at Lincoln, the local course which was just one hill after another. Then we drove to Carmel, which is quite awesome, nearly as much so as the drive there. I didn't get to experience the unique feeling of an earthquake, it didn't seem feasible and I really couldn't imagine what that would be like, maybe one day I will. The whole trip was fun, and I was happy for my sister, though I likely never expressed it.

The next thing I recall after we came home is a bike ride to Fred's house on July seventh, nineteen-seventy-seven. I was going about forty or fifty miles an hour down Diamond Hill road, and a school bus was coasting along side of me. At the bottom of this road is a traffic light, and the intersection is level, then it goes up a small hill, and at the peak of that hill is a little rock wall on the right holding a home's property line off the street, and then the road continues down another small hill.

The light was green, and I stayed right next to the bus, or vice versa, and at the crest of the small hill were some rocks on the street that had fallen off the wall, and the bus just kept getting closer to me by the second, till I bumped my shoulder off the bus, hit a loose rock that was in the middle of the side of the road, flew over my handle bars, and stopped myself on another rock with my knee. As I lay there bleeding, someone going the other way stopped and said, "Are you OKAY?" I said no, and I tried to move a little but couldn't, and he just drove away, muttering something as he left. The bus never stopped either, it just kept rolling along like nothing happened.

Then an ambulance came by, the same direction I came, went by me to the bottom of the hill and about a hundred yards further, then stopped and backed up to me and gave me a ride home. Why not the hospital, I didn't know, but that's where my mom brought me immediately. There was nothing broken, just a badly bruised kneecap. This kept me on crutches for six weeks, it would have been less if Peter didn't kick my leg behind the knee when I just began walking on my own again, just to make me fall. His grandma and my parents lifted the rule of not being together by then, which was a bad idea I thought at that moment. I used my crutch to chase Peter out, got him once too, the stupid dibble. I got even with him later, too, by pouring itching powder, which is really just loose fiberglass I learned, down the back of his shirt one day. Peter used many curses that day, which I never really did usually. I also learned that it's very hard to go to the bathroom, when your knee is hurt.

I spent the first few weeks in bed with my TV and stuff, basically bed ridden during the next major event in our area, July thirteenth, when all the television stations went out. The great New York black out and I was crippled. How poetic. While I was disabled, I talked to Fred, Vera, and Peter by phone a lot. That was the most debilitating injury I would suffer in my life, to this point so far. When I slid on my shoulder down a ladies driveway because I took the turn off a hill too wide on my bike, I was in shock, but only scraped.

The next biking accident was while riding bikes with Fred and I ran his arm over, with my bike, because he fell in front of me. I landed in the front yard of a house and a guy came running out yelling, "are you OKAY"? We both just started laughing hysterically, not being one bit injured, this time. He just looked at us with a confused look, and went back inside. This knee injury took about two months to recover from, the time was quite boring and gave me lots of time to contemplate my own mortality, realizing injuries can happen that change lives, never knowing when the next debilitating injury could or would occur.

I remember another day going down Johnson Road on my bike with no breaks, before route seventy-eight was completed across this road. At the bottom of this large hill was a stop sign, and a fifty-mile an hour speed limit street called Johnson Drive was the cross road at this stop sign. Across the road was another road, mostly dirt, and it led to the deserted village of the Watchung Reservation.

I flew across Johnson Drive just missing a car by inches; my only concern was if I could catch a wild pine or corn snake in the village. Never mind being inches from death, that wasn't important. It seemed that nothing was going to break my bones, in my own teenage indestructible mind. I never did catch those species of snakes, either. The biggest snake I ever caught was a six-foot common water snake, which put up quite a fight. It had thirty babies two weeks after I brought it home, and those I let go, back in the village where I found their mother. No wonder the snake was so displeased with me.

Once my knee healed, I heard from Eric again. Eric's trip on my life's path with me ended after Eric's Bar Mitzvah I had went to some months before. At the party I sang Bad, Bad Leroy Brown and The Cats in the Cradle, then stayed overnight at his house. I took something out of his dad's office at some point, and had not heard from him for a while after that. He called me one day to ask me if I took something of his dad's, and when I told him I had, he became quite pissed and said he didn't need friends like me, he got blamed by his dad for this at first, and don't call him or come over anymore. That roads exit in Wayne closed down permanently; no signs for Eric's house existed anymore.

I think my reply was just "OK Stymebob", and I hung up. I don't even remember what the thing was, probably a paperweight or something. It didn't matter; I had some other closer friends to occupy my time. Plus, his dad was a furrier, and I thought this was a very environmentally unfriendly business, along with cruel, inhumane, needless and stupid, to be used only if your survival requires it. Though our trip across the country together will always remain a high point memory in my life, I could live without ever seeing him again. Thanks for the memories, stymebob.

Vera was whom I considered as the girl I had my first deep relationship with. Vera refused to be hindered or intimidated by everyone's attitude towards me, didn't care what anyone thought about her sitting with me. She enjoyed talking and I did too, she knew me, knew how I really was and thought I was interesting to talk with, telling of all my adventures and experiences so far, and how open I was in discussing any topic she could think of. This was fine with me, I thought she was fun too, and I liked talking with someone who could actually respond in a normal way, express normal viewpoints and the philosophical ones, much like I did, and look good doing it, since she was quite attractive.

Vera was who I discussed all my life's events with at that time, and most of my thoughts and feelings of what love meant and should mean. She was my listener, as I was hers, and I did hope one day she'd be considering me as a future possible soul mate for life, but was content to just be around her. We did science projects together, talked on the phone continuously, and always got along. We studied things like telekinesis, psychology, and social behavior in general together as part of science projects, which overflowed to our personal lives, and she would always be quite open and truthful, in all ways.

We'd observe others and enjoy their predictable reactions to certain events, knowing what they'd do before they did it. She was only four foot eleven, brown hair, and her eyes, though I don't know what color they were, always caught my attention. They were very sexy and deep, and it amazed me what I could feel just by staring into them, and we had played staring contests, I had seen them happy and crying, wasted and indifferent, angry and confused, truly a window into the soul, and her window I liked looking into often.

She liked drugs like Quaaludes, Valium, and alcohol, which made her very open. She would call around two in the morning, to discuss why her boyfriend acts as he does, if I thought he would cheat on her, what she can do to prevent this, and why she's always afraid of losing him. She always wanted my viewpoint and comments on things like how she looked today, and if her scar looked too noticeable. She was hit in the upper lip by a football once, and was a little sensitive about how it appeared.

I had at least twice talked Vera out of suicide by drug overdose, because she thought her boy friend cheated on her or was leaving her. I convinced her that she was a good, valuable person, if to no one else, at least to me, and her dying would hurt me a lot and accomplish nothing. She saw the logic of not taking the easy way out eventually, and decided against dying just for some guy. One time I told her I would have to join her, if she really wanted the ultimate final life experience, I would have to come along for the final ride of life, which I think convinced her not to try.

One day, her and her friend, also named Vera, went skinny-dipping in Vera's pool with Peter and I. Swimming in her pool was nothing unusual, we all loved to, but on this occasion, they decided to take it all off, completely by surprise. This was some time after Vera overcame Peter's habit of lifting dresses, obviously, and they actually got along after a while. We had a diver's mask, and that underwater view I will never forget. We let them look, too. They weren't un-eager or bashful either, but did stay on the other side of the pool anyway, just far enough for no contact but plenty close enough to view clearly all details.

Nothing actually happened, neither Vera was going to make things go any further, which I had to explain to Peter, told him to just enjoy the view and don't be concerned about what can you do next. It was a surprise to both Peter and me, all we were originally doing was going for a swim, and then the Vera's just starting throwing their bathing suit pieces out of the pool, it was extraordinary, just that they felt comfortable enough around Peter to actually do that.

EXIT TWELVE

The Road to Procreation Pass

About a month later, Vera called me around the usual time, midnight, and said, "Chris, I need something from you". She and I were much closer than we knew or cared to acknowledge, she was for all intent and purposes my best friend of the time, including Fred and Peter and she was a hell of a lot prettier to look at that than either of them. She was the only person at this time in my life who never called me Greenie.

I would do almost anything for her, which she knew, and I figured that eventually it would pay off with reciprocal feelings, so when I asked her what she needed from me so late at night, she said she had to try me. She told me she was extremely horney, and her boy friend was gone for a week now working, and she needed some relief. I assumed she liked what she saw in the pool that day, since water can arouse me, I find it quite erotic.

She told me she was deciding about if her boyfriend was really her best choice, and wanted to know that night if I may be a better choice, and to get there as soon as possible. She decided that in choosing a mate for life, that testing the only other guy she knew in a physical way would decide who was best suited for her, she already knew who was better in a communicative way, and I did too.

This I discussed with her for a while, and tried to demean the meaning of such impulsiveness between us, how this may ruin a good thing, but how honored I was feeling for the offer, and I would enjoy honoring her request immensely, to a degree even she would probably not believe. She claimed it would have no effect on our friendship at all and understood my concerns and apprehension.

I did not want to make light of how deeply I felt for her or how good I wanted to make her feel, or how good I wanted to feel, and that this should be done under better surroundings, or another time. That was the only stipulation she gave, it had to be tonight. I understood her raw desire, which of course sparked my own, and this was normal, but I wanted the first time to be special, and still not reveal to her that it would be the first time for me, fearing she'd rescind the offer after giving it some thought. My own virginity was oddly missed in every conversation we ever had somehow, it just never came up for some reason.

I really could not think of any good reason not to explore, it would be a new path, but it would also shape my belief that our level of communication should be attained before indulging in physical contact, or ideally anyway. So I told her I'd be right over, and I ran, singing the whole way "Girl I've known you very well, I've seen you growing every day, I never really looked before, but now you take my breath away . . ." she did, too.

I never ran that consistently far before, either, never having been that intensely motivated. Had to have been thousands of thoughts running through my head on the way, wondering if I could finally say I had a girl friend, or if I would disappoint her instead, every high and low thought, was I just getting used or using her, could this be the beginning of the ultimate relationship to last eternity, or the end of a great friendship, but the consistent one thought was to keep moving, don't stop till your there, and be as open as she was, as I've always been.

I got to her house, she was out by the pool, and she asked me where we could go. I tried to explain that this would be much more fun if we had all night for me to really show her how good I could be for her, but she claimed that it wasn't possible, not having much time to spare, and she needed me now. She looked determined, and really good for some reason, excited by the opportunity to do something no one she knew would approve of.

Eventually I thought of Peter's house, about one hundred yards from her house, and we went there. She was only wearing slippers and a robe, nothing else. I told Peter I had to talk to Vera privately, so we went into his grandma's bedroom, she wasn't home as I already knew and that's why I thought of his house. Vera said I didn't have to kiss her, even though I wanted to pretty badly, but I didn't get the chance. Her body was nice, definitely wanted her for my first, I don't think she knew it, probably still doesn't.

She began by dropping to her knees and undoing my pants, not wasting a second. I remember thinking if I had showered that day and if I smelled bad or not, always conscious of how clean I was, hoping I would not ruin this with some stench from my body caused by running strait for ten minutes. Her lips were like silk, as if I never had felt silk before in my life and this was the first time as a new born. She didn't need to be there long, or even at all, as I was sufficiently aroused already. Then she stopped and jumped up on the bed, making noise enough to have Peter ask us what was happening.

She just asked him to please not bother us now, and everything is OK. Then she pulled me on top of her, and she maneuvered me in, saying "yeah, just do it, it'll feel great"! She was right about that and just as I peaked, which was pretty quickly, Peter started banging on the door again. She jumped up and wrapped her robe around her, and I was back in my underwear and shorts almost instantly, still shaken from the force of the orgasm, shaking and sweaty, wondering if she was disappointed with the briefness of our encounter and feeling inadequate for the showing I made, peaking much too fast.

Peter said, "What the fuck are you doing in there?" Which made both of us almost laugh out loud, I just replied nothing, and we came out. He asked Vera if she was getting laid in there, she just laughed in his face and we left, leaving Peter confused as ever. I told him what went on the next day, made him giggle too, after punching me out of jealousy. Vera eloped with her boy friend shortly thereafter, and I never saw her again. I talked to her before she left, as often as I usually did, told her do whatever your heart wants, and I never told her she was my first, and I'd remember her forever even if I never saw her again.

She apologized for her actions, understood I never took advantage, and she wanted it this way, and I was the only person she could do anything like that with and still feel comfortable being around or talking with afterwards. She said she would always remember me as the one person who never took anything from her, never manipulated, misguided or used her for anything, the one she knew she could say anything to, and not be held in contempt for her feelings, thoughts or faults, and the only person she could honestly trust implicitly.

She said she did not expect it to be as good as Danny, and understood that the circumstance was unfavorable, and I just said that I had hoped she enjoyed some of our time. She claimed to, and she thought I was OK, but not great. She didn't think she loved me that way, which was why. Doing it at Peter's house made Peter jealous, because he always wanted her too, so we had to go to New York to get him laid as well, he figured, to be fair.

I only wished for a fair chance with Vera, never got it. She would not be my destiny, this one; I lived to love another day. Vera was headed for problems I figured, from drugs or alcohol, since she indulged in them quite often, a problem I didn't believe she could solve without me, and I always wondered what happened to her, still do. Many times I've been better off without following my heart, and I never regretted where it led me, or what path I followed or avoided guided by the pure emotion of lust, love or desire.

Peter and I began to ride the train to Hoboken out of the Murray Hill station often, and then the PATH train to Thirty Third Street, Manhattan. One time upon arriving back home, the extended stairwell from the Erie Lackawanna train car hit me while it left the station, but I was only scraped. I was standing too close to the train as it left, and Peter saw it coming and didn't tell me, I was facing him with my back to the tracks talking about the trip.

He broke out in hysterical laughter as I was knocked to the ground. He thought it was pretty funny, getting hit by a train and not dying, I thought he was an idiot at that moment. I would have to say this was when I was about sixteen years of age still, and I was not a virgin anymore, I could drive and stole a car, I cruise through school with C's and D's, I've seen the country, and now it's time for the visits to the sex dens and whore houses of New York's forty second street area.

We went to a few strip clubs, one favorite I recall, and probably the first one we ever walked into, was the Golden Dollar. This was a place where we eventually knew all the dancers, had sex with none of them but touched them all, drank thirty-dollar tiny bottles of wine, champagne, and soda, the soda for me because I still didn't drink at all. To impress my newer friends I met through Fred like Elton and Jake, we would all go there and I would have the girls sit naked on my lap while I fondled and caressed them, and watch them give Elton or Jake the cold shoulder.

Elton was shocked, Jacob was Impressed, we had some fun there, that one time, hanging out as though we owned the place. I felt like I imagined Fred would, the one with all the female attention, not a virgin, the roles reversed for a change. Though Fred never went here with me, it was during one of the separation times our parents tried often, which only worked when we had others to hang out with, other things to do. Fred said once he didn't care about bars, since it never gets anywhere and he'd rather have his girlfriends.

The bar owner liked Peter and I, because we spent money and we were not assholes, meaning we didn't give the dancers a hard time. The dancers liked us because we weren't just some perverse old men, who they usually had to deal with, and we were young and good looking. They seemed more pleased to have us come in, even though they knew we didn't always have much money, unlike every other bar we tried and were ignored in due to this fact.

They knew how young we were, but the fake ID stand a few blocks away made it hard for some business owners to distinguish, and we were regulars, kind of, going maybe ten times a month for a while. In fact, it was the bars owner who originally suggested the IDs to us, so he wouldn't get in trouble for allowing us entry. Peter would take things from his grandmother and others and sell them in New York, where anyone can sell anything, so we'd have money to spend.

One time when I held up a ten dollar bill in a store on forty second street, a guy standing in the store with us snatched it, ran, and Peter started to give chase, since it was his money this time and I was just buying some knife or switchblade for him that he was too scared to ask for himself. He figured the cracker storeowner would never sell a weapon to a young black kid. Very dangerous and depressing, that area in the seventies, entertaining only in the context of being the sleaziest place anyone could possibly visit. Peter never got his knife or his money back. We were much more careful about showing money anywhere after that.

I always mused at the drug dealers trying to sell us their products, or give us free samples in hopes of causing us to become addicted and return for more. Every ten feet on the street or in the urine smelling tunnel from 33rd to 34th street there was some extremely shady character saying things like: "Good smoke y'all, blow, horse, trips, you name it, ten bucks'll do ya! Got the best shit on the street! Check it out homes!"

We found it hard to keep a straight face and show no concern or fear when we'd say no thanks to each person. I believe half of the degenerates were just undercover cops, anyway, trying to pin users on the spot. Fortunately, though Peter would probably indulge in anything, I still wouldn't. My signature difference with the crowd of my peers throughout my teen years was non-indulgence in any drug or alcohol, which was a strange viewpoint to most of the people I knew, but a great vantage point for me.

Other times, just for a change of scenery, we'd take the path train to its other destination, the World Trade Center. Here, in its massive basement, was where we would slide down the many escalators, years before they put some hardware between the escalators to stop people from doing this. I always marveled at the size of the place, like a city of its own within two great pillars. I remember looking up at the towers at night, thinking that Mother Nature would certainly fell these massive buildings eventually, with a hurricane, tsunami, earthquake or tornado.

I didn't think it wise to build something that large and high, and if they did fall, what a nightmare that would be. I remember wondering what would happen if a plane accidentally flew into one of them, creating a domino effect that would no doubt kill thousands, and hoping that I wouldn't be there if or when it did. My mother was an eyewitness to a famous plane crash when one hit the Empire state building many years ago, and it seemed as if humanity was again tempting fate, or getting too big for our britches, by making these humongous structures.

The escalators led you to the mall portion, but everything was closed when we went, because it was always late at night, so going there was not in its self entertaining, but lying on our backs between the two buildings looking up at the stars was truly poetic and like a scene from a postcard. If you watched close enough, you'd see them move, a really odd feeling, wondering if they'd fall in either direction, not fully comprehending what keeps them from doing so with each forceful gust of wind they endure continuously. It gave the appearance of the earth moving, you could feel the ground pitch as the building did, Peter told me it's how you feel when you do some drugs, just as did Fred. With or without drugs, it was an impressive view the few times I saw it.

Inside, we'd jump turnstiles, ride between the PATH cars, and one time we got back to Hoboken too late for the last train back to our town, around five in the morning, so we slept in the terminal with the homeless. I remember thinking that if I were homeless, I would head for Florida, where I could live by the ocean or bay without the danger of freezing in the winter, and I would only need a fishing pole, shade and a lighter to survive off the land. The tri state area was just too cold to be homeless during the winter. Any southern location would be better suited.

Up on forty second street, Peter tried endlessly to win the three-card monty card game street hustlers play, losing money quicker than if he just burned it. I finally convinced him it was impossible to win after a dozen tries or so, these guys knew their business, and I probably saved Peter a lot of money by stopping him from playing. Told him the bar would be more fun to spend it in, which was true of course. But even that was becoming boring, and there was nothing in the place that would direct our futures, just some naked bodies to look at, always pleasing to see, yet inaccessible to real contact.

Occasionally, we would just ride the subways, the D train through Brooklyn, very late with lots of strange people hanging out or sleeping. We didn't have or carry anything of value visibly, just the money we had to get there and back hidden in our pockets. One time on the subway we had two drunken girls throwing confetti and glitter on Pete and I, then make out with us for a while and leave without a name or phone number exchanged.

I remember one time when three guys who were apparently gang members wanted some money from us; I knew something was up as soon as they walked into the train. One guy just looked at us and said, "hey punks! What do ya got"? I just answered: "nothing, what do ya need"? "We need some bucks" one guy chuckled, "for my girlfriends' birthday, so give it up". I said: "well, I got your bucks swinging, boy, and if you're tough enough, come get some". As I spoke I laughed, then turned around to face the end door and I smashed the subway door with my head, cracking the glass like a rock against a windshield. The guys just laughed and said: "we were just bustin, you're cool with us, fuckin' crazy dude"!

They did appear a little concerned that they may be in danger instead, I found that amusing. Then one guy asked me: "you wanna join our gang?" I said: "Nah, I don't join gangs, we are a gang!" A gang of two, I said, with Peter in full agreement and trying to look intimidating, and that made them laugh for a while. Then they just left, after talking about some good-looking women we saw there, like most guys do, and listening to a stream of pure fiction I created with feats of my strength and endurance, some of which made Peter look at me strangely and as impressed and confused as the other guys were. Too bad I don't remember any; they were pretty funny as I recall, possibly related to events with the inmates of Bonnie Bull.

We also helped homeless get dinner, lunch or whatever, and basically just had fun wandering around the massive city. I had this jacket, the lining in the pockets were cut out purposely by me so the pockets had no end and just went through the whole jacket's lining. Peter and I would go into supermarkets, I'd fill my coat with food, snacks and stuff, and then we'd give the stuff out to the homeless, except the stuff we wanted to keep, like lighters or candy, Peter liked the cough medicine. You'd think that the people in an area with such high crime statistics would be weary and ready for shop lifters but they weren't. Stealing from those who had, giving to those who didn't, seemed honest to some degree, though I knew it wasn't and we weren't Robin Hood and his merry men.

We eventually went back to Forty-Second Street to an upstairs whorehouse we found, where this nice black girl couldn't arouse my interest at all, and I began to realize the lack of feeling I had for this person did make all the difference, Vera spoiled me with friendship and trust, plus an awesome body, I was totally comfortable with her, my disadvantage. The extremely worn out persona of the hookers drug filled body left me as limp as a noodle.

She was definitely stoned on something, and totally drunk, which I suppose was her way of dealing with the embarrassment and humiliation of the acts she performs in the career she selected, this was my first thought. She said I don't have to tell my friend, he'll never know, she was trying to be kind enough. I said I was nervous, which I was, but her looks just didn't do it for me, and I didn't want to tell her that either. Though the sensation of touch was fine, it didn't excite me the same way Vera did, it seemed really like a waste of money to me more than anything else. I told Peter anyway, which just made him laugh and call me prejudice, which he knows I'm not. Just a mother fucking crazy cracker, as he'd say before butting heads with me and laughing hysterically and obnoxiously. The two hardest things in my life at this point were trying to decipher taxes and trying to convince Pete that life doesn't revolve around pussy.

When you entered this whore house, the palace of pleasure or whatever it was called, the room you first walk into has couches, with all the whores available sitting around on display and you get to choose which one you want. The first time we went there only that one girl was left, Peter took the other, more attractive one, quickly, and so I had no real choice, unless I wanted to wait, which I didn't. Peter rushed right in as though he'd been there many times before, though I knew he had never been there, he went running up the stairs singing: "Greenie! We're gonna get lay-aid, Greenie were gonna get lay-aid", making the last word sing as two, giggling the whole time. You hand over your money, I think it was around twenty bucks, through a little hole in a bulletproof glass window that this guy sat behind like a bank teller, and then you wait for room availability. That was strange, just sitting there with everyone knowing what you're waiting for, a chance to have sex that was paid for already, wondering if they were just gonna say leave and then keep my money. My biggest wish at that moment was to grow up never needing such a place at any stage of my life, for any reason. I certainly wondered if we'd survive our little exploits, or if we'd get mugged, shot or stabbed, luck always seemed to follow us around here, and although I didn't feel like we were in danger, I knew we were at times.

It was all very cut and dry, you pick the girl, and then go through an electronically locked door they buzz to open, and you go into a back hallway that has very tiny dressing room type stalls up and down both sides, like an extremely cheap hotel. You get a little room with a single bed and little bowl of water with a wash cloth on a little table, and the whore washes your gonads to make sure you're clean before putting the condom on you. At least that felt nice. I kept thinking: "how can I determine if she's clean"? "Can I wash her"? Of course, you can't, and I got laughed at for actually asking this question.

The second time we went, a few days later, the girl I wound up with was overweight and Australian or something and she had a very nasty attitude, saying things like: "come on! Hurry up!" This may have been because she knew what kind of tip she was getting; guess pleasure can't be bought for thirty bucks. She was only slightly more attractive than the other girl, but just as depleted looking. I did manage to reach my peak, though, and even that was less than exciting, especially when I was done and she said: "OK, you done? Go home, little boy! I'm busy. I find someone with real money!" I said thanks anyway, and wondered later what I said that for when I could have had the same amount of pleasure just hanging on some object somewhere. At least the first girl had a very pleasant attitude.

Peter enjoyed it, thought it was the greatest thing ever, but I needed more. Just physical satisfaction isn't worth it; the emotion must be there as well. Those two times were the only times in my life with an actual hooker, and two of the five one-night stands I've ever had, and I shouldn't even count the one where nothing was really accomplished due to my lack of attraction.

I was and always have been a one-woman man, going through their heart and soul, looking for the connection to mine, the missing part of my being. I enjoyed the sheer pleasure, but if it lacked emotion, it felt unsatisfactory. I need to feel at one with whoever the girl was. There can be only one opening for that position at a time; only one female applicant need apply. I never felt deprived, since I knew something about orgasms that no one else did, and knew it for many years before anyone my age did. I decided the whorehouses weren't that much fun and never went to one again after that, no matter how much Peter would try to convince me to go.

So Peter would meet Fred around this time, and all Fred would do upon meeting Peter was give him the name Peter the Raisin. I didn't know what that was supposed to mean, but found out later that it was racial in nature, and I only thought it was because of the shape of his head. I was pretty naive in that department. Peter was into trying anything, so one day Fred had some oregano, and he told Peter it was pot and we could all get high together. He rolled a joint of this stuff, passing it to Peter and even I pretended to smoke it. The point was Fred's experiment about the power of suggestion, using Peter as the lab rat. Peter became very giggly and disoriented, and acted like he was smoking real stuff, which we pretended to do also, asking Peter every few minutes: "so you like this stuff?" and "isn't this strong?" laughing the whole time about it. Peter would just agree, and figured we were laughing because we were stoned too. It proved to me that it's all truly in your head, which I suspected anyway.

Fred also introduced us to Pink Floyd's Dark side of the moon, as I mentioned before, Peter liked it, but eventually this bands music would become my all time favorite music, after the guitar rift of David Gilmour following the vocals end in the song Time sent shivers through my spine like no other musical moment. No wonder it became the greatest selling album of all time, probably still will be once or if this book comes out. The guitar rift in time was only equaled by another rift, the end of the second chorus's lyrics in the song comfortably numb, same effect, and two awesome songs. Fred always liked the Floyd, wondered what took me so long to like them too.

Fred would go to the city with us a few times, all three comprising the "triple threat" according to Peter. Peter, Fred and I also liked making phony phone calls, an activity that never seems to stop amusing, especially since there was no general caller ID yet, so most people didn't have it. I would use my strange French accent to talk with people, calling myself Jacque Lepeur, and would ask directions from the people to get to the French Consulate, the Empire state building, and just anyplace that popped into my head.

Once I called the operator from my house while my parents were out and Pete and I were hanging out, and I said: "Take off your pants, honey, I'm coming home!" She froze my line. She just sat there for an hour with the line open, no dial tone, just her. So I faked an older woman's voice and convinced her I was my mother and I'd be punished somehow. I just kept yelling "Christopher, what did you do now! What did you say?" at the top of my best woman's impression voice. Made sounds like banging and whining, told myself how sorry I was in my own voice, thinking the operator would hear this. I told the operator, in a woman's voice, "That won't happen again, I'm so sorry he did that", and a few seconds later, dial tone came back. Peter almost died laughing, as did I, and I never cranked operators again from my house.

This was around the time Peter and I decided our town sucked as well as the people in it, and we had to explore elsewhere, someplace less expensive than Manhattan; money sources were fewer these days since Pete got caught by his grandma. We went to Blue Star shopping center in Watchung, which was the closest shopping mall to our homes.

We'd either walk or hitchhike there, and it was only five miles from my house. Fred, Peter and I had been there before, seeing some movies on different occasions, and I had been there before with my sister and parents, which is how we knew about it. It had a bowling alley with an arcade that had video games like Asteroids, Missile Command, Space Invaders, and they just ate quarters all day. I was never best at any, just good competition for anyone. I did own my own bowling ball eventually, and that's where my parents brought me to bowl, so I already knew about the arcade.

There was a Radio shack, pizzeria, Hallmark, Baskin Robbins, men's and women's clothing stores, a head shop, a bank, and a supermarket, which is where I shoplifted many bags of candy and food. It also had Kress, which was renamed Caldors, which was renamed K-mart, which was renamed Mandee's which was later called Kohl's, and is probably something else by now.

I remember going into the supermarket, down the cereal aisle, and setting up the large cereal boxes in a square around a Sterno stove I put behind the front box. I lit the stove, and would put a can of tuna or Vienna Sausages on top, letting them heat up, then I would eat them right from the can while still in the store. Supermarkets had everything I needed for this activity, can openers, the Sterno's with the little stands they go under, and even forks to eat with, along with enough space to set up my dining box.

Fortunately, the shelves of the supermarket were all metal, and wouldn't catch fire from what I used them for, and the stoves were quite small. Just to be inconspicuous, I would carry around the hand basket, putting random things in it as though I was really shopping, and I'd just leave it full in some isle when I left, maybe just buying one or two things on the way out, made me look like a normal customer. I recall one lady taking my front box and finding my in-store cook out one time, at which point I had to leave, annoyed and hungry. I also realized they may be watching from now on, once the lady reported what she found.

While hanging out at Blue Star, Peter and I watched Animal House at least ten times for free, sneaking through the back door of the theater, it's still one of my favorite movies. Then, one night the manager said to us while we were sitting watching the movie "come with me, boys, you're up shits creek". Within seconds, I punched Peter's face, with not much force, and said: "I told you there was no such thing as a free ticket asshole!"

At first, Peter was a little confused and didn't know what I was doing or why I hit him so lightly, but he was aggravated enough to begin hostility towards me anyway, as I knew he would. Eventually he realized I was staging a fight as we had done many times before for fun, so he threw me passed the guy, who just stood there shocked, as we pretended to beat the life out of each other, like professional wrestlers, moving steadily away from the guy. I threw Peter through the exit doors, and the guy followed us. We continued to toss each other around, chasing each other towards the end of the mall and the woods.

The front windows of Kress at the end of the mall were painted glass windows, we didn't know they were glass, and Peter threw me against one thinking he was throwing me against a wall, which I crashed through impressively, like a stunt man in a movie. It's a wonder that I didn't even get one scratch that day. I jumped out of the stores display window, shook all the glass off myself, and said quietly to Peter: "run idiot, run away towards the woods!" because he was just standing there in shock, along with the manager who was just far enough away not to hear me but approaching fast. Then I yelled: "I'll fuckin' kill you, you fuckin' asshole!" and I started running toward the woods, with Peter pretending to run away from me. The manager stopped following us when we both fell over the short guardrail at the end of the mall and out of sight into the woods. Once in the woods, the laughter could probably be heard throughout the valley. We decided to continue our direction, into the valley to see what was on the other side.

We found a combination roller rink pool hall video arcade food stand called Fun Time. There I met Keith and Mustafa Rollins, two brothers, one a martial artist knife expert and teacher, the other a happy go lucky, crooning, pool shooting, girl chasing idiot. But I liked him, he was at peace, somehow, and tried hard not to "worry shit too much" as he'd say. Mustafa was supposedly extremely dangerous, though I thought he was cool enough, and he didn't scare me one bit.

He created his own method of martial arts, where he had two knives linked together with a chain and they were like extended knife nun-chucks. Very hard to use and practice with, since they were so dangerous. I saw the scars he got from practicing with them. Keith and I would begin hanging out together for a while when Pete wasn't around to hang with, walk around route twenty two at all hours, dodging cars, throwing stuff perilously into traffic with no regard for anything, singing funk songs, and I had even slept over his house once. His brother, I believe, thought I was pretty cool for a cracker, or so he said. Neither of them particularly cared for white folk, but I was ok, the coolest cracker they ever met, as they said.

Peter and I went to Fun Time often, and I went alone sometimes, and I would hustle some pool games sometimes, but only a few times because large men don't like little boys taking their money. I was pretty good, and that's how I got most of the money I used for video games or food and drink. Peter was OK, but he wanted to skate around the chicks in the rink down stairs more than shoot pool, always thinking with his dick. Though I hate wearing belts, I wore my money belt, usually, it's the only belt I liked to wear, and it's where I kept most of my money. I bought it on the trip across the country, don't remember where. Keith would shoot pool with me endlessly, and hours passed very quickly here, along with money disappearing just as quick, while playing till the place closed around two in the morning.

One time I was by myself, just shooting pool as usual, and some big black guy wanted to play for some money. I played for a couple of bucks the first few times, letting him barely beat me some of the time and keeping things basically even between us. Then he put a hundred down on the table and said it was serious shooting time. I agreed, and let him break.

He got two of his shots in then missed, and I ran the rest of the table, never giving him another shot. He said: "you little honkey cracker fuck! I'll break your little fucking neck, hustle me, bitch!" So I grabbed the cash on the table as he spoke and ran out the door, with this guy in close pursuit. The highway was the front yard of this place, down a small hill and about fifteen or twenty feet away from the back edge of the front parking lot, and it was nighttime.

I ran onto the highway and jumped the divider, just missing a car coming down the fast lane on our side by inches, then I looked back and watched the guy try to jump the divider, but another car was coming down the fast lane on the other side, and he wasn't so lucky. I did feel a little guilt as I watched him get hit and thrown down the highway, but it was his own fault for chasing me. I didn't stay around to learn of his fate, I just walked away, back to the woods leading to Blue Star where I watched the ambulance coming and then I called my mom for a ride home from the theater payphone.

Going to Fun Time eventually led Peter and I to Mount Saint Mary's Academy, the back yard of the place I taught handicapped to use the dibble, which was really under the school's umbrella of care. It was a young girl's Catholic boarding school. I will drive a school bus for them later in life, but till now I didn't know what the place was, looking like an expensive mansion on the top of a hill with a great view of the valley below.

So if you stood on the highway at the intersection of Terrill Road and Twenty Two and looked up the mountain from the highway, you'd first see Fun Time off to the left, and a hundred yards behind that more to the right was the Handicapped building and some tennis courts, and two hundred yards behind that as you follow the winding road up the rest of the mountain was the academy, visible for many miles around atop its mountain nest.

Peter had only one thing in mind as usual, and I was never really against a good time with some female contact, at least these girls were closer to my age. We went around the back of the school; coming from the hill and woods, and all we got was yelled perversions at, whistled and flashed at. You really can't get in unless you scale the wall, some thirty feet; we both were not into that, since there were no protrusions to assist with the climb up.

The school has the cute nickname of whorehouse on the hill. More like dykes on the brink. Many years from now, one girl from this school while riding in the back of my school bus decided to spread eagle with a skirt and no underwear on right in the middle seat so only I could see her clearly. Not your average girls next door. I laughed, of course, and said something like better keep that overgrown bush covered, before something goes and builds a nest in there.

We did get some of the girls to come down, they were cute, and we made out with a couple of them in the total darkness, and never knew their names. The house mom as they called her eventually found these girls missing and she came out of the side door, the same one the girls came out and began yelling: "trespassers! I got you now! The police are coming now! Don't move or I'll shoot your asses!" But I saw she didn't have anything to shoot with, so I yelled back as we ran for the woods: "what are ya gonna shoot us with, your ugly face or a dibble super dinodyke?"! That made Pete nearly fall laughing, but we kept moving and never went back again. We never found out if the girls got in any trouble either.

Blue Star is where we would wind up going, bowling alley time. I think this also was during one of the times Fred's parents and mine would not let us hang out with each other, not that Pete was really any better. They pretty much never wanted us to be together, they knew no good could come from it. Of course, we never listened. The last thing Fred and I did before taking a break from each other for a while was shoplifting a canoe from Two Guys, which was also behind Fun Time, we just put it over our heads and walked out.

We let the canoe go down the Passaic River, after riding around in it awhile. We couldn't go too far, we didn't get any paddles and used our hands for rudders. But Fred would not be with me in the beginning of the Blue star days, he wouldn't be there or at fun time for a while. I met and re-met many people at Blue Star, most of whom were younger than me, like Reverend Ed, Ernie Church, whose sister Madeline will make it to other chapters in my life, Barry Gant, Lilly Longe and Betsy Black who I did know before, Jan Bowes, Eric "Fucking" Lee, Reggie Arnolds, Biff Pots, Danny Gall, Reggie "Spike" Brown and his brother and sister Barney and Natalie.

Natalie holds the wonderful distinction of being the only girl I ever hit in my life on purpose. She would be the only girl ever I would actually hit. Peter and a dozen others were standing around in a circle in the parking lot of the Blue Star bowling alley, while Natalie would hit my arm, which had no effect what so ever, then she would try to slap me, and spit on me, and I don't remember what her problem was or what she was arguing about, I think it was just a test of my patience.

So everyone was eventually chanting, "Hit her! Hit her!" So as I turned away after she spit in my face, I turned back quickly, and with an open backhand I slapped her across her face, and landed her flat on her butt. I allowed the reaction to happen, didn't give myself time to think at all, and though I knew enough about conversation to end nearly any confrontation, I knew I could not with her, she wanted someone to do this for some reason, and I still felt guilty when I did it.

I did it so quick and accurately I surprised myself, nearly had to laugh, but I didn't. She wailed off shouting and cursing about how dead I would be within a day, how her brothers were going to get me, which I knew they wouldn't, and didn't believe they could. They were pretty tight with me and liked most people more than their sister. They just called her a bitch that finally got what she deserved, I heard later.

We did standard teenager stuff at the mall, climbed in the six-foot sewer known as the pipeline or hell, the same one Fred and I walked through years ago, hung out by the head shop, rolled shopping carts down ramps into moving traffic on route twenty two, spread graffiti all over, vomited from eating too much candy or drank too much alcohol then passed out.

I'd entertain myself by watching them all drug themselves on occasion, watch them fall down the hills in back of the mall, and just laugh at their general state of confusion and disorientation. We would actually bowl at the alley sometimes, I had a hundred-eighty bowling average at one time. We also would go to movies, through the front door and back. I think the biggest movie of the time was Star Wars and I liked the Pink Panther movies, science fiction, and James Bond flicks, perhaps some horror too, but none stand out as a great horror movie till Carrie came out. Well, maybe night of the living dead too, but horror was in its infancy at the time I believe, at least the graphic aspects were.

Here at Blue Star I got along fine with everyone, very unlike my own town. I always showed up at the arcade with bags of M&M's, or other candy I took from the supermarket, that I'd share with everyone, which they all liked. Everyone there knew me only as Greenie, which is how Peter or Fred always introduced me since that's what they knew me as. I had the leather jacket, customized by me of course, so I could fit vast amounts of stuff within the lining, and I never got caught shoplifting again. Eventually I grew up and discontinued the practice, realizing it wasn't smart, necessary or impressive, and doubting my life would ever reach the point where it would become necessity, I also knew it was socially wrong, according to the majority.

While hanging out between the bank and theater, which was the only space between buildings in the whole strip mall, and the banks' designated driveway for the drive thru window was there too; Peter asked me what would happen if someone pulled a knife on us. He was acting like I was supposed to be scared by the possible circumstance, giving all kinds of wild scenarios, none of which made any sense, like in the subway in Brooklyn that night where words disarmed the situation.

He kept going on and on, till eventually he pointed one at me because he happened to have one, as did I most of the time, and as soon as he spoke some sentence about a gang of guys coming over to us, and ended the sentence with the words: "like this", I did a spinning heel kick and knocked it out of his hand and sent it into the woods. He was pissed he couldn't find it because it was dark at the time. I really impressed and shocked myself, I was only playing around.

I took karate for a few months when I was around eleven years of age, and I was quick enough to kick the teacher square in the stomach, and he was a black belt. He asked us all the first day to show him what we thought we knew, and just from watching old karate movies, which I loved to watch, I could determine how to move without actually knowing, and was able to make firm contact. I don't think I hurt him, despite the fact that he moaned as though I did.

I couldn't block well at all, but that didn't seem to matter much to me. It really took a lot to hurt me, as anyone who knew me had discovered, and one or two shots would not do it. I would not work out or practice enough to continue, and became bored with lessons. I knew enough self-defense in my mind to show no fear of anyone. I thought I knew enough, along with the wrestling mix I use, and have never really been tested yet; I figured I'd get by most situations with language and have so far with few exceptions.

Blue Star was where I got to meet one of Fred's current girl friends, Crystal Langly, and her younger sister, Shelly. Fred and I would go there often too eventually, mostly to walk around it and go onto the roof to hang out and distract people with odd sounds and falling objects, never hit anyone except Pete who knew we were there. Shelly and Crystal would come with us at times; I met Shelly before Crystal, found out later her sister was Fred's girlfriend.

Both girls were Irish, and Crystal was a self-proclaimed super bitch and nymphomaniac, who said she had to have sex every day to be happy, though I never tried to fill that void in her life myself, not that she would want me to or ever offered me the position. She was way too defensive and insecure for me to want to deal with, but I liked her as a friend, she was funny at times and gave different perspectives to things, in a bitchy sort of way. Shelly became the equivalent of my little sister, and she thought like me as much and sometimes more so than anyone else I knew. She looked like Janis Joplin and loved Pink Floyd as much as I eventually did. She had to be about twelve when I met her, I called her sis.

They both hung out at Blue Star, and I would have married Shelly, if I had been her type or had she had any interest in pursuing me as more than just a big brother she liked. We became instant friends, seeing things so similarly it was eerie. I thought I had met my true soul mate for a while and watched for openings in conversation or action where I could assert or display my feelings, but she was destined to spend her immediate future with her boyfriend Donald Valentin, who I only came to know as a bi-sexual cocaine slut, when I finally met him years after meeting Shelly.

I don't believe Shelly knew at first about Don's lifestyle, it was a long time before she saw him again after meeting me. She would talk about him though, like her great mythical knight in shining armor, whom she was dedicated to. One of Shelly's favorite sayings was: "I was mortified!" and that applied perfectly to what I felt about her devotion to Donald. I think that phrase came from a Bugs Bunny cartoon.

Watching Shelly devote herself to him was quite heart breaking. But this wouldn't happen for a few years, me meeting Don and his nearly toothless brothers Billy and Danny. All they would do was mass quantities of drugs and drinking, which I was opposed to at that time still, I wouldn't even try them till I was nineteen. Never drank till I was around twenty, and then for only a short time, since I hated it. Made my crap smell really bad, my stomach hurt, and gave me a headache.

I was only sixteen at this point. Crystal was Fred's girlfriend, but I just couldn't see what she thought was so great about Fred. I thought the girls around him were fairly empty-headed, just toys for him. That was a shame, because they were all usually fairly decent looking, and I realized that the old rumor could be true, that pretty women like ugly guys, and obviously all guys like attractive girls.

I would talk to Shelly, much like Vera but in her language, she was younger than me so it wasn't quite equally comparable, just because of the school grade differences. Otherwise, she was definitely another favorite of mine to hang around, very entertaining when she drank, I had to carry her around some times, she being too wasted to walk. She would drink anything, from one fifty one proof rum to wine coolers, though I don't recall how she got these drinks, since she was very under aged.

I took her home one day and her parents figured I got her drunk and took advantage or something, plus I was friends with Derf, as they called him, who only seemed to make their other daughter cry, so they looked down upon Shelly and my relationship quite a bit. Just like Vera and her boyfriend, I built Shelly's relationship with Don, though I don't know why, just being a normal Greenie, she'd say. And her questions about why guys do things seemed oddly familiar, a script from Vera's mouth only less advanced in thought process, younger viewpoint with different wording.

We all went to Blue Star, this new crowd of friends I had, at one time or another, like Craig Elston, and his brother Garret. Craig introduced Peter and me to Carol Birney and Darcy and Ramona Sampsin. Ramona, unfortunately, will get hit by a truck and turned into a vegetable right in front of Shelly's eye's, in front of the high school, in about five years from the date I met her.

Darcy and Carol were Peter's and mine first dual date experience. I got all the way to second base with Carol, Pete and I spent many days hanging out at Darcy's house. They faded from the scene after a few months, and their friend, another Carol, dumped Fred, someone finally realizing what an idiot he was. Carol was ok, but she decided Reverend Ed was cuter. She was no great catch, though. Quite large in size and red pigmented, if you know the type. Good times were had by all. I do remember kissing her though, it felt slightly empty, uneventful, no connection made internally though pleasant, still exciting enough to be lustful, but this was simple petting I assumed out of her own curiosity, like I was warming her up for someone else she desired.

One of the more dangerous activities I did was with these Blue Star people, was behind a Friendly's restaurant in Scotch Plains, where the railroad tracks were. There was a rope tied to a tree, and the train tracks were lower than the street, and we would swing on the rope a few feet over any moving train, literally coming inches from death if one happened by at the right time. One kid did slip and die there, some time before I went there. It was known as the grope for some reason. Eventually I figured it was more fun to swing over water, since you could fall with little danger of injury, and I only participated a few times in this deadly activity before deciding it was stupid. What's the fun of swinging from a rope if you can't jump off it? Bungee wasn't invented yet.

Another activity with pending danger was when some of us would go to the water tower in the reservation, the same tower some young black kid had committed suicide on some years earlier by jumping off it, though some say he fell by accident. The gate around the spiraling stairway was less than proficient at keeping trespassers off, and we'd go to the top and have bon fires, for cooking marshmallows and hotdogs. Just the thought of the fact that someone died there was enough to make the experience kind of eerie, though no one I went with was pondering a repeat performance of suicide.

They eventually fixed the fence and access was lost, thus we never went again. These things were all done with some, one or all the people I mentioned, I just cannot recall which did which with me, so I apologize for the generalizations. They were all good times, simple teen adventure that seemed to have no point, end or purpose really, but fun anyway. Once we grew tired of these wanderings, or were in circumstances that wouldn't allow for this activity, we found other ways to spend our time. I do remember Shelly walking along the edge pretending to have no control over her steps, trying to scare everyone with nearly falling to her death; she found strange ways to entertain herself.

EXIT THIRTEEN

Long Distance Love Boulevard

When not at Blue Star Pete and I looked for some other activities to occupy our time. So one day Peter and I decided to make phony phone calls again, with Jake and I, the first call was to Clare Goins of Berkeley heights, and her friend Alice. After some conversation above the usual crank call type, what they looked like, what we looked like and such topics, these girls decided to have us come to their house for some swimming, since Pete told them where he lived.

Jake was visiting his sister, and Peter and I just ran into him on this day by chance, and he was into doing phony phone calls as well, so he joined us. On the way to the girls house, we told stories about Fred and Elton while we danced and sang old radio tunes and some Floyd while walking down the tracks from Murray Hill to their house, about two miles away in Berkeley Heights. They were already hammered from drinking by the time we got there. We never saw any adults in the house for some reason.

They went into the other room to get us drinks, and Alice, who drunkenly stated she liked me by whispering in my ear: "you are so sexy!" passed out cold in the other room and wouldn't wake up. Then Clare began to pass out as well, and we never got to do anything, except to spend about an hour trying to revive them, and we wound up going home. This, of course, was around three am. Jake and I had to stop Peter from disrobing them while they were passed out, too. "Can't I just get a peak?" he begged. We wouldn't let him. They were quite gorgeous, and it was tempting, but Jake and I knew better.

Outbound crank calls were fun, but we also did inbound calls, the phone would ring in Peter's house and I'd answer and say things like: "Morgue! How may we dispose of you? Bake, burry or dump? Davey Jones locker available for a small extra charge! Let the Vultures do the work for you with our special desert drop off!" We would both enjoy this, especially if it was a telemarketer, and we didn't actually know the person. The other end didn't appreciate our game usually. Opportunities for these types of calls were rare, and doing outbound ones was much more fun.

The next time Peter and I made a crank call, we decided to make it further away, so we don't get screwed again. The single most important phony phone call ever made, for a change of destiny and our path though life was to a south Jersey number, in Princeton Township, to a girl named Dora.

The initial call went something like this: "Hello?" a young female voice asked. "Hi" I said in a relaxed tone, as though I knew her all my life. "Who is this?" the girl asked. I said; "Oh, this is Chris". Then there was some silence, and the girl said; "I don't know any Chris, are you sure you have the right number?" I replied; "It doesn't matter, I just like to call numbers to talk to someone new and you sound very sexy and interesting".

She replied; "Well, I don't know who you are, but you really shouldn't call people that way, and I should hang up now". "No," I said, "wait, I'm not just some nutcase, I'm Chris from New Providence, and I'm just sixteen, six foot three two hundred pounds with blue eyes and blonde hair. I'm not out to hurt anyone, I just like to talk with different people".

She replied; "Well, that's cool, but don't expect much from me, since I don't know you, although you sound kind of cute from that description". I said; "Really? Good! Because you sound very sexy, am I right?" She said; "I've been called that". Then I continued; "Could you tell me a little about yourself? Something small that couldn't matter who you tell? Like your name?"

"My name is Dora, I'm nineteen, and five foot two one hundred fifteen pounds, black hair and brown eyes, I'm Italian, that's about it". Then I asked her; "Do you have any friends?" She said; "of course I have friends, but most of them are younger than me". "Well, I have a friend with me now, Peter, and he wants to meet your sexiest friend sometime, that is, if I get to meet you sometime too", I replied.

She said; "We'll see, but I still don't know you well enough to meet you". I answered; "That's OK, I'll call you back tomorrow and tell you everything you want to know about me and my friend. Don't get me wrong, I'm not a loon or anything, you just sound really nice and I'll take all the time you need to feel comfortable enough to meet me". "Uh huh," was all I heard in a rightfully suspicious tone.

So I said; "I'm really a nice guy who's just tired of the bullshit people who surround me here are full of, and you sound intelligent, and very sexy, so kill me for being curious!" She replied; "I can understand that, I'm kind of sick of the people around here too, but I gotta go now, Chris, I'll be home tomorrow, if you feel like calling me". I said; "OK, Dora, I'll talk to you tomorrow then, bye!" Then I hung up, and Peter asked me if she had a friend, I told him she said she did, and we'll find out tomorrow. That made him giggle in anticipation, along with giving the usual head butts.

Dora Fresse from Princeton would wander into my life, clueless as to the change of directions our lives would take from this simple phone call. Though the phone calls eventually became very explicit, around topics like oral sex, I never did a thing with her. After giving all the physical descriptions to each other, she agreed she would meet me if I came down alone to a place that we decided was neutral. She didn't want to meet two guys she never met, since she was afraid we might take advantage of her, and she wasn't into black guys she claimed.

I walked and hitch hiked to a movie house on route two-o-two in Belle Mead about thirty five miles one way from my house in pouring rain, so I could sit there and talk to myself while waiting for her to show up and keep her promise of some great oral sex.

Occasionally I would call her house and get no answer, after waiting several hours. Dora never showed up, and I'd have to walk back home. When I called her later asking for some reason for not showing, she gave me some excuse about her brother or father not letting her out, and she would definitely be there the next time I came down her way.

Peter would eventually go to Princeton with me, and once was on Christmas Eve, and we went down to meet Gertrude, Dora's friend and a supposed easy slut according to Dora, but closer by. That's all Peter was interested in, and that is exactly what he asked Dora, if she had a slutty friend he could fuck, since she wasn't into him. Gertrude was Dora's answer for Peter; she lived slightly closer, five miles back up two-o-two, by a place where the signs read: "Don't pick up hitch-hikers, mental facility nearby". The facility was called Carrier clinic.

This made it tough to hitchhike, and I refused to drive Peter and me down in my dad's car. So we went, met no one since no one was at the Dairy Freeze Dora said she would meet us at, as usual. We got a ride most of the way there, and had to walk the thirty miles home on Christmas eve, and no one would stop for us. Eleven hour walk through an on-and-off blizzard seemed almost poetic justice for our high expectations of some girls we have never seen. Only got splashed a few times, But we were soaked from head to toe and slept almost all day when we got home. That was, I think, about the sixth time going down to meet girls, and we were beginning to wonder if Dora ever planned on really meeting us, how naive we were.

Then I called Fred. He knew people who drove, or could get a car, and would understand the motivation and wouldn't accept any excuses from Dora. He and Dora became close fast. I gave him her phone number, and that motivated him to go, which he did. Dora worked at a supermarket, which was on route two-o-two, and she drove a sixty-nine Olds Cutlass, candy red, and she was quite promiscuous, except with me, facts learned over the phone during weeks of conversations.

Her brain didn't function sufficiently to have normal conversation, but the long distance cloak and dagger, sex line type game was interesting. Once Fred discovered where Dora worked, I was finally able to meet her, we just went down to the store and walked in, and somehow, I knew who she was without ever seeing her yet, and Fred had seen her already a few times, I was not surprised by her appearance when Fred began walking up towards her, I knew it was her. She didn't seem remorseful at all about never going to our arranged meetings, but I think she was sorry when she saw me, because her eyes opened very wide when she realized who I was.

This is when Elton joined the search for women in the Princeton area, because he began hanging out with Fred and me more often at this time. Fred usually fixed Elton's cars, being mechanically inclined, so I think he gave Fred the first ride down to Dora. If Fred found some girl to have sex with down there, only Dora at this point, he'd get Elton to give us a ride down, then he'd lose both of us, leaving the path open to admired hatred, and much conversation. Fred didn't care, he'd get rides home from Dora, but she wouldn't come pick him up for some reason. Elton was the one who taught me the Itenditen song during our cruises, because Fred taught him and Fred didn't have enough patience to teach me he claimed. Elton smoked but wasn't into drugs, just like me, and this commonality stood for a while.

We would go to diners and get a bagel with coffee and we frequented literally almost every New Jersey diner there is, in his sixty-nine Firebird, listening to every imaginable Elton John song ever written. Our purpose was to try finding and meeting different women to fool around with, for years, and we never did. Elton, as Fred, only thought about sex. But unlike Fred, Elton was usually unable to get any, but never stopped trying.

We diner hopped from High Point to Cape May, from Staten Island to Allentown, usually all night long, after dropping Fred by Dora's house. Elton was the kind of driver who would go painfully slow at or below the speed limit, claiming to be avoiding tickets, never driving with any purpose or intent to reach a goal, though it was true we were in no rush, didn't have a destination really so it didn't matter, but he'd race if challenged at times.

He was content to have his car be the hang out, with his music playing, not caring one bit about getting where he was going, making a game of it, seeing how annoyed other cars could be driving behind him. Sometimes this was fun, mostly it was boring, even when he did race, he'd only go about a quarter mile or so then quit after he believed he "made his point". Most of his dialogue were jokes he heard, he remembered most and repeated them often, whether I or anyone else wanted to hear them or not.

So Elton at this point was about to meet Gertrude, who I think also wasn't into Peter as I recall. Elton talked to her on the phone and decided to go right to her house instead of meeting somewhere, knowing how often Pete and I got stood up doing that with Dora. Peter, Elton and I went down to her house, and all Elton remembers about that day is that I asked for a tuna fish sandwich.

He believes to this day that I almost got us shot for that, but I was hungry, and Gertrude asked if we wanted anything. She lived in the middle of the woods, by cornfields and forests, the town was called Hopewell. We went to meet Gertrude and some friends of hers, a black girl for Peter named Maria, about twenty years old, and Wilma Timbers, about twelve or thirteen, but slightly older looking.

All Wilma and I could do when we met was stare at each other, in that infatuation type look, like there was no one else standing around, instant love at first sight, for me, anyway. Peter was already making out with Maria in Elton's back seat. He just walked up to Maria and said: "how ya doin' sexy"? As he put his hand on her neck and gave her a kiss, right on the lips. He just kept calling her fine, sweet, and things to that effect, couldn't believe that blatant method worked. Gertrude's father kept yelling about something from the house, but we couldn't make out what he was saying from where we were.

Later, I found out that the yelling was about, as he said, the slut Dora, and all her weird slutty friends, including his own daughter. We were just the next victims in line for them, but Dora wasn't even there. I didn't care, when Gertrude offered something to eat, I said yes. Then we went inside. Peter didn't, he was busy. Elton got stuck being told off by a hick about what a stupid person he was if he thought these girls gave a rat's ass about him. I thought it was funny Elton didn't find any amusement about this scene.

The tuna sandwich was fine, and too bad about Elton. Plus I thought I was in love. I got Wilma's phone number and began talking to her regularly; talking to girls on phones was nothing new to me, except this time. Dora was right about Gertrude's promiscuity, and Elton took full advantage of that fact and went out with her for quite a while. My own mother would describe Gertrude as 'dumpy', after meeting her one day at my house. I think Peter was glad he never went out with her and his relationship with Maria was short lived.

During the next few months, I would walk and hitchhike thirty miles one way to just talk to Wilma, discuss life in general, philosophize with her, and make out in her basement, so I always wound up leaving very excited. I felt that by showing such patience and never forcing myself upon her, she'd get the message of true care and love from me.

I never tried going past first or second base, just holding her in my arms and consoling her on her life's main issues, like her perverted bisexual ex-marine sergeant father who sexually and physically molested her, or so she said. I knew the physical part to be true from the evidence of bruises on her, but Wilma claimed he'd say she did it to herself when confronted, which may have also been possible.

I knew he was an ex-marine Sergeant as well. I know I was suspicious about some things she claimed, just not about how she said she felt about me. She was also into doing drugs, and that added to my suspicions over all. I didn't care about the fact she did them, just like anyone else I knew, but I also knew her judgment could be impaired by them and could do damage eventually.

She was the first girl I had ever been attracted to enough to be able to physically express myself to her, and the only one comfortable enough to reciprocate and accept my feelings almost immediately. We did not begin as only "friends", like Vera or Shelly; it was actual attraction in every way from both sides. I remember how wonderfully special she made me feel, like I was the only choice worth making in her life as a lover or partner, and she felt natural to me, as though this is the way life should be. I felt like I was whole and my search for the meaning of love and relationships had ended with the discovery of this girl.

We'd kiss, touch and contemplate infinity and destiny while watching a full moon for hours, or whenever we could, I was her knight in shining armor, she was my long lost princess, and her dad was the great evil dragon I had to avoid or slay. Nothing and no one ever made me feel as important or loved as Wilma did at this point in my life, she was my motivation for living and growing, the only focus of my passions and attention, thoughts and feelings.

From the day I met her I knew she'd be a big part of my life, and I was certain she would be my soul mate forever. Just the sound of her voice was enough to make me feel that life was meaningful, relevant and had purpose.

Her conversations with me involved a lot of "I miss you", or "I love you" with heavy sighs in between from both ends, and topics like how the years needed till we legally could be together seemed a life time way, and how to avoid her dad the next time I came or avoiding getting caught on the phone with me. She always said I deserved better, or I shouldn't wait for her, but she was always amazed to the point of tears with my devotion, my words of comfort and ease, knowing I would never cheat on her, lie or cause any harm, she was to be my paths destiny, sharing the roads of my life, and nothing could change that. Now I had the long distance love, like Vera and Shelly experienced, now I saw from their perspective the 'excuse' for not seeking another's love, or passionate attention. I was the only one I knew, of all the guys I hung out with, that held this devotion with such high priority.

I had many thoughts while I walked, always full of anticipation, but also lots of time and random contemplation. As I walked for hours on end in all possible weather, I thought at times it would be easier and more fun to have my five iron and a ball with me, like one continuous hole of golf, which would have passed the time well. It would have amounted to five continuous games, since it was twenty five miles to where I was going, plus I figured no one would pick up somebody carrying a golf club and ball. I'm sure I'd lose the ball quickly, and I didn't want to carry anymore than one.

No friend of mine believed that one girl would be worth going through all I went through just to see her, their opinion was that girls were a dime a dozen, and the choices were plentiful, no need to devote all feeling towards just one so far away, I disagreed, though had no evidence to back that feeling.

A little more about Elton here, since I'm mentioning friends who aren't as monogamous as I and to describe events around the time I met Wilma, but wasn't around her. Elton indulged in drugs for a while, as everyone except me did at that time, but once in Peter's grandma's house while smoking pot and snorting speed, he claimed to go on a hallucinatory experience, and walked fifteen miles home in the middle of the night, being lost the whole way and going through the mountains on his version of what I would call a vision quest.

I wasn't there for that, only Jake and Peter were, and all they said was he disappeared at some point from the party, they didn't see him leave. He didn't touch drugs again for a while. He was a unique character, who had his leg crushed between two car bumpers prior to my meeting him, so he wasn't athletic, but he was pretty big.

He was philosophically weak, and if I pointed our conversations towards religion, or life origin, he wouldn't discuss them with me. He'd just go into some comedy routine he knew, and he knew many, he would only make light of the topics. He had an uncanny memory for jokes, stories, and trivial bits of information. Unfortunately, all who knew him got to hear most of them several times over and over again for years.

He was a two hundred fifty pound Sicilian kid singing Elton John songs, with various perverse variations on other songs. We all liked the "fill in the word" type songs, with a disgusting twist or replacement of words, the worse, the better, like musical Mad Libs. A habit I figured he got from Fred, though that could have been generated from either direction, ultimately being some real comedians' work they just mimicked.

One of Elton's favorites was the song 'How deep is your love' by the Beegees. He changed it to say: "How deep is your love, about six inches, I really mean to learn . . ." and I would interrupt by laughing and saying: "don't you mean two inches in your case, fag?" and laugh harder and more obnoxiously, then he'd try to punch me. I would just call him a gay Tunisian toenail twister and laugh some more. Another favorite activity of Elton's and mine was cruising around the town of Belle Mead re-arranging all the house for sale signs, which we would take from one property and place on others, like the police station, the high school, the Dairy Freeze, and supermarkets. Probably very annoying for the realtor, but extremely funny to us, especially selling the police station, and we did that one a few times. It was the Hillsborough station mostly, along with Princeton Township's once.

Elton is a pretty nice, happy person, for the most part, but suffers big self-doubt, not that I haven't. He and Fred had the habit of trying to punch me for some reason, thinking I would be complacent or a punching bag, but I wasn't bothered by it. They were not unlike bullies, the differences being that they actually enjoyed my company, and never pushed things so far as to cause any real injury.

Fred was abusive only because he's an idiot Derf, and knew no other way to convey friendship, and had always been this way since I met him and he stopped as well, since it had less and less effect on me as time went by. Elton's attempt to emulate this behavior did not work with me, since I'd hit him back before Derf, hitting Fred didn't do much and it seemed to confuse and effect Elton, I never hit anyone as hard as I could except Pete once or twice.

They would sing a song and try to use me as the drum to beat in step with the music, and Elton hit like a little girl, so it didn't bother me as much as me hitting him. Neither of them could cause any damage to me anyway. The spider bites Derf used that left a black and blue wherever he used it was probably the most annoying,

I would hit back repeatedly for that, but at this point in our lives hitting Fred was much like hitting a wall, didn't faze him either.

Another of Elton's favorite things was criticizing my nose, he'd say if it were turned upside down people would try to drive through it believing the Holland Tunnel had moved, and things like that. I believe I actually thought of that one, I was best at insulting myself first, then anyone around me after. I get different reactions to that, Elton's reaction was usually: "you're such a Greenie!" Also, Elton's nose is actually larger than mine, a fact he couldn't come to grips with.

Elton got along with almost anyone he talked to, being open to small talk, even specializing in discussing basically nothing. He liked to attempt feeling superior by commenting negatively on any situation that arose, continually trying to belittle any statements made by someone else, like a putdown contest with no winners. Eventually, you'd have to ignore his chatter, not take it too seriously, or beat the shit out of him, if you cared enough about what he was commenting on. I never had a problem ignoring his attitude and tolerating his endless comments about my nose, intelligence, or my way of viewing life. One person we knew later did have issues with Elton, and Elton paid for it, never knowing when to close his mouth. This was due course, I figured.

If you look at pictures of Elton's dad or grandpa when they were his age, they look exactly like Elton. This became apparent one day when Jake and I went to his house to pick him up. He came out, and I saw his dad in the top attic bedroom window just slightly moving the curtains to see outside. I asked Elton what his dad was doing up there, and he said, "Greenie, nobody's home". I said bullshit, and told him I saw his dad, and he told me that was his grandpa, whose spirit lived with them and moved here to Clark with them from Newark.

His grandpa hated Elvis Presley and Elton's mother had many statues of Elvis, which mysteriously would break when no one was home, or while everyone was sleeping. We did go back in the house, just to prove to me no one was there, and he was right unless his dad decided to hide from us for some reason. Both Jake and

I saw the curtain move some, only I saw his face. We left after that, wondering what his grandpa's spirit thought about who was hanging out with his grandson.

This made some sense or logic regarding another event that happened some years later, where Elton, Jake and Elton's brother Cosmo were doing the Ouija board, and recording on a normal old-fashioned tape recorder with no radio the events in the attic bedroom of Elton's house. The board went nuts, the pointing device supposedly moving without anyone touching it, and when they played the tape back for me, the sound was cut off slowly by the ham radio signal of Voice of America, which got louder and louder as it played.

Since the recorder wasn't a radio, it's impossible to overlay any other sound onto it, and no one knows how it got there, but Elton lives in fear of Ouija now because of that. Elton won't even go near a board. Jake would, just because he's that type of person and doesn't show fear about anything, if possible. Figures what's dead can't hurt him. I would have to agree.

Elton's mother was somewhat psychic; she had predicted fairly accurately all the trouble Fred and I would get into. She was a very nice lady, who always invited Fred or me to breakfast, lunch or dinner if we were around at the time she was serving. His dad liked motorcycles and owned a Harley or something; Elton would follow those footsteps later on. They were both nice people, who seemed to be the only ones who could tolerate Fred most of the time, but wished their son had different friends, perhaps normal ones. They liked me, but I was friends with Fred, my only fault they knew of. Elton's' family loved Jake, who always helped them and never caused any trouble.

Elton saw things in different perspectives, as do I naturally, so we could collaborate endlessly about almost anything or nothing at all. Things like a good song verses a bad one were discussed, mainly because he was a music addict, and it was a topic he could handle. Happy as long as his music played, this was easily ignored by me, since music played almost no roll in my life. That is, till I heard Floyd for a while. We probably went through thousands of different topics, which would comprise all the things I had wanted to remember, but naturally years later remembering them all would be difficult, lost during the span of time, as most dialogue with my friends would be.

Elton also liked politics, which I didn't, I would cause him to get annoyed when I'd ask him the difference between Democrats and Republicans, stating there is none, and we're all the same in our wants and needs. Then he'd try to tell me that I was being a Liberal, one more useless classification to people with one common goal, a good productive, happy life.

I kept telling him the government should be more like star fleet, which he couldn't fathom, didn't take much of what I said seriously. It was fun cruising to Princeton and Belle Mead with Elton anyway; it certainly beat having to walk and hitchhike there and took much less time. I think my record for time used to hitch to Belle Mead was about seventy five minutes, two back to back rides within five minutes of walking, very lucky, and rare.

I remember the dangers I encountered hitching, the first being one day coming home from Fred's and one of the first times I hitch hiked, long before going to meet Dora. A big guy in a pickup truck with a little feminine looking guy stopped for me, I got in, they started going up diamond hill road, and the big guy says to me: "do you like to party?" I said something like it depends on the party, didn't dance or anything, liked lots of chicks, and they said they knew of one going on right now.

I didn't really think about it, but never worried about much, so I said cool, let's go. They both started talking about how much they hated fags, so I just chimed right in about how sad and disgusting that is, and how it made no sense. The driver pulled off the road into the woods, heading into the reservation which I knew possibly better than anyone, and drove up the mountain, both of them laughing, smiling and having a great time. The big guy stopped and said the party was here in the middle of the woods, and to get out and let his "girl" suck my dick.

I just laughed, after inquiring about where all the chicks were, thinking he was joking, and we had gotten out by now and he came around the truck to where I was and tried to punch me. Missed the nose of course, not much force behind it anyway, so I just stood there and said "do you really want this much trouble, or can I leave now fag?" He tried punching me again, missed.

I started to laugh now, which really pissed the guy off, and his little friend jumped me from behind wrapping his arms around my neck. I just threw my head between my ankles, and felt him fly over me and land on his back on the rocks and dirt. While I was bent in half and the other guy was watching this, I found a soft ball sized rock between my feet, which I grasped with my hand. The guy tried to knock me off my feet then by throwing a body block, and as I pretended to fall, I bounced off his trucks door and stood up quickly and smacked the side of his head with the rock I was still holding. He didn't see it coming and fell right to the ground, apparently knocked out, leaving his shocked gay friend sobbing over his body.

That was possibly the closest I ever came to killing someone. I stood there to see if he'd come to, which he did, his buddy didn't budge from his side and probably couldn't figure why I was there still, but I really felt as though I should know if I killed someone by accident or not, I don't like to hurt anyone, even this low life pair of strangoddities.

After maybe five or ten minutes, while the little guy cried and cursed at me, he came to, and the little fag began massaging the bewildered guy's crotch, I decided it was indeed time to depart before vomiting. The big guy jumped up and gave chase towards me, ignoring his boyfriends' attention and telling him to watch the truck, and I laughed at him as I did what I do best, run though woods. It only took me a few seconds to lose this fool in those woods. What kind of life they must have had to be like that was beyond me.

The only other predicament I had hitching was not with a ride, but with a loose pit bull I ran into one day on the highway. I was going down route twenty-two in Green Brook when I noticed a fence door slightly opened to a junkyard. I also noticed it was clean up day in the area because there were large piles of refuse on every driveway and curb in the area. Fortunately for me someone was throwing away a baseball bat right next to the junkyard, because I saw a dog come out of the open fence and start growling at me, moving slowly closer each second I watched.

I started moving slowly towards the heap of garbage where I saw the bat. As I grabbed it, I saw the dog start to move quickly towards me. I took the bat and swung as I usually did, very hard, right at the dogs' head. This knocked it sideways and back for a second, but didn't deter it as much as I thought it should. I held the bat like a lacrosse stick or wood chopping axe and within seconds, as the dog came at me again, I whacked it right between the eyes, grounding it with a sledge hammer type blow.

Still, the animal didn't have enough and it got back up stunned but barking, trying to shake off the damage I did and looking clumsier, looking for some opening to get me, then it jumped towards me again, I gave it a sledgehammer again right on the top of its head. That finally did it, laid the dog out on the ground, still breathing but not moving much now.

So instead of keeping the bat and walking away, fully expecting the dog to recover and come for me again, with sheer insane adrenaline I pounded the bat on its head about three more times, till it was bleeding out the eyes and nose and I heard crunching as if I crushed its thick skull. Then I left, walking down the road as if nothing happened. I was going to see Wilma, and nothing was going to stop me, including a mad dog.

As dangerous as it is to be a hitchhiker, it's also dangerous for the people who pick you up or sometimes even the ones who refuse to pick you up. I was by a traffic light on the highway one day, about fifty feet before it, with my thumb out. The light just turned red, so I knew the next car would have to stop and I may get a ride then.

A lady was coming towards the light, the traffic already started through the intersection from the cross direction, and though I thought she would stop, she didn't. I think she was either afraid to, because I was there begging rides, or she just didn't see the light. I watched her go right through the light and get hit by a car turning onto the highway going the same direction we were.

Her car was flipped into the front yard of the Holiday Inn that was on the corner, and I just continued walking right past this whole thing, like nothing happened. If she had picked me up, she would have avoided wrecking her car. There were always people who seemed to aim their car at you, just for spite, and I could never figure if any of it was intentional or not, they'd be past you so quick that you decide since you're still standing and uninjured, that they had no idea how close they came to killing you.

Since Princeton was so far away, Fred and I would go and camp out in the cornfields near Wilma's house for days at a time, once spring like weather came back. We'd also camp close to some other girls house Fred met there, Pam was her name. I don't even remember where Fred met her, but he had a habit of meeting women anywhere he went somehow. She would let us sleep in her garage sometimes, as long as we promised to be quiet enough not to arouse her parents' curiosity.

We would just eat raw corn, which is quite good believe it or not, live off the land, and attempt contact with Pam, Dora or Wilma at night or during their school or working hours. Yet another school for me to trespass upon, I loved Wilma's look on her face as I would peak into her classroom at her. But we couldn't do that for long, since we both did go to our own schools most of the time. Summer was coming, and it was going to be time for more fun, adventure, freedom.

There would be many trips Fred and I would take to Princeton. We would get there in Elton's dad's car, which Fred stole one time, I think it was one of the first times going there, and he had me drive, so he could throw stuff out the window, and do things, plus I had my beginners permit. The battery died as we pulled into Dora's apartment complex's parking lot, and Fred had to steal one to get us home, he knew he'd have to wait till very late to try and do this. We were hanging out with Dora all afternoon, and couldn't leave till late enough for the battery switch.

We had dinner there with her family, which was very strange, it was the first time I actually met Dora's family, and seeing all the people she always mentioned, like her dad and brother. We cruised around with her in her car, going to the mall where she seemed to know everybody, and then they'd drop me off at the other car and leave for some sex someplace for an hour or so.

I think Fred was fingering her while I was in the back seat, could tell from some of the faces Dora was making while she drove along, which I could see clearly in her rear view mirror. When we finally did leave, Derf got spotted during the theft, and Elton's dad was almost arrested after the police ran the license plate back. We got out before the cops got there, didn't even know till we were back home again that someone did see us. Elton's' dad had to pay the guy we stole the battery from for his new battery, Fred was supposed to pay him back, thereby avoiding jail, don't remember if he ever did.

Another time we took Fred's sister's car, Cindy's, and I got to drive her yellow seventy-one Camaro down to Princeton again to see Dora. That was as fun as driving a Camaro could be, a lot. On the way home, I got pulled over and ticketed for taking a car without the owners' permission, which was worth four points on my license, and failure to yield to a traffic signal worth two, which I wasn't guilty of, but for some reason the cops didn't arrest us and let me drive away.

Cindy didn't realize Fred took her car and called the police. She didn't press any charges, and it had more gas in it than when we took it. I did get to see Wilma on the way home, though, and do what Fred always did to me. Only I just talked, since I never pressured Wilma into anything physical. Left him outside in the cold for once, but this didn't appear to bother him at all. Derf waited in the car, I had to hide twice in the closet since Wilma's dad wandered inebriated into her room a couple times, looking for his gun.

He would just start cursing at Wilma about where she put it, she dealt with it better that I could have imagined, like standard text lines from a bad soap opera, very deliberately with high levels of exasperation in her voice, she kept explaining to him that he left it in the garage, where he always left it, as she pushed him out of her room onto his ass, this was amusing to him.

Fred would be waiting to hear if I got any, just sitting in the car waiting, and he'd get annoyed to hear that I wasn't into just screwing Wilma, which made his wait a waste of his time supposedly, but the drunken hide and seek part was amusing to him at least. He called me a fag for not trying to get laid, of course.

Most of my junior and senior years of high school were spent going everywhere but my school. I would leave like I was going to school, but I'd wind up either going to Wilma's, or to Scotch Plains Fanwood high, to hang with Fred, and be chased around by Steve Obrien, the vice principal. He never caught me. I did actually go to my own school, just enough to pass my courses with exactly the number of credits needed. If New Providence had a truant officer, I don't recall ever meeting him since he never found me. But Steve was stuck chasing me all over his school.

I remember Fred making fun of one particular teacher, Mr. Eberstock, who would say to his students: "my name is Ebers, like the candy, and Bock, like the composer". Fred would yell down the hallway: "Hey, yeeeeberstock!" with great sarcasm, which was amusing to everyone but the teacher. He only mocked him because he thought he was a good teacher.

We both used a high pitched voice signal, a sound we both could make and you could hear for miles, Derf's was lower pitched due to his maturity, but mine took some time to grow out of, and it's how Derf knew I was there at his school, he knew where to meet me already. From my parents roof Peter could hear me five blocks away at our grammar school, in the school I would do the yell from the front doors and that would be heard throughout the entire building.

SPFHS was considered one of the best in the country, but twenty years of budget and demographic change ended that. I discovered that one English teacher there, the one who took Fred and Reggie and several other degenerates to his farm to work, was really just a gay guy who liked to watch teenagers doing physical work with no shirts on. I learned about him from a bi-sexual guy named Craig Chargil, whose idea of fun was rolling his own cigarettes and making it look like he was smoking pot, letting cops pull him over so he could make them look stupid and possibly to sue them for harassment.

I thought that was pretty funny, and he was ok as a person by me, not like Troy. Fred and Reggie never went to the teachers' farm again after hearing about the guy's true motive, naturally. It was fun roaming another school, one where you didn't actually have to go to class ever, and no pressure to be somewhere or finish any work. I would hang around the gym, outside, in the ductwork, basement, roof, and anywhere I was capable of reaching.

The school had a sub basement that spanned the entire floor of the place, and you could get in from almost anywhere around the base of the walls, where the exhaust ducts were. Derf and I would go there at night, just to get in and eat stuff from the cafeteria like we did in camp, and get supplies Fred thought he needed, mostly audio visual equipment or chemicals.

My true goal in life at that point was to save Wilma from her life, get her into my life, and show her more love and care than any human possibly could. Many times I'd get Elton to drive down with me, so I can hang out at her window and talk to her, or climb in to visit. Her house was a one level ranch, as most houses in the area were. The front yard seemed like half a football field, fairly big. A few times Fred went for the walk or ride, and once we were there eating venison burgers on an open fire in her front yard around three in the morning, one of the times we were staying in the area and were hungry. We built the fire far enough away that if anyone came outside, we could extinguish it and disappear into the woods before anyone could get close. Her father was passed out drunk in front of the television often and she would give us the burgers out the window without him ever knowing.

Other times Elton and I have been shot at with his gun, the same gun he used to hunt the deer with that Fred and I were eating, the same one he always looked for in his drunken stupor. Sometimes I'd be in the middle of talking to her, and he'd come crashing in, which would send me diving out her window, hearing him yell as I ran: "I'm getting my gun!" Other times I would be hiding in the closet in her room as I had done before when I hear him coming, and one time he did find me, then he would run for his gun.

He had three kids, the oldest brother Chip would chase Elton and I in his Mach four, but Elton drove a little better than he did. She lived next to a nice, long, deserted road, oddly named great road, very long and roller coaster like with almost no traffic. He lost Chip easily. Wilma always claimed the bullets were only salt pellets, but I didn't really want to know or cared to find out for myself anyway.

I have dove into Elton's moving car more than once, with bullets flying behind me, and Elton yelling about how I was going to get him killed, and what a Greenie I was. I think her dad missed me only because he was usually pretty drunk by nightfall, since I knew he hunted and was probably accurate otherwise, no possible way it was simply out of the kindness of his heart, he had none, I was certain.

This didn't deter Elton from going down there with me, though. It also didn't prevent me from getting Elton a ticket one night. The Hillsborough police were following us, after I had spoken to Wilma for a while, and I tossed a cigarette butt, I think it was my second or third one ever in my life, out the window of his car He got a ticket for littering, even though I threw it, because he was responsible for the car it came from. This left him quite unpleased for the rest of this night, and he remembers it very clearly, always mentioning the incident when it becomes pertinent to the conversation's topic.

Little did Elton know that when we cruised around looking for women, that I couldn't care less if we found any, because I had Wilma in my heart and wouldn't cheat on her no matter who we found anyway. That, plus I knew how unlikely it would be to find any girls interested in Elton. He was just too forward, obnoxious and over anxious, as a big shaggy dog in heat would be, if males could be in heat.

Wilma told me once while talking on the phone she was afraid of the consequences of seeing me, after the beating she took after the last time we got caught, and I told her I was coming down and I'd be better off dead than living without her. The only way I would leave her was while dying in her arms and I told her I took an over dose on something so I could die where I belonged. She only restated how she wasn't worth the effort, but I said I was coming and would see her shortly.

I hung up, then I swallowed a bottle of Tylenol and walked to her house, which did nothing but give me a stomachache. We talked for a while through her window, because I refused to go to a hospital, and she understood I would never give up on her and as long as she said she loved me, I would just go home and wait for the right time to see or talk to her again. She agreed and told me to call her when I got home, and then I walked away.

I couldn't get a ride this night, so I called my mother from Somerville to come get me because I was very tired, and she came and brought me home. I called Wilma when I got home, to prove I was fine and to apologize for showing such drastic devotion, but that's what teenagers do, and I was not really going to end my life for any reason I assured her. I only wanted to prove a point, that she was not the only one who could be that drastic, given that she often told me she wished she were dead and the only thing keeping her going in life was me and our love.

My devotion was to Wilma and nothing would change that. I realized that this devotion would have substantial effect on my path, leading me into a vast labyrinth of emotionally charged, drastic measures and poorly planned rendezvous. My main stream of thoughts revolved around the one who best suited me, showed equal emotion and as much passion as I showed, with a logical view of how obvious it was that we were meant to be, no matter what anyone believed.

Fred and I were often discussing our path, searching for a new beginning to a story within our lives, one that would make sense, create wealth, direction and invention, find humanities weaknesses and resolve them through knowledge, and we both knew eventually it would be time for a new road to travel. We could do nothing here since no parents wanted us to hang out, as Wilma's and Dora's families didn't want to acknowledge or support the associations their children had with us.

My parents only explained what needed to be done by me to get the things I would need, to get what I desired, and I foolishly never really listened or gave much weight to their knowledge. They supported my feelings at all times, usually very logically, calmly and with good insight. But even that could not prevent the next turn in my path.

One summer day Fred and I decided while walking to my house from Blue Star that we should take off soon. We began this topic once we were in front of Bell Labs, someone who worked there gave us a ride from Diamond hill to the main entrance. I lived a two minute drive away from Bell Labs, which had huge parking lots on both sides but none in the middle, just a small visitor's lot for maybe twenty cars.

Fred knew how to hot-wire anything, he claimed, as he began walking towards the parking lot on the left side of the enormous building. Why he picked a nineteen sixty-seven Beetle that day I'll never know. Gas mileage and ease of hot wiring, he claimed. I think he just didn't know how to get a different or better car, plus I didn't believe he would do it at first.

He did, very easily, and we drove off to my house for some things, leaving the car at the dead end and gathering some clothes and things I normally liked to carry. Then we went to his house for some stuff, he took a few grand from his dad's sock drawer and other necessities, and we were off, headed out route twenty two west, a very familiar direction to us. He knew where I wanted to go, and for some reason, he agreed with me, and we didn't even speak a word about it. We knew exactly where we were going.

We made some stops first on the way to Wilma's so Fred could extend our escape offer to both of his girlfriends individually, or to say good bye to them if neither accepted, and neither did. Now it was around midnight, and I woke Wilma by knocking as usual on the window, I explained that this was it, we were all getting out of this state and leaving everyone behind, to disappear and go find a life in Florida. She responded to the initial shock with disbelief and a mix of jubilation, excitement and relief, trying not to make too much noise so she wouldn't be heard, as she gathered some stuff from her room. She gathered a few of her things, I got her out of her bedroom window, and off towards Florida we went, after flying down this road with a large hill and bump at the bottom making you go air born of course. Fred couldn't resist one last flight.

It was quite an awesome feeling, beginning over again with no barriers or rules to follow, both Fred and I figured there had to be a better place, a bigger purpose to our existence, in which Wilma was included on my side of the quest as my eternal partner, and my best friend Fred who would steer us through the exit at this next turn of our collective destinies. Fred knew he'd find a woman no matter where we went, he always managed to and he was not concerned about it at all.

Thus as we left our state, the one we each grew up in and knew as well as we knew ourselves, it felt like my other cross country trip, only no return ticket was waiting this time, no adult guiding our trek. The sights we'd see, the places we'd be would all be very different than those I had seen before, and this was true for all of us. Wilma brought some food, which we ate as we drove, and the last thing I remember was going to sleep in the back of the car with Wilma riding shot gun, someplace around the Delaware-Virginia border. The owner of this car created a bed type area in the back seat, quite small, but I was very tired and fell asleep quickly, while thinking how different things would be once I awoke in the new land, with the people I knew best at my side.

EXIT FOURTEEN

Future Slippery When Wet

So here begins a new direction, forged with the imagination and belief that a fresh start far away would help me find my destiny, set my path, pleased and surprised that the woman I loved the most was willing and able to come along to share the destiny that awaited us in the southern states, breaking all ties with the people and places we knew so well, disregarding the finish of high school, and with my best friend along to share the drama and discuss it's philosophical intricacies.

Since I didn't know how to drive a stick shift yet, Fred drove; Wilma and I took turns sleeping in the back. It was one of the only times I had my girlfriend along, and Fred didn't, but he didn't care, he knew he'd find a girl wherever we would wind up. Fred tried to conserve gas by getting inches away from the bumper of a truck and letting the wake of wind from the truck pull us along, which is exceptionally dangerous, because if the truck hits its breaks, were dead. Going eighty to ninety miles per hour two feet from a wall going equally fast was not how I planned to die.

I figured we could live simply, getting work here and there and live off what we caught in the ocean or bay, plenty of fishing to be had in Florida, and we should make it there in twenty or so hours. I had some peaceful dreams, images of island type living, knowing full well Florida's not an island but wanting to live on one anyway,

279

palm trees, perfect beaches with room to spare, some isolation and solitude, perfect for beginning a life with the best people I knew.

We had a nationwide alert out on us, and never knew it. Wilma's dad saw to that. In Richmond Virginia, I woke up with a shotgun barrel in my face, and a voice saying in an extreme southern accent, "O.K. boy, get out slowly, lie face down on the ground, you're under arrest". I did, and then they discovered we were all minors, me by a year and month. Fred and I were put in the juvenile facility, and Wilma I didn't see till the courtroom.

They said they would extradite us back to New Jersey, to face charges of theft, and if I were one month older, seventeen, in Virginia I could have been charged as an adult for bringing minors across state lines and corrupting the morals of a minor. That would include Fred, as a minor I corrupted, which I found absolutely insane, and oddly ironic. The car was only worth three hundred dollars, and fell completely apart on the road back we heard. Fred told me Wilma had been waving and shouting at every car that we passed, or passed us, turned out some of those were undercover cops.

No grand theft or larceny, since the value has to be over five hundred bucks for that. I think we got reckless endangerment, but I don't recall the exact wording on the conviction. I remember the plane ride home with Fred, my mother, who came for us both, Wilma, and her father who came for her, sitting just a few seats in front of us. Wilma and I were making very sad eye contact all the way home, her saying with her lips "I'm dead", me answering, "I'll save you", her saying "please don't, I want you to live", and "don't worry about me", which she knew I could never stop doing.

Strange ride, I still recall thinking about getting a window seat and how fun flying is. When we got home, we were given probation. I continued to talk to Wilma on the phone, showed up once at her school and met her one time at Dora's work, this was the time she said I had to move on, to keep living a normal life, and if our paths were to cross again, it would be a matter of destiny in our future, but now was just too dangerous. Naturally I disagreed and told her I'd never quit, knowing we were meant for each other, but suddenly her number was disconnected, and I eventually discovered from Dora that they moved to Manville and she didn't know where, she also didn't tell me how she knew this.

Strange, because that was even closer to me than before, and I made many efforts to find her, but she was quite out of reach now. I knew she still had my phone number, and hoped that she'd reach me, but I felt lost and hurt, not knowing what she was going through or if she survived the incident when dealing with the consequences her father would subject her to, I was very worried. When I saw her at Dora's work, she didn't look beaten, no bruises could be seen. I knew they were trying to move, because their for-sale sign was one of the signs Elton and I had so much fun with once. So we were partially responsible for the length of time it took to sell the house.

During the next few months, my senior year of high school, Fred went out with a girl named Sophie Reyblat. Sophie spent more time hanging around me talking about Fred and her problems than was digestible, but I loved talking humanity with anyone. Analysis of things was my specialty, and I just explained her obsession to her, and attempted to direct her towards her true goals, and not the idiot she thought she loved. While I explained things to her, Fred would be at her next-door neighbors' house, the Peruchis. Fred was trying to have sex with Debra Peruchi; at the same time Sophie was pouring her heart out to me about how much she loved Fred. But Debra was only twelve and her vagina was too tight for him to get into, which I thought was the sickest, funniest thing I ever heard. Yes, he actually told me about it. That's why I was even there talking to Sophie, as a distraction for him. Of course, I never explained that part to Sophie in so many words, I just implied that there were better people than Fred out there for her, and she was wasting her time with him. Debra's' brother, also named Fred, wasn't too pleased, but could not do much about it, since he knew how Fred was, and knew he couldn't beat him up.

In the beginning, I think Sophie was only around me to discuss Fred, and Fred wanted me to hang with her because he knew I wouldn't try to seduce her, and he could go mess around with

Crystal or Missy Snell or someone else somewhere else. Sophie would discuss what she felt and I would rationalize, analyze, and explain her every emotion, and I always made sense to her.

Some years later I helped this girl walk and hitchhike to a home for pregnant run away teens in Trenton, where Christopher, Fred's first born would come to be. She was eight months by then. It was winter, and we hitched for hours in the two feet of snow. I got her there, without knowing or caring about how I could get home. People stopped, seeing a pregnant woman and me hitching, but not always, and naturally those who did stop thought I was the father, which made Sophie laugh. Getting home was slightly more difficult, and it was further away than Princeton.

Other times Fred and I would go to Sophie's house, I would pretend to sleep while Fred and she would begin to have sex on the couch only a few feet from me. Must have been a fetish of theirs, and I thought it was pretty funny. Didn't care at all, didn't even try to watch. I knew the eventual "Greenie go someplace" was coming. But she was kind hearted, for the most part, just her own worst enemy.

Sophie was short, heavy, but had a relatively nice face. She dated Craig Chargil for a while, which is how I knew he was bi-sexual, since she told me so and he confirmed it. He was a nice guy, and she probably would have been better off with him instead of Fred, in the long run. She tried killing herself many times; I rescued her each time, just like Shelly, Wilma, and Vera. Fred I would have helped succeed, if he were to bother trying. Doubtful he would ever try. I do remember him pretending to overdose on various over the counter drugs, which he did take, but only to get attention and concern from one of the current women he was seeing.

I talked many people out of suicide, because I knew the drive for attention could be satisfied with just some simple conversation and attention. I could lift their self-esteem with but a few words. "That's the easy way out, don't give satisfaction to those who hurt you, your life is of value, at the very least valuable to me" were just standard replies. Finding the reason behind their desire to end it while knowing the person was the easy part. I realized it worked better for me than when a paid doctor tries to console or understand, being personally involved.

My philosophy helped, too, since I knew or believed very deeply that the people who terminate themselves are not pleased with the results, which had always been an instinctual feeling for me. I could convince them that it's a chance they better not take, and there was no way to prove me wrong, or to change your mind and come back. Just sheer logic, that's all it took. With Sophie I knew exactly where to go and what to say. I wonder if it would be considered suicide if a person with diabetes decided purposely to not take insulin, or if an anemic person decided to stop giving themselves the shots to keep them alive. Guess we'll all find out one day, whether we want to or not.

I explained to Sophie how the Freds in the world function, why men do what we do, being one myself made it simple, and I used sheer honesty. All men are capable of having sex with all women, given any specific circumstance, and vice versa. Choosing to or not to have it was the hard choice and potential live changing event, for both sides. Those in between, attracted to the same sex, good luck to ya, I could only explain why that's wrong in my opinion.

Sophie understood all my chatter, amazed by the simplicity of it all, understood the complexity too. Go for whatever you want, try to be happy when you get it, see the best, and worst of most things. Find the medium. Watch out for number one, if you can. What you give out will come back to you one day, stop the self-pity and selfishness, and standard common sense phrases like that usually worked well as suicide inhibitors.

I remember one mistake I made talking with her, while she was sitting on the ground in front of the high school. I told her that pulling my hair didn't bother me, so she grabbed two handfuls of my hair and I proceeded to lift her off the ground and had her standing, which didn't bother me at all. She was fairly impressed, and never disbelieved anything I told her after that. She also had an uncanny memory for dates when things happened, and I could have used her assistance a lot in writing this book. She'll probably call me if she ever reads this, to try and correct some of my time framing or small details, but since this is how I remember things, it would be pointless.

Later on, I think soon after the Virginia trip and while Peter lived at my house, Sophie was at a party at my house. Sophie was two months pregnant by Fred and I think my parents were out for the night for some reason. The party was inside and outside my house, basically there were people all over. Elton was there, Reggie, Carol and Darcy, Craig and Gary, Barry, and Jake, Shelly and Crystal I think were there as well. Fred was not for some reason.

Sophie never Liked Peter, told him so, and they had an argument this day that got out of hand, because Peter was drinking some of my parents alcohol collection and cannot handle alcohol, I think he was drinking Saki. Sophie slapped Peter's face because he wanted a blow job from her, and as she went to go down the front steps of my house, Peter, from the bottom step, kicked her in the stomach and caused her second miscarriage. She had a few of those, possibly due to the fact that she liked drugs, and this time because of Peter's foot.

There were many parties at my house throughout the years, but I was nearly fanatical about cleaning and never left any evidence that a party had been there. I was always extremely neat and organized, and my parents wouldn't believe I ever had a party at our house, almost never having seen any evidence. The only evidence that was apparent to them was because my friends all drank and would take liquor from my parents den, which they did notice, because they bought very expensive stuff, all from different countries, but they knew I would not drink any. They didn't appreciate my sharing their liquor with underage friends, but did appreciate the fact that nothing was ever broken or stolen, or left in a mess.

Then one day, shortly after her miscarriage, Sophie decided to invite me to a party at Madeline Church's house. I went to the party walking from Blue Star, since that's where Elton had dropped me off for some reason, and all I heard walking up the street as I approached the party was Sophie yelling "Greenie's here!" over and over like I was some great celebrity, hero or politician. I found myself confronted with a very drunk Sophie, who I had to convince it was not me she wanted, but Fred being like me, and though he's capable of being this way, he chooses not to be most of the time. Sophie had been gloating about our relationship, the way I could understand and discuss things, to the point where everyone there couldn't wait to meet me, this surreal emotional super hero.

After hanging on me a while telling me she loved me, I convinced her to go home, and I wound up making out with Madeline on her couch. That was odd, since I wasn't looking for a girlfriend, never did because of Wilma, but she seemed attracted to me and I'm not totally unapproachable when it comes to women, just thick headed, I don't get flirting at all and never assume any girl had interest in me. She was pretty enough, so I didn't see any harm knowing she wouldn't change how I felt about Wilma, who seemed pretty unreachable by this time.

I guessed that Sophie convinced her I was worth pursuing with her drunken ravings before I even got there. Here at this party I met people like Oscar Mahon, Kirk Delugh, Phillip Goth, Ruth and Barney Vince, Frieda Kissler, Barney Pate, Fred and Stu Arnok, Jan Bowes, Walter and Craig Noteli. Craig was one of the two hundred fifty marines who died over seas in the terrorist attack in the ninety's. Or was that the eighties? Anyway, I also met Ida Marsh, who would be Elton's next girlfriend some time later for many years, Herb Carthal, Ashlyn Trink, who will be Mrs. Carthal later and was Madeline's best friend, Russell Bender and Wilma Bumstead.

Russell was the kind of kid who knew how to make explosives, batteries, radios and things like that. He built the only pipe bomb I ever saw, and he, Wilma and Brad Bumstead and I set it off in the reservation, to a very entertaining display. It was very loud, poked a five-foot hole in the ground, and was a big success. That was when I was around eighteen years of age. But when I met them I was sixteen or just seventeen.

I became instantly popular there in Scotch Plains as some sort of emotional hero, or over experienced teenager. I was inundated with people's phone numbers, addresses and party schedules, as if I had always been a member of the club and just returned from a long absence. These people didn't mind much that I was Fred's friend, but couldn't understand why anyway, though Fred never socialized with this crowd much, they just all knew him for one reason or another. At least they accepted me for who I was, just a friendly happy secure emotional icon of sorts, who had positive answers for any problem they faced and shared with me, along with a lifetimes worth of experiences already.

This was also around the time I started working again in my father's laboratory, where he specialized in the dehydration of waste for fuel. His challenge was to create more energy than is used to make it, making one ton of material yield two tons of energy. I got to measure results, clean equipment with sixty-three percent caustic, play with raw mercury, and had access to ninety-three percent sulfuric acid. It was like an advanced college chemistry class with true life applications, very interesting stuff.

I started working for my dad at age sixteen, and I did a good job, and had an aptitude for science, I was told. I got to take readings from the plant and monitor the process, and work with Troy, the technician who worked there who was pretty nice and down to earth. He also was a chemical engineer and very good at his job. I had to clean things that were so incredibly dirty, I had to use caustic to get any results. Caustic, for those who don't know, is a base like Drano, only a hundred times more powerful. The process, my dad's invention, was for converting many waste products into fuel, and light oil was the preferred tool of filtering or dilution.

So I had to clean the main pilot plant, and the miniature version, the test tube plastic clear tube with a Bunsen burner type of process, which was also very impressive looking. It made me theorize and realize that the conversion of human waste and garbage into energy with no environmental impact is the only way our planet will survive in the long run. Build a car that you crap in to make it go, the fuel being a process of Methane consumption, find the key to producing the most energy out of the molecules, solve the worlds fuel consumption issues. This is a substance I know we'll ever run out of.

The lab was my second paying job right after a two-day job in a pet store in Fanwood, which was my actual first paying job.

Acme supermarket stock boy was my third job, extremely boring and mundane, having to clean displays after people knocked things on to the floor, real generic job. Roy Rodgers was my fourth job, cooking food, cleaning and such. That got tiresome fast, though I liked getting free food and their fried chicken I thought was better than any.

So I worked for dad again after Roy's, with equipment capable of producing nitroglycerine, had I chose to make it. I knew not to mess with highly combustible unstable material having some common sense. Russell didn't, good thing he didn't work there. I copied the door key so I could get the chemicals I wanted whenever I wanted. Elton had driven there once; we just hung around looking at all the stuff. When Fred and I went, we filled small beaker type jars with some acids, bases, mercury and the like. We figured we would have some use for them sometime in the future, like a very advanced and dangerous chemistry set.

Wilma T. was talking to me again, called me out of the clear blue and she told me her father almost killed her little sister Natalie, and beat her too. I was amazed that she reached me again, so soon after all the drama we went through. I was not going to allow Wilma to give up, which I knew she never thought she would do. I told her about the party, how it didn't mean that much or have any impact on how I felt for her, which she claimed to know already and not to worry since I didn't fuck anyone, and she loved me no matter what.

She claimed she had an inside source who told her everything I did while not in her sight, thus proving my loyalty to her. I think that was fairly fictitious, though, unless Fred and Sophie have some long time un-revealed secret I know nothing about to share. I explained how kissing Madeline paled in comparison to kissing her, and no one ever would compare to how I felt about her in any way, and how happy I was that she reached out to me again. She gave me her new address and phone number but told me never to call, which I never did, so her father would never know I was around again.

Fred and I went down to her house in Manville, broke in since no one was home apparently, found some homosexual videotapes, which we saw were homosexual after running one in the VCR, causing us to almost vomit and make many disgusted noises, and then we just left. Before leaving, I painted a line with a slow dripping stream of sulfuric acid, right down the center of her dad's car, from bumper to bumper. We couldn't wait around for the results, and went on to Dora's, who Fred was still seeing on occasion. A while later I did go back, about two days later, when Wilma called me again. She made no mention of her dad's car, like nothing happened to it, but wanted to see me. This time Jacob and I walked down, we hitchhiked with bread trucks in the wee hours of morning, since they're usually the only vehicles on the road that early besides police. Jacob said he had nothing better to do after sleeping over my house the night before.

We were supposed to meet her at the Manville Elks club around ten in the morning, but we were very early. Jake decided he wanted to meet the Wilma I always talked about. I never really called him Jake but everyone else did, I just called him brother or geek, and we both called each other geek and brother all the time. Jake had to use the bathroom when we got there but the men's room was locked, the place was closed at six a.m. So he decided to use the women's room, which someone forgot to lock.

This set off a silent alarm, and when he got out, we stood there a minute, then we heard change jiggling like a Vegas slot machine was coming around the corner, and when the person turned the corner, we saw that it was a Manville policeman. He had his gun out and he jumped back, and we just stood there amazed. He said we scared the shit out of him, and he almost shot us, and we were under arrest for trespassing.

No one pressed charges, since we did nothing wrong really, so we were let go, and the story stood that we were arrested and nearly shot for taking a crap. We walked back to the club, which was open now, and Wilma was there. She told me that for her safety and mine, not to try to see her again, because her dad would kill us as he threatened to do many times before. I told her I'd never give up, I was not afraid of her dad, and not to be surprised when I see her again, and that she should call me whenever she could, her turning eighteen years old wouldn't take forever. I agreed to disappear from her life for a while, and we agreed to not let our love stop any opportunity for finding someone else, and if we truly loved each other, we'd come back to each other in the end.

After Wilma was out of my reach again temporarily, I hung around Scotch Plains more, and the Madeline crowd. She was a musician, and artist, playing flute at high school football games, and went to college for six years for art eventually. I went out with her for a few weeks before she announced to me she found interest in another guy, but it would have no effect on her feelings for me. I explained where my heart lied, and the story of Virginia always showed impressive devotion to anyone I told it to. Madeline claimed she had another boy friend too now, and that Wilma T could never be a problem for her. She felt we were too young to be too serious, but age never meant much to me in that respect.

Phillip Goetz was her other boyfriend, for a while, and had the dismal distinction of being the first person I ever knew to die about two years after I met him. Up till then, only the aged did I see depart. Like Rene Cobler, my live-in nana, my mom's mom. She went when I was six, and I told everyone not to cry because she was very happy now. And Grandma Ida, who made the best Jewish delicacies I ever had, like matzo ball soup, chop chicken liver, boiled chicken. Sort of boring cuisine, but good I thought. She passed away when I was fifteen or sixteen, I think. Anyway, I liked Madeline, and didn't mind the circumstance. I enjoyed going to parties and watching them all get drunk, or stoned, and dance clumsily around, vomiting every so often, found it quite entertaining.

So while hanging around these people, I saw that they all thought this one girl was a little strange, demented, and not really part of the group in any normal way. She did odd things, like laughing at nothing out loud, talking to no one usually, and acting drunk though she didn't usually drink, and if she did talk she talked in metaphors and rhymes and colors, and generally just acted strange for attention.

I remember her while I was with Madeline one day at another party just laughing hysterically out loud about nothing, which made everyone except me look at her with a peculiar look, as if she were insane. She couldn't surprise me with abnormal behavior, and that's where her attraction for me came from, someone on her level of understanding, or so she thought. She would become the other Wilma in my life, Wilma Bumstead.

After going to her to discuss what she was laughing about, and showing her that her fear and defenses were unneeded against me, and her cries for attention would be answered, she became another girl friend, along with Madeline. I was attracted to her I believe because of the different ways she saw things, in a unique way that was not like most people, which is how I saw things, uniquely.

She initially was confused about why I was showing interest enough to talk to her, and didn't know what to do about it. She thought no one could have genuine interest in her due to her attitude or appearance, not being the prissy make-up type, and I explained that I was not like anyone she ever knew or ever would know, and that attitude is exactly what I liked about her. She enjoyed watching others be drunk or stoned for the same reasons I did, entertainment. She eventually agreed and dropped the facade and let her true feelings out, and let us explore each other on an honest level.

At one point I explained to both Wilma B and Madeline I would not choose between them, so as not to be unfair to either, and neither would have been my only choice, especially since Wilma T was still in my thoughts and heart. Madeline had Phillip as a boyfriend, so she had two boyfriends and I had two girlfriends, or three depending on how you looked at it.

I greeted Phillip with open friendship, seeing how we were allowed to share affection for certain girls and still be close to each other and neither he nor I felt jealousy towards the other, as far as I could tell. Wilma would have been his girlfriend too, she had once said she thought Phillip was cute, and that would complete the circle, but Phillip wasn't into strange brew. Wilma thought he was somewhat shallow, but good-looking. He liked to smash beer bottles over his head, she liked purple.

So we went on, as we were, Madeline drifting away slowly, and Wilma taking full advantage, since I unleashed her inhibitions. Once I did that, Wilma became in touch with her desires and passions, expressing them to me freely. Madeline was far less willing to free herself of inhibitions, and she remained in her immature world of puppy love and crushes for a few years.

Madeline and Wilma were friends to a degree, and used to hang out together in the cafeteria of their school, and I always wondered if they would discuss me at all, and how odd that would be. They weren't initially too close, Wilma being too philosophically different for Madeline to communicate with rationally, but when I became a common factor their friendship grew some. They were both quite intelligent, never struggling with school and ready for college. Wilma was very abstractive and argumentative, like purple was the only good color, for no apparent reason. Madeline was more rational, into crowd pleasing, involved in all the things like football games, where she played flute in the marching band.

We went to a few Scotch Plains versus Westfield games, and I was there when Westfield kids did donuts in the Scotch Plains football field with a car, destroying it as part of their rivalry. Madeline was the first person ever in my life to get me to dance, which I don't do since I am a horrible dancer, plus I never saw the point of it. I used to go to their high school dances with her and Wilma, never bragging about having two girl friends, but loving every minute of it.

I was very proud of the fact that I out did Fred's habit of having multiple girl friends, with the most distinguishable difference being the fact that I was honest with them about it, Fred never was. Plus, I wasn't having any sex with them at this point, which did not matter to me at all, that was not my immediate goal. They knew about each other and about Wilma T, and accepted this fact easily; I guess they thought I was worth it.

I went to Scotch Plains high more than my own high school, to hang out with Fred, or to see Madeline or Wilma B, showing up at their classroom door often, peering in the window on the door and making anyone who knew me laugh out loud, until the teacher had to chase me away.

One time while I ate lunch in their cafeteria with them a kid named Bert Burroughs became pissed off at me. He told me to go to my own school, and leave "his" chicks alone. When I started laughing in his face he decided to throw a punch. Aside from missing, he left himself open, but I took no advantage and just kicked his shin, and pushed him away by the collarbone, still laughing in his face the whole time. I told him these were not "his" chicks, by any means.

I said that hurting him wasn't my goal, and unless he felt lucky, to go away somewhere, and so will I. He decided an after school confrontation was needed, which made me laugh more. Fred told me not to kill the guy, said he knew I could, but don't be a fag, either. So when we met outside, with an audience of kids surrounding us who heard about the fight, and as I squared off in a martial art position, he asked me if I knew Karate. I just said "you'll find out", and suddenly he didn't want any part of fighting with me. So I told him it could just be a wrestling match instead, since he was scared, and I wouldn't try to disable him.

He agreed and the crowd left disappointed, then I grabbed him in a headlock and just laughed while he made futile attempts at breaking the hold. He gave himself a DDT, which one wrestler used a lot, Jake the snake Roberts. So he wound up on top, his heads in the dirt, I'm laughing there on the ground with Fred sort of laughing about the whole thing too, and I told Bert we could just quit, or eventually I'd break his neck. He stopped, and asked me to show him the moves I knew, but I told him his attitude was all wrong, and he'd need a few years of growing up first. Never saw him again.

Peter, around this point in time, had to move into my room for senior year, because his grandma kicked him out for stealing from her, plus she was moving back to Georgia and didn't want him to go with her. My parents let him in, too. Then at one point he stole eighty dollars from my aunt Elvira while she was staying over in the attic bedroom, which no one believes Peter did and think I did it.

Never did convince my parents or aunt that I was not the thief, even though it was the truth.

Fred had already lived here, up in the attic, out in the storage room under the porch, this during the times we were not allowed around each other. Fred liked to run away from home a lot. Fred didn't cost my parents much money, really, just hung out, getting women and Elton to come pick him up, like another home base. While Fred was in hiding at my house, he would drive us around in my parents' cars, since I had keys to both. He was the first to show me line locks, which is when you rev the engine in neutral then drop the car's shifter into gear, thus causing the tires to spin and leave tracks, which is very bad for the car's transmission but lots of fun.

This we did several times, and I remember letting him drive one winter. He never crashed, but would slide around in the car on snow covered roads doing around thirty or forty miles per hour, and I thought we'd both die a few times. He would have the car going down the street sideways, and I'd yell at him to knock it off before my parents wound up with a wrecked car. He thought it was pretty funny to worry about, though while he was doing it, I didn't think it was that funny. He would call me a paranoid dibble brain just for worrying.

He said he learned from some guy who was from Wisconsin, and they're apparently very used to driving in snow, according to him. I got to ride around with Fred and this guy as well, and he kept the car basically sliding sideways driving down every street he drove on. That, I thought, was very stupid, you're just asking for trouble, and eventually he did slam his car against a large snow plowed hill in a parking lot, getting stuck while I laughed at him for being so stupid. Don't recall exactly when this was or the guys' name, I just remember having to walk home from Chatham someplace, while Fred and the guy waited for a tow truck to pull them out. I was home by the time they were rescued.

Peter, while living at my house, ran up a three thousand-dollar phone bill one month looking for a wife in a foreign country, through the stupid ads in Hustler and Penthouse magazines. The teen line in my room was brutalized. Dora and Wilma T were as much to blame for the large phone bills as well, along with Maria and others. I spent many long night hours with phoneitis, my own created word for over extensive phone use.

But we did actually go to school sometimes. I even went to Plainfield with Peter for entry tests for the National Guard, and my score was officer, his was ineligible, and we switched tests. We entered our names and other information on the top of the exam, and switched them before taking it. Of course, once he got there, he was honorably discharged for cheating, giving away his level of intelligence quickly. The National Guard had been embarrassed by us and had to give him honorable discharge, otherwise looking less than intelligent for not screening candidates better, and this gave Peter the opportunity to get jobs he wouldn't be able to under his own merit. I am unaware of any penalty or repercussions for my part in that, and never received any.

I had no desire for the trauma and brutality of the military. Become responsible enough to kill someone, big accomplishment. I won't say we don't need order, but it has to come from the individual, as they say, "do unto others". Obviously, the whole world will never agree upon just one ideal. Perhaps the instincts we all have for survival will induce the need to fix this world, since our language, which is the rave of our homo-sapient accomplishments, should find a way to make life more meaningful, purposeful, and remove the need for anger, hate and destruction.

I would agree with Gene Roddenberry's message, in my own way, get along with all people, abolish hunger, hate, poverty, pollution, and we'll live well, through traveling to the stars, or not. Humanities common goal should not be that different than Roddenberry's vision, and hopefully we will never evolve to the level the movie Soylent Green depicted, or any other negative representation mankind has thought of.

At this point Madeline began seeing more of Phillip, and less of me, and I was seeing more of Wilma B, because she was around more, never being too distracted by group activities like Madeline. I even got to go skiing with Wilma B's family once, which Wilma did well, but I found it a little tough to really do, they make it look so easy, it's not. I went down three times, snow plowing my way down the slopes of Vernon Valley Great Gorge.

The last time I went down I found the top of the mogul course a few feet away, sliding uncontrollably towards it on my back, and I went bouncing down the moguls, on my back. My skis were down the hill already, at the bottom of the other course I was on when I fell, and I used my heels and hands as breaks all the way down, but they didn't do much to slow my decent. Never went, or had opportunity to go skiing again so far. Wilma found me asleep on the floor in the big house, or lodge or whatever, my legs felt like I ran a marathon that I trained poorly for, or not at all. Plus, I had bruises all over from bouncing off moguls.

I still went to the parties with both Madeline and Wilma B, the one at Phillip's house being the most interesting, due to the relationship web that existed. I was always the indestructible one of the group, doing the dangerous climbs, the weird stunts like swinging on a rope over a moving train, or scaling bridges or trees, dodging or bouncing off cars, bouncing off walls, the ground and such. I never wanted or needed any drugs for stimulation or to induce such actions.

I was always trying to entertain everyone with feats of balance, strength or philosophy. According to this crowd, I was one unique geek. I seemed unaffected by anything, taking all events at their face value and never over reacting to anything. I must have appeared a little Vulcan like, for lack of a better comparison.

Madeline, would never partake in the same activities I did and wasn't into drugs either, but she could drink. I remember the taste of wine or beer while kissing her and it wasn't always pleasant, though I didn't care. Wilma almost never drank, which was more like me since I rarely drank any alcohol, even to this day. Never found any need for it, and when I have, I usually got sick, and I always regretted it. In my opinion beer is disgusting. Elton worked for Budweiser, as his dad did, which is how he got in.

Elton was at this one party with Ida, Fred and Sophie were there, Sophie was crying about Fred as usual, one big fat soap opera, and it was the last time I saw Phillip ever. While I watched them all play drinking games and get inebriated and stupid, I realized again how much more entertaining it was to observe than to participate.

I noticed that Stu Arnok, who was also at the party, was particularly interested in Elton's girlfriend Ida, and anywhere she was with Elton, Stu was there too. He would never leave her alone, and called her often, which Elton didn't like much. Stu eventually married her, getting what he wanted by being patient and consistent. He was considered by Ida as just a friend at first, but I could see how intensely he wanted her for himself, and he took every opportunity to talk to her and be around her when Elton wasn't around.

Ida knew his motive as well, but she wouldn't acknowledge him at this point and played him off as a child with a crush. She was not to be Elton's destiny, and I knew this long before he did. I believe Elton is happy with the path he eventually followed ultimately, but it was interesting to watch him stew in jealousy and anger for a while. I don't recall exactly when or why he and Gertrude broke up, but they did.

Shortly after that party is when Phillip died, riding in the back of a pick-up holding the roll bar when the truck rolled, crushing and killing him instantly. Madeline came to me after he died, but all I would do is console her, never taking advantage of such situations. She became attached to Kirk, who was willing to use the stepping-stone of a friend's death, and was also best friends with Oscar, and Oscar was going with Madeline's best friend Ashlyn at the time. That made sense, and I hoped she would be happy. I never held any grudge, and allowed destiny to control what it would control anyway which is why it's called destiny.

I was pretty far along with my relationship with Wilma B at the time, and even though the other Wilma was always in my mind, I was showing the complete devotion to Wilma B that I always show any relationship. I was Wilma B's escort for her junior prom, and that was the last picture there is of me with really long blonde hair.

I got through her little girl games and psychoses, and showed her how pleasure filled life can be. I was her first, and she was actually mine as well, as far as a lasting sexual relationship goes, or if I were to not include one-night stands, namely Vera and the hookers. Her family seemed normal enough, they never allowed drinks with meals, and their mom smoked pot while walking the dog. She believed or just stated her husband was Satan, and this guy was champion skier Jack Bumstead, who obviously pined for something other than his wife and three kids. Her little sister Cheryl was a basket case as described by Wilma, though I thought she was nice, and her brother Bradford was lost in his own little world, with no known friends. I pretty much fit right in.

Too bad I went and got her pregnant, since I had to tell my mother so the abortion could get paid for. The same doctor who delivered me gave my mom the name of the place to go, very safe, but also expensive. Her family wasn't very pleased with that, so we became sneaky, which was OK too. I was kind of used to that from experience, but her dad wasn't a psychotic bi-sexual abusive pedophile ex-marine Sergeant, and no danger loomed for either of us.

Just for an opinion on abortion, I realize many people believe this to be wrong, and many believe it to be right. I think that any woman should have the choice, to abort or not, and that no one has the right to force their opinion about anything upon others, no matter how right they think it is, even though I was adopted myself. If the right to choose faction is wrong, they'll find out after they die, and the same goes for the ones who think it's so wrong they're willing to commit from minor to capital crimes to stop it. I guess they believe it's the lesser of two evils, or two negatives make a positive somehow, as long as their point is made, which is scary since that's what terrorists believe.

They will discover in the end if they're opinions or actions were justified. I don't believe it's a simple matter of right or wrong, either, since I also believe in the problem of over population, which can take a back seat to nothing and will have an impact on future generations that we cannot possibly realize or predict now. Only now is China actually doing something about that, and even though it may appear to be a barbaric solution to some, they do have the right concept and goal.

Just like fossil fuels, what idiots decided these could never run out, and we'd never need another source of power in the long run? The question of "is the world half empty or half full" is irrelevant. Do I care that I may not have existed had my mother decided to abort me? Since it would be a non-issue if I was aborted and this text would have never been written, how could I? That would be acceptable, because I would have had no choice in the matter or conscious knowledge of this existence, theoretically.

Wilma B and I were good for each other, getting what all youths need around that time in their lives, love, communication and sex, though I felt some guilt since Wilma T was so deep in my heart still. We had sex almost everywhere we went, outside in the reservation, on the sky ride at Great Adventure, up on my roof, in many hotels and motels, in cars like her AMC Gremlin, along with inside every room of both our houses. Like some song said, "I used her she used me, neither one cared, we were getting our share", I think Seger sang that and we were the epitome of that verse.

Although I am not that comfortable with the term "used", since I don't believe it was just use, it was more like a learning from each other experience, in both directions. I knew Wilma B could not change my feelings for the other Wilma, and I told her so since I didn't want her hurt or surprised if Wilma T came back in contact with me, which she claimed to understand. Oddly, I have never used anti pregnancy devices in my life and neither did she, and she never became pregnant again after that first time. At least she kept me too occupied to cause trouble most of the time.

That is, till one day Peter and I, about a week after graduating high school, went into my neighbors' house, with the keys Mrs. Fisch gave me to watch her cat for her. We sold her gold and silver at a pawn shop n a nearby town for cash. Peter and I had become acquaintances of a pawnbroker and antique storeowner, and I even had the guy come to my own house, to pick out things of value.

I sold three things to him that day, which my mom had to go and buy back from the guy, and she was pretty upset this guy would buy things from minors with no parent in sight. I confessed to her about what she found missing from the house and she was just happy to get the things back. Pete and I were in the habit of looking for things of value, and once Peter led me to rob his own church, where he said he saw money one day, as I think I mentioned earlier. I didn't feel very good about that, but was able to overcome the shame anyway, possibly by letting Peter do the actual stealing.

I was held in Juvenile detention for two weeks for my neighbors' house incident, they called it entering without breaking, and I had to take high school classes by requirement while there, even though I did graduate a month prior. Ron Preting was my roommate, and we got along fine, no issues between us. Two weeks was all I suffered through there. I watched Fourth of July fireworks all over the county from the top floor window in Elizabeth, about seven or so floors up. That was two weeks before I turned eighteen years of age, and I got out a day before I would have had to be transferred to the adult jail.

EXIT FIFTEEN

Blind Hairpin to Sex, Drugs and that Desisto Glow

My sentence was to either go to private rehabilitation school, or jail. Naturally my parents and I thought the school would be a better idea, and we drove to Stockbridge Massachusetts in august of seventy-nine to the Desisto at Stockbridge Gestalt therapy school. Most of the kids there were there because of drug or alcohol use or suicide attempts, and this place was the most expensive non-affiliated school in the country, I think to the tune of twelve thousand dollars a year.

I was enrolled in their supposed college program, since I was eighteen already and graduated high school months before. What I didn't know was that when we got there, I was going to stay that day and not go home again. Their rule was not to leave once on the premises, which my parents didn't know either, but accepted. My parents sent me my clothes later. The school sat on about 200 acres I think, with a front yard at least five football fields big, with a full gym, four dorms and a huge mansion that served as another dorm, cafeteria and game room and was actually quite nice, if it were a summer camp. There was a large vineyard and a big barn for equipment as well.

I lived there from August of seventy-nine till January of eighty. My picture is in Time magazine in the November twenty sixth nineteen seventy nine edition. The picture was during a senior English class, because I was not advanced enough in their therapy to go into the college program they said. The title in the magazine read: "Getting that Desisto Glow". The picture showed the director Mike with a kid sitting on each side of him; I was one of those kids.

So once again I was taking high school courses after graduating already. My parents weren't pleased and had nearly no confidence in the place anymore. I was to attend the Berkshire community college from the beginning, and that's what they told my parents would happen, and it did not. My parents came for a family group session once, and had to stand around the bed of the founder Mike Desisto, while he lay in his underwear, large, hairy, fat and smelly, my mothers' own words for describing him.

Gestalt is known for structuralism, giving set goals and patterns of behavior as a common factor, every one equal, and punishment equally structured. For instance, if something is stolen in a dorm of twenty people, the whole dorm must sit quietly in a circle doing group therapy till the guilty one gives him or herself up. The only break was for meals and sleep, there was no time limit for resolution, and we waited until the person confessed.

If a theft occurred somewhere the whole one hundred and fifty students in the school have access to, we all had to sit in the cafeteria, with Mike leading the group therapy, till a confession is obtained. No activities or schooling would continue, just bed check, dorm therapy, and chores. If someone tried to run, the dorm members were allowed to pin the person to the ground and talk the feeling through by rubbing their stomach, giving blind support, and talking about the negative feeling that made the situation.

Weekly individual therapy included things like picturing yourself as an eight year old, and trying to determine how you felt then. It was interesting, but only for meditation purposes. I never thought this type or regression therapy was useful. It was always one on one, or with a parent present, to offer moral support, hold your hand, talk softly, to really cornball the mood. Very uncomfortable, and only effective for a few days, because your mind moves on, to important issues, like not getting work duty. The point was to try and determine what in your past caused the issues that got you to the school to begin with.

One kid was there because he covered himself with gasoline, and lit it. So when I made a comment about how he looked and the fact that he was gay, the person hearing me told, I was brought in front of the idiot to be yelled at, and criticized for commenting and judging, but I was able to convince these fools that I was eternally sorry, cried for added endorsement, and made the guy feel better.

Still had to do extra chores for the offense, called community hours. I couldn't believe the gall this guy had, because he still would light his farts with a lighter as entertainment, obviously never learning the lesson of don't play with fire or you'll get burned. This was the first time I ever saw anyone do that, though I knew it could be done and never felt the need to try it, and it seemed pretty stupid to me, especially since it was him doing it. He went from gasoline to methane, never learning the lesson about flammables he should have, or so it appeared.

My roommate the whole time was a little guy named Fred. He was fifteen I believe, and besides looking as fearful of the world as a possum might, he was really quiet, nice, and I could never figure what he did to need to be here. He seemed just too afraid of life, he didn't do drugs or drink, and didn't try suicide, so self-confidence or lack thereof was the only issue I could find for his being in this place.

He was very advanced in the program, and very young, I felt bad for him, thinking he didn't believe in himself, and this place over emphasized his problem, he was just timid and I thought they should just leave him alone. He was subjected to many anti-depressants, which I thought weren't that necessary. He and I never had any problem, and worked together well when chores and clean up was the activity. Ours was the cleanest room around, since we both were neat freaks. He was a small, frail guy with big raccoon eyes and black hair, with a scratchy, between ages voice that wasn't fully childish and not yet adult that cracked when he became emotional.

Another guy would just sit in meetings and philosophize. He was Indian or middle eastern, and he was always happy, very content, and liked to eat paper. We discovered after someone else read his mail, which somehow was legal in this place since we were mostly minors, that the letters he was eating were coated in liquid lysergic acid diethylamide, better known by the acronym LSD. No wonder he laughed at everything. He was never the same person after Desisto started intercepting all his mail, I don't think I ever saw him even smile once again after that. His friends that sent the letters were turned over to authorities, as I heard it.

Off school suspension was another punishment, in which you were told to leave, and your parents were instructed not to let you back home, so you'd have to go back to the school to face hundreds of hours of service. You would have to walk to town and call Mike Desisto himself to ask permission to come back, which I thought was quite strange.

Shoveling snow was one of these chores, and in the Berkshire Mountains a writer once said there are two seasons, winter and July, and he wasn't lying or kidding. It was brutally cold, sixty below zero with the wind sometimes. Snow shoveling was nearly pointless, because it never stopped coming down until spring. It was a lot of work for anyone to do.

Most of the kids took thousands of milligrams of Thorazine, Stellazine, Meleril and the like every day at breakfast, lunch or dinner and sometimes at all three. One day it was forty below zero outside, and someone switched their milk with mine and I received about a thousand milligrams of Thorazine with my breakfast. I didn't even feel the walk back to the dorm, and I forgot my coat.

I wound up unconscious on the stairs to my dorm, and when I woke hours later, the kid responsible was gone from the school, without hope of returning, and I was given the rest of the day off. I agreed with their philosophy in part, that we should all communicate much deeper than we do, but on large-scale population that doesn't work often, too much selfishness and difference of opinion blocking the way. Desisto drove you to confront feelings on the level they're on, distinguishing them from thought completely. Just feel what you do, get over it, and learn from the experience.

It's true that thoughts drive some emotion, but emotion drives thought more often than it should. So the basic Desisto breakfast food for thought was: "think with your head, not your heart, confront your heart, and let it feel". I came to realize there that what you feel, negative or positive, remains within the acceptance center of your mind forever, and generally doesn't influence your actions too often. The larger the trauma, the more frequently we access the feeling, like a bad memory to compare the current issue to with regards to the level of severity.

We do not actually forget most events; we just suppress to allow ourselves to get beyond the event. When we die, they say our lives pass before our eyes, and it makes me wonder about how much of my life I'll see that I forgot to write about here, and it's relativity to what lies beyond this mortal existence. I guess I won't be too surprised, since I did write much of it down, creating the ultimate flashback.

In Desisto, there were no locks except where required by law, like the pharmaceuticals room. You were free to go if you didn't relay the urge to leave to anyone and just left so they couldn't pin you down, but it would cost you and your parents if you did. That's what they thought. They didn't enroll me in Berkshire community college as promised. They tried to decipher me by having me picture myself as a youth and talk to myself, asking how I felt at the age requested, which is a stupid question. I went along and let them drive the wedge between emotion and thought, which was my specialty anyway and I never had trouble making that distinction. In fact, that distinction is so second nature for me that I couldn't understand others problems with comprehending it, or why they believed I didn't know it already.

There ideal was sound only within the point of view that any psychological aid given for forty-five minutes a week in some doctor's office is insufficient to help make a difference, since you walk out into the same surroundings and situations as when you walked in. They thought that by being consistent, where you live your days and nights with this help, it would have a larger impact on your personality, because it surrounded you twenty four hours a day.

Unfortunately, when the psychological help is insufficient to begin with, or just plain lousy, it makes no difference how long you subject yourself to it. The dorm members I did live with were still degenerates, with much larger problems than I supposedly had, thus making them your counselors was self-defeating and ironic I believed. They really had no influence over my choices or views, or input to any issues I tried relating to them from my own life, which seemed incomprehensible to them; just made up stories I created to mask the unthinkable Greenie side. No, they never called me Greenie; I didn't bother giving them that nickname to muse about.

I could literally feel that the other social outcasts here hated my guts, because they were all convinced I had things to hide, big unknown horrible thoughts and feelings, and was wasting their time with my patronization of their ideals. Plus, I was continuously smiling as I always did, without chewing drug laced paper, which they thought was just a cover for something, they didn't know me too well.

That's what I always do, but convincing them I was usually happy was impossible, I guess because none of them were. A good thing about this place was that no one could abuse anyone without extreme repercussions, so I was completely safe in that respect for a change, and I took full advantage of it. It was an entire community where being the "rat" or telling on anyone was the right way to be and looked upon as a strong positive trait. I could express myself anyway I chose and not have consequences for it, up to a legal limit of course.

I remember a basketball game, and I was playing with some other residences that were basically my age. I was continuously knocking the ball away from one of them, to the point where he became so frustrated he tried to knock me over with a shoulder block the next time I came for the ball. He failed, I knocked him over instead, laughing at him the whole time, and he wound up on his ass on the floor.

He then jumped up cursing me and started to square off with me, he took a swing at me, which missed, forgetting about where he was and how wrong this would be viewed as at dorm therapy. Of course, three other residents immediately grabbed him and held him down right in the middle of the court, telling him to relax and that I meant no harm to him, while I stood over him smiling confidently. I was just better and quicker at basketball than he was which is what really pissed him off.

He was very advanced in the therapy, and that simple game of basketball sent him back a year in stature, and he was forced to confront me at dorm therapy apologizing about how he acted, thanking me for not reacting similarly, as if I would. I could see how meaningless his words were to him as he spoke them, and how much he really wanted to try and hurt me, which made me laugh inside pretty hard. He had to do hours for it, and could do nothing in retribution to me. If he wasn't such a geek I might have felt sorry for him, or if I didn't see the pure hate he had for me. Poor, stupid, misguided fool, finding my own method of retribution or revenge, or kicking his ass myself would do so much less than letting the school handle the discipline, and that's what I let them do.

During a senior English class Mike ran himself as the "teacher" he asked everyone to find three boys and girls they found sexually attractive. It was a simple exercise in honest physical attraction, the only problem being that I never met a guy that excited or interested me in that way. Admiration for superb physical condition is possible, but that's just more like jealousy or envy, not sexual attraction.

I picked out three girls easily enough, but simply wouldn't state a non-truth, as my parents always taught me. No one was pleased with my answer, and figured I was just lying. I told them that only while hitch hiking did I experience that type of perversion, when a guy picked me up once, offered me fifty bucks to let him perform some oral sex on me, I accepted, and when he pulled over and handed me the money, I just got out and walked away. I watched, of course, to see if he'd try to run me over or something, but he just left.

They were not amused, probably didn't believe that story either. I didn't bother telling them the other story of the two fags in the woods that day. Incidentally, the great Desisto and all his therapists had no answer to my tickle problem either, not that I expected one. They also blew my problem off as psychosomatic, fictional or unheard of. Somehow I was not surprised, just disappointed as usual.

I was not liked, just accepted, and most knew nothing could be done for me, in their environment of fantasy and semi-reality. Mostly, we all just hung around listening to Supertramp, Zep, Beatles, Stones, Who, Floyd, and watched a guy chewing paper, till he was caught. I think some kids, like Fred, did like me but seemed unable to express and mutual interests with me, like that would deter their own therapy or something.

While I was there we went bowling, boating, canoeing, mountain slaloming, water skiing, hiking, camping, archery, and there was a large gym, pool, and many games of capture the flag. All paid for individually by parents who could afford it, except the free ones like capture the flag. Usually, I would be close to winning it, as I always was at summer camp, but these times I just observed. I wasn't into it anymore, and just enjoyed watching the lack of strategy on display. I captured many types of wild things, mostly snakes and turtles there, because that's what I do.

Once while doing mountain slaloming down a fiberglass track, I came upon two others who had crashed ahead of me somehow. I had to ditch my cart as well, which wasn't fun. But one kid was still on the track, just laying there not moving, across the track in a U like the track was his reclining chair. The curve was only a few feet from him, and the only reason I didn't hit him is because I wasn't going too fast, and I was able to get off the cart, which I got burned for because when you slide on fiberglass, it burns you, like a rope burn.

This is also why I wasn't flying along, like the people behind me. I landed against the kid on the track on a roll, got up and pulled him off, just as another cart missed his head by a few inches. The person he originally crashed with had left unaware that the kid was knocked out. The kid I saved didn't even know what happened, and I didn't offer information since there was no need to make a case out of the accident.

There was one guy in our dorm; he seemed to not have any real problems except with acne. This poor guy was covered from head to toe with zits, and when he sat back in any chair you could audibly hear the squish of his zits crushing on the furniture, making it very unappealing to sit anywhere he had been sitting. He spent his day releasing the fluids on his skin, and changing his shirts and pants many times a day. He was a really nice kid, and I felt pretty sorry for him, but he seemed at ease with his condition and utilized it every chance he got, like a weapon of filth. If he wrapped his arm around you, there would be an irremovable stain left where his arm was. He thought it was comical, everyone else was fairly disgusted.

I do recall one other English class, because the subject fit my realm of thought, the philosophical ideal that there really is no such thing as right or wrong. When someone does something, they inevitably, while doing it, believe it to be right, or they would not do it. This does not mean every action is right in the view of society or just a few others, and no two people would necessarily react the same way, but even a killer thinks he's doing the right thing while killing. Fortunately, in this case the majority of society sees this as wrong and will take exception to the act. I don't think killing is right, therefore I never killed. Even stealing, while you're doing it seems correct at that moment, though minutes or days later you may feel differently.

It's what the majority of people believe that make laws, but it doesn't mean they are correct all the time either. If someone were to injure my offspring, I would be correct in feeling that I should injure them, whether I do or not, and if I did, I would feel that it was correct at that moment. Feeling correct and acting correct are truly separate issues, one having no bearing on the other, since acting correct is based on what the majorities and society believe, feeling correct is what you do or don't feel. I can always feel the desire to have sex with every gorgeous woman that I'm attracted to, I can think about it or fantasize about it endlessly, but doing so or trying to do so would not be correct, or even realistically achievable. Naturally, I spent many hours happily discussing this particular issue, since I found this topic the only one worth discussing with anyone there.

I seemed able to make these other kids more disturbed than they were before they came in, more violent, hateful, less confidant and apprehensive, simply by being myself. I could beat them all in most sports, out psychoanalyze them, and basically prove that all the intense structure was not needed, that true control comes from yourself and your family, not strangers or friends holding you down rubbing your belly telling you it's ok. I don't think they appreciated my insight. I won't say this place didn't help anyone, I'm sure it aided many kids in finding their own way in life and to help them understand themselves, but they didn't really have anything to offer me that I didn't have already.

I wrote letters to both Wilma's while there. Wilma B was sending me fifty and sixty page conversations, which I would answer each and every line of, and Wilma T just sent me her news, like that she was moving to a new foster home, she loved me more than life, and she only wrote a few times in the beginning, ending with the usual I'll find you, don't find me type of message. I couldn't write Wilma T back, she never gave me her return address. I had not made love to Wilma T yet, but had to the other Wilma. I was her first. Never hid the fact from either and the two Wilma's actually became friends for a while, just discussing me and whatever girls talk about, while I stew up in Massachusetts in Desisto land.

I discovered that Wilma T called Wilma B out of nowhere, arranged to hang out together in Manville, and brought my two worlds together, which I wasn't sure if they could handle or not. That's how Wilma T got my address in Massachusetts, from the other Wilma, but I don't know how she even got Wilma B's phone number. They wrote a combine letter once as I recall, and everyone I showed the letter to in the school, camp, prison was envious, jealous or thought I just made these people up in my mind. I found elements of all three places existing at Desisto, it was actually how I would imagine a prison would be in some ways, appeared to be like a summer camp in others, and was always like a school.

I was allowed to go home for Christmas, since I wasn't for thanksgiving, I was not "advanced" enough yet. During my Christmas break I could only remain home a day before disappearing to Wilma B's house, for the night. I was there in the basement bedroom with Wilma, where I would hide often, since her parents didn't want me there, and I made her go upstairs after some fun, since it was too cold in her room to sleep. Then I went home.

Around three am, my phone rang, and it was Wilma. I asked her what was wrong and she said I just saved her life. Her house just burned down, the basement was totally destroyed, due to her dad's home furnace repair work. The bedroom we were in a few hours ago was gone. They moved across the street, to a house that was up for sale anyway, and they arranged to rent it till repairs were done. There was pretty massive smoke and water damage, and it would be a couple of years before the house would be back to normal. Of course I went right over, now that I was considered a hero. Her parents couldn't argue about my presence anymore.

My parents told the school about my disappearing act, and also said I had contact with the one person I was disallowed contact with, Fred. And even though I convinced my parents I didn't hang out with him, by having Wilma B. tell them so, which was the truth, I was still requested to return. They drove me up there, dropped me off, and I had a personal counseling session with Mike Desisto himself.

He confronted me with the usual type of dialog I had heard him using before on other crushed souls, till they were broken down to tears, begging for another chance. He told me I didn't really work hard, didn't try to undergo some type of metamorphosis brought on by their caring and love, I could do better, leave or work two hundred hours to stay, a simple decision for me. The "Desisto glow" had become nothing but a dull, black tiny windshield speck to me by now, and for as fat as he was, he couldn't crush my spirit. So I packed all my things into my duffel bag, except for my own bowling ball, which wouldn't fit, and windshield wiped away the annoying little speck from my life.

Now I was leaving, and a kid named Larry Taddei from Cranford was going to leave the same day, basically for the same reason, since he was eighteen also. Legally, if you were under eighteen, the school could force your presence. Larry was born the same day in the same year I was, we left the same school for the same reason in the same direction the same day. His problem was alcohol, and Mike Desisto gave him the same speech and ultimatum as I got, and the decision was as easy for him as it was for me. The difference was that Larry had already been there for over a year I think, and he believed he was much more advanced than most, so he was pretty pissed about Desisto's attitude.

Of course, we had to walk, all the way to the Massachusetts turnpike, the New York thruway, and the Garden State parkway. This took eleven hours, walking with our bags, sitting on them every mile or so to rest, in the middle of the winter of seventy-nine, between Christmas and new years. I would describe it as fun to the coldest degree. The first night I stayed at Larry's house, sleeping on a couch in his den.

My parents refused to let me come home for the first time in my life, deciding to follow the schools rule, so I slept fully clothed under four blankets in a sleeping bag in Wilma Bs' parents' bed, in the burned down house. They were not using it and it wasn't badly damaged in the fire. I even slept on a roof of a realtor's office in Fanwood a few times, on those first nights, right on the busiest intersection of the towns' center.

Eventually, my parents took me back, but only after I got a job at Friendly's restaurant. Then a few days later, I got a little room in Fanwood, forty-five bucks a week, and my parents gave me the security. They weren't letting me off, and if I wanted to live my way, I'd have to move out. This is when I collected every picture I could of me and destroyed them in a little bon fire, a useless effort attempting to rid the world of any physical evidence that I existed, just because I felt like doing that.

My landlord was Mrs. Bullock, a ninety-year-old woman, who lived in the attic, and she would come downstairs slowly and noisily at various times. I had to use the hall bathroom, which was decorated as an old woman would, nothing masculine anywhere. The room was just that, a room with two windows and a bed, a dresser and desk, a chair and closet, very droll.

It was around this time I started experimenting with drugs. A friend of Fred's named Reggie Arnolds I had met before, was born the same day I was, two years earlier, was my primary supplier and participant, along with Sophie, who couldn't believe I finally gave in to peer pressure, which I didn't really. I just wanted to see things from a different perspective, and knew my experience would not be as hers was, mostly bad.

I felt that I needed to find out what all the commotion was about with using them, having never wanted to before, and made a conscious decision to try something completely new, without anyone tempting me. No one needed to twist my arm, I wanted to explore the other aspects of consciousness and thought, wondering what creative discoveries awaited me in these altered states of mind that some great artists found using the same method throughout history.

I was certain that I would not become as lost in addiction as I saw the kids in Desisto were, and wanted to prove to myself that drugs could be handled if done right, just like over the counter ones, since it was an issue within your own mind and therefore, controllable. It seemed much like the famed Ritalin I had taken for so many years, which failed to have any significant effect on me, as far as I could see.

Before I began partying with Reggie and Sophie, Herb Carthal was the first person I ever smoked pot with, in January, nineteen eighty. We cruised through the town of Westfield looking for chicks, playing Saturday night fever's soundtrack loudly in his seventy-nine Firebird. I knew every word to that album at that time, not the greatest of accomplishments. We cruised for chicks, just like I did and would do again with Elton, and we also never found any. But we had fun, anyway, racing around all over the state, just cruising wasted, laughing at everything.

Funny thing about Pot, when you drive, the road seems to be going extra fast, while you're moving slowly. You tend to be a better defensive driver than usual, not caring about how much traffic is around, or how badly people drive or who cut off whom. Quite the opposite of alcohol, which makes the road appear to be moving slowly while you're actually moving fast, and road rage or anger can surface much more easily or frequently. Herb was a motor head, and I was not, so that party ended shortly thereafter, with him finding his time manipulated by Ashlyn and the mechanical workings of his precious car.

That was fine, since the new drug venture occupied much of my time, in a deeply creative way. I found it to be a near religious experience, as if I'm in touch directly with the forces that there are. I could comprehend some things much clearer, yet others less, and it appeared to me as though portions of your mind that had no use before or were idle were now active, and if you're not prepared for the expansion of thought, you could become quite frightened by it, not understanding where these new and different thoughts or ways of seeing things were coming from. Plus, it was the only thing on earth that allowed me to go to sleep without the tickle, which gave me the greatest relief in my entire life.

Finally, I was allowed to forget about it, my mind was elsewhere. Made me wonder why I didn't try street drugs earlier, and if the tickle really could be psychosomatic, but the memory goes back way too long and even now still persists without some chemical aid to suppress it or by sleeping in a completely stationary position as I tried to do for many years.

The mind is a powerful thing, when you think about it. I was just thankful to find temporary relief, regardless of the legality of it. Nearly twenty years of suffering finally ended with the discovery of a simple, naturally growing herb. Now this usage did not stop the feeling completely, and I still had to begin sleep in the familiar position as I always had, but passing out became quicker and easier, and no dream tickle ever occurred. The only thing I did like about alcohol is the fact that it simply knocked me out, and I could fall asleep in any position, but I've dealt with the tickle for so long that the down side of drinking made it not worth the effort. Perhaps, as Elton will discover later, I have his affliction where a vein in my head is vertical and it's supposed to be horizontal.

This condition of Elton's made him black out, but he appeared like he was fine, eyes wide open, just unresponsive to anything like he's in another world. Once we were sitting in a diner, he, Jake and I, and Elton didn't notice the sugar and pepper and stuff Jacob and I kept dumping all over his hands. When he woke out of his daze, he was extremely upset about what we did. He didn't, even to this day, think it was funny. Odd, being the clown he is. We should pity and console him, instead? Yeah right, right after he's done belittling someone I'll do that.

Anyway, the way I saw pot use was as the Indians used the peace pipe, and it certainly does make peace. I know many people who could use this as medicine, for various reasons. But the paranoia will get some people, just a bad experience amplified. It's all still in your head, so if you believe you'll have a bad time, you probably will. I'm relatively certain that if the Palestinians and Israelites would smoke the peace pipe, the killing would stop. They would both possibly forget what they were fighting about.

In the end, it can lead you to stronger more dangerous things if you allow it, which alter your life usually. My additional use of other substances only altered a short span, and was helpful in the discovery process of what should or should not be done. I think everyone should be allowed to live as they see fit, and it's humanities responsibility to assure it happens, as long as the method by which we live doesn't affect anyone else negatively.

Perhaps more like Amsterdam, allow the weak willed suicidal people to just do away with themselves by over dosing, and everyone else can be peaceful for a change. I'm only assuming the peacefulness, don't know if it is peaceful there or not, never been there, thought I'm certain it's more sedated than most places. Let the pigmies be pigmies, the Indians be Indians, and the Asians be

Asians, along with the Eskimos, Africans, French, and all of us mutts.

I also discovered that the destructive or vengeful side of me was less apparent or needed, and calmness reigned more often, since this chemical tends to make one somewhat lethargic and content with current surroundings, which can lead to laziness if you're not careful or aware. It also makes things much more humorous than they would normally be, allowing one to laugh at nearly anything, which is quite entertaining.

Your mind can suddenly visualize so many different aspects of simple things simultaneously, logical or not, that would have never been thought of as amusing normally. Having a pleasant life with little catastrophe is probably most humans' goal, and should be realistically reachable by most. I believe the national debt would be gone if they were to legalize pot, which would also alleviate some of the paranoia for users since fear of authority is what causes the dilemma, and I wouldn't care if they brought back prohibition.

I have personally seen people do more stupid and dangerous things drunk that I ever saw them do stoned. I know alcohol is more dangerous than herb, so this "buds" for whom? Not me, or not that bud anyway. Just breathing the air in certain cities is probably more toxic than smoking herb, I would believe. Alcohol doesn't occur naturally either, at least in a form that's usable to humans, Pot does.

Around this time, somewhere near the end of 1980, Fred and I went to New York occasionally, just to ride subways and goof off, as Peter and I had done many times. Fred thought it was pretty funny that I decided to party now, and he was still into it, so we added that twist to our adventures. We would party together in his garage, singing a tune re-worded for our use, and it went: "Wasted away again in my garageville", as opposed to Margaritaville, which was very funny, of course, in that state of mind.

One time we decided to go to New York the same day John Lennon was shot, December Eighth. We were just two blocks from where it happened, walked right past the doors just minutes prior to the event. We heard a commotion, basically ignored it since New

York always had a commotion somewhere, and heard later over the PATH trains speaker that Lennon was shot dead. We realized how close we were to the event very quickly, thinking we might have prevented it somehow, if we weren't walking quite so fast at the time. Didn't do much else in the city, helped a few homeless, bought some stupid things, but really didn't care for the crowds too much. Plus, women cost money there, Fred would never pay for that, and neither would I anymore.

So I was living in my Fanwood room, partying with Reggie, Sophie, Fred, and a slew of others I care not to or don't recall, and one day I get a call from Wilma T saying she left her family and wanted to come to live with me, since I was her only reason for living. Wilma B lost contact with Wilma T shortly after hanging out with her in Manville, and neither of us heard from her till this moment. Though I was still with Wilma B at the time, she understood what Wilma T's arrival meant and claimed it broke her heart and changed nothing as far as how she felt about me.

She picked this moment to tell me that she had sex with some black guy she worked with while I was in Desisto, so it was OK to have sex with her some more, even with Wilma coming. I disagreed, and I forgave her at that moment, it didn't bother me much, but I made sure she understood who my priority was, and I would never cheat on anyone, including Wilma T with her, and the sex was over for now and possibly forever. I also told her I could never feel as I did for her again, but I was glad she was honest about it anyway, and it may have no effect on our future, if there were to be a future with our names written on the proverbial stone.

Wilma T. did come, Reggie picked her up for me, since I had no car and rode my bike to work, and when she got there I was talking with Wilma B. she had come over looking for some sexual fun. I refused to give in to her, and was telling her goodbye basically, and Wilma T thought I had been cheating on her already, seeing Wilma B leaving my house as she arrived. Knowing the kind of person I am, I thought she understood my truthfulness, and she lived with me for weeks happily after I explained to her that nothing went on.

She never called me Greenie, only Christopher and she said: "Christopher, I guess I'll believe you, you've never lied to me before, and I love you so much!" which I agreed with and returned the sentiment. She also said she was scared that Wilma was going to take me from her, which I told her could never happen, she was the only person I needed or loved, and I thought she understood.

During the weeks Wilma T lived with me, I went to work with Reggie and she hung out with Shelly, Crystal, Fred, and whomever they hooked up with. I heard the album The Wall for the first time at Reggie's, listening to side three over and over, doing snow bongs with Wilma and Reggie, and basically having tons of fun. Wilma T was fairly shocked when she saw me take hits on the bong, having known me long enough to know I was against drugs most of the time, but she accepted it anyway, since she always did them.

In this time frame was the first time I made love to Wilma T. She had such a powerful orgasm that she pissed the bed, and it felt so natural to have her with me I thought we'd be together forever from that point on, now that she lived with me. It was the happiest time of my life at that point, all seemed to be fitting perfectly into place, and we were close to our roads exit where sharing the ride would be permanent.

But she eventually, after I had made love to her for her first time and many times after by her own choosing, cheated on me with Reggie in his car. Reggie told me about it, and she did too eventually, and I did blame her for it. That was one of the few times I almost cried, since the time I cried angry tears when Craig and Edward jumped me so many years ago. I suddenly didn't feel her in my heart anymore with the same overwhelming, complete, all out, "kill for her if I had to" feeling that I had felt for so many years. The great wall had pushed the sorrow deep inside me, never to be heard from again, sinking to the bottom of the off ramp construction site of my life's road that never gets repaired.

She did move out, saying her sister needed her badly and she felt obligated to go to help, as she always did. I told her she didn't have to and I forgave her, but I knew our path was not going to be shared any further. So I wound up back at Wilma B's door, just to tell her what transpired. She was very receptive and probably happy that the great Wilma T. was no longer an issue, and we resumed our relationship right where it left off, only now I was also a little more receptive, yet still apprehensive since she had her other experience.

Reggie I didn't blame since I wasn't in love with him, and I hung out with him anyway and Wilma T went on to a new foster home somewhere in Bridgewater. I told her I'd be around, and I'd always care, but my deepest love for her died that day, so the intent for going to her was only to be her friend and help her if I could, hiding the pain she caused as well as possible if I did see her again. I would have had sex with her again if possible, but I was never that into pursuing sex without feeling and those were crushed from all sides at this point by both Wilma's.

So I was free again, just having sex with Wilma B. whenever possible for the sake of having it after having been dumped on by both my emotional partners at the time, never feeling the same about either after, but it was interesting. I even got Wilma B to start using some drugs, very controlled and supportively, and she enjoyed the mutual feeling we'd share on a drug induced plane of reality. Everyone I partied with who knew me as a nonparty person was going to experience some revelation while doing it with me, not just the usual blank minded incoherency, because that's what I believed it should be, along with the experience being entertaining or fun.

After I quit Friendly's, Reggie got me the job with him at Glass Flex, the place where airplane windshields are made, along with U.S. Bongs, and we went to work together. Reggie had a seven-foot plastic tube pipe, which is what we did at work, polished and finished these tubes, and he brought the imperfect ones home and turned them into paraphernalia.

He made many devices for smoking herb, and his friend who also worked there had a dresser in his house, with each drawer full with dozens of bags of different herbs from around the world, from the traveling he did. I don't recall his name but I believe he was quite rich. He had stuff that made blue smoke, and when he put some in his seven-footer, he would force the smoke down your lungs by blowing in the shotgun hole at one end. No one but I was able to continue standing after receiving one of these shotguns, and since I was considered an amateur user, that was impressive to the other burnouts. Reggie turned out ok though, removes trees for a living in Myrtle Beach and is quite successful. Quit drugs, too, which I never thought I would see.

Reggie was a known psycho, as far as anyone I knew thought, and we had much in common, besides birthdays. He, Fred and I comprised the triple threat, thought Elton and Jake may argue that point, we wreaked havoc on many levels throughout the state, without hurting anyone, including ourselves. We liked climbing trees and high places, our motto and Jake's and my motto later would be "let's smoke a bowl and think about it". Once Reggie and I went to rock climb in the Weldon quarry, and we sat on a log near the top and smoked for a while, then left. Reggie left his whole bag of herb on the log.

Two days later we went back expecting to find nothing, but the bag was there, even after a good thunderstorm the night before, right where he left it. We just sat back down and smoked some more and thought about it, this time remembering the bag when we left. Reggie also worked for a car repair shop, the type that fixed Lotus', Lamborghini's, Maserati's, Bricklands' and Porsche's, and he had keys to the gate at all times.

Once he took a Lotus out and picked me up, and we went to the parkway for some fun. The ten-lane Driscoll bridge between Woodbridge and Perth Amboy is where Reggie really opened up the throttle, and though the cars' speedometer only went up to two hundred, he pinned that and was going fast enough to make the dotted lines for the lanes look solid. That was the fastest I had ever moved by ground transportation in my life. My guess was about two-forty.

So now I'll go off on yet another tangent, and I'll try to cover the jobs I have had throughout my life. I was just now choking down some lumpy pumpkin paste, which used to be a pumpkin cake with nuts, right after the dinner of some corn and meat granule stew, when I thought of the first job I ever had. At sixteen years of age I worked at Pets and their People pet shop in Fanwood, for two days. I was the reptile expert.

The owners' son took over, Pinhead we called him, but George was ok, just hated Fred and couldn't and wouldn't understand or tolerate anyone who hung out with him. Fred was the only one supposedly who could get away with calling him pinhead. They had a pretty good selection, but not much in the reptilian department. So, the kid realized a fast buck was to be made, and he wasn't going to let me get it.

The next wonderful job was the handicapped home for which we have the dibble experience, and I think I covered that, and that was voluntary, no pay. Then was my dad's lab, which I also covered. Roy Rodgers was the first true hourly job, which was the second most filling yet the single most annoying job I ever had. Very disgusting, handling all the food that other's were actually going to eat.

They actually fired me, wasn't fast enough, so I went to work in my dad's lab again. That worked fine, for me, but no one else, as I already explained. Here, the order of jobs will not follow any real accurate time line, but are all former jobs of mine nonetheless. I've been a Roofer for Mahon and Barett companies, a Haynes salesman in the Livingston mall, and a telemarketer for the Police Reporter newspaper, and Telco in Westfield.

I was a school bus driver for Brunner, Villani and Hiltbrunner bus companies, a telephone survey worker for TRAC, an AT&T company, a hotel desk clerk and night auditor for The Ramada Inn of Clark and Somerset, Holiday Inn of Springfield, Days Inn Coachmen restaurant in Cranford, and The Grand Summit Hotel in Summit.

The Grand Summit was over a hundred fifty years old. I have stayed in all these hotels for free, in their most luxurious rooms, which was a lot of fun. I was the midnight security guard for Van Nuys Airport, while a nationwide warrant was out on me, and the airport director that hired me was a cocaine and pot fiend and dealer, as well as a beautician, but a nice guy anyway. I was an Electrolux door-to-door vacuum cleaner salesman, a stock boy and bagger at Acme supermarket in New Providence, and a salesman of fine china with a lifetime warranty, and worth thousands, for mostly engaged people with a lot of wedding money to waste.

The Ramada Inn of Somerset is where the Durham road explosion occurred. I was there at the desk, the sky lit up around two a.m. after a loud explosion, and five minutes later a lady comes in and says she just lost everything she owned, and needed a room pretty quickly but had no identification or money. I requested she wait a few for the manager to come check the situation out. This made her and the manager mad, and I was told to write an apology note, which I did, but I felt that as unfortunate as it was for her, she shouldn't blame me for wanting verification from management. Once thirty people showed up in the lobby with the same story, I instantly gave her and everyone else a room anyway.

I have been an Amway representative, which does make sense if you want to live on planet Amway, the rest of us can go to Pathmark or any other local supermarket. Most of Amway is sub-quality, yet some small fraction of products seemed actually superior. Make the people on top happy, keep their unearned income.

The point is that unless you get several hundred people to join under you, you go nowhere. To work that hard with the possibility of eventual death as a lowly direct distributor doesn't seem worth it. Very over capitalistic, I think, and I currently refer to it as scamway. They even had Amway tampons, which my wife and I call Ampons. We have a lot of fun with their name, Amjuice, Amsnacks, Amscum remover, etcetera. I worked for Qualco of Fanwood with Bif Pots, where I packaged super glue and lock de-icer.

I was a telemarketer in Corporate Telecom, a pager company, and worked at Thul's auto parts. I also worked at Friendly's in Scotch Plains which was already described. Driving a school bus for years was my favorite job of all. Driving along a five-speed fifty-two-passenger big yellow bus, having a cigarette, a coffee, and eating a bacon egg and cheese sandwich was my idea of fun. I would also party on occasion, which would take place after all the kids got off the bus, of course. Sometimes, I would use a Marlboro hundred cigarette as an alarm clock, being so sleepy around five thirty am. I would wedge it in the crook of my middle and index finger, keep it in my lap, and take a nap. It only fell once, and I awoke sweating around nine to mass confusion and disorientation wondering why I was still there and no kids were around. I was a little late.

I was an Herbalife distributor, a Sears basement stock retriever, and I was a bus boy and dishwasher for Tarpley's on the Square. The square is now all condos, and historic Murray Hill Square is just another expensive place to live. I preferred the greenhouses that used to be there so much that I delayed construction by draining the onsite oil tank used for the machines building it. Didn't work, they built it anyway.

I worked in Livingston in a place I don't recall the name of. They made those sandwiches and burgers you find in machines, and I'll probably never want to eat anything out of one of those machines again as long as I live. I got to eat the fresh, just cooked stuff, which was great. Then I took one of their big roast beefs and twenty pounds of bacon and got told on, don't even know by whom. I didn't really care, I was disgusted by the whole place, and by everyone else who also helped themselves, but got away with it. Plus, I was starting to gain a lot of weight, which I didn't like at all, since I never had that problem before. That was the most filling job I ever had, as far as food products go.

I worked, with my future wife, at a place called Network Publications in Springfield. We called help wanted ads and offered the people looking for help another way of doing it, like through us and our targeting method recruitment service. Interesting, but completely mismanaged, and they went under quickly. My mother in law worked there too, and others. I remember one girl we worked with there, her name was Colleen Thigpen, but we called her bitch lips, for some reason. Another girl I recall was Shelly, and I only recall her because she used her boyfriends' semen to clear her acne, which I thought was mighty funny. And there was Glass Flex. I was a class five switch transmission technician and a VOIP third level phone support technician.

That covers all of my jobs that I remember, in no particular order after the first three; because I'm sure many of them will appear later or have appeared already in the midst of some other tale of life. The last two are accurate and up to date and I don't believe I missed any.

So now I was living in Fanwood, Wilma T was gone for now, and Fred and I decided to leave town. We couldn't deny the cultured sense of adventure we both had, and it was time for one. He took some money from his dad, called a cab to bring us to the airport, and we headed towards Miami, because he always thought that since he was born there, he should live there. We brought some stuff, like Reggie's roller skates, and winter coats, which are all probably still sitting where we left them, thrown off the side of Miami Airport's exit ramp where we were walking.

From seven degrees to ninety, I thought I would get sick, but Fred did instead later on. First, we stayed in a hotel on Collins Avenue at about one hundred sixty third street in North Miami. It was six bucks a night, but had two beds. The first night we went to the beach, looking for stuff to do. From the Cubans who all hung around there, Fred got two of the Quaaludes that were laced with PCP, which were notorious in that time for many deaths.

Of course, he took them, but I wouldn't, since I never tried that and this wasn't the place I felt like attempting something so potent or powerful. I spent the night fighting him off me because he kept jumping on my back, and getting the sand he threw out of my hair and clothes. Then I was watching him bounce up and down on his bed like a trampoline, spinning from his front to back in between each bounce, and doing that over and over, for about an hour, screaming wildly, till he passed out like a dead person on the bed.

I finally got some sleep. He lived, and he claimed he didn't remember anything. Then we went to Miami, and started hitching up route one, towards New Jersey. Fred got sick right there on the side of the road, so I did some gardening for a Chinese restaurant to get food for us, since we were out of money. Fred just slept for the whole day on the yard next to the place, and I brought him food once in a while. Then a day later, we got a ride.

The first time I ever drank a sip of beer in my life was this day, and the trucker who picked us up certainly had a few already.

It was very hot, and the beer was very cold, but I had to spit it out the window, because it was disgusting, tasted like someone stepped on my tongue after walking through a manure field in the rain. The king of beer did nothing for me; I called it pawn of raw sewage water, for a more accurate comparison.

The guy and Fred thought that was pretty funny. Then he dropped us off, and we started hitching again, but now the police were starting to take notice and a patrol car swung a big u-turn and stopped by us. We said we'd like a ride anywhere with a population, and the officer drove us out to the middle of alligator alley, and left us, saying this is as far as he goes, and don't hitchhike around his area anymore.

He sounded very southern with an inflection in his voice attempting to generate fear in us, trying to frighten us into going home, and he said: "y'all keep the hell out of my jurisdiction, now. Have a good day!" Going home is what we wanted too, and after playing around with some baby alligators we found, we hitched back to Miami to call Elton. We did discuss how to get the gaters back to Jersey while we were there, since they would be worth a lot, but it wasn't possible to do on foot, so we let them go. Never saw the mother either, fortunately.

Before we called Elton, we started hanging around this guy and some of his girlfriends, and they seemed like they thought we were the coolest people they ever met. Fred got to have sex with one, which is when I discovered they were really hookers. The same girl Fred just had sex with slept in my arms all night, because she felt safer she said, and I did nothing with her. Tried some, but she said she was tired, and I didn't really care.

No feeling of lost accomplishment or missed opportunity there, although she was far more attractive than the other hookers I had experience with. Later on, Elton sent us a couple hundred, which Fred and I spent on food, drugs and alcohol, though I still wouldn't drink. I looked at a newspaper down there and found an ad to get money, a place advertised that they would give you two thousand dollars to let them stop your heart and restart it, but neither of us was that desperate.

Fred told Elton we were robbed, and wire some more money so we can leave. We were both very familiar with the Western Union system, having used it several times before in separate circumstances. Elton bought the story, and he sent I think three hundred this time, and we went home. That whole trip only lasted about two weeks total.

Since I still lived in the apartment in Fanwood, it didn't feel as though we left at all, being in the same place we were just days ago, only cold again. Nothing changed, except that I didn't work at Glass Flex anymore and I lost Reggie's roller skates, having tossed them off the airport ramp into a pond in Miami. I was still seeing Wilma B now, her understanding the fact that I could no longer promise faithfulness to her, but would still give her my undivided attention. So she wasn't worried, because now she was going to go to a Pennsylvania college and figured she'd meet other guys there.

That same winter after Wilma left, I was ejected from the room I had for too much noise at odd hours, which wasn't really the case, she just didn't like my smoking in her house. I moved into the burned down house again with a sleeping bag and many blankets, using Wilma's parents shower and food, which Wilma usually suggested. There was a lot of sex and drugs, those days, and during the day it was not too bad to hang around in. The smell stays with you, though. Tough to get jobs smelling as if I just fought a massive forest fire. But I didn't need one; I was able to live off little, just hanging around the people I knew. Unfortunately, the time line will be difficult to follow for a while, since the drugs haze the sequence of events, accompanied with the stretch of time involved, but even if the events are not exactly in chronological order, they all occurred almost exactly as I will describe.

This was a winter Fred and I were still wandering around aimlessly creating havoc, and one day we were walking east on route twenty-two through a blizzard. We started in Scotch Plains, and when we reached Mountainside, a bowling alley called Echo lanes, we decided to take a break and warm up in the bowling alley.

When we left, Fred noticed that a pick-up truck with a snowplow attached had the keys in it, so Fred decided to take the trunk, and I went along, of course. We drove around my parents' neighborhood, plowing people's driveways for a few bucks, helping people stuck in the storm, even though we were in a stolen vehicle. The trunk also had an oscilloscope in it, and Fred rented a hotel room in Union with the money we made and we hung out there playing with it all night.

His parents were still upset about the money Fred took for Florida, so he wasn't in any hurry to go home again. His dad didn't believe in banks and the money he made from his Elizabeth shoe store he kept in cash in his dresser, which Fred knew. When we left the hotel a few days later, we put the oscilloscope on the divider of the highway, about a hundred feet from where we took the truck. We also left the truck undamaged in the same parking lot for the bowling alley, and locked the keys in it and walked away. Fred finally had to move back home, due to a court order making him do so, I believe.

I began hanging around Jake and Elton after that, who had known each other since their middle school days in Clark. Jake's family was originally from Newark, back when it was a safe city to live in. Elton was usually busy working seven-day weeks at night at Budweiser in Newark, so he wasn't around much then. I started going over to Shelly's house and living off her hospitality, too.

But she was like a sister to me and though I had slept with this girl while she was nearly naked in the same bed, I never tried any physically suggestive contact, respecting her as if she was really my sister. I loved her a lot in many ways; more than she'll ever know, but would not do something that would have that much impact on our friendship, or change how she felt about me.

I remember her getting frustrated listening to Fred and I converse, never knowing what we were talking about in our own weird language. She always would ask us what the hell we were saying, like it was some big dark secret about her, which it wasn't. Pot use left her slightly paranoid. She was so shocked that I smoked herb now, that she pinched me to find out if she was dreaming, which I though should have been the other way around, so I pinched her back. Then she shot a stream of spermicidal ooze at me, and we had a little war with that, much like a silly string fight. I didn't ask her why she was carrying this substance around, it was pretty obvious, but I knew it was not for our hair, which is where it wound up on both of us, along with all over our clothes.

After a few weeks of living nowhere, my parents let me move back home again. During this time Jake and I would go to scale quarry cliffs, bringing Shelly along sometimes too. We would listen to Pink Floyd's Atom Heart Mother overlooking the dark crater, with some office lights shining like tiny candles down in the distance, and the music echoing incredibly around the mile wide place. The Floyd song Echo's was impressive and fit in this setting, as if it was written just for this place and scene. We sat upon giant rocks, smoking a bowl usually, around two in the morning, watching for the dogs rumored to live here, and thought about it. Jakes thinking was philosophically close to my stream of thought. We liked to believe we were actually brothers, separated at birth by our parents somehow, and finding each other by sheer coincidence later on, as unlikely as that was due to our totally different physical appearances.

Then one night we shared a Pepsi, which in itself isn't unusual most of the time. While leaving the quarry, after hiking thirty miles or so, jumping off massive fifty to sixty foot high mountains of sand, hoping not to hit an air pocket, Floyd-ing out, watching dozens of shooting stars from the September meteor showers from the rim of the quarry, we walked down the street towards the car from the back entrance to the place.

We both had always believed were observed, by someone not alive any more or some other omnipotent force. Later on a friend of ours told Jake he saw three distinctive spirits following him around, but the same guy couldn't figure me out at all, and my aura scared him. On this night we were dying for a drink after our hike. One thing about hiking while under the influence of substances or not, it makes you thirsty, and this night we were not under any influence at all, other than our own spirited exploration habits.

So when we walked around the corner towards the car, we were discussing proof of existence after death, and we both drew the conclusion that a sign was required. This time there was no drug smoked or taken, just good hiking through the place. Just as we rung out our shirts from the sweat, thinking how we'd never make it back the mile to where the car was parked without dying, we looked down simultaneously to see, on this eighty-degree night, an ice cold, sweating, undamaged, un-opened, standing up right can of Pepsi. Good old super natural event? That or someone just stopped their car and put it down, carefully by the side of the road, in the middle of the night, then drove off. It wasn't even dirty. We were quite amazed and thankful. That event we've pondered for the rest of our lives, or at least I do.

Madeline was going out with a guy named Phil by now, but she had me come to her house one day, I believe it was around this time, basically just to see if a sexual connection could exist between us. Since we never actually had sex before, this was going to be the time for us, and it was the most awkward, uncomfortable thing we ever did. She was a little too late for exploration of her libido with me, I thought. I obviously reached my peak, don't think she did, but it didn't feel right between us.

So I told her we could always be friends, and think of me when the moon was full. She always believed that a full moon had some great influence on her personality for some reason, though I was the person with the astrological sign of Cancer, and it should affect me most if there was any effect. She said the Meatloaf song "Two out of three ain't bad" is how she felt about me, and that made sense. I said I'd come visit her eventually at school, because she was leaving soon for her college in Indiana for art, and would wind up spending six years there.

So once again I had a girlfriend, Wilma B, but Fred had found Wilma T somehow, and called me to inform me of her whereabouts. She lived in a foster home in Bridgewater, right on route two oh two. I went there, of course, again feeling compelled, even in lieu of her betrayal. I guess we both needed something, to at least say it's over, which I was beginning to believe anyway. Fred came once, and he noticed that there were huge jars of coins in the house, large spring water type bottles, and full. So after weeks and a few visits, Fred planned out the hours at which time no one was home there.

The last visit was the one where Wilma T and I decided we'd never be the same for each other again and called it quits finally with no blame either way, though I still felt in my heart that she was at fault really. This was the end of Wilma T within my life, never saw or heard from her again, and the chapter of my life including her closed forever, not what I expected to happen at all, my hearts strongest path to that date led to a dead end and vanished, never to be found again.

A few days later, we went down, Fred, a guy named Albert Stunky and I.

I believe Albert was there because he had a car, I know I met him through Fred, and it was at his house that we checked out the loot, but I wasn't that comfortable with him around for some reason. Fred just kicked in the door of the foster home and we moved very fast. We had thousands of dollars, bringing all the coins we rolled by hand to a bank near Morristown to cash in. The Stone House Coin shop in Scotch Plains is where we went with rare looking coins.

I think we each got about eight hundred, and blew much of that on good living, limousine's to the city, renting expensive hotel rooms, buying drugs, food and things like that. Albert even indulged in heroine, which I never had and never would do. Possibly the only drug I never did and would never try, though I probably have accidentally, since there are no Food and Drug Association inspections for illegal substances. Imagine asking your local drug dealer if what you bought was FDA approved, and get shot at for your trouble. We all decided not to hang around together for a while, to avoid suspicion, and thus I began hanging around with Jake.

Jacob was a unique person. He was dating a mother daughter pair somehow, and worked for his dad most of the time. He was a carpenter and cabinet maker, built bars and used lamination, since he was five supposedly, and he knew his stuff around wood and tools. He will be my best man at my wedding, and now another partner in partying, crime and philosophy. He was also as much a male whore as Fred, but better looking and much more honest.

He was the biggest self-proclaimed American gigolo I ever met, and had an ego to match. His girlfriend, whose name escapes me now, was going to school in Rutgers at the Douglas campus, in New Brunswick I believe. I went down there with him, and his girlfriend had a roommate named Barbara, who was attractive enough. Elton came with us, and while Jake was indulging sexually with his girl friend, I was giving Barbara some oral satisfaction even though she was having a menstruation cycle at the time, which never bothered me. Elton was just sitting in a chair, pretending to sleep, but stewing in a jealous rage in reality. He was why we had to leave before I could get any satisfaction from Barbara, but she was willing to see me again.

Unfortunately, Jake's girlfriend, while riding around in Jake's car a day or so later, was cross examining me about what Barbara and I were doing, what I thought about her, and being the type of person I am, I naturally told her everything, which she seemed a little surprised by. She didn't think Barbara would let someone do what I did without knowing the person for more than a day, and I found out she was laughing at her friend later, for being so promiscuous, which turned her off of me, and I never had another chance to see her again. That was obviously her jealousy showing up, and I never respected her again, to the point where I can't even recall her name. But it didn't stop Jake and I from hanging out, he was pretty upset that she did that I think, but never really said so; he seemed amused by the whole thing.

After all that was forgotten and laughed about, Jacob and I decided on a new phrase. We would just say to each other it was time to get money and we were able to find some most of the time, so our new catch phrase was "let's find money". I knew my school in Massachusetts held a few things dear, like no locks except where required by law, and no one outside anywhere, unless accompanied by another. Plus, they stole my bowling ball, or at that point only misplaced it, so I was going to find it.

They also had a video arcade, that took money, and some students were allowed to play, if they deserved to and their parents allowed them the luxury. So we at least knew of that money, and it made it worth pursuing. Jake had some money he was saving for many years, and it was time to spend some, at least I think some. He was one tight Greek geek, when he wanted to be. Jake was kind of like Elton, but not quite as bad a workaholic, he didn't do seven day weeks usually but was working often enough to be busy most of the time.

Drugs became desirable to both of us, I'd have to admit, and it became a battle, overcoming the nightly tickle event of mine by any means possible, without being arrested or dying of an overdose. Alcohol worked, too, but left me feeling so incredibly shitty that I never found the necessity or desire to use it yet. It feels like it makes more organs in my body sick than drinking gasoline, or falling from a tall building. Not too natural, in my opinion. I believed at this point, and still do sometimes that the world needs to smoke a huge peace pipe, and stop destroying each other, for ANY reason. The Indians knew what they were talking about. We are part of this earth, and it us, even down to the nice little hallucinatory mushrooms that grow around cow dung. No processing needed there, let the hops and barley grow free, without our desire to ferment them.

EXIT SIXTEEN

![road divider]

The Dark, Unlit Road to Crime and Punishment

The summer of nineteen eighty was the quest of our life, to that point. Jake was bound and determined to find some adventure, by whatever means necessary. We would siphon cars for gas, which we got a summons for in Edison when we were caught once. We decided to head towards Desisto, for some fun, change of scenery and to find money. As we rode along the highways towards Massachusetts, we were smoking a pipe, and a bong, and had the windows up; just as the movie characters Cheech and Chong had done in the movie Up in Smoke.

The Lady, a car named by Jake, a seventy two brown Dodge Challenger with no working lights except for the two headlights, was seen by the New York State Troopers. We were listening to some Floyd, our combined favorite, and we were feeling pretty comfortably numb and mellow, when Jake saw the police car coming in his mirror behind us.

He doesn't panic, neither did I, and I stuffed a full film vile of pot into the hole in the carpet under my seat, along with the bong, and put a small bag under my crotch. We pulled over fine, very cooperative, and when they came up, we rolled down the windows, and it was no movie anymore. As the smoke billowed out the window into the cops face, the cop asked the obvious question, we admitted the truth since it was pretty undeniable, and then he said, "Got any more?" I said yes, and I pulled the one bag out of my pants.

I asked the officer to borrow his flashlight and pretended to look under the car seat for more, of course not finding any, just getting the bong instead. He took the bag I gave him and opened it, then dumped it out on the road while we watched it blow away in the wind. I said "what a waste", as I watched the herb scatter in the wind all over the ground, and the cop said, "What do you mean, boy? I could take your car and everything you got here, tow you away and lock you both the hell up!" Looking as stern as he could, "get back in the car, and wait here" he said, but he kept talking to the other cop, and seemed pre occupied. Then he just took our bong, and put it in his pocket. When he asked about more again, I said there was none. He said this was our lucky day; we were just getting a ticket for not having any exterior lights, because we were so honest.

The first cop said: "wait here; I'll be right back with your ticket". We were sitting in our car for a long time, it seemed, and when we finally turned around to see what was going on, they were gone. They had to have backed up, turned around with no lights, and left. If we sat there and waited long enough, I'm sure they would have been back for more than just issuing a ticket to us.

So we left, and Jake thought we lost all our stuff, but we didn't. I watched his eyes pop out happily as I took the bulk of our stash in the vile out of the hole in the floor. "Alright geek!" Jake exclaimed. "Let's smoke a bowl and think about it," we said as we both laughed. So we rolled up the windows and smoked our way up to the school, this time with just the pipe.

I hoped the schools' office would have a good deal of money, located in the mansion, but it didn't, wrong season for finding cash here apparently. We waited till two am, parking on a dirt road next to the school that I had been walking on just about a year prior, then, like the marines or soldiers of fortune, we scoped out the school with binoculars and crept slowly towards the house on our bellies.

We used the front door since no one was out and about, and it's never locked. We scoured the whole office, but found nothing. We moved around the place, upstairs, all over, and almost got seen a couple of times. We hid behind doors while people walked in and out of the bathroom, just inches or a slight noise away from a real hazardous situation that could have become ugly fast.

We got out without being seen somehow, and went to the arcade. I used my scuba knife, which was strapped to my leg, and ripped the machine's coin slot open. Felt very satisfactory, they may like to know, getting back some of the thousands of dollars my parents wasted, and thousands of hours I wasted there, even though it was only a fraction of what they took from my family. I think we got around two hundred, which was plenty for getting some stuff somewhere in Plainfield and to finance our return trip home. Plainfield, though, was hundreds of miles away, and we'd waste half the money before getting back, paying for food, tolls and things with the quarters we had. So we'd have to find some more money once we got back home.

Before leaving Massachusetts, we decided to go on to Boston, since Jake knew some people there. I don't recall who he knew, I think he had an ex girlfriend or something there, but I'm not sure. I do remember going by Fenway Park, and Jake and I were always big Yankee fans, so while he was driving by, I sat on the window sill of the car, and yelled: "Redsox suck, Yankees rule!" This caused all the people who were waiting to get into Fenway to start running down the street towards us, cursing, screaming obscenities and throwing bottles and stuff at us, but we were able to get away quickly, and we laughed about that for a while.

Then we found the people we were looking for, some girl who had a house in the middle of Boston. We stayed there over night, listening to her and who was apparently her girl friend having loud, lesbian sex in the next room. They didn't offer any type of indication that they would include us, so we went to sleep disappointed.

When we awoke, we left and headed back to New Jersey. I was living back at home now, so I forged and cashed a check from my parents' account. Did that three times, getting about six hundred each time. I also got the Sears credit card, and used that for Jake and I, and Albert, who got back into the scene at this point too. We stopped for a light in Fanwood and there he was standing by the Sip and Dunk, a local doughnut shop. That was a while after Wilma T.'s house, and we figured enough time passed to allow us to hang out again.

I already knew him, so I said what's up. He said "nothing", and Jake asked him if he knew some women. He said he knew some girl, Annie Smearing and she had some friends, and he could give her a call. So Jake naturally wanted some action, and I was not opposed to that, though for some instinctual reason I was still apprehensive of having Albert around. They lived in Cherry Hill, and that's where we went after the splurge in Sears.

We were living pretty good, big hotel rooms, mounds of drugs, mostly pot and a little coke. This was the first time I indulged in the powder a little, and the high is terrific, like a powerful burst of emotion, thought and senses. And thought it makes you feel more in touch with yourself and others than anything I ever tried, it's very short lived. The down side is way too strong and overwhelming, making you feel like death is not far away and your mind feels empty and useless, unable to communicate or want to, and it causes the crave for more to become extremely intense to equalize the down, along with being much too expensive.

The consequences your body feels for such a great feeling are ten times worse than the positive feeling you get, so you pay dearly both for usage and cost. You need to either drink a lot of alcohol, which does alleviate some intenseness and helps you go to sleep, or do more to restore the euphoria. It's a very wicked circle this drug puts you in; I can see why people die and go broke using this stuff.

So onward to Cherry Hill we went. When we first arrived, we checked in to the hotel at about three in the afternoon, and since Albert couldn't reach Annie yet, Jake started looking for other women in the hotel, and found many things, along with a girl. After we settled in, we took a picture of an ounce of pot spread over a hotel room table in a pile with a piece of foil on top like the mouth of a volcano with some coke and Quaaludes in it. We all had new clothes and toys, like knives, cameras and radios. We didn't keep any of the photos we shot, they were all too incriminating.

The first time Jake came back to the room from one of his wanderings, he had a projector, the kind from school you put the transparent on and it comes up on the wall. Then he came back with a massive tray of food, mostly sandwiches, and he said if he had one more second, he'd have had a whole roast duck dinner.

The last time he came back, right before we began the party with the girls who finally showed up, he brought two twenty-gallon ice cream barrels, one chocolate, and one vanilla. I took a shower that next afternoon with my feet in chocolate ice cream up to my ankles. Hillary and Chyna were the friends of Annie who came, and we all hung around smoking, coking and chatting for a while, listening to tunes, then Chyna decided to go get more liquor with Annie.

This night I had my only two girls at once experience, which was a shame in a way, not because I didn't like the idea, but because I had never done Quaaludes before. They were Rorer seven one fours, and I didn't think they'd do as much to me as they did to Fred that day in Florida. I took two before crawling into bed with Hillary, who stayed behind in our room and had gotten naked already and was waiting under the sheet for me when I came out of the bathroom.

Then Chyna and Annie came back from the liquor store, Chyna got naked as well, and asked me if there was room for one more. Though I felt honored and surprised, I thought I was also on the verge of passing out, and I felt I almost robbed myself out of the full pleasure of this once in a lifetime experience.

But with both of them getting into it, I was able to maintain arousal and complete consciousness for hours. I just put more effort into Chyna after a while, and Hillary eventually got out and went and had sex with Jacob. He just got through indulging with the other girl he found in the hotel in our bathroom, and was just sitting at the table after she left, smoking and observing all this perversion, and taking pictures.

He took Hillary back into the bathroom. But before Hillary got out of the bed to go with Jake, Jake got a picture of Chyna riding me like a horse and Hillary sitting on my face, facing each other, both rocking back and forth and bouncing up and down like I was some sort of great, perverse carnival ride. Had to destroy that picture as well, too pornographic. Albert and Annie were already heavily into each other in the other bed by now, totally oblivious to everything going on around them.

Hillary liked having sex in the bathroom, since it was out of sight from the others, and Jake and I both gave it to her there separately at different times. None of these girls ever did anything like this, supposedly, and we hadn't either, and after some hours of free for all sex on the two twin beds and in the bathroom, we all passed out for the next twelve hours. Neither Jake nor Albert had the twosome I did, so it was quite satisfying to rub it in their faces, the only thing missing was rubbing it in Fred's face too, which would have been perfect, since I knew he never had this situation either.

We crashed hard that first night, with the sex, drugs and all, and we slept for twelve hours strait. The girls even left and tried to come back, but we weren't answering any phones or knocks. When we did wake up, I was first, and I went to the door and got the ear-full from Chyna and Annie, but it didn't stop them from initiating a separated, more monogamous type of orgy all over again. Fortunately, I remember thinking; we were out of Quaaludes now.

Albert only had sex with Annie and vice versa, Chyna and Hillary with me, separately this time, and Hillary with Jake but not Albert so as not to piss Annie off. Jake never had Chyna; she didn't find him attractive, apparently. They were all acting very surprised by their libidos, passion and forwardness, still claiming not to have done this kind of thing ever. I just felt like royalty, the three kings were we. We eventually ran out of money so we had to leave after a couple days of unlimited room service, sex, drugs, and rock and roll.

When we returned to the area we lived in, Wilma B's parents fell victim to Jake, Albert and I. I really didn't trust Albert, and later he would give the police a description of our actions, his, mine and Jake's about the robbing of Wilma B's parents house

He and Jake did the actual stealing, while I was with Wilma in the burned down house, and as Albert said in the police report, I "was across the street laying her". This was a planned distraction, according to authorities, which it wasn't really, we didn't go there with that intent, that heist was spontaneous.

Jake found some coin collection, Albert got some silver and jewelry he found, and we threw out the car window a platinum ring purely by accident. Albert and Jake were seen by Brad in the parents' bedroom in the act, though. We only got a few grand for everything, and we spent it on Pot, Coke, and hotel room living. We sold many things, dealt with pawnbrokers, antique dealers, jewelry stores and banks. Many drug dealers, as well.

At this point we all felt we needed to go further south, and we headed down route one from Newark, after scoring some herbs for the ride. I still have the picture Albert took of the Lady that day, the only picture from that era left, with Jake and me in the front seats on route twenty-two just before we left the state. Jake named his car Lady simply because the car would not function right, or even start sometimes, if any female sat in her or drove her, as thought it had a mind of its own and was a jealous female.

I saw evidence of this myself more than once, and it was strange, perhaps I'll give some examples latr. We left route twenty-two and took route one to Route Thirteen, to Seventeen down to route A1A in north Florida. This took us over the Chesapeake Bay Bridge Tunnel, which I always remembered, from my dad taking me over it many years ago. Unfortunately, it was nighttime and the view was not quite as spectacular as it was the first time, but it was still interesting, how the lights ran out towards the pitch blackness, disappearing in spurts every now and then where the tunnels were. Of course, we stopped in the middle somewhere to smoke stuff, admire the scenery, and think about it.

We stopped at each state line so we could smoke a bowl between the states and think about it. I'd hand the pipe to Jake who was in North Carolina, and he'd hand it to Albert in South Carolina, then me right on the border, switching places every so often and so on. We thought it amusing to be partying in two states at the same time for some reason, saying things like: "I wanna party in Virginia now Geek!" With replies, "Nah, go to North Carolina instead fag boy!" laughing much while switching that line and other similar one's between us.

We used all night gas stations where you feed the machine a dollar per liter of gas, fully automated and unmanned. If you didn't have singles, you couldn't get gas. Jake and I drove mostly; Jake didn't know Albert well and wouldn't trust him with the Lady.

On the way back, the one time he let Albert drive, in Virginia, with the Cars "let the good times roll" playing on the stereo, me in the back seat with Pam's head in my lap sleeping, who I will explain about later, around three am, we got hit by a drunk lady with no insurance who blew through a stop sign onto the highway we were on. It wasn't Albert's fault, because I was the only other one awake at the time and saw her coming at the last second. Albert never saw her. Jake was damaged and made money off the deal later, but now sciatica will torment him forever.

On the trip down, we went through most of the states at night, ending up in Daytona Beach, swimming in the ocean from three am to five, since you're not allowed on the beach at that time. We just hung out in the water and watched the police cars drive back and forth; ducking their spotlights and headlights till it was legal to come back on the beach.

If I had to be homeless, the south makes the most sense for living without extreme weather conditions threatening my life, which I tell every homeless person or beggar I ever met in the city who ever asked me for change. We eventually got another hotel room, I believe it was the Holiday Inn at the end of Daytona's boardwalk, and that was nearly the end of the money we brought with us.

Jake and Albert went dancing in the club on the roof of our hotel, Jake met a girl from Muncie Indiana, Albert met a hooker named Pam, and they basically bought us all our food from that point on. We realized we couldn't stay there since finding money was much easier in New Jersey, and started pawning off the items we bought in Sears just to get food.

Pam decided she was my philosophical soul mate, and came back with us, mainly to get away from her pimp, I think. Though Albert thought she was his woman, she went skinny-dipping with me in a KOA north of Saint Augustine, while Jake and Albert jumped a fence into a junkyard to get the starter and plugs the car needed to move on.

They managed to get some gas, as well. I did not have sex with Pam then, or ever actually, even though the circumstances would appear favorable for such action, but I was still me and I don't compromise my beliefs under any circumstances. She showed no physical desire towards me yet, and I never force myself on anyone, and even though we were both naked in this pool together, I could wait. She was a hooker anyway, so how could I tell? Probably avoided some disease again, now that I think about it, likely a wiser choice that I figured it would be at that time.

Further Along the way, I remembered this the town in Georgia, I think it was Statesboro, where Peter and his grandma lived, and decided to stop there to find him. We did, found him walking down the street, and he had his usual over excited reaction and started head butting Jake and I as soon as he realized who was standing there looking at him.

Pete kept screaming and yelling, "Greenie, you freaking bastard! Jake da' snake you idiot! How the hell, why the hell are YOU here?" He carried on for several minutes, sweating under the intense Georgia sun and cursing us out about not telling him we were coming. He didn't know Albert, but that didn't matter, gave him a head butt too, and tried to kiss Pam, who just pushed him away when she introduced herself to him

His grandmother was happy to see me, and she let us stay for a couple of days. This is where Pam and I really began our rapport together, and we spent hours talking. Jake, Pam and I had a plan to leave Albert there with Peter, and I took about ten Vivarin capsules to insure I didn't fall asleep so I could wake Jake and Pam later. Albert woke though, because Peter heard us getting ready to leave and started talking all loud about why we were leaving so early in the morning. Albert wound up leaving with us anyway, and I wound up with a stomachache and a case of the caffeine shakes. Pete's grandma gave us a few bucks to help, she was always very giving.

A little further north in a Georgia apartment complex parking lot, as we just started siphoning a tank, I suddenly felt that it was important to leave at that second. I pulled the hose out of the car, Jake just asked me what I was doing since we only got a few gallons, and I wouldn't say anything except we had to leave, with a very anxious tone and in a hurried fashion.

As we raced out of the complex on onto the highway again and got fifty feet down the road, three cop cars appeared, flying from the opposite direction behind us and turning into the complex with lights going but no sirens. They all thanked me later for not letting them end up in a southern chain gang.

Shortly after that and two states further north was the time of Albert's accident, and the Lady was damaged but we were able to fix her enough to get back home from the Fredericks Virginia hospital they took Jake to. Pam's money was gone, so was ours, but we did make it back to Johnson drive in Watchung, the street directly behind Blue Star, where we went to sleep the first night back.

Pam had sold all her jewelry for money to get us to New Jersey, which turned out to be quite a waste. I never was able to try and become intimate with Pam, because the police found us the next morning, let Pam, Jake and Albert go, and took me away to the county jail. Jake said the first time he visited me that Pam let him drop her off on route one that day, and she was headed back to Daytona hitch hiking.

So here I was, in Union county jail, on the forgery charge from my parents, who dropped the charge eventually, and luckily the prosecutor dropped it too. I was already in court once before, for the neighbor issue that got me sent me to Desisto, and now I was nineteen and ready for the big time. Wasn't till I had called my parents pleading for bail that I got out, I would never jump it, just because I like nothing hanging over my head. They agreed, but not till after a scumbag named Shameel Moronk showed up on the same tier and a few days had past.

Most of a county jail day is boring as hell, I would sit with an old roommate of mine, Ron Preting, who happened to also be caged with me on the same tier. Of course he remembered me from juvenile hall, and we wrote down every rock band we could think of on the wall with a pencil tip or something, and we filled the whole wall, along with spending hours discussing how coincidental it was, our both being here at the same time.

When you enter there, you get strip-searched and all you have goes in a manila envelope with your name on it and into some unknown place. You get the temporary tier first, A or B, which are larger with sixteen cages as opposed to six to twelve in the main house. All entry doors are on the end, which is where the shower is too. The rooms are divided into three long rectangles, about six feet wide each. One side has walls every six feet or so which are the individual cells with sliding doors on each unit, the center is the hall for the common area and entryway.

On the opposing side from our common area view, there was the third rectangle, the one the security force could walk, where food was served through a special opening, through horizontal bars as opposed to the vertical bars that are between us. The whole place was made of very hard iron, or steel or something, and a bench ran the length of the bars, from one end to the other, solid metal, about two feet off the ground in the common area. The television was in the area we had no access to, and guards had to change channels for us upon request.

There were two, three and sometimes as many as five people per cage, but only in the first two temporary or holding tiers. During open time, you could hang out and watch soul train, since the majority of other prisoners watched it compulsively. The show had some impressive women, nothing fantastic in music in my opinion.

Most of the people I met certainly belonged there, guards included. So since one has to take a shower occasionally, I did so, many times, stopped being paranoid about the whole thing after a few times. I kept forgetting how actually large and strong I was.

Three guys decided to try and pull me out of the shower once, just making a game of it to test my strength I would assume, and they beat my wrist and arm I was holding the prison bar with, and none of them were able to dislodge my hand from the bar.

I heard from Ron they wanted to get some ass, Ron or me, but I wasn't too worried, since the assholes usually left me alone. They liked to beat on Ron, though. He said it didn't bother him, and I understood that, but watching a guy get beat till bleeding with a shoe tends to make you wonder what you ever did to categorize yourself and imprison yourself with the likes of the guys doing it. This wasn't Ron I was talking about, just some other poor soul who was hospitalized.

Even the guards were surprised; looking at me, most of them said you don't look like you belong here. They were right, but I was still young, and worrying about it wasn't my way. Then, on August eighth nineteen eighty, I was given the challenge to either fuck or fight. They all said that before, but never did anything. Shameel and a couple other prisoners surrounded me, so I said, with real base in my voice while trying to sound for real, threatening and calm, "what's up punks"?

I looked around and realized there were no guards in sight, as if they purposely avoided this tier knowing the little obnoxious white boy was getting a lesson. Shameel said, "We aint no punks, punk! Shut up and fuck or fight bitch", with the other guys just saying "yea, yea cracker, bend the fuck over" and things like that. Then he punched me right in the face. How everyone misses my nose, I'll never know. Being very quick, I'm usually able to defend any hit from causing damage, and I turned just right so as not to accumulate pain in a bad place.

This just made me mad, and I saw his fear, as his blow had no effect on me, much to his surprise, he seemed like I was supposed to cry or something. Instead, I jumped up and kicked the jerk right in the face, and that caused me to lose balance and fall backwards, since I had no shoelaces, slamming my head onto the bench we all sat on. Besides having my wisdom teeth out and recently a colonoscopy and upper endoscopy, I have never been rendered unconscious till that moment, and I have never been knocked out except that one time.

When I woke, I was in the middle of the floor of my cell, face down with my pants not completely closed, with a pretty big headache. After taking a shit that didn't feel right I realized what the gay scumbags did. Apparently being labeled as bi-sexual is better that being labeled a bitch in jail. The calls of "here pussy pussy pussy!" were somewhat amusing, but no one tried that ever again. I'm not even certain they did anything, just making it look like they did, but who would believe them?

I asked them "what did you faggots do"? Only Shameel replied, saying: "what do ya think? I fucked a bitch, ya bitch! And I ain't no faggot!" He claimed that since he was looking at a picture in some magazine of some black chick, he wasn't gay. He showed me the picture and said he fucked this chick. Truthfully, I felt sorry for the weak willed low intelligence assholes. They all claimed they saw nothing and thought only Shameel took advantage, but that didn't make it better. After I explained this to my parents, they agreed to bail me out the next day.

I thought about killing the guy, just removing his windpipe with my hand, but wasn't bothered all that much by the whole thing, and I didn't need murder charges against me. Plus the nice bruise I left on his face was adequate to me at that point, even thought barely visible. Everyone left me alone after that, and it seemed as if nothing happened at all in the area.

The guards were obviously in on the whole thing, suspicious by their absence, which is as close to police brutality as I've ever come. I assumed the inmates on my tier learned from the kick in the face I gave Shameel that it wasn't worth the effort to mess with me anymore. Plus, I knew I could get out now. I guess you could say that I wouldn't mind running into Shameel again one day, in a nice dark alley with no witnesses around, so I could settle the score once and for all with that brainless homosexual asshole. I'm sure he'll get his, whether I run into him or not.

I will forever be under the impression, perhaps incorrectly, that fifty percent of inmates have the potential for being homo or bi-sexual, having seen some evidence myself. Thinking that since their looking at a picture of a naked chick while their acting homosexual, and that if you believe hard enough in the picture, your with the girl in the picture itself, doesn't make it true or them normal.

They appear unable to control that instinct, even to the point of homosexuality. How sad, to live life feeling so deprived and driven, just by a stupid bodily function. The whole purpose of existence is to multiply and pass your ideals and philosophies to the generations to come, not to shoot your load anytime and anywhere you can. Naturally, since the ratio of black inmates to other races in this area of the country happens to be ten to one, perhaps in other areas it's more evenly distributed, but that's what I had to go by for my hypothesis through experience.

As far as racism is concerned, I have only witnessed a few examples of this within the past few years. Many years from this time period, when my son is six and he attends class in Linden, he was subjected to racism in first grade. A black girl called him a fat white bastard, a little six year old girl, and when he came home confused and hurt, not even knowing what she meant, I had to explain the differences between races, which he never even noticed, and I told him to continue his viewpoint, that there really is no difference between the people on this planet, no matter what color their skin is.

This little girl obviously learned racism from her parents, and she got no reprimand or punishment for her statement. I couldn't help but wonder what would have happened if my son called this girl a fat black bitch in retaliation, which he didn't even consider, but I can guarantee he would have had some punishment set upon him if he did. Since most of his class is Afro American, I'm sure they would have reacted completely different had he done so, not just a slap on the wrist as this girl got, figuratively of course.

I thought it was very sad that even in the year nineteen ninety-eight, when this occurred, that people are still so ignorant as to teach hate for those different in appearance to them, and how humanity hasn't really advanced as much as we think it did. The incident made me recall how much I hated how my peers treated Peter for years, thinking them extremely mean and shallow and never understanding what the big deal was, just because he was black. He would still be my friend, regardless.

So my parents bailed me out after hearing this story and because they knew I had other warrants out for me, so I was not going to just go free. Upon leaving, a Middlesex county sheriff was waiting for me, to escort me to their county jail because Jake and I were caught once, siphoning gas in Edison, and he had to appear there too. That was given to the lowest court, and we were given a fine. Middlesex county jail was just one big dormitory, completely metal with individual cells on the sides for solitary. It was comprised of long rows of metal bunk beds, and I always managed to get a top bunk. I only spent three days there and no stories were generated, very boring. as jail was designed to be.

As I stood there in the court when the judge was done, I knew Somerset County had a warrant on me for Wilma T's foster home. Albert ratted me out on that one as well to get himself a lighter sentence, and they should have been there to bring me to their county, but there was no one there looking for me.

I could have just walked out free as a bird, right past Jake's dad, who kept giving me looks like I killed his mother. But I was honest, and figured they would just be looking for me anyway, so I stood there and waited for the officials to come to their senses. They did, after the judge asked me if I was waiting for something, and I just said: "no, but you should be", so on to Somerville and the Somerset county jail I went. Good thing, too, since the judge wasn't happy about me making his judicial system and deputy's look so disorganized and stupid, and he probably would have gotten me with contempt if he could, but court was already dismissed.

This place was almost exactly like Union, but much older, darker, and a little more even in racial distribution. Barely remember there, except for the fact that I played spades and smoked almost non-stop. My parents said they wouldn't bail me out this time, just because it was a lesson, and because the conditions were a little better there as I described them.

But Jake decided to get me out this time, and I Elton helped him as well. This took a couple weeks, as I recall. My parents were a little mad, but accepted me home all the same. Elton picked me up, and decided we needed to stop at a diner on the way home, after I had been incarcerated for over a month and only wanted to go home. He just kept telling me I owed him while we ate our usual bagels with butter and jelly, which I thought was pretty ridiculous. For the charges regarding Wilma B.s' house, I was eventually given Probation for three years. The case of Wilma T's house was still pending at this point.

So I was back home again, and I called Shelly first for some reason, letting her know I was free. She invited me over and then introduced me to the Waldwick family, comprised of Crystal, Gloria, Maria, and my next girl friend, Cheyanne. They were hanging around Blue star with Shelly when I was released and were part of the crowd now. I was Cheyanne's first love, her virgin experience, and I thought she was interesting, but she was a little far from herself, and really had no clue what to do with life.

She enjoyed my philosophies in a layman's sort of way, never completely grasping the ideas, but thinking them unique and interesting. She of course, came to me, and I moved in my usual way, slowly and with great care and patience, allowing her to control the pace of our contact. I believe I ruined all my former girlfriends with the all out devotion and depth of communication I showed, but true love needs no boundaries, and honesty with truth is very powerful.

I boasted love and uniqueness to all, hoped I achieved it for most. I entered all relationships for deepness, which most people find odd. I had my share of ruthless, meaningless, fun sex, but only that one time so far, and probably will never again due to current circumstance, which is fine by me. So once again, Wilma B was cut off from contact with me, but she went to college and didn't care that much anymore, knowing this is how I am, and believing it was probably a temporary situation as it was before. Obviously, her parents did not want me near them.

The mother of these Waldwick girls was a very nice person, and I called her ma because she wanted me to. I ate dinner there frequently, even after her boyfriend Rodney spit his fake teeth out onto his plate to make Crystal scream. She was ten or so. The whole family was dentally challenged, looking a little horse like for lack of a better caricature, very large, noticeable front teeth. They were all from the south, and I would introduce the oldest daughter Maria to her husband and ex-husband Herb Slunct, later on down the road. They were very giving, kind people, who accepted anyone into their home for meals, and I ate with them often, good food and fun, these were good people.

Gloria, the second oldest, was a good person, but a little shallow, much to learn like us all. Very defensive, didn't want to hear anything. The whole family was pretty cool. So I was going out all day and most nights to Cheyanne's with my new Plymouth Horizon that my parents bought me so I could work.

I was doing work at Thul's, which is where Cheyanne also worked after school. I got one ticket in that car, right in the middle of Fanwood. I was going over a hill that was the railroad tracks bridge, and there was a stop sign at the bottom. I heard a bang from the engine; it stopped running, right in the middle of the hill. So I rolled the car out of traffic, through the stop sign and into the train station. If I stopped I doubted I could get going again, because I was no mechanic. That's why I didn't stop fully at the stop sign, the car wasn't even actually running, and a cop gave me a ticket for not completely stopping at the stop sign. I think it was Officer Jarvis.

I tried to explain the circumstance, but all he said was "tell it to the judge". I did, and even thought the car wasn't running, I lost the case since I actually did not stop. I was trying to not cause a massive traffic jam, being considerate to the people behind me, and thought it was the right thing to do, but that made no difference. Next time I'll know to just stop, no matter what, regardless of the inconvenience it could cause everyone else.

I began to spend more time back at Scotch Plains Fanwood High, going to see Cheyanne and Gloria, Shelly and Crystal. Cheyanne was president of the school store business, and the lead in many school plays. One of my more memorable moments was when Cheyanne was playing a part in which there was a ship and a rock on stage, the guy was on the rock and she was on the ship, and it was a very dramatic separation moment, as the two sides of the stage began to separate, with Cheyanne and her counterpart reaching longingly across the stage to each other, and I yell from the back of the silent gymnasium "jump!" the whole auditorium laughed pretty loud, and Cheyanne Knew who did it.

I was a guest speaker for Cheyanne's psychology class, because of Desisto, and got to tell forty kids about the experience. I always had perfect grades in those types of subjects, even through thirty-five years of age, when I went to Devry institute; I got A's in Philosophy and Psychology. This time the school didn't mind my being there, having something positive to contribute finally.

This was around the day Craig Elston, Cheyanne, another girl and I were robbed at knifepoint by Louie Flugger, the only time I've ever been robbed in my life. It was out in back of the school, going away from the school into the back streets, and Louie with a couple of his friends decided they wanted our smoke, all for themselves, and held a knife out trying to be all cool and dangerous.

I was just about to knock it out of his hands and drop him, I already had my knife opened in my pocket if needed, but Craig kept motioning his eyes to me like I should cooperate, and be careful, like he was scared and not about to back me when I nailed these jerks. Cheyanne was also there and didn't need to see this, so I gave Louie the bag I just bought. They just walked away laughing, but I didn't really care, thought it was pretty funny later on to realize what a wuss Craig was. They also didn't try taking any of my money, so it wasn't all that bad, just annoying.

I spent this time working for Thul's then Sears and seeing Cheyanne, her family, Shelly, Crystal, Jake, Fred, Elton, and Theo Hilten. Theo was black and about six four, two hundred thirty pounds, and liked playing the drums to songs from Rush, Zeppelin, and the Who. He hated Elton, and actually beat him up one day later on. He did this I think because if Elton had a point to make, he'd

349

make it regardless of the consequences, and Theo didn't appreciate the way Elton did it this time.

He also liked Karate, and accidentally kicked me across the head while practicing with a high front leg sweep kick once, and couldn't believe I was un-phased or at least knocked down. Guess that's why he didn't mind any point I made, though I don't convey points exactly like Elton does. He was nice enough, but unpredictable at times. Good drummer.

I also began hanging around Reggie Brew and his crew, Reggie being the one who saw spirits around Jake, most of the rest of the crowd were forgettable, so I don't recall their names or any significant events in my life they generated. The only interesting fact about this Reggie was the fact that he became Cheyanne's next boy friend. Reggie told me once he never saw an aura like mine, and didn't know anything about what it meant, just that it was very unique, and it kind of scared him.

Around the same Jake, Gloria and I, went cruising through Plainfield around midnight. Jake had a Dodge Aries K car then, since the Lady was gone now, considered totaled after the accident and trip home. As we drove down the main street, route twenty-eight, someone from the sidewalk threw a whole McDonalds soda into my open window, missing me and hitting Gloria in the back seat.

Jake was a very large obnoxious person, who was afraid of nothing, a short temper, and he got out of the car and in the middle of the street yelled: "you fuckin niggers! I'll kill all you fuckin bastards! What's the matter nigger pussies? Can't handle some white boy? Come on, let's find out how tough you all are!" and he yelled like that for a few minutes. The people who did it were long out of sight, and no one who heard him did anything, much to my surprise.

I was poised and ready for a big time brawl, expecting everyone within earshot to be offended enough to actually confront him, but Jake was very imposing to look at, being six-two two hundred fifty pounds, and he was pretty maniacal during his fit. Gloria was scared to the point that she thought she wet herself, even more so than with the soda that just soaked her.

The cowards wouldn't come out of hiding, and we didn't have to fight anyone. I thought the whole thing, besides the mess it made, was pretty funny. Gloria thought we would be killed. I would have backed Jake, and he knew it, which was possibly why he was ready for war that night, or perhaps because he was pretty drunk already.

In another scenario of Jake's drinking moods, Wilma B and I had dropped him off at home drunk one night, and we sat in her car across the street out of site of Jake's front door. We watched Jake beat up the seven cops who showed up to try and get him into his house. He was being noisy or something, and in Clark, that was a bad thing to be late at night outside your home. So I knew what kind of fighter he was, and wasn't all that worried.

Jake and I did have to go to court for the siphoning and he was forbidden by his parents to hang around me, even though he was well over eighteen, ever since that day in court. Why his dad blamed me, I have no idea. He still did occasionally come around, just to be defiant and for fun, but I was mostly around Cheyanne, and Wilma B was going to college in Pennsylvania by then. I still saw Wilma B, but only as a friend, since I only allowed one girl into my pants at a time normally. Less confusion and apprehension, plus, I always thought it was fair and the right thing to do.

I wouldn't want my girlfriend seeing anyone else, even though I had not a jealous molecule in my body. Wilma would attempt seduction often, telling me how good it always was and that it didn't matter since we'd been doing it for so long, but I felt this wasn't right. Acting upon desire never clouded my judgment of the correctness of my action, and though it would be fun sexually, I felt it was wrong in my heart. Not sure why I didn't feel this way during other offenses I committed.

This was also the time of my experimental usage of things like Butyl Nitrate, Mescaline, Lysergic acid Diethylamide, but still no alcohol. Mescaline came first, right after inhaling Rush bought at the head shop in Blue Star, which caused an interesting and intense trip. Shelly, Cheyanne, Gloria and I were doing it, and ten minutes after we ate the little blue dots we did the rush. I remember everything going dark, and I was suddenly dreaming that I was out in space in a ship, fighting like Luke Skywalker would, but without knowing how all the controls worked. I was getting hit and bounced around, and just as a large ship hit me with something resembling the energy weapon Nomad used in Star Treks episode "the Changeling", I felt my head being bounced off the back wall of the ship, and all went dark again. As I regained my sight I discovered Shelly straddling my chest banging my head on the ground trying to revive me, yelling "Greenie, Greenie, come out of it!" which explained the bounce feeling on my head I was having in the dream.

I just sat up that second, hugged her and said "wild!" and Shelly couldn't believe I just got up and was fine. I couldn't help but feeling, for that moment while we were holding each other so close, that we should be together this way forever, she felt quite natural and comfortable, what a shame she didn't feel for me that way. Since I was now going out with Cheyanne, it wouldn't have been possible at that point anyway, but the thought did cross my mind.

Shelly said she wasn't sure I was even breathing and was ready to call someone since I was out cold for at least ten minutes, but shortly after that the Mescaline took hold, and everything was hysterically funny, no matter how significant, including them thinking I was dying. We all started laughing hysterically.

This was the second time I tried it, since the first time was with Sophie and it did nothing, as she said it would. I didn't think the second time would accomplish anything either, but I was wrong. Yes, I knew it was really rat poison, or better known as strychnine, but the senses, internal and external come to life like a flood. I can understand why people go insane on this stuff, if you're not prepared for the intenseness of the feeling.

You can see in the dark like a cat, have seemingly unlimited access to controlling your adrenaline, which explains why some idiots believe they can fly I believe, and it gives seemingly endless strength and endurance, which certainly could be a bad thing. Acid or LSD had the same effect on me, and for all the people I tripped with, according to them.

It's like an out of body experience while you're fully awake and conscious, very intensely over amplified in every aspect of the senses. I have never actually seen anything that was not really there. Hallucinations are just in your mind, and mine apparently would not allow such irrational or illogical thoughts and visions to exist.

No pink elephants, thinking I'm a bird, just the sinking or floating footsteps, which is really just the sensation of becoming highly aware of your leg muscles flexing and relaxing when they're tired, walls bleeding, breathing, or hair growing, just the usual refraction of light experienced with greater intensity and sensitivity.

If you actually stare at a wall or door long enough, you'll see it move slightly, just like I did as a child by concentrating. With this stuff the concentration state is more permanent, and you can't shut it off. After twelve or thirteen hours, you usually feel the need to end the trip, and some people become panicked that it won't, but logic should reign since the mind is in control, and acceptance that it's over should be easy, but it's not that easy for everyone.

The wearing-off ending effect was nothing near as bad as coke, and really easy, which I found odd. You're just strait again, no overwhelming feelings of needing more or dysfunction, it's over, period.

I guess what interested me in the hallucination experience was a story my mother told me, where a friend of hers daughter was given some LSD in her drink at a party, without her knowing it. She went completely insane, and wound up hospitalized for seven years after the incident. She continues to get flash backs, and needs constant therapy. The person who did it was jailed.

So I needed to find out what could be that overwhelming, and I did. I felt sorry for anyone who was given the experience without their knowledge, understanding how they could think they're dying, going insane or something. All someone had to do for that poor girl was to explain what she was experiencing, talk to her and tell her she's ok and stay with her, and the entire trauma might have been avoided.

I agreed that it was a very bad thing to do to someone, but if done properly, with a lot of time to spare and a much sedated atmosphere, with people you know and care about or trust, it can be just as enlightening as it can be destructive or dangerous.

I have climbed through mountains, valleys, up trees, bridges and buildings while tripping, mostly at night, never having any doubt of my ability, since I did all those things before utilizing drugs anyway. The insight into your own persona is incredible, and I understand why American Indians felt so strongly about vision quests and peyote buttons, or peace pipes.

The strength of the mind in that state differs from the usual, and unlike the cocaine horror, there is no down, wish you were dead, empty feeling, an hour after coming down from doing it. Trips just end, and contrary to popular belief, I recall nearly every trip I ever went on. Like when Cheyanne, Shelly and I hiked the mountains nearly all night, or when Jake and I went cliff climbing in Weldon quarry, with Shelly sometimes, we both thought of her as our little sister. I have never had a flash back, as some people claim to get, though I've wished for some occasionally, just for entertainment purposes.

One time, I was at Sip and Dunk in Fanwood tripping with Shelly, and I felt the need to go home. So I started walking, hearing dogs bark from miles around, sirens, TV's, and any other noise my oversensitive hearing could get, and decided to call my mom for a ride home from Blue Star. I told her what I was doing, and said she just needed to talk with me, because it would be a while before I could go to sleep, and it would make for some interesting philosophy with her.

I had her laughing after an hour, she was pretty mad at first. Of course, I told her I wouldn't do that again. She was afraid I'd wind up like her friend's daughter, and I had her wondering after an hour why it affected her friend's daughter so much, when it didn't seem that bad for me. I tried to explain what just not knowing could do, but that's hard for someone who never experienced it to understand.

Another trip was Jake and I playing a good two back-to-back games of golf at Oakridge, Clark's local course. We both played well that day, and joined up with an elderly couple on the second game that were very nice, but couldn't understand why we were always laughing at things. This was the day I shot the eighty-six; I was unable to miss the greens from the fairway for some reason.

Most of the trips I took were with Jake, always a long journey somewhere through the woods, looking for the supposed witch cult that was said to exist in the reservation, but we never found them. We went to the quarry too, and had one great night of watching the September meteor showers from the quarry all night, counting at least a hundred between us. Jake thought we were just hallucinating, but there was actually a shower, and I discovered later that this occurs every year anyway. Our supplier was a girl who lived two houses away from Jake's in Clark, not where you'd expect to find this type of deviation, but we got a sheet of acid from her once, sold some and in total, perhaps took ten or eleven over time.

I have never had a bad experience from this substance, but I did know that it may not be good for long term exposure, just like anything else including alcohol. The myth that it causes insanity I believe is just that, a myth and fright tactic in most cases, unless you want to believe it, then anything's possible. Naturally, if some people are susceptible to negative or self-destructive thought patterns, I would highly recommend avoiding this stuff.

Back to Cheyanne's roll in my life, I would describe her as thin and small or frail, with a pretty face and a boney body and black hair to the extreme, more on her chest than mine. That's not saying much, since I didn't have to shave regularly till I was nearly twenty-two. She was one bad driver, needed to take the test a few times to pass and get her license, even thought she took lessons prior, and it was the same with Gloria.

EXIT SEVENTEEN

Skidding Off Road into Incarceration Circle

Cheyanne's heart was always looking for the right place, much misguided devotion, ideas, very insecure, but kind and a real good natured kind of person. Her innocence was never compromised, not by me anyhow, and she stood by me faithfully on May twenty fifth, nineteen-eighty one. This was to be sentencing day for the foster home incident, and Albert Stunky has his way in pleading out of that one, too.

Albert eventually married his large ugly probation officer, so he got his. Fred had already been sentenced to prison, Annandale, two five-year concurrent sentences, with parole available in nine months, for something he did without me for once. I was unaware of that fact at this point, wasn't really hanging around Fred for a while. He robbed someone's house while they were eating dinner, without them even knowing he walked in, and the tracks he left in the snow leaving the house lead officials right to him.

Prisoners do about one fifth the sentenced time they are given for first conviction, a third for the second time, half for the third time, and then you do the full sentence or just don't get out ever, or shouldn't. The problem is the lack of space. I don't recall the exact percentage of criminals to the general public, but prisons need a new idea, and not something like Australia, just dump our problems elsewhere. Space, perhaps, but that would be the same thing, send the problem elsewhere. They call it a correctional facility, but what exactly are they correcting? Just keeping you out of society to protect everyone else is more likely a valid explanation.

Give the non-violent ones a planet to screw up themselves, uninhabited of course, and keep all the violent ones except murderers on a colony separately, but confined. Killers are another story, and determining the guilt of one should be the priority, because they should all just be hung from a wall for the victims' families to torture and kill, if they're truly guilty. Burn, or not to burn, vengeance or forgiveness that is the question. If someone killed another person who was related to me, I wouldn't even have to think about it, I would want their death, and no one I believe can honestly say they wouldn't feel the same.

Of course, it's beyond me to actually do that much harm, for fear of any possible repercussions, because I do believe that ending anyone's or any thing's life will weigh heavily upon what happens to your bio electric energy after you die. This is possibly the only thing that weighs. How many bugs or animals did you crush as a kid, Christopher? Oh, around a hundred thousand. I would not want to be an executioner, either. I think they're in for one nasty surprise when they die, even though they believe they were only doing what justice called for, or their job.

The only events I do recall about the months prior to sentencing were the cliff climbing, hiking, and going to Blue Star of course. Shelly, Cheyanne and Gloria had even gone hiking with Jake and me a few times, and I remember having to carry Cheyanne on my back down the side of the mountain one of those times, since she was too wasted to walk that type of terrain, or any other terrain, really.

At this point I was working in Sears, which was as dull a job as any could be. I would reflect on more of the time spent with Cheyanne in the months before this day in may, but all I remember besides the accident in the Plymouth Horizon with Shelly and Cheyanne was that it was just a big, wasted, endless party, which ended the night before court, with Reggie Arnolds driving me home so wasted he couldn't see.

He was taking a turn heading up Diamond Hill road at about ninety miles an hour. We both heard the tire pop; the car started spinning wildly across all the lanes at three in the morning, luckily there was no traffic. If we had flipped, we were dead. Never got that out of my head for the next year plus, and I would on occasion wish he had flipped that night.

It didn't seem quite right, this man in a robe with the power to send people to some common place where they can no longer interact with society, not really knowing who or what type of person they are. It's more power than I could live guiltlessly with, even though the cause is just, so called justice.

But speak the words he did, saying, "I sentence you to two five-year sentences concurrent, in a state correctional facility beginning immediately, bailiff, do you duty", which was sort of a shocking thing. To have someone decide to take away some years of your life, beginning at that very moment, can be an extreme shock to the system. Especially since everyone expected me to walk out and go home that day.

I could see the disbelief and tears of Cheyanne and my parents, and I was surprised, and even a little pissed at the public defender, who really does nothing spectacular for defendants. It was due to prior trouble, according to the judge. I felt more trapped than I had ever before. When they put me in the County holding cell for transport to Yardville, I met Herb Slunct. He had just received a similar sentence from the same judge, and from that day, for nine months we would be side by side almost the whole time.

Yardville is a maximum-security short term, fifteen to fifty year sentence type of prison, and a processing center for new inmates. Eight eight four three eight was my new name and prisoner designation number, and his was Eight eight four three seven. I felt like Patrick McGoohan from the show, the prisoner. My parents had to get rid of my last pet, the boa, since I wouldn't be around to feed it for a while and they refused to.

Herb and I would share the bunk bed; I always got the top, because we trusted each other more than the other prisoners. That was only because we shared our shock with each other about how stupid people could be, meaning us, to allow such atrocities to occur and basically throw away a portion of our lives for nothing.

Herb was a chef, thus became useful to the rehabilitation process by utilizing his skills to get himself transferred into a satellite minimum-security facility, no fences, gates, or locks, located in High Point State Park. He was, for all intent and purposes a good guy, just a victim of himself, his fears and addictions. We usually watched each other's back, if we could, but it wasn't necessary most of the time.

It appears to me this was the way the philosophers lived, all isolated, brilliant, and somewhat sociopathic. Perhaps it was just chance that the right people had been drawn together in that ancient time, isolated, as any humans confined to debate life would do, with nothing else to contemplate.

So by implementing prisons, we create the opportunity for great philosophy, since no one there has anything else to do. Perhaps take inventory of the foot locker they give you to keep locked by your bunk, bathe, eat, smoke, play spades, and either try to intimidate, defend, or ignore others, and philosophize about what the hell you're doing there, and how you got there.

When society puts enough mentally unbalanced people into the same environment for long periods of time where nothing is the main topic, you wind up with fighters, victims, and philosophers. Cast out as dangerous or unproductive by society, all different in their methods, thoughts and actions, either there is war or peaceful discussion, and war does win out in many instances, among such unbalanced individuals, but not always.

The only other discussions revolve around stories of other illegal acts committed before reaching here, that they got away with, or describing different women you screwed, or wish you did. Also common memories of places we've been would occupy time, sharing knowledge of areas where others may know of as well, all being from the same state usually.

When you arrive in Yardville, you're subjected to medical exams and a six hundred question psychoanalytical profile test. This was the most interesting accumulation of multi lie detecting tests I ever saw. Asking things like do you hate your mother, and sixteen other questions with the exact same purpose, to determine your feelings about your mother, asked sixteen different ways. If your mother had a million dollars and was dying, would you pull the plug? The whole thing had me laughing so hard I could barely contain it inside.

I clued everyone in the room in on what was being done with repetitive questions in many forms about the same things, which some inmates already knew. We had no idea what classification we faced. Yardville only lasts a couple weeks, sort of the prison prep holding area, very secure and full of the basic scum of the earth, and there I was sitting having breakfast, lunch and dinner with rapists, arsonists, armed robbers, and even killers. Some of these guys were going to be staying there for a very long time.

Others, like Herb and I were never told too soon that we were leaving, but after much wondering about what was going on, we just heard from others that we were being classified into which facility we were going to serve time in, Annandale, Leesburg, Bordentown, Rahway, Trenton or stay here in Yardville.

Herb somehow knew we were going to Annandale, since our crimes were minor and nonviolent, along with being our first offenses, and that's exactly where we were sent. Upon arriving at Annandale, there were already fools yelling "were gonna turn ya into the homo's you are, mother fuckers!" "Give up the money or the ass bitches!" and other kind, cute welcoming phrases meant to frighten or intimidate new arrivals.

We were assigned cottage number eight, and given a big footlocker with a lock and combo you had to remember, or suffer the consequences. Cottage eight was the "college" cottage, with classrooms in the basement, and we were there because we showed potential for educational rehabilitation. I was also in the bible school, because you got out of the routine of the day, and so I could study some philosophy.

The Priest wanted nothing to do with that, and just had us sing mostly, and read. They also had inmates from the women's prison in Clinton join us for bible school, and I remember some of their stories, like they are not allowed a push broom or a whole banana, or anything else they could use like a penis.

Fascinating book, the bible, like a two thousand-year-old message from another world, handed down for so many generations, no one really knows for certain what it's about. Herb was religious, so it made him happy. That and being the cook made his time very pleasant and not very stressful. He got what he wanted, as far as things to eat anyway, and always had good stuff in his locker from the kitchen.

Your locker was where you kept everything you owned, and you owned very little. You're allowed care packages of clothes and food from home, all incoming material thoroughly searched, of course, they even stick a knife and stir peanut butter or jelly to be sure nothings in it. I had a supply of tuna, sardines, jelly, deviled ham, canned chicken, Vienna sausage, and all canned stuff that needed nothing more than a cup of hot water to cook or bread slices to stick it between.

The heating device that almost boils water by putting a metal ring in the water and plugging in the other end to a socket was allowed. They had a store, called the canteen, and people outside could put money in your account and you could spend it there. Cigarettes are a big sale item and very cheap too. Candy, supplies, magazines, games, cards, and necessities were all at the canteen. They give you a hard plastic twelve-ounce cup upon arrival, and I still have it to this day. Never found that kind of cup anywhere later and I wanted to, since they are very durable and apparently can last decades.

You play spades all day; try to brew hooch, which is illegal alcohol made with apple peels, bananas, or whatever ferments, which I would never drink, naturally. You could lie in your bunk and contemplate infinity, while counting the squares on the ceiling. You make speedballs, which in jail are a pound bag of crushed peanut M and M's mixed with a bag of crushed Herr's potato chips, not a mixture of cocaine and heroin as it is named for on the streets in the real world. You wait endlessly for the day you get your date, the date you get to leave if you behave.

Mine was given to me over five months in advance, which makes it that much tougher, since most find out two to three months prior.

They call you short. You're just short of release, and other inmates will do anything possible to make your stay longer. Knowing your date makes the countdown much slower than if you don't know the date for some reason. Mine was slightly longer due to an incident I had.

When Herb and I first arrived at the cottage, we went in the door, which was like a big hotel lobby with chairs and couches and tables. The TV was up in the corner, with no knobs on it, controlled by the one guard they had for the sixty inmates on each floor. There were more doors, going up the stairs to the second floor and through the front into the dorm, and a set going into the basement. The main dorm is where both sides had end to end from front to back double bunks, and as usual, Herb took the low bunk and I took the high one. We were located almost as close to the middle as possible. There were fifteen bunks on each side, two sides, thus sixty beds total

I remember walking in with Herb, and another guy was on his way out, shouting things like "later homeboys, I'll think of ya first bitch I fuck" and "all you scumbags can kiss my big black ass, I hope I never see you all ever again"! Sounded more like someone who won the lottery instead of just getting released from prison. But that's the topic, when are you leaving, how long have you been here, and what did you do to be here. Nothing else really mattered to them.

As the guy leaving looked at us he yells "hey everyone, fresh pussy in the house", and "have fun NEW guys!" We just ignored him and his maniacal laugh after each sentence he spoke. There were several inmates yelling back at the guy as he left: "get some pussy for me!" and "I'll see ya back in the hood in a few days when you fuck up again", or like some bon voyage speech given to a passenger you're related to: "have fun!" or "don't do anything I wouldn't do!" Most of the comments were obvious painful yells of "go fuck yourself", or "suck my dick, asshole". Painful because they realize they were not leaving with him and much resentment was relayed as he left, though some actually seemed genuinely happy that someone finished their sentence, even though it wasn't them.

As you walk through the door into the dorm, the bathroom is immediately on the left, behind a three-foot cinderblock wall. There's a two-foot opening in that wall for entry, and the urinals are placed four on each side, to your left and right as you walk in. Past those are the commodes, also on the left and right, which have only three-foot walls around them on three sides. You got to face someone directly across from you while shitting, if it was a full house.

On the right across the main isle and entryway to the bathroom were the two showers, made like concrete closets without doors. As you step in the two-foot wide opening, the nozzles are against the right wall, with a four-foot section to wash in. The idea was you were never out of sight, and could be seen from the guards' viewpoint if he walks by. Then about twenty feet after the bathrooms begin there was a ceiling high cinderblock wall separating the bathrooms from the bunks. In fact, the whole place was cinderblock construction with bars across all the windows there were.

Occasionally the inmates would drape their sheets and blankets to section off areas between the bunks for privacy, which no one really needed but did anyway. Most guards just overlooked it, but some made you take them down, and you were never allowed to do that at night, for obvious reasons. Taking a shower was never comfortable, you made them fast and thorough, and I hated being watched, though people usually didn't bother. It was just plain humiliating, the tiny shower area, but if you didn't take regular ones, the guard would hose you down on work detail, if you smelled bad enough.

On nearly my first night I got to watch a blanket party, which is where they throw a blanket over a guy while he's sleeping and beat the life out of him with any heavy blunt or sharp instrument they could find, or just with their hands. A guy on each corner would use his body weight to hold the blanket, and another two or three guys hit him.

Never happened to me, or Herb, but did happen to Fred in cottage seven. Yes, Fred Finally saw my speech come true, that I told him we'd be here seven years ago, because that first day when I was walking to breakfast, there he was, coming down the walk from the next cottage towards mine. He was pretty black and blue, finally became the punk, which made me laugh inside hysterically, since I thought that should happen to him one day.

He was much more calm and reserved, and he said it's my fault we're there for saying that it would happen so many years ago. Anyway, he was not popular in his home, the crowd found his brand of bullshit boring. He was released before me, just because he was hurt, he was able to get out after only nine months or so, which is almost un-heard of, unless you're a rat. They thought at one point that I was. They were wrong.

Every day was spent doing all the seasonal farm work, raking leaves, mowing lawns, shoveling stuff and the like. Paid a dollar ten a day. Other activities would be to hang out and go to classes, or played spades and chess for pushups. I played chess with this one guy, beat him a few times, much to his shock, since he was dorm champ and very good. He beat me as well, a couple times before he wouldn't play me again unless it was for a carton of cigs. So he never got the chance to play me again, which I considered his loss.

I refused to gamble with the little money I had, which pissed some people off for some reason. But I saw what happened to people who did gamble, and lose, they spent their time bumming cigs and supplies from everyone else, which I refused to do so I never gambled for any reason, even to swap chores.

I was also privileged to witness the other inmates sexually relieving themselves in the middle of the night in the bathroom to some magazines in a semi-private circle jerk while I tried to take a crap or piss. Quite disgusting to see, though I wasn't trying to look, it's kind of hard to miss, unfortunately.

It actually becomes an acceptable normal activity for some, since there aren't many other activities to indulge in, and its effect eventually matches that of being in the same room with someone brushing their teeth, and just as easy to ignore. There aren't many shy inmates in jail, and for some, this was a daily activity, but it still made my stomach turn for about a month just hearing and knowing it before becoming immune.

After a month and a few weeks, Ron Preting came to my cottage. He brought the story that I was fucked in county, which I couldn't really verify but suspected, so the word spread and I was pretty much forced to confront him about lying about me. In the back of the dorm the guy who slept there had the blankets up, and Ron was being interrogated by some other guys since he was new, and out of fear he brought up my experience in the county in an attempt to draw attention away from himself. I went over to him because a guy named Louie came to me and told me what Ron was saying and how bad that would look for me if I didn't do anything about it.

Usually I ignore such things, but I'd have to live there for an unknown time frame and I didn't want to have to really hurt anyone later on. So I used pussy punches that wouldn't hurt my mother along with some wrestling sounds for authenticity, and when he panicked and covered, I swept him off his feet first so he'd be down and unable to hurt me, and I could make like I was pounding the piss out of him, cursing about the way he lied about me the whole time. I just used lines from Sergeant Slaughter, seemed to work, especially when I smacked Ron with the mop ringer, I think he caught on.

Didn't enjoy doing that much, but it was quite a convincing show because Phil and Louie, two fellow inmates, said I should never fight anyone strong, after seeing the lack of damage to Ron, because I'd lose. If only they knew I was only proving a point without hurting anyone. I staged it myself and I never had to fight before or after that in prison.

There was only one other jail fight, where I beat myself, which I described earlier. Phil was a nice guy, in jail for drugs, but he was well established in the cottage and usually Herb, he and Louie were the ones I played Spades with the most, along with a large black guy named Pinnel. Pinnel liked me for some reason, he was a thinker and very mellow, and understood all my chatter about life. I cleared his name later, since he was always nice to me.

I had many visitors, my parents, Jake, Elton, Reggie, Gloria, Cheyanne and Wilma B, and Even Maria, Cheyanne's sister. Their mom and Crystal even came, and everyone usually brought me something and was very supportive. Maria discovered Herb at one point, and he would wind up marrying her after our release. Herb de-invited me to the wedding for some forgettable reason, but they're divorced now anyway. Fred and Sophie were married just before his sentence, and I wasn't there either, now they're divorced as well.

My priority during this sentence was dealing with the tickle, as usual, and this made it very annoying, as you cannot possibly imagine, since I've never met anyone with a similar condition. Somehow, I was able to remain just about completely still every night and all night, Herb used to tell me he almost never heard a sound from me, like I were dead, not so much as a breath.

There was a small guy there, Barney, I think was his name, but he played that game where you rest your hands on someone's, and try to move before they turn their hands over and smack your hands with theirs as hard as possible. Idle entertainment for the idle minds. He made anyone else he played with bleed, and though he turned my hands red, I beat him for the most part and remained less damaged than he was.

So he was a quick little guy, I was a quick big guy, which I proved all day working and playing softball, football and other idle time activities. Even found a guy who sung Bike by Floyd all day, and though I liked it, he was too hooked on just that song, not most of them, as I am.

The main undesirable person of the cottage was this big doofy guy named Louie Flunker from Union. Louie was the living proof of a botched abortion, and basically didn't have a clue or care about life, even though he cried to me about his girl friend once, and I got by in jail by knowing why people do things, and being very calm and logical and using easy psychology to rectify problems. I solved his issue, making him realize that his position isn't what she would look for, but telling her what he was telling me would be a good start if he had a chance. Stuff like he can't live without her, need and want her etcetera. But his only real interest was causing trouble for anyone else.

So he devised a plan. I was dumb enough to mention that people I knew outside could get weed whenever they wanted. So I thought it would be profitable, since a joint sold for five to ten packs of cigarettes each, and it would be easy. Letting Louie in on the deal was the dumb part. He let the guy Barney I mentioned before in on it after the first time but before the second, and Barney was short of leaving by weeks, so he ratted me out for no reason other than he said he hated every one of us, after he was beaten up one day in his own personal blanket party. I never did anything to him; in fact I knew places he went, like Scotch Plains, the gas station Reggie Arnolds worked at about three years before this day.

Barney told me the story about a Cadillac parked there, I remembered it, Reggie never knew who's it was, and we used to sit on it wishing we had something to smoke. It was under police custody, we thought, because it was always there. This guy told me there was at least fifty pounds of pot in the trunk, and it was his car. That was interesting, and other than the fact that we were prisoners I thought he was OK as a person.

When they caught Gloria bringing me some balloons stuffed with clean, powdered herb, I had to claim I was under pressure from other inmates. I called her, who worked in collaboration with Jake, and said I'd get beat up if she didn't get some for me, which was just plain lying. Even though Louie knew I wasn't afraid of anyone, he liked to play the game of pressure by saying things like if I ever see you outside, I'd get you, or find you, or whatever, and that gave me the needed excuse for finding the scapegoat.

The first time Gloria came loaded, it worked, sort of. You see, the way it worked was I would swallow the balloon with a drink during a visit, thus bypassing the strip search performed after all visits. Then by drinking shampoo and giggling myself a little, I would vomit the balloons back up. Unfortunately, only the true pros can do this without making a sound, and I am no pro. Everyone in the whole dorm knew I got something, and I was too paranoid to even smoke any, much less hold it in my locker.

So back to the cottage after visits we'd go after the strip search, Herb having the same visitors as I for a while till he was transferred to the honors camp at High Point. Then Maria went there to visit him, and that was nearly a conjugal visit according to Herb. Gloria was quite into the cloak and dagger game of running illegal drugs to me, thought it was kind of fun, till the second time she tried.

Barney went to the director of security, a guy named Aronski who was an ex police man busted for drugs and given the choice of being an inmate in Yardville or heading security here. So he intercepted Gloria, who told him I was under pressure to have this done by other inmates, mainly because I told her so, and they brought me to the office in hopes of opening the information path for all the others who smuggle things in.

I basically cleared everyone of any wrongdoing; even the ones who were doing it like Phil and Pinnel, but not Louie since he was such an asshole who everyone hated, and he was the cause of this predicament anyway, because he tipped off Barney.

In return for the info, which was mostly false, I was allowed to go to my bunk and clear it out, and was sent to cottage nine, the isolation cottage. Everyone in eight was yelling rat and other nice names at me, thinking I blew many whistles on people, but I just laughed in their faces as they threatened all kinds of bodily harm to me, that was nothing new to my ears.

Solitude seems so actually rare, that only a few are able to bask comfortably in the "alone" climate, or afford such a luxury, or prison, which would be decided depending upon how the solitude was reached. Michael Jackson desired solitude from fear of disease, and was able to achieve it through his wealth, and now I had my own, without a dime to my name.

It was the simplest part of my sentence, spending all my time with myself in deep contemplation, not needing to work or interact with others. The only down side was the rumor of how kitchen workers would vandalize the food sent to solitary. Otherwise, it was like a vacation from being in hell, if it were not for my usual sleep problem. Cheyanne would visit me often, and eventually she would tell me that she was dating someone else, Reggie Beer, and that I was still a good friend to her. The same song Madeline sang me from Meatloaf came to mind once again, two out of three ain't bad.

I didn't blame her or even care that much, considering where I was and not knowing when I'd get out, and Wilma B. was becoming a regular visitor for a while and appeared as if she wanted me back in her life, which was always the case with her and she knew there would be a chance usually, with the right circumstance.

Herb was already transferred to the High Point satellite facility, an honors camp which is as minimum security as possible, and has no bars, locks or cells in it. The site is in the state park, and the inmates were the ones who maintained it solely. After three weeks of solitary, keeping me there in a room where the last person committed suicide by hanging himself, I was transferred to High point too.

The place was built for about thirty people, had one guard on duty at a time, and had a pool table, a basement with TV and ping-pong, and was more like summer camp than prison, except for the lack of girls, money or freedom.

I had my first surgery done there, by the local Sparta dentist, and this would be the second time I ever was allowed to lose consciousness without effort, for my wisdom teeth. They came in rotten, in fact, my mouth had more than a million spent on it, and twenty-six cavities in one check-up was my record as a kid. I remember this dentist saying the Sodium Pentothal was the truth serum, and he wondered if I had any good stories or crimes I wanted off my chest. So I started babbling out all kinds of lies, talking about major drug dealing bullshit, people I've damaged and other tall tales.

Gave nothing but lies based off slight truths, and since then I always wondered why they don't call it the lie serum. He was impressed, and I think believed every word I said and even became fearful, because when I woke, he was gone and the guard was the only one left in the room with me.

Guards there didn't worry much about escapees since all the residents had many guns and dogs, and it would be very dangerous to try and escape. Only one person did it successfully in its history. The work was much more physical and dangerous there.

This place was very cold in the winter, and work details had to go shovel mountains of snow covering the parking lots. I personally swept the stairs in High Point's needle like monument from top to bottom. We had a warehouse where the wood burning stove was maintained by us if we wanted to keep warm. In the warehouse one work detail would split logs all day with a wedge that one person would hold, and a sledgehammer that another person would hit it with while you held it. Letting a convict swing a sledgehammer inches from your face and dangerously close to your hand was not a reassuring or comfortable feeling to say the very least.

Other work details maintained all the buildings in two parks, High Point and Stokes forest, we painted them, raked leaves, picked up garbage, took care of High Points resident caged bear, and gathered wood from the sides of mountains. We did this by hand, to be brought back to the house where the people on disciplinary action would stand outside with a two handled saw and saw two-foot sections off every log.

All this would go on whether it was ninety degrees outside or nine below zero, which it had been at least a few times each while I was there. Another disciplinary action was a cold shower in the basement, which I never had to do.

There were also traveling work details, and I got to work at Saint John's University with the religious guard, who also taught bible and held masses on Sundays. He was a minister. He also brought a few of us down to the Manville army depot to work there, which sparked some obvious memories for me. We went to some summer camps for clean-up type activity, and it was nearly like a good physical job, but only paid one to two bucks a day. We could almost forget that we're in prison at times.

It was the hardest physical work I had ever done to that point. We would pull the van with ten of us over next to any point along the road to the monument, walk down the side of the mountain and put two or three hundred pound logs on our shoulders and walk them back up the mountain and load them into another truck to be brought to the lodge or warehouse all day long.

The guard for that duty only carried his chain saw to make long logs a little shorter, but he went after dead trees like a maniac. Of course the food was good because Herb was again the cook, and since I knew him the whole time I was able to get preferential treatment, as well as access to the kitchen to cook my own stuff my way.

The house had great scenery; a pond in back where I caught many snakes as usual, and my first porcupine. The porcupine had just been in some fight it appeared, and not many quills were left, but I brought it back to the house anyway where half the guys ran in fear and the other half couldn't believe their eyes. I let it go, of course.

You could get lost easily in the vast woods of Stokes and High Point, very scenic and natural, but I never did even though I wandered around whenever possible, and even made it out of site a few times. We also maintained Stokes Forest because it was just across the street from high Point. I had the opportunity to fight a large forest fire there, where they gave us shovels while a helicopter flew overhead dropping rain from a large bucket onto the fire. We went around and put out the small fires still burning around the ground. It was very hot and dirty and dangerous, but rewarding and exciting at the same time. To be in jail and still contribute to society with importance was interesting.

We cleaned, repaired and maintained the forest cottages and shacks, some were extremely poorly maintained before, and some weren't that bad, which made me wonder how long the state was involved, maybe not till recently, cheap labor and all. We even had a work detail that went to Lake Hopatcong and built a dam in it, for no reason we were ever made aware of. We just filled steel cages with rocks, for endless hours, or at least all day. Some inmates were in unbelievable shape, very strong and the exercise didn't hurt me either.

They had a few of us work directly with park rangers, and on Christmas that year, one other guy and I, Eric Steele, were working on the monument with a ranger, and he took us through the drive thru at McDonald's down the street near Matamoras, Pennsylvania. I never before had a big Mac and fries that tasted so good, and never would it taste that good again in my life. He made us promise to never tell anyone we went there with him, which was a simple request, but this book coul d cause him trouble, If it weren't for the fact that the whole satellite camp is now gone.

I learned this by visiting there recently, since it was such a great park anyway. Eric was from Roselle, and I would hang around with him for a while, after we got out. Not for too long though, he was definitely simple-minded and cost me a traffic summons once when a cop pulled me over for going the wrong way down a one way street in Elizabeth one day. The cop was going to let me go till Eric opened his mouth and made some comments to the cop. The cop said: "your friend just cost you a ticket", which I was not pleased about. Plus, he thought he was in love with Gloria, and he hounded her endlessly, and she couldn't stand him for some reason she wouldn't make clear.

In the High Point house, it was divided into three dorm-type rooms, again with bunk beds, and this was the first time Herb and I didn't share a bunk. Here is where a guy taught me transcendental meditation one night when I was complaining about my sleep problem.

First he said concentrate on any noise you hear, allowing no two parts of your body to touch. Then you have to tighten all your muscles starting at your feet and hands, one by one, all the way up to your head, neck and face, then relaxing them one by one as you go. Then just picture a table in your mind, then picture another one behind it, and another till the whole view was just a giant line of tables as far as you can see.

Then picture one in front of the original one, and one in front of that, and repeat that till your whole mind is full in all directions, then picture yourself rising above the tables and floating above them, then fly through the tables right through the middle of the earth and out the other side, and that's usually where people lose consciousness. I was hoping it would trigger more lucid dreams, but it didn't, even though it did help some.

He said he did it using pinheads instead of tables. The next level would be to fly through the air like superman, level nine, which is a true out of body experience if you can remain aware, but very few people can. I don't remember his name, but he told me he had only reached the eighth level, breaks through the other side of the earth, and then he's out cold. I was unable to do the relax part, due to the circumstance of my problem, but I was still able to concentrate enough laying on my right as usual to go to sleep somewhat easier. That and the fact of all the physical labor was enough to tire you into a good night sleep.

Then one day a guy from cottage eight came here, getting the same high honors as the rest as being a non-risk. He remembered me, and one day in the basement where the showers were, just three faucets on each wall on the left and right with no walls or doors, he was coming out in his robe, and he grabbed me in a bear hug from behind and said "you screwed a lot of people that I knew, they all got sent to Bordentown with more time because of your fuckin ass". I just did my usual and whipped my head between my knees, making him come flying over the top and landing on his back on the floor, naked.

Herb happened to be downstairs watching TV that day, and he jumped out of his chair and told the guy "Chris didn't do shit, he probably saved more of your asses than anyone would, and definitely more than he had to, asshole! Just leave him the fuck alone!" The guy just complemented me on the move to toss him aside, and that was the end of that. Barney, the little guy who was long gone, was the one who got everyone in trouble and tried to leave the blame on me. Herb knew it already, now everyone knew. It was nice of him to do that, though unnecessary, but I let him anyway.

When we weren't working, we were shooting pool, which I also could defeat anyone anytime in, and had received great respect for that and for my strength in the work force. The pool table was in the middle of the dining room, used as a table when not in use for pool, and one guy always wanted to play, and of course I did too, so we played many games for months.

Time was finally getting short, and I was scheduled to be paroled in early June of eighty-two, finding out in February, which was quite early. Most inmates find out their release date within sixty days of it, I had to wait over a hundred. So after watching people leave with the ceremonial tossing of the person into the pond, including Herb, I decided to try and figure a way around that.

I stayed up all night that night, out of excitement and sheer adrenalin from the fact of finally being freed, and I sat by the night guards' office door all night. I didn't have to work either. They got me the next morning, but could only manage, between the five guys who tried, to get me in up to my knees. They threw me, but I landed like a cat, on my feet. They tried dousing me with a hose instead, which I deflected and made everyone else wet for their efforts. I wasn't shy about being happy to get out of there and couldn't belive the time was here.

Then they took me back to Annandale, which is where you have to be released from, for some reason. They give you your original possessions, things I had not seen in over a year, some money, and of course my parents with Wilma B were there to pick me up.

There are many feelings in this world, good, bad, indifference, sadness, pain and pleasure. Nothing I know compares to walking through those gates for the last time, walking into freedom and actually into a new life. It's a bone chilling sense of accomplishment and relief, or elation, even though I put myself there to begin with. I had goose bumps as I looked back upon the place that took away my twentieth birthday, twenty-first holiday season, and thirteen months of my life. I believed I would never be back, but I'd never forget. I had still not slept due to the excitement of leaving, and was completely exhausted on the way home.

EXIT EIGHTEEN

New Path, New Road, and New Life

Eating my mom's cooking was nearly like having an oral orgasm that night, and I celebrated with Wilma B the other thing imprisonment took from me, thirteen months without any sex. We went to the Holiday Inn of Clark, got a room on the second floor facing the parkway, and had sex at least three times before passing out.

Unfortunately, the room we had must have had some horrible things occur in it once, because in the middle of the night I woke up screaming and kicking, which I have never done, and kicked Wilma clean out of the bed, because I felt something dark, feminine in shape, but very bad or evil in that room. So we wound up going to the restaurant around four AM and staying there the rest of the night. She thought the room was spooky too, but we couldn't decide if it was the trauma of the first night of freedom and lack of sleep, both, or something more.

This was around a time when Fred and Sophie lived in Somerville, and I went to visit them one night. Sophie wasn't home, she left Fred over some fight, and when I walked in, the floors were covered with clothes and garbage, wall to wall. Freds' son Christopher was in a crib, and he had pulled shit out of his diaper and painted the walls with it.

Apparently, Fred and Sophie's fight was about who should clean what, so nothing got cleaned. Wilma B had gone with me, so for lack of anything else to do she decided to clean the apartment up for them, just enough to be able to get around without stepping on things. Wilma B was the only Wilma left in my life so I will refer to her only as Wilma from now on, with Wilma T long gone from my life, never to return.

We were both pretty fresh out of jail, and we were listening to WNEW on the radio. The station was having call in sessions about criminal behavior, so we decided to call in as living examples of what they considered to be people who express criminal behavior. We were asked many questions, and the station was glad to have us participate, but all people wanted to know was why the punishment was so light, or how could we do such things.

No one questioned us about what it was like, how we survived, or had desire to hear stories about life in captivity. We were basically normal citizens by then, but most of the callers seemed to believe that rehabilitation is just some myth used to keep prison population at a tolerable level, doubting we should have ever been let free. They just wanted to know why we did what we did, as if they never did anything wrong in their life, like a bunch of saints. We held on the phone for a couple of hours, and that was it, since people didn't want to hear about circumstance or behavior, just consequences.

This is when I started to work out with weights, and conditioning myself, thought I now smoked and should have quit, but I didn't. I also began my favorite job to date, driving the school bus. I loved being able to stop traffic legally anytime I wanted to. I was taught by a sixty year old, seventy percent legally blind driver, who knew the routes better than anyone, though I would not want him to drive my kids anywhere.

I knew one girl who worked there, Marlene I think was her name, who claimed she had to be stoned on every route, or she couldn't remember where to stop. Odd collection of people, school bus drivers, including myself, since I was on parole at the time and anyone would figure that parolees weren't the best choice of employees, especially when working around children.

Naturally, I didn't tell them, and they never made an effort to find out, which surprised me. I worked from five AM till nine, then from about one thirty till four thirty or so, pumping iron in between. I still went to hang around with Cheyanne and her family, sharing life in jail stories, and Herb was there for Maria, courting her to be his future bride.

Bus driving had many advantages, it was the only job I had where I could sleep and still make money. I would bring a football team to a school, and then while they play I could sleep on the bus, like a taxi with the meter running. One of the saddest school bus stories I have happened on Cooper road in Scotch Plains.

I had a full bus, and was going about thirty, thirty-five miles an hour down the road. As I reached this little bridge, I saw a Doberman and Sheppard appear from under the bridge and give chase to my bus. Since there are mirrors everywhere in a school bus, I could see exactly what the dogs were doing, and hoped I could out run them before they got hurt. But in the millisecond I had that thought, it was too late to react.

These two dogs, running side by side decided to try and run under my bus to the other side, and all I felt was two bumps from the rear of the bus, like mini speed bumps. As I looked back, I saw two large lumps on the road, which used to be the dogs and were now just piles of road kill, and I looked around at the kids, who were being less observant than usual, because none of them saw or felt anything.

Busses run on time frames, so I didn't stop to see if anything could be done, and I knew that nothing could be, since the double back tires carry tremendous weight and the dogs didn't stand a chance. Felt worse than when a pigeon slammed into my windshield on the parkway and was stuck on the hood dying for about ten miles before it fell off. All the kids got to see that, Lucky them.

On another day, I was coming up Vaux Hall road in Springfield, and I went to stop at a light, there were only three kids on the bus in the back two seats, one on each side another somewhere in the middle. The light was red, by the Seven Eleven, and a garbage truck was backing out of a driveway next to it, the one I was approaching as I slowed for the light.

The truck just kept coming, and it caught the last window on the back left side and popped the bus open like a tin can. The girl sitting in the seat saw it coming a second or so in time, fortunately, and she jumped into the lap of the kid sitting on the other side. They both got cuts, but were ok. The driver was drunk as hell, and I did all I could not to try injuring him on the spot.

I couldn't believe that this idiot had a license anymore than I could believe the chief of police of Irvington telling my boss there was nothing he could do about the fifty or sixty license plate numbers I gave him of people who would not stop for my bus. I think about ten percent of cars did stop in that city, but the police chief's kid didn't ride on any bus, so why should he care?

Once I was driving for Governor Livingston high, in Berkeley Heights, and I was into chatting with one of my female passengers, who was only four or five years younger than me. I don't remember her name, but she was the last drop off I had to make for the day, and she decided to invite me to her house to hang out, eat, or get a drink.

I agreed, since I was always sociable, and figured why not? So I went in, she went upstairs, and her little brother came over to me and asked me while giggling: "are you gonna pork my sister?" with a little sarcastic grin on his face. I asked him where their parents were, and he told me they don't come home till around five.

Then I said, just as this girl was coming back down the stairs dressed in a bathrobe, "no, she's just a kid, I couldn't do anything like that". This girl heard my reply, and she became quite different than the friendly girl I knew from the bus. She said things like: "what, I'm not good enough for you?" and: "I've been with men before, older than you". I just chuckled, and drank the soda she brought me, then told her how much trouble I'd be in if I did anything with a minor.

She said she would say I did something to her anyway, and get me in trouble if I didn't "screw" her. I laughed pretty hard at that and just left, never hearing from her again, and when I told my boss about the little game she played, he acted like he knew and gave me a different route. Apparently, I was not the first driver she tried this with, just the youngest and best-looking one. This job was an absolute Trip, but when not working, I still enjoyed familiar activities and passions.

Jake and I went hiking again one night through Weldon Quarry. Local roads in two towns surround Weldon quarry, Watchung is their mailing address I believe, but they border Berkeley Heights as well. One side is the road I was pushed into a rock by the school bus on that day I described before, which is called New Providence road. That road is the only separation of the Watchung Reservation and the quarry, and a stream runs along it on the reservation side, which has great cliffs and trails on the other side of the stream for hiking.

There is also a waterhole the stream feeds from Sealy's pond, deep enough to swim in, and I have many times with many different people. The other side of this road, the quarry side, is just a two hundred foot steep wooded hill, and rocks, trees and things usually fall off that side during bad storms and block the road occasionally.

We would park on the stream side and go across the road and up the hill, using trees for leverage and about two thirds of the way up is an old, tree beaten fence that makes a poor attempt at keeping trespassers away. Once you go over, or under this fence, and over a narrow service road for the quarry and up the rest of the hill, you reach the edge of a hundred foot drop very suddenly, and if you're not careful, it's quite easy to just fall off.

Ruth's cousin I was told, did fall and die there, and she was the one spreading rumors about guard dogs residing there. That was probably what sparked my interest in hiking in that place; just the danger and excitement of doing something few have done without devastating injuries. No one I ever went here with got hurt, including myself.

This time we walked there, and began with our usual tour of the different levels of the place. We enjoyed yelling down the two inch diameter holes the workers drill, for putting dynamite in and listening to the odd echo it produces. We wondered occasionally if that would set off the explosion, not knowing or caring if there were any explosives currently in the hole we were entertaining ourselves with.

These holes were always just feet from the edge, and you could see the pattern used to make controlled explosions to loosen up rock for processing. We decided that one wall at the bottom of the quarry would be a good place to climb to the next level.

Jake began to climb, and I started to follow, but the quarry was mainly comprised of shale, and every time Jake took a step, he'd dislodge pieces of the rock that would fall on my head. So I got down and told him I'd follow after he reached the top, which was about a hundred feet up. I couldn't see him too well, but I heard him talking to me clearly. He said that he was stuck, and only a few feet from the top, and all the rocks he grabbed were just falling out under his hand. Then I heard him slide down the side cursing, which I thought was the beginning of him falling onto the big rocks below.

I heard him say: "Oh shit! Oh shit! I'm gonna fall, oh shit!" Then he said he fell but found a ledge somehow, and was OK for now, but couldn't go up anymore. He told me to go for help. I ran the mile to Blue Star and used the payphone to call the police, who didn't believe what I was telling them anyway.

They sent a car, and I had them drive to the entrance of the quarry. A guy who lived across the street had a key for us to get through the gate, so we went in. I called Jake, who answered sounding very far away, but we heard him. The cop called for the Watchung fire department, which came and put a spotlight on Jake, and he looked like a little fly on the wall.

He was about eighty feet up, and Watchung's ladder was only thirty feet long, so they had to get North Plainfield's' ladder company to come, with their hundred foot ladder. This was taking hours, and by the time North Plainfield got there, there were two ambulances, three police cars, and a few Watchung fire and rescue vehicles all hanging around waiting for the big ladder to get Jake off the cliff.

They did, and when Jake came down they had him get into an ambulance to check on his condition. We were both given summons for trespassing, eighty bucks each, and we both made the newspaper the next day. The paper had my full name and address, and it had Jake's name misspelled and no address, and the caption read, "two climbers stuck on a cliff in the quarry", or something like that, I don't exactly recall.

While we were in court, the owners of the quarry were there, and I guess they thought we had ulterior motives for going because they said to us, "now you guys know about our whole operation". I knew from the past that people would break into the offices of their quarry to steal scales and things, but we weren't interested in that, just the climbing and hiking. They said this like they were keeping some big, dark secret hidden in the massive quarry, but we found nothing that interesting to speak of.

That was the last time Jake or I ever went to that quarry, life's direction pointing us elsewhere after that. My favorite part of the quarry experience was when we'd jump and sail thirty to forty feet through the air from the top of a sand pile to as close to the bottom as possible without hitting the actual ground first. Like stunt jumping, it was nearly as exhilarating as the falls in dreams I had, and landing in the last ten-foot slope of the pile was like landing in a bed of feathers.

Fred now, was working at service merchandise in Woodbridge. He had a girlfriend named Robin, and I would go to visit him there. Service merchandise is odd, you pick items out of their catalog, then you go to a large counter where the people behind it take your order, then you see your product come up from the basement on a conveyor belt, like luggage at and airport does.

You weren't allowed to pull most merchandise from the displays and carry it around; they were only there for those who wanted to see the products before buying them. This was supposed to promote security, and this place sold everything from toys, tools and guns, to furniture, jewelry and clothes.

Unfortunately for them they hired Fred, who realized that products came from the basement with or without a work order, so he managed to have other people come in, like Elton, and take items never paid for out the door for him and others. I actually bought my hundred-dollar Swiss army knife there, which I still have today. I know he had taken many thousands of dollars worth of electronics, clothes, gadgets and things, I guess never learning his lesson in prison. Naturally, they all got fired eventually.

At this point, I heard from Peter out of the blue. He Lived in New Jersey again somehow, and went in to security work, and was the security guard for a large office building in Bernardsville. He was working for Burns security. I went to visit him and hang out, just to look around the offices during their off hours.

They had a computer that was calculating the value of Pi, which was running for months apparently, another one made to play tic-tac-toe and never loose, and of course chess as well.

Too bad it didn't play Monopoly, because I have never lost a game of that in my life, mainly because when I was young I cheated sometimes. But it was interesting to see how much trust and responsibility they gave Peter, knowing he couldn't even keep his eyes open the whole night. He fell asleep while I was there and let me do his rounds with the security keys.

Very tempting, but there was nothing to really take of any interest, and I didn't want to get him in trouble, plus, I knew I would not do anything to put me back in jail again. My parole had nothing to do with drug testing, since I have never been in trouble for drugs, and they were never considered part of my problem. So my partying would continue for a while.

At this period in time I believe Jake was working with his dad, and driving a Dodge K car, which he almost killed us in one night. He was drunk, going down Inman Avenue at around one hundred miles per hour. He was dodging around what few cars there were, going up lawns and on the shoulder, and he never slowed as he approached the short hill for the railroad tracks. After we went airborne and landed some stretch away from the tracks, he finally slowed his pace. I didn't know why he was driving this way, but it was fun in a deadly maniacal sort of way.

Now I was still seeing Wilma and she'd drive us, with others on occasion, around in her AMC Gremlin. I remember once her driving through Westfield one night with me and Shelly, and some other people, though I don't remember who, maybe Cheyanne, who was no longer my girlfriend, just a friend. We got to a light in the center of town, and I had my window down.

Shelly decided to yell at some black teenage girls hanging out on the sidewalk, she was quite obnoxious at times and enjoyed irritating people for some reason; it was one way of entertaining herself. She started calling them black bitches and things to that effect, and a black guy about the same age came from the store as we pulled away, and I saw the girls telling this guy what Shelly did and they were pointing at us.

The guy ran after the car, and we had to stop at the next light, so he caught up quickly. He said something about asshole crackers and punched me in the face, and as usual, he missed my huge nose completely. So I kicked him in the head with my boot through the window from a sitting position and knocked him to the ground and told Wilma to go, which she did when the light changed. Shelly thought that was hysterical, but Wilma was pretty pissed about the whole thing, and said later she was tired of driving me and all these weird friends of mine around, which I thought was very funny.

Then shortly after that experience, Shelly brought a friend of hers to Cheyanne's house one day, someone who would change the course of my life forever in many ways, a girl named Bethanie Engle. Beth, like Shelly, was as close to being the perfect soul mate for me as few girls could be, she could have been my choice of destiny in life, as Shelly would have been, which would make the choice if I had one or ever achieved one impossible.

The day I met her, not quite like when I met Shelly, she and I took a walk together and talked for hours about life, philosophy, and everything this world had to offer us. Shelly was only less instantaneous because there was a crowd around us usually, and we didn't get to be alone together much, as well as being much younger when we met.

It was actually a little scary, how similar Beth and I were. Beth was basically identical to me, laughing at everything for the same reasons I did, seeing most things as I did, and she actually understood some of my deepest thoughts and philosophies, which is not an easy thing to do. Unfortunately, though I was instantly attracted to her as any normal male would be just based on looks, she had a different view of the perfect mate, tall dark and handsome. Though she was blonde, she didn't find blonde men attractive.

We had a relationship without any bounds up to but not including sexual contact. I had never gone after a girl in my life, allowing them first contact always, and she was the same. Thus, we spent a lot of time together, enjoying all the humor the world had to offer from our unique perspectives and generally had continuous fun whenever we could, without compromising or confusing our relationship with sex or misplaced loyalties.

I used to call her diz, because I would always throw her on my shoulder and spin around till she was dizzy. She enjoyed it, I believe. I also believed, as she did, that you could love almost anyone, if the desire to give effort, faith and patience is there, as long as the basic attraction is there. I think the saying opposites attract is more from the female perspective, since I'm a male and I know what attracts is just plain physical appearance first, no matter how similar or opposite the girl is, until we learn a little more about attitude from being around her. Beth's attitude was absolutely perfect, as far as I could see.

She thought at one point that she was in love with Jake, had even been his girlfriend for a while, but like Shelly and Donald, she had a guy she knew from Newark named Roland, who was not at all like Donald. Her first real love, she thought. She believed he would eventually come back for her, and though she deserved it, he didn't.

Bethanie, Shelly and Cheyanne all went to Scotch Plains Fanwood high school, so I spent many hours between school bus runs going there and peering in on them in class, making Bethanie laugh continuously, and causing Obrien much grief as usual. Cheyanne was amused, but much more composed.

Bethanie's laugh is quite unique, and could be heard and identified for miles, and the echo through the halls was amazing. In this school, as I would walk the hallways I would recognize and be recognized by more people than in my own school, and most of these people actually liked seeing me, much unlike my high school.

The difference between Shelly and Beth besides appearance was the fact that Shelly's parents hated me because I hung around with Fred, Beth's mother and family liked me a lot. That, and Shelly drank much more than Beth, claiming it was the Irish in her that allowed her to out drink most guys.

Beth was one of the few to make the transition from calling me Greenie to calling me Chris, which took many years. Shelly, I'm sure, would call me Greenie if I saw her today, which would be fine. Shelly was also quite defensive and insecure, which Beth was not or didn't show it as much as Shelly did. Neither was insecure or defensive around me, which was a relationship characteristic I was happy to have

Shelly's parents eventually accepted me, realizing I was not exactly like Fred in his many negative ways. I had even gone out on Shelly's dad's boat, a fifty-foot sailboat, for an overnight party, where everyone except me was drinking all night long, and did some fishing and swimming too. That was a lot of fun, even when the boat ran out of gas and had to be sailed into dock, which took many hours.

I know Shelly was there, but don't recall who else came, and there were a few of us, all I know is that Fred was not there. I recall sleeping with Shelly, very close and cozy, hoping at some point she'd acknowledge some deeper, more passionate feelings for me, but as I expected, she wouldn't.

Bethanie had more friends than most people, mostly guys. Most of the guys around her seemed obsessed with her, due to her unique personality and outstanding body, an unintentional trap she had no way of knowing she set simply by being herself. I did try to explain it to her, and I believe she understood it eventually, but still didn't like it. Perhaps wondering what made me different.

She also had many female friends, like Cindy Pratt, Frieda Blue, Cori Scardia, and Michelle Duville. The ton of guys after all of them were now hanging around with me, perhaps four years younger, but I've always enjoyed watching and talking with women much more than hanging out with other guys. They're much prettier and pleasing to the eyes.

Since I wasn't really "after" any of them in particular, they seemed to prefer my company more so than most guys. We all would go to Don Billie's in Newark, to get the Portuguese food, until one day the owner tried to molest Beth, in the ladies room. He was a big time pervert who tried to corner young girls in the bathroom. Too bad, because the food was great, my favorite being their shrimp and garlic, which I could eat twenty-four hours a day, if it wouldn't kill me to do so. Beth's boyfriend Roland took Billie by the neck and beat him, once Beth told him what happened in the bathroom.

I always had fun and felt appreciated hanging out with four or five eighteen and nineteen year old girls in Newark, knowing their safety and integrity couldn't be bought or stolen from me. I had a girlfriend, Wilma. who was still around me when she could be, and I'm a one-woman man usually, just not in Wilma's case because of prior circumstance.

I was always in complete control of my own hormonal instinct, even at the age of twenty or twenty-one, when control is unlikely for a man. Thanks, Desisto. I would have shared myself with Beth or any of her girlfriends, giving them anything they wanted, had they shown any desire or physical interest, like any normal male would where pretty women are concerned.

None really did, they just partied their asses off, falling into me when in need of a lift or help staggering back to my car. Needless to say I had a blast too, and I never had to defend anyone from anything, nothing ever got out of hand to any significant point while I was around. I'm sure all these girls wondered at times why I wasn't aggressively attempting to get passionate or physical with them, but eventually I believe they realized this was not my style, which I think they appreciated, hopefully not thinking they were unattractive to me, because they were all quite attractive.

I remember all their conversations about guys, and how I was the one exception they knew of and most stereotypical rules or profiles didn't apply to me, which gave me a lot of satisfaction. I was available to any of them if they chose, but I couldn't care less one way or the other since I was having fun anyway.

I was their well of information from a man's viewpoint, and they all looked pretty descent, so I had all this beauty surrounding me without the fear of hidden motives. It was like being the night guard in a sexy art gallery; all the good views were my own exclusively. Even guys in the bars of Newark or in the dance club called Studio One would ask me which of the foxes I brought I was "doing", not understanding or believing that it wasn't my priority in life, and it appeared that they thought I was possibly a pimp or gay or something.

That amused Beth and I for a while. I guess they were impressed or confused by my ability to hang out with all these gorgeous girls and not need to try and take advantage of any of them, or they thought I was the biggest idiot they ever met, being too immature or narrow minded to understand my way of thinking. Trying to explain the difference between desire and need, aggression and patience to mostly drunk guys, especially around great looking women, is a pretty futile thing to do. The easiest thing would have been to screw any of these drunken beauties; it took real manpower not to take advantage of their weakened drunken state of mind.

Beth was another rare dance partner for me, along with Michelle I believe. They were quite adamant about me dancing with them sometimes, so I appeased them when I could, even though I suck at dancing. I think Shelly became jealous of how quickly Bethanie and I became close, and how much time we spent together. She told me how she felt replaced, but Shelly was my sis, the mini-Janis Joplin, and she could never be replaced by anyone.

I told her so more than once, while playing hours of Yatzee at her house, her, Crystal, Beth and I. We did that frequently. She was likely too drunk to comprehend or remember, but she was never uncomfortable about what she and I shared while she was in that state of mind, I never let her loose too much control, or took advantage of the situation. I think she knew that too.

I recall once Jake, myself, Shelly and Bethanie all cruising in Jake's fifty seven Willie Jeep he recently bought, and Jake tended to drive like a madman. The Jeep would not do over forty-five miles per hour, and when another driver tried to pass us on a four lane road, Jake kept positioning himself in front to prevent them from getting around us, just being obnoxious.

Then the road narrowed to two lanes and went from forty-five mile an hour speed limit to twenty-five, and the guy was still behind us honking like an idiot, with Jake zigzagging in front of him to make sure he couldn't pass us still. As we approached a traffic light, we were going to turn left, and there was a car coming the other way much closer to us that I would ever had allowed it to be for us to still make the turn, if I was driving.

Jake turned in front of the car anyway, and the idiot behind us in pursuit also tried to make the turn, apparently not seeing the car we just missed, and they crashed into this car head on. Jake and I laughed, and we went around the block and came back, and the driver of the car that was playing road games with us was standing in the middle of the street with his whole face covered with blood, and he recognized us and started shaking his fist at us and tried to point us out to the other car's driver, but Jake just honked his horn, waved and laughed at the guy as we passed him within a few feet of where he was standing.

When Shelly, Beth, Jake and I got together, it was as if the perfect crowd of four was formed. We all fit together perfectly, and though no sex was involved for me, there could not be a more perfect combination on earth of four people at this point in my life. Jake was as close to me as my brother would be if I had one, and we referred to each other as brother always, and Beth and Shelly couldn't be closer to me than if they were really my sisters, though I would have given up that comparison if they felt as passionately for me as I could for them.

I would have married either of these two girls, and I never thought to ask them if they knew that or not. I had occasionally wished I were a Mormon, just as a fantasy, because I would have married both of them if I could legally, though I doubt they would have appreciated that sentiment or felt the same about it.

They both reached the level of communication I saw as important for a long relationship, so only time would tell. I allowed destiny to march on, I was far from through. I loved them both a great deal, differently as individuals, as real friends. Either you love someone or you don't, and I was accustomed to beautiful women showing no passionate desire for me, and I cannot change that, nor would I ever care enough to want to. I respected the one-sided physical attraction element of our relationship, and I would never impose myself on either. I allowed them to control the pace or level of our relationship, based on what they felt it should be, which may be part of the reason they liked me. I would pose no threat to them.

As long as they were comfortable, so was I. The feelings I had for both of them was reciprocated with honest open communication and feeling, and I felt for them deeper than I did for any of my other girlfriends, since neither of them would ever assault my emotions and heart and lay groundwork for distrust and deceit as the other girls in my life had continually done.

I had my sexual partner in Wilma, no love from my perspective anymore, just lust, and my love for my friends Bethanie and Shelly, with no lust from their perspective, just love, and I realized that it didn't matter that love and sexual aggression were achieved through different girls, because as long as I had both, I was happy. Physical attraction is simple, and takes much less time and effort than building the real friendship we had, which can make it more appealing and lasting in the long run.

Granted, I would have been ready and willing yet scared shitless to make love to either, which would be normal since I found them both physically attractive, but that didn't weigh as an important issue to overcome, since our closeness was so rare that I was happy just to be as close as I was with either of them, just by being myself, their friend forever.

Being close friends with any girl, as it was with Vera so many years ago, was always more important and acceptable to me than getting into their pants, unlike most guys I knew. I couldn't understand guys who thought they were God's gift to women, and figured every woman wanted them, which was way more egotistical than I would ever want to become, and oddly, that described most of my male friends' attitudes. I've often wondered what Shelly or

Beth would have thought of me if they knew me at age ten through fourteen, if they had been the same age as me, that would have been interesting, yet I doubt they would feel the same about me as they did around that time or even now.

Wilma was my friend, as it was, not the type I could project long term happiness with but I always told her the truth, spoke openly about everything, and figured if this was to be it would be. I never allowed the possibilities to fade until they were gone from the view of my destiny, and accepted what was, always building upon what I had learned as I experienced it with Wilma. We were safe to each other.

When I held parties at my house with twenty hours of strait Pink Floyd, Shelly, Beth, Wilma, Jake and I were the only ones who could stand it, and we all loved it. That tended to clear the house of people we didn't want, without having to get violent or rude.

Jake lived at my house at this point, his parents had moved to Florida, and every night we'd go to sleep to the sound of one of my Floyd albums, Wish You Were Here being his personal favorite. My parents adored Jake; he was always very nice to them and even installed their garage door opener for nothing. He cost my parents nothing, unlike Peter, and we had a lot of fun living in my room together without causing grief to my parents.

We had many parties, always making certain my parents house looked exactly as it did when they left, and usually with only the same four or five people. Shelly would challenge Jake to a drinking contests, which no one won because after a couple hours they would be so wasted that they would forget that they were competing. I would cook for everyone, making my homemade specialties, while Jake and Beth would disappear into our bedroom for some intimacy and Shelly and I would just listen to more Floyd. I walked in on them one time after a while, forgetting they were even in my room after some time and many pipe hits with Shelly were taken, but no one in this group in the house would feel embarrassment of any kind, we were all quite close. Wilma and I would also disappear frequently, letting Shelly, Jake, and Beth have run of the kitchen, stereo and such.

This brings me to recall a story I wrote, since I mentioned homemade specialties, written on November fourteenth nineteen eighty-three for an English class, as an exercise in descriptive writing. It also was one of my favorite activities to do during the Floyd fest, and I called it: "The Cheddar Cheese Bacon Burger Bagel". I made many for Jake, Beth, Shelly, Wilma and myself, and here's what I wrote about it.

"Some of my favorite foods I like to create myself. I strive to create incredibly unique and delicious foods with the use of only my kitchen. One day, I decided that I wanted the salty splendor of bacon, along with everyone's favorite, the cheeseburger. Then I thought to myself, what would make this meal unique? It hit me like a ton of lox. The infamous unique, scrumptious bagel! This presented one more problem, what type of bagel? I chose the onion between the choices of onion, plain and sesame. Now, throwing the bagel into the toaster oven at three hundred fifty degrees would give me fifteen minutes to prepare the burger and the bacon. I grabbed a half-pound of bacon and a burger, put the burger in a small fry pan and the bacon in a large one and began waiting. While I waited, I prepared myself by getting the cheese, mayonnaise, spatula and tongs ready for action.

Keeping an eye on both frying pans, I cut the bagel in half and put cheese on both halves, knowing the heat from the bacon and burger would melt both sides. The burger was done first, so I placed it on one half of the bagel to melt the cheese. Then the bacon was done, so in three rows across and up and down I stacked the bacon high, spreading mayonnaise generously between each layer. Then I closed my creation and crushed the extra space left by the pile of bacon with my hand. I got a tall glass of chocolate milk, sat down, and experienced what could only be described as a totally oral orgasm! Since then, this creation has become commonplace in my house, and I would willingly share the recipe with anyone" This essay got a B plus, for some reason, from my professor Doctor Serafin. I thought it should have been an A, but what did I know.

Onward with my life, Jake at that point had the Willies Jeep, and we'd all go cruising and partying all over the state, on road and off.

This is when Bethanie showed us an incredible place, the Oxford quarry that she and Roland knew of, since Roland was a cliff diver in his country, Portugal or Brazil I think. I still have pictures of this place, and Beth, Shelly Jake and I would all go swimming and skinny-dipping during the day or in the middle of the night there, jumping off the sixty foot peak unable to see the water below.

You had to wear shoes at least while jumping, and we never jumped that far naked, since it could be too painful. Only Beth and I were brave enough to jump off the sixty-footer at all, much less at night, and we all went off the thirty foot one. The place was about a quarter mile long, a tenth of a mile wide, and was surrounded with ten to ninety foot cliffs, overlooking hundreds of feet of water.

The scenery looked like a tropical paradise had been pulled out of some tropical place and moved to New Jersey. I would eventually go there at least a couple dozen times. I would travel there with each and every one of Beth's friends, individually and collectively, Michelle, Cori, Frieda, and many others. Even if we didn't swim every time, it was worth going to see just for its beauty and utter uniqueness.

When Jake and I went one day, there was a private security cop there, and he told us that a guy who parked exactly where we were was found by him with his head blown off by a shotgun, and we should not come here to trespass again. He believed Jimmy Hoffa's body could be in this place, since it's around four hundred feet deep in spots, and so narrow that the pressure made it near impossible to scuba dive to the bottom.

He said he was positive there were dead bodies in this thing, and for many years' kids would come drink on the ninety foot concrete platform, and a few times the drunk kids fell off the peak and landed on the water wrong, and were never found again. He said they tried to retrieve a body once, but the police diver could not reach the body due to the pressure, even though the person was only a few feet below him, and in his sight.

I told the guard I didn't quite believe that, because I knew they could drag the bottom if they had to, or so I thought, but the guy claimed there was too much debris to do that and it wasn't possible.

He also told us that there are telephone poles under the water, only a few feet from the surface on the sixty-foot cliff side, and if you hit one, you would certainly be badly injured or killed.

I never landed on one, and no one I knew did either. I only jumped off the ninety-footer once, it took seven seconds to hit the water, and it took me over ten minutes just to build up enough nerve to actually step off the platform. Needless to say, it was an incredible feeling. Obviously, the day this guard was there we had to leave without doing any swimming, which was disappointing.

Bethanie was the first person I ever drank alcohol with besides the one sip of beer that day in Miami. This time, it was in a bar in Linden, we were drinking wine, and I discovered I'm not that great at shooting pool while drunk. She and I spent many nights after that cruising around with seven-eleven's largest cup full of ice and wine all night long.

We also had a tendency to go to Newark for coke, which we liked as well, and that insured an all night event. This was indeed the most drug filled portion of my life. She, Shelly, Jake, Elton, and even Wilma would all indulge massively in the killer powder for a while. As good as it makes you feel initially, it took me a while of remembering the down side before completely quitting the giant money burner.

Beth and I did many things together, like going to Chinatown in New York since we both loved Chinese food. We'd park on the roof of the Port of Authority and walk through the city, marveling at the vastness of the place and all the odd people in it, similar to when Pete or Fred and I went, yet so much more fun, we laughed at everything.

One time in a little restaurant I ordered something that I had no idea what it was, and it came to me as chicken feet. The waiters and Beth were all laughing at me, watching me trying to get something edible off them, and I never knew how or what to do with them, neither did Beth. Mostly we just wandered around the city for fun, seeing all there is to see in this huge place.

Then one day Jake, Beth, Wilma and I were playing truth or dare at Beth's house. We would all just say truth usually because none of us felt we had a lie or anything to hide between us, which was true. Wilma asked Beth on a truth, that I could predict coming from her before she asked it, if she would ever have sex with me, and Beth said definitely not since I wasn't her type.

I knew Wilma was just weighing the likeliness of Beth and me getting together, and getting between her and me. Beth and I have never found anything negative to say about each other, and probably never will, always pointing out the positive points or humor of any situation. A trait I hope we never out grow. And even with this gaming statement I never gave the possibility a second thought, I figured if we were to be we would be, and life would go on.

I often felt she had no attraction for me in that way, much like any good looking woman, and though I had held her in my arms while she cried, because Jake loved someone else, and stood by her under any circumstance, I would never think to make any type of contact to ruin the comfort and closeness we had shared for so long.

It was nearly identical with Shelly, I held her close when she had bad trips, abortion, and just needed to be held, never pondering my own desires even with her lying next to me in just her underwear, with my arms wrapped around her like a teddy bear. Shelly was a lot more cynical about life than Beth, more negative and paranoid due to drugs, and deep into drinking her life away, and thus she eventually lost touch with me, because I couldn't bear to watch her demolish herself, feeling as I did for her.

I have no doubt Shelly would accept me as a friend anytime in the future, as would every friend I had like Elton, Jake, Fred and Reggie, unlike a few former girl friends, whom I just never trusted again as I did, thus the level of emotion drops significantly. They were who I considered as my family, handpicked and closer to me than anyone in my real family was.

In Peter's case, it wouldn't matter that much to me if he didn't ever see me again; he became a little strange and distant later on. Fred was like the brother who always wanted to be better and smarter than everyone else, Elton was the comedic brother who sought only to get laid on a regular basis, Reggie was the less sane brother, who's sanity was never in question in my own head and realized for the act that it was, and Jake was the combination of all three traits, with the ability to speak a foreign tongue to add confusion to the mix.

Beth and I began attending Union County College in Cranford together, studying, working and cruising together for years, and Cheyanne and her family moved to Kissimmee Florida after her graduation from high school. I took a writing class there at the college, Allen Ashtill was the teacher and he claimed, by writing it right on one of my assignments, that I showed "wasted talent" for writing. I hope I have proven him wrong with this piece of work.

I'll reprint my assignments and early writing samples, maybe even some of my poems, perhaps later on. This is a reprint of one, the "wasted talent" one, mostly fiction and partly fact, it's quite long and I think it's a really good story. I wrote it in May of nineteen eighty-four and I call it: "The Dreamer".

"The day was young. He awoke to the sound of water dripping methodically against a glass he had used the night before. This made him think of the dream he just experienced. Or was it truly a dream? As Chris sat up, he wondered what it was exactly that he was doing there in an old, rat-ridden hotel somewhere in the Florida Keys. Suddenly, a huge black bird appeared upon the windowsill and a streak of horror overwhelmed the boy. The bird's eyes reminded Chris of the same ones that, not too long ago, had sealed a short portion of his destiny. But wasn't that just a dream?

Then the bird did something very odd; it spread its wings as if to leave, then with its right claw it exposed a small stone pipe that it had concealed behind its tail feathers. With a knowing look at Chris, it was gone. The boy instantly jumped to his feet, went across the room in what appeared to be one sailing step, and grabbed the small stone object. Now he knew. He shook his head frantically in hopes of waking up for good, but found that reality had already brought him to consciousness. "There could be hundreds of reasons I'm here and not in my bed in New Jersey", he thought to himself. As for anyone waking in a strange place, there had to be an explanation. "Why am I here?" These were the first words uttered by a totally confused person who, not twenty-four hours before, was hanging out in a coffee shop in Fanwood, New Jersey.

Chris remembered the events of the last day as someone would remember a daydream, especially if it came true. He had just returned from a very strange encounter with the head shop owner in Plainfield. The keeper, who looked as though all his years of smoking herb had finally vegetated his brain beyond all concepts of reality, greeted him as if he had known Chris for many years. This shop, randomly placed among the business district's many other stores, was cleverly concealed by its front entrance, which jutted out nearly to the next shop. This only left the front door visible. Once a person would enter, he would immediately be greeted by several slogan banners hung with great care, the less that intelligent shopkeeper and a rather large German shepherd named Bugs. The store dealt mostly in paraphernalia, but had a small supply of tee shirts, jeans potions and curios.

Then, while browsing, Chris saw it. The object he was looking at could be no larger than a Bic lighter, yet it was slightly wider. It sat alone on a top shelf of what looked like a three-dimensional chessboard. Chris asked the keeper what was so special about this item that it had its own little plateau, but he just looked confused by the question. This frustrated Chris, so he took the pipe off its perch, motioned to the keeper with it, and said: "How much?" The keeper replied: "I know not of what you are asking, my friend, but if you see something that pleases your eye, I will make it a gift to you". This startled Chris, and once more in plain English he requested the price of the pipe in his hand. The keeper, looking ever so confused, stoned and disoriented, simply said: "Take that, for I do not see it". Chris agreed quite readily, one can't frown on a free token of friendship, and Chris never could.

As he left, Chris noticed a slight burning sensation against his right hip. Digging into his pocket, he found the pipe he had just acquired from the shopkeeper. It was very hot, as if it had already been used and left in his pocket to cool. Then the stone began to smoke, all by its self! Chris dropped it, yet it did not break. The pipe lay there smoldering, so Chris quickly picked it up and returned to the shop. Upon entering, Chris noticed something very unusual. The man he had discussed the pipe with wasn't there. Instead, an elderly, white haired man stood fiddling with the numerous headbands that were hung on nails several feet apart and camouflaged against the back wall.

Chris caught the old man's attention, held the pipe up to him and asked: "What's wrong with this pipe and where's the other guy I talked to?" The old man took the pipe in his withered hand, looked at it carefully, and then returned it to Chris's hand. He said: "Son, there is nothing wrong with the pipe, and furthermore, there has been no person here other than myself all day. You are my first customer". Chris suddenly felt a great chill in his spine, starting from his lower back and working its way up to the back of his neck. He turned around to point out the three level shelves where he had found the pipe and then his breath left him. The shelf that had held six pipes altogether was no longer there. Instead, there sat an entire display of porcelain bongs, which stretched from one side of shop's back wall almost out the door.

There is no way this old man could have possibly moved all these items by himself, Chris thought. Then the old man spoke to him. He said: "Son is there something wrong? Can I help you with something? You don't look well". Chris said nothing for a long time. He ran over in his mind what had just taken place in the past few minutes, and could find no logical explanation. At least the dog was the same. Then, without warning, he began to yell at the old man. "What, are you crazy? Is this a joke? Where's the other guy, you old fart?!" This startled the elderly man and even Bugs got to his feet and began to growl threateningly. "Leave!" the man said. He said it with such authority that Chris was a little surprised. Again the man said: "Leave!" only he added some words about the police and his faithful friend who was by now only inches from Chris's leg.

Chris stood very still for a moment, wondering why he had gotten so upset. He apologized to the old man and said that this was not how he is usually. The man said: "Listen, you little brat, I don't know what kind of trip you're on, but I could have the cops find out for us!" Bugs was now carefully measuring up Chris's weak points, sniffing inquiringly at his ankles, awaiting his masters command. The man told Chris to leave again, which he finally did without any further hesitation. As he left he couldn't recall if the pipe had been returned to him. While he stood outside his car door, a small white dog trotted playfully towards him and proceeded to urinate on the left rear tire. "Scat, you little peeve!" Chris said. He figured that this must not be his day. There had to be some logic behind all this. Then, without any warning, blue smoke curled its way around his nose and drifted slowly out into the atmosphere.

Chris looked for the source of the smoke and nearly had a stroke. It was coming out of his own left front pocket. His skin became clammy, his eyes started to water, he felt the previous chill reasserting itself up his back to almost unbearable stiffness, then he found the pipe. He pulled it out of his pocket and found that it wasn't as hot as it had been earlier. In fact, the warmth was quite pleasing and he felt his back begin to loosen.

Chris sat now in the front seat of his Oldsmobile Cutlass, looking at the small stone object in his hand with the fascination of a child viewing a mouse for their first time. The pipe was no longer smoking, but it was still warm. Then a small stream of the blue fragrance tempted his nose soothingly. Chris inhaled deeply, as if he had filled the pipe himself with some rare treasured herb. The feeling of incoherency was overwhelming. Suddenly Chris failed to recognize where he was and why. The mystery of this pipe vanished as though this union was meant to be. Through all the disorientation, Chris managed the six-mile drive back to his house as if he floated the whole way, occasionally sniffing the sweet blue smoke that was unceasingly rising from his newest possession.

It was a beautiful Saturday afternoon, so peaceful and so quiet. Upon arriving home, Chris wondered why. What could be the purpose of this pipe that cost him nothing, yet gave off such a sweet, mellow high that you had to appreciate every living thing just because it was alive. Just then, the overwhelming urge to cruise took control and Chris found himself driving effortlessly across the mountains, his small possession wielding ever so intoxicating fumes. Then he saw it. He was driving along a fairly narrow road when a large Buick came careening over the solid line, causing Chris to eat the shoulder of the road with his tires and skid to a stop some fifty yards away.

The Buick wasn't so fortunate. There was no shoulder on the opposite side of the road and the car had become air born over a gully that led to the construction site that ran parallel to the road. It flipped over several times, and then stopped upside down against a tree, its nose upon the tree, and its trunk against the ground. Chris was suddenly and inexplicably aware of the events. He immediately jumped out of his car and ran towards the crippled car. Standing next to the wreck he noticed three people sprawled throughout the interior and at the same time, he saw smoke begin to swirl around the usually unexposed gas tank. This made Chris's adrenaline flow, as he never felt before. Without thought, he pulled with all his strength at the car door, feeling his stomach and groin begin to give.

Then the door sprang open with a snap that caused the remains of the window to break off completely. Frantically and feverishly, Chris pulled the first and the biggest of survivors, threw him over his shoulder and carried him to the opposite bank. Then when he returned to the car, he saw the flames begin to lick the side of the car where his entrance was. Two girls were still in the car, and for a split second Chris wondered why he had rescued the guy first. Ignoring this though, he managed to pull out one of the girls and lay her down beside the car, while he went in for the other girl. This girl was very conscious, and her screams were deafening. Chris asked her quietly if she could walk and help him, but the girl just sat where he put her and screamed. Chris was on the verge of panic himself.

The flames were now encasing the whole inside of the car, and the smell of burnt hair was nauseating, especially when he found out that it was his hair burning. Then Chris lifted the screamer to her feet, praying that she could stand on her own. When she did, he picked up the other girl in a fireman's carry, held the other girl up by the waist, and struggled across the road to the spot where the unconscious man was lying. Before he reached the other side, a resounding explosion rocked him to the ground, dropping both girls in a pile of flora very close to the other side. His last thought was how he got from the yellow line to the other side so quickly. Then a subtle dull throb started in his back and he passed peacefully into shock.

He lay there in a fog for what seemed to be an eternity, and then a face appeared through the mist before him. Chris thought to himself that his maker had arrived to claim his soul. He wasn't sure if he was pleased or not to find his best friend standing over him. Then his friend spoke. He said: "What happened? I was on my way to find you when I saw smoke and your car!" Chris lay there thinking about what had just happened, when the sound of ambulances startled him to his feet. The smell of smoke and burnt hair was abundant. Chris said: "Man, we've got a lot to talk about!" He then told his friend Jake about the events that had transpired a few hours before. He showed him the pipe and Jake sat there in disbelief.

The cops finally arrived, and an officer of Union County came over to where Chris stood trembling. He asked what had happened, and Chris gave him the details. "They say I saved these people's lives, did I?" Chris asked Jake. "I suppose you did," Jake said, "That must have been pretty wild!" After Chris gave the cops all his information, like why he was there and where he lived, he said to Jake: "Let's go man, I need a shower something fierce!" Jake replied: "Cool, let's drop off the Jeep and then I'll drive". Chris and Jake started for the car, and then they stopped where the medics were working carefully. Then they saw it. One of the stretchers, the largest one, was covered with a sheet completely. Nausea flowed freely through the boys' stomachs, and Chris told Jake that this guy was the first one he rescued. The thought of carrying a dead man made Chris feel utterly ill. But a warm feeling that he had done all he could swelled from his heart.

Then he remembered the pipe. It felt warm again, and Chris couldn't resist showing his friend what had started this whole day's events. Jake stared in disbelief, wondering just how much damage the accident caused to his friend. Then he remembered. How did he know where Chris was and that he was in danger? An uncomfortable feeling in Jake's chest made him realize that there was more to this situation than meets the eye. That was when the pipe Chris handed him started its familiar, unnatural blue smoke. Jake dropped it in fright. Chris said: "Fear not, my friend, I feel this artifact has much to do with the course of our future. We can actually get high as you've never been before, without paranoia about police, and I don't understand it anymore than you do". Then Jake remembered the signs they saw over the last few months, the soda can, the mountain, and he looked at Chris with great understanding.

Chris and Jake have been the closest of friends for many years. To this day they both believe that they are really brothers, separated from infancy by some fluke of their parents somehow. The events Chris had just seen were very clear to Jake, and it did not take any time for Jake to react. If one was in danger or hurt, the other knew it. The two boys had gone exploring often, not knowing what it was they were supposed to find, and they had found some rather inexplicable things along the way. The most favored example was the ice cold sealed can of Pepsi, which they found as they were walking, dying for something to quench their thirst. It was taken as a sign. Now they possessed the pipe. Chris explained to Jake that the urge to cruise had been stronger than ever before, and when he did, the Buick was what he found.

So the two went riding around, inhaling the free smoke, which had been flowing steadily since they dropped the Jeep off at home. They went to Scotch Plains in search of a friend that they could share their smoke with, yet every time they found someone, the pipe would cease activity, and be cold and as clean as a new pipe again. They began to wonder about their sanity. Chris had been paid the night before, so both of them decided to cruise for a while. They drove semi-consciously across many mountains. Neither could have cared less about their destination and within hours they realized that they were in a different state. Then they stopped for food and fuel.

The station was some fifty yards off the main road, in an enclosed area surrounded by high greenish brown pines. Once inside the area, the road was not visible. Jake carefully pulled the car into the gas lane, remembering how stoned they were. The closest approximation as to where they were, was someplace in Pennsylvania, this was one possibility. Next to the pumps on the other side was a dark blue Mustang with some six people stuffed into the small interior. The occupants appeared none too friendly. Then someone dressed in dark gray and quite tall came out of the restaurant that looked quite empty. The two decided to go for some munchies, even though the usual need for them wasn't felt by either. Jake told the attendant to fill it, check the oil and transmission fluid, and that we'd be inside eating. The man nodded and the boys went to eat.

Chris and Jake sat against the window that had a full view of the car. A beautiful blonde waitress appeared out of nowhere and offered two menus. Chris said that two bagels and coffee would suffice. She agreed and wiggled her way towards the kitchen, with both boys following her walk closely. "Ah, what a sight!" Jake said. Chris agreed. Just then, Jake turned around to see how the attendant was coming along with our service when he noticed that the Mustang was still there. Looking closer, he noticed that the attendant was moving very slowly around the pumps, as though being overly cautious. This made no sense to Jake, and he pointed this out to Chris, who was awaiting the waitresses' magnificent return.

As Chris looked out at the two cars and the man, something glared in his eyes. He felt the same as Jake, something wasn't right. As they looked on at the Mustang, the glaring object took shape in both boys' eyes at the same time. One of the people in the car was holding a large machete to the attendant's throat, which explained why he was lingering near the window of the Mustang for such a long time. Suddenly the feeling of prey and predator, life and death streamed through the boy's veins. Without words, Jake got up, motioned to the waitress and asked her where the back door was. She told Jake that there isn't one, at which point we heard the screech of tires, and the Mustang had fled.

Chris was outside in seconds with the fallen attendant who had a large gash across his chest and the guy said: "I was robbed!" Chris told the wounded man that he and his friend would go after the Mustang, and before the man could answer, Chris ran back to the restaurant and nearly collided with Jake who was just coming out. Jake told him that the police and ambulance were on their way, and then they both jumped into the car to give chase, with the adrenaline of a new and excitingly real adventure flowing through both of them.

As Chris drove, Jake opened the glove box and removed the solid steel bar they kept for emergencies, kept there so that if the odds were ever against these two large boys, this would make up most of the difference short of having a gun. Within minutes, Chris had closed in on the Mustang, and they were riding alongside the fleeing crooks. Jake motioned threateningly to the driver to give up, and that's when he became aware of the passenger raising some object and pointing it at him. Jake yelled to Chris to hit the gas, which he did as if he too had seen the object. Then lee lifted himself out of the window and with his right hand, he hurled the solid bar at the driver of the other car. The object sailed true, and with a great crashing of glass, the bar penetrated the right side of the windshield.

This time, there was no saving the occupants, as the car took a flying leap over the sunken shoulder of the road and hit an oak tree head on. Then it burst into flames, inside and out. Chris congratulated Jake on his aim, once he stopped the car and got out to look for damage. A small hole had appeared on the door, one that Chris was sure had not been there before. "I guess they had a gun", Jake said. Well, let's split before we have any explaining to do" Chris answered. Both agreed. As the boys drove down the road a mile or so, they saw numerous cop cars heading in the direction of the crash, and they also noticed that the print on the sides of the cars said: "Jackson County Police, West Virginia". The boys exclaimed: "wild!" in disbelief and how they got there was the topic of conversation for a long time. They finally decided that the pipe had wanted them to come here and as they smoked from it, they found that again their direction was unimportant.

The sun had just receded behind the mountains as Chris as tried to capture the great natural beauty of the colors that swirled just above the horizon. There was such unspoiled beauty, so unlike the familiar gray patchy skies that New York had been known to give off into the atmosphere. The peace of this scenery was so intense; Chris and Jake felt that nothing could spoil it. That is, till Chris saw the familiar rotating, flashing red and yellow lights growing closer in his rear view mirror. The word cops scrambled through the boys minds, like some forbidden taboo as Chris pulled cautiously to the side and stopped. A pair of large, blue uniformed officers walked slowly to either side of the car. The cop on Chris's side asked him to get out, and upon doing so, Chris found himself sprawled against the hood, with the officer searching through his pockets. The other officer subjected Jake to the same procedure, neither of them explaining the intrusion.

Chris said: "Did I do something wrong, officer?" knowing that his Jersey license plate must have been the reason for stopping them. The cop, who must have stood six foot ten, simply bellowed: "Shut up boy, if you want to walk again!" Then both cops started asking questions, the same kind of questions Jake and Chris had been asking each other for a while. Why were they here in North Carolina? North Carolina? Both boys wondered to themselves. What did they want down here, and where were they going, and the usual cross-examination. After the boy's had evaded all the questions, the officers started searching the car. The smaller cop found a pipe in the front seat between the cushions. "Well, well, looks like we got us here a couple of pot heads, what do you think Luke?" the big cop answered, "listen boys, tell us where the stuff is and we'll let you slide this time". In a polite voice, contradictory to his nature when dealing with authority, but knowing enough about southern cops not to mess with them, Jake said: "We don't have anything, sir, if you'll notice, the pipe is clean". "So it is, so it is" the cop reflected. "Well, we'll keep it so you boys don't find any temptation to fill it".

Chris and Jake stood quietly, knowing there was nothing they could do about the situation, and utter frustration flashed across their faces. The cops, looking very disappointed in the fact that they could not find anything illegal, got back into their car. Pulling up next to Chris, they said: "Now we cut you boys a big break, so get your Jersey asses out of our state or we'll bust your asses good next time". That's what the boys interpreted, but they really said: "Get out of our state and maybe we'll not bust your asses good next time", which wasn't true English, of course. Chris ignored that improper language and just said: "Yes sir, thank you sir!" and the officers were out of sight within minutes. Chris said to lee: "Damn! They got the pipe!" Jake started to chuckle.

"What do you find so funny? The pipe is gone!" with this statement of no real hardship, Jake broke into uncontrollable laughter. Finally, he managed to say: "I'm glad they didn't strip search me, because they found my old pipe, not the pipe!" Then he stuck his hand down into his sock and pulled out the nearly lost device. At that point, the blue, sweet smoke began to drift thicker than it ever had before. Both boys broke into fits of laughter that lasted the rest of the ride out of North Carolina. After they left the state, Jake said: "You know, I always wondered what happened to my pipe". Chris said: "Well, I'm glad it was there, and we didn't really do anything wrong". Ever since they had left Jersey, this pipe they had seemed to give them directions, and also appeared to have some hidden destination. The two had traveled from New Jersey to North Carolina in what seemed to be one afternoon, which was impossible, as they knew. They figured that the pipe must distort time as well as space, and makes the days seem like hours.

The road stretched out before them, like one of those video games, where as long as you insert quarters into it, you never have to stop. Unfortunately, their machine was low on fuel, and there was no station in sight. They decided to drive until the car was empty, and worry about that then. Chris was thinking about how much he and Jake had been through, and what else may happen down the road. He fell into peaceful slumber, and Jake must have found a station since Chris's dreams seemed so long and complete. Dreams came about the people they had recently encountered, faces faded in and out like a poorly focused movie with no plot. The whole trip must have some purpose, yet it made no sense. There was no feeling of danger, or that the whole thing had been just a waste of time.

Then the car stopped, and Chris remembers Jake telling him that this is where they would be staying and asking him if he wanted something to drink. He drank, he thought, and then he lay down on a comfortable bed and continued his sleep. The last thing Chris remembers Jake telling him was that they were in the Florida Keys. So there Chris was, sitting on a single bed with pipe in hand, wondering where his friend was. He had honestly hoped that when he woke, he would find himself in his own bed, back in New Jersey.

Accepting the circumstance as real, Chris went outside to find Jake sunbathing in a lounge chair. Jake asked him what was going to happen next, and Chris only said he wished he knew. The two sat and smoked the blue smoke in hopes of an answer. Jake said that they were out of money, and that they should sell the car for more, since it was apparent that returning home was not possible. Chris agreed apprehensively, and they got nine hundred for it, and then decided to seek employment. The entire time the pipe would smoke only in their presence, and it seemed they were the only two who would know of this phenomenon, since the pipe would stop smoking as soon as they came in contact with anyone else. Chris and Jake went walking along the beachfront, which is kind of hard to avoid in the keys.

Their conversation was in mostly half sentences, since they understood each other so well, and if one were to listen, the meaning of the conversation would most certainly escape them. "Listen man, we've both been brought here for some reason, don't you think?" Jake said. "Yea, but I honestly don't have the slightest idea of why" Chris replied. "Me neither, but I'm starving, man" said Jake. "Cool, let's eat and replenish, our energy, because I think we'll need it. Jake said: "I get that feeling too, so let's get some supplies first, while we still have money". The boys decided that the basic survival tools were needed, so they went to the town's sport shop. Hunting knives, compass, tarp, fishing line, hooks, tool belt, pole and a snakebite kit are some of what they bought. They also bought a tent, propane stove, utensils, a long life flashlight, inflatable boat, and a forty-five pistol, which they convinced the store owner they needed in case of encounters with crocodiles in their college study of the Everglades and other desolate places. The man in the store convinced them they would need a bug light and hip boots.

All of this they packed into backpacks, except for the gun and knives, the knives they strapped to their new belts. The gun made them both quite paranoid, and they took turns stashing it down their pant legs. Neither Jake nor Chris could conceive of keeping the gun for any reason other than the one they had given the storeowner. They headed north, hitch-hiking up the main road in the keys, and no sooner had they reached North Miami than the pipe, which had been smoking steadily except when they got rides, was finished. No smoke, no high, just the reality of being in Miami on foot for no reason at all.

The boys were feasting at the corner of Collins Avenue and one hundred sixty Eighth Street at a Stewarts in North Miami Beach when they began to realize that looking for a substitute for the smokeless pipe was useless. Chris' car, their only transportation would be the only true loss in this experience, but what they felt was that they lost the confidence that this trip meant something. "There has to be more to this!" Chris complained. Jake answered: "I think we've been taught a lesson here. Let's face it; the force that made the pipe smoke has abandoned us. Something is still not right, though." And as the words left Lees' lips, Chris noticed that on the overhang of Stewarts, a large black crow, very much like the one in the hotel room, perched watching Chris closely. "It's that bird!" Chris exclaimed. Jake said: "What about that bird? Are you high?" "No!" Chris replied in a vicious tone that threw Jake off guard. Jake asked for an explanation, Chris told him about the bird.

By now, the boys had finished their food and were about to leave, when the screeching of tires caught their attention. A large, black Cadillac came flying around the corner and as Chris and Jake saw it, and they noticed that it was coming right at them. "Oh, shit!"

was all they had time to say as the Caddy decided to use the very table the boys had eaten on and several more in the row outside the restaurant, to stop their momentum. The car flipped on its side when it hit the unyielding concrete parking stop, and four cop cars nearly smashed into each other trying to stop from repeating the Caddy's performance. Chris and Jake were standing under the huge sign, each behind one of the iron pillars holding it up and more or less in between the cops and the Caddy. Both fell to the ground when the sound of gunfire started and four men climbed out of the car with all arms firing.

The cops returned fire, obviously not seeing Jake and Chris sprawled out on the ground praying to their maker. Chris realized, in between prayers, that he had the gun on him, and he thought he might be up shit's creek again. Chris and Jake watched with mixed curiosity and fear as one by one the cops were losing and had only managed to hit one felon. As the third cop fell, Jake said to Chris: "Give me the gun!" Chris reacted quickly, and knew what Jake had in mind, so he decided not to waste any time and proceeded to aim the never fired gun at the criminals. The crooks as well as the cops took no notice of the boys and this gave Chris a clear, unobstructed target. He had never fired a handgun before, which made him hesitate a second. He knew that once he fired, a return fire would be unavoidable.

Boom! Boom! Boom! Boom! Boom! The gun sounded. Had he hit anything? He thought so. The firing had ceased and all you could hear was the police radio squawking. He picked his head up, and never felt so lucky in his life, as he saw that he had hit all the crooks, who had just robbed a bank. Chris was grateful to the riflery teacher he had, many years ago. That was when he felt a metal object at the back of his head, and someone said: "Drop it and don't move!" This he did and then he heard Jake say: "Wait a minute, he just helped you!" The voice that lay heavy on Chris's back said: "I know! Who are you?" Chris said: "I'm Chris and this is Jake, We're from New Jersey and we're campers. We keep this gun in case of emergencies, like crocodiles." "Well," the cop said, "we need it for evidence now." Then a voice interrupted and said: "One dead, the rest wounded, one severely." Chris felt disgusted. "One of ours was wounded, all the rest are forty-five calibers except for the deceased."

There were many questions asked, and Chris and Jake decided to stick to the student story, since they really were students. The Dade county police station kept Chris and Jake for two days, returned all their possessions except the gun, which they shouldn't have had in the first place, according to Florida law, and since they helped the police, they were set free. Now the two were walking up Route ninety-five discussing the events that had transpired. "Where's the pipe? Chris asked Jake. "I thought you had it man!" "No, and stop bullshitting, you had it last." No, I didn't, seriously!" "Well, I can't remember putting it anywhere, and I know we didn't chuck it. It stopped working anyway". "True, I guess it really did lose its purpose, but I still would have liked to keep it". "Think the cops found it?" "I guess so, man." "Damn, and now we don't have enough money to fly us both home! What are we gonna do?" "I don't know, I guess we'll just keep walking.

This they did. The boys were walking on a road that wouldn't end for thousands of miles, and neither really cared. They were both quite used to walking great distances, and this place was really very pleasant. The sea breeze was sweet, an unceasing vent that kept the sweat to a minimum, and even cooled them at night. Food was abundant, in wild rabbits and birds, and the two felt in tune with nature, nothing modern could spoil it. They were on their way home and decided to stick together as always, saving the last of the car money for desperate situations. The road stretched forever and time was on their side. Every once in a while, Chris or Jake would spot their newest guardian angel, the large black crow, which seemed to be around whenever the boys would think about it. If they caught food, the bird was there. The creature followed them throughout Georgia, South and North Carolina, and up into Virginia. It seemed to guide them in the direction home even when they were so far from the road that the sounds of traffic were gone.

They discussed things along the way, such as how the pipe deceived them and betrayed them and how things kept happening around them. It was almost believable, as though fate needed them in Florida and all their actions were part of the grand plan. It seemed that it had taken hours to get to Florida, and now weeks were lost retuning. In their minds, the trip was true, yet they doubted that anyone would believe it. "We'll have to keep this to ourselves, you know" Chris said. "Yea, I don't know if I believe it myself! Let's see, we stopped bank robbers, thieves, saved some lives, and partied the whole time. I don't think we need that anymore." "What, the adventure?" Chris asked. "No, the drugs." Replied Jake. He also said: "I mean, the smoke couldn't have been real, right?" "I don't know, but when those guns went off and we chased those people, I felt perfectly strait" Chris said. "So did I, my friend, so did I" Jake stated. "We came to rely on the pipe to set our direction, but maybe that was fate's way on convincing us to go on in the first place. And something like that would certainly do it." "Yea, sort of an attention getter, huh? I think so"." It served its purpose up till Miami, and then it stopped. I don't have it and I know you don't either, so did it actually exist?" Jake puzzled. "That, my friend, is the best question I heard in a long time, so let's go home and think about it!" "Amen, brother!"

So both Chris and Jake set off for home, no longer wondering about the pipe or the bird, which disappeared once Chris said he recognized the road. All this would just become as a memory of a dream, and neither boy was sure it really happened. They were used to strange experiences, although this one, both would admit later, was of an exceptional nature and it would never be completely forgotten by either."

This piece of writing got an A, but also was reprimanded for the content. Oh well, can't please everyone.

Here's another shorter example of writing, since this would be the time where the essay I wrote would give the most accurate account of my creativity at this time, as if the last story wasn't, and I called it "The Machine". Here is what I wrote:

""Ladies and gentlemen", a mechanical voice said, "Welcome to the machine. Please remember during your visit to please not touch anything. There is no smoking, and due to security precautions there are no emergency exits. Once the tour has started, there cannot be any departures from the group. Zog, your mechanical tour guide will answer any questions that he is capable of answering. You are all his responsibility now, enjoy your visit!" I thought to myself as the door we came in closed, what have I gotten myself into now? I looked around and felt as if I were in the heart or stomach of the death star in Star Wars. The only difference seemed to be the small touches of humanity. The display cases, photographs, soda machine and robot constituted all I could understand about where I was.

As I looked at the display of our star system, I thought for a moment that I must have been dreaming. I thought about what this small world of ours was coming to. Could humanity be so unfeeling as to let so many good people remain idle? The very same people who constructed this technological wonder known as our Earth could now retire to sit back and watch it work, or not work. I thought back to the failures I knew of, the chemical dioxin or Three Mile Island, and I knew these things didn't affect me directly. Some things did, though. I found myself in this giant machine in space, reminiscing of my hometown, the woods that surrounded it, and the hikes that made them forests. Then technology showed its ugly face, and despite protest they tore the forest from existence. They did that a lot, back then. The awesome power of technology soon ran out of places to be awesome, or people to be in awe of it, having been replaced soon after it began and becoming themselves considered as outdated or obsolete.

I walked over to where Zog was showing people different styles of anti-gravity shoes, took an axe in hand, and proceeded to cut Zog into two separate parts. I know they will arrest me, but for what? For killing a robot, or destruction of private, expensive property, no doubt. I looked around at the shocked and panic ridden people and said: "Don't you see? This robot is showing us our future! These intergalactic space cubicles might as well be your tombs!" I said with some urgency. "Surely we have a better chance of survival on our own planet, don't we? Just tell them the robot attacked me, and that will be one more step to slow technology down before it destroys us!" But no one would listen, they just coward in a corner and waited as several more Zog's came through a door and trained their electronic eyes on me, as I took an escape pod and headed for home, Earth." That exercise essay only got a B, but I liked writing it. So now back to the real deal, like bus driving.

EXIT NINETEEN

Last Lonely Path

Beth, Shelly, and Jake all went for joy rides with me and my bus many times, partying the time away and stopping traffic for fun. I would come to their houses and park my bus right in front, which was pretty funny to them. I was fortunate that my ability to drive was never impaired, and I never had an accident or ticket related to drugs or alcohol in my life, or drove under any influence while kids were aboard.

I figured if one wants to use controlled substances, they should remain in control. I'd let my friends hang out while picking up busloads of kids, and since I never drank and drove my bus, I'd just watch them drink vodka and orange juice or wine coolers and smoke after dropping the last kids off on my route. Then I'd usually bring them back to my car parked by the office, drop them by it, and go park the bus, and no one would know I had passengers other that school kids on the bus.

Union Catholic high had a name for my bus, the "canna-bus", because I took the late disciplinary problem kids, who always had a bong or pipe in the back row going strong. I made it clear to the kids that if I was pulled over, I would turn them in quickly, but I didn't care as long as they remained seated.

I also drove for Mount Saint Mary's academy, a totally female school, and the girls here were quite unbelievable. Some would sit in the back row spread eagle with no underwear, trying their hardest to get some reaction out of me or distract me, as I described before. Of course, they always failed; I would just laugh or ignore them till they stood up. Standing on my bus was a real bad idea, and I have done some nasty things to ensure safe passage to and from school at all costs.

Like slamming the breaks on the parkway and stopping till they sit down, yelling back that all your lives are in these two hands and unless you sit down I'll crash the back of the bus first to kill you, but I'll survive.

Some must have thought me a lunatic, but I was not going to let anyone on my bus get injured out of stupidity. Beth thought that was pretty funny. I always passed her or any friend of mine off as a new driver learning the route. Driving a bus comes with many stories. I can say from experience that most of the people doing stupid or drastic things around my bus were women.

I hated to even think that since it sounds so chauvinistic, but I saw it with my own eyes. Women would do amazing things to get around me, breaking several laws, because no one likes being behind a school bus during school hours. The only other type of person I saw driving badly besides a woman would have to be really old men, but the ratio was roughly ten to one or less for them.

One time a senior girl of Union Catholic high took her brand new two day old Camaro Z twenty eight and swung out of the parking lot in a semi-circle left turn trying to pass the line of busses going the other way parked in front of the school at the curb. Once she was on the street, she continued the circle and couldn't stop because the road was wet, and she smashed and totaled her car against the front bumper of my bus, which was parked and not even running. She hit a parked bus. Mine. I sat and watched the whole event in amazement, and then they towed her away, and I did my route, since the bus had no damage.

Another time I remember was driving the bus in snow and ice. They get great traction since they're so big, but this day I discovered what all vehicles do upon reaching icy curves in the road, they slide uncontrollably. There were no kids on my bus fortunately, and as

I turned, the bus kept sliding forward towards a small creek that paralleled the road up to this curve.

The bus finally turned some, but only enough for the front of the bus to slide off the road sideways onto the little bridge over the creek, balancing precariously on the edge like a teeter-totter. I opened the passenger door and saw only the creek below and the ten-foot plunge my bus almost fell into, then I called for help on the radio and they pulled me off the bridge. I could not leave the bus from the front, only the back door was a possible exit. That was in Edison right down the street from Saint Thomas Aquinas high school.

A different time while delivering kids to the same school, I remember picking up kids at the top of a hill somewhere in Edison. It was one of my first driving experiences in snow with a school bus, and as I started down the hill, I noticed the bus began to turn sideways. Luckily, there were no cars coming the other way, because the bus was occupying the whole street, both sides, as it slid towards the traffic light at the bottom. I remember the kids screaming, some out of fear, some just for fun, as we headed apparently uncontrollably towards certain doom. I was able to stop at the light, before shooting into traffic on the main street, avoiding any collisions.

I liked driving my bus over giant leaf piles people leave at their curb, scattering them for hundreds of yards down the street, as well as large snow piles, crushing and spreading the slush while soaking anyone who was unfortunate enough to be too close to the mound when I drove by. I thought it was fun to utilize my bus for these forms of entertainment, since it was so large and I knew no damage would occur.

After I drove for a few years, the state changed the law, and anyone with over twelve points on their license was not allowed to drive a school bus. Without a reckless driving or DWI charge ever, I had managed to accumulate fifty two points on my license, going through the rehabilitative course three times they offer you when you don't surrender your license to them.

I just kept telling them that I lost the physical license, so they had no choice. They were able to suspend the bus license, though. The bus company wanted me to drive anyway, suspended, like no one would notice. But I wouldn't. I could have written a whole book about the school bus driving experience, and if asked one day perhaps I will. There was that much to write about, if I detailed it sufficiently. Amazing job, too bad it paid so poorly.

I will now recreate a writing essay I wrote, simply because it fits this segment of my book. I called it "the Road", and I wrote it in November of nineteen eighty-three for my writing class in college. "As I look upon the road ahead, I seem to realize how many different types of drivers there are. I can tell differences in attitudes on the road, since I am always driving. What seems to be the most common are the aggressive and the paranoid drivers. Another class besides normal ones I can identify are the sick drivers. I cannot imagine a non-aggressive driver in New York City. Such a person would get absolutely no place; therefore, aggressiveness becomes sadly mandatory. I also noticed that aggressive drivers tend to have the attitude that they are the only people who need to get where they are going, regardless of other traffic. These people appear to be in a constant state of panic, and are usually late. I can relate to them, since I drive with a tight schedule. This aggressiveness, whether it is hereditary or chosen, is widely recognized by other drivers.

This brings me to another class of motorists, the old, frightened, paranoid type. These people seem to realize and believe that driving is the single most dangerous thing in the world, and everyone except them take it for granted. It is true that the masses of humanity cruise around in what could be called one to twenty ton projectiles, leaving themselves open to instant death. But does this warrant the acts these people undertake? Most people would swear that the little old lady, who has reduced the speed limit from forty-five to twenty directly in front of you, and glares at you in the rear view mirror as if you've committed mortal sin as you screech to within five feet of her bumper, has done so intentionally just to aggravate you.

Same conclusion for the ones who find driveways in the middle of nowhere, as they proceed to enter at a speed that suggests they're testing the ground for land mines. Indicators must be a thing of the past. I see that the paranoid driver's intent is to get off the road, and I believe they should do exactly that. Thus, no matter how often we try to have a smooth, constant comfortable ride, the same paranoid person is more than likely to pull out in front of you, causing massive break application, and inevitably ruining your whole trip.

This brings me to the final and least understood of all drivers, the sickies. These people, whether it's because of lack of sleep, drugs, alcohol, or simple insanity have no business being behind the wheel of anything. I know this, for I am a school bus driver, and I have observed the people in this area, and I have realized that a person will do nearly anything to avoid being behind me. They range in all types, all ages, races and nationalities, and spend their entire driving experience tempting fate. I personally have had the entire back end of my bus torn off with kids aboard by a very drunk garbage truck driver.

In conclusion, I will say that driving is not as totally hopeless as I have depicted. In fact, when you look at the number of people killed each year, and you contemplate the variables involved with driving, you might consider the human race quite lucky. The scared, tough, insane and sick constitute ninety percent of drivers today in my opinion, varying only in temperament and patience. Are there people with the sole intent of getting where they want to go? Of course. But it's how they do it that concerns this driver. The human race is not a road race, but a people who use roads as such much too often." This work got an A plus, which I thought made sense.

Now was around the time the movie version of The Wall by Pink Floyd was coming out, so Jake, Wilma and I decided to go to New York and see it in the largest theater I've ever seen, it held over a thousand people I think. It was around some Irish holiday, and we waited in an overcrowded pub for the movie time to get closer. We were all tripping, and Jake was drinking.

We all had our tickets already, and Jake got separated from Wilma and me, since he had to go chase some girl he saw. So we figured we'd watch the movie and meet Jake back at Penn station afterwards where we left the car. When Wilma and I went in, I was continually looking for Jake in the mass of people. We went to the seating area, and I decided to yell: "Yo Geek!" Amazingly, Jake was right behind us about ten people away, he didn't see us and we didn't see him till I yelled and he answered, and we somehow found each other, like this is what this trip was about, beating the odds of running into each other in such a crowd. The movie, of course, was awesome.

I think this was the time Elton was going out with a girl named Joyce Rice from Cranford, having recently broken up with Ida. Joyce would eventually seek my company, but only for a short time, her interest in my ideals limited. I cannot recall why Elton and she broke up, but they did shortly before we got together, possibly because she liked pot and Elton didn't.

We never had any sex, but rented separate rooms in the Ocean Grove area during one summer. I drove a school bus for Hiltbrunner Bus Company in Tinton Falls, now that the suspension was over, for about three weeks before we left. I was not her type, once again, nothing unusual there. Nothing I can even say regarding her, she liked body oil and smoking herb, but she was pretty dull and limited in the philosophy and conversation department.

So I found another girl, through Fred and Shelly, named Darcy Brookman. She was an outright alcoholic, who looked rather rat like in appearance. Her vagina was capable of holding a two by four without touching a side, and it only took one visit to that crater to convince me she was wrong for me. Perhaps an elephant or horse could fill her gap, no normally endowed human could.

I did get to eat goose and duck for Christmas that year, which was quite good. Her family lived in the woods of Warren Township, hunted food and lived in a shack that appeared to be brought here from some distant remote swamp down south. They were nice people, though, and shared whatever they had, showing little faith in Darcy being able to straighten out her life, even with my help.

Darcy was friends with Lana Janes, the pool player, and that's how I met and played pool with her that one time, in her own pool hall in Green Brook, on route twenty two. The girls name was Lana, but it could have been another one, though I do remember her being very good at pool and having to run the whole table to win one game of eight ball.

Then I began working at Centercore, I remember this job mostly because of these incidents. I was using the fork lift, getting fifty sheets of five quarter inch flake board on a skid from about thirty feet up when the fork lift tilted sideways and the whole skid fell off, destroying all the sheets and the circular table saw it fell on. That was pretty impressive, I thought, since I was able to get out of the way in time.

They didn't fire me over that, which I sort of expected, but it was an accident after all. That was when I worked with Jacob, running a multi-million dollar table saw to make office furniture on the mass production level.

Then, one day I was driving to work there, and a woman going to work off a side street blew threw a stop sign and hit my seventy-five Cutlass, sending me into the telephone pole, I bounced back and she hit me again, then I hit the curb, and she got a ticket for ignoring a stop sign. I got out first to ask if all were ok, the woman driver said no, but they took me away in an ambulance. Jake picked me up from the hospital, and then I went with him to upstate New York to do some work, even though I still had a headache.

This occurred on Rock Avenue in Dunellen. I have a picture of Bethanie standing in front of that car, wrecked, and she and I with Jake and others spent the seven grand I got for that on many drugs, and I bought myself a new stereo. Beth's friend Frieda Blue worked for a lawyer, and she advised me to sue, which I did, though I couldn't feel totally comfortable with that since I didn't feel all that injured, except for the day it happened. I had what they call soft tissue damage to my neck, which did bother me some, and it took over a year to complete the suit.

Now Jake was still living at my house because his parents moved to Florida, and we would begin to go on many trips again. I wasn't going out with Wilma really but she called me and we decided to go visit her at the college in Pennsylvania. Wilma has tripped too, so we brought some acid and we would listen to Pink Floyd in a room of the house she lived in. One guy there had a copy of Dark Side of the Moon live, and it made for the perfect environment for a head-trip. We left the guy's room after the album was over to do some nighttime climbing and hiking.

Wilma came with us and fell down one small cliff, but felt no pain whatsoever due to the acid, and she laughed about that till the next day, when the bruises she got became sore. She didn't break anything or suffer any permanent damage. Jake and I went on a fifty-mile bike trip with two guys there the next morning, keeping up fine after climbing cliffs all night with Wilma and with no sleep.

We shocked the other guys completely, since they were very experienced bikers and thought they would need to wait for us to catch up, they didn't. Jake and I brought a sixteen pound roast beef and twelve pounds of bacon I took from my next job and brought them to her school. Since Jake was a chef in his experience, we feasted there, feeding everyone in the house for days. The job I had immediately after Centercore was this one, I think, which lasted till this particular day. It was the job where we cooked all the vending machine foods, in Livingston I mentioned before.

During this time that Wilma was off at college in Pennsylvania, we had both decided to follow the old adage "if you love something, let it go and if it comes back, it's yours," and we would just do our own thing. Now I was hanging out with Jake, building bars and cabinets in his dad's shop, with Elton too, along for the experience and because he had nothing better to do at the time.

Elton had found a girl, Alice Peterson, whom he was dating for a while. She was a waitress at Friendly's restaurant, which is where Elton met her, and the exact same Friendly's I worked at years before. Then one day Elton invited me to a comedy club with Jake and his current girl, who I don't recall right now, but I think it was Frieda. We saw Johnny Valens; I think was his name, nicknamed doctor dirt, who just used profanities for his entire show, like the script was built specifically for profanity. A song like: eat, fuck, suck, bite, gobble, nibble chew, nipple, bosom, hair pie, finger-fuck, screw, was the headlining song, just try to imagine the rest being equally profane.

During the whole performance, Alice's foot was finding its way to my crotch, and I realized she was just a whore and Elton didn't need that type of thing in his life. Turned out she was a complete nymphomaniac, and thought she wouldn't kiss you, there was little else she wouldn't do. I indulged myself for a while, pissing Elton off for his own good.

He was way too sensitive to be involved with such a free spirit, and it turned out to be in his favor, considering how his life went after that. As fun as she was, it wasn't that satisfactory after a while since I could never seem to get her in a state of orgasm. I never did like one-way pleasure, it had to be mutual, or it didn't excite me for long.

She was nice enough, played violin with her old lady friends, worked in Friendly's, and was pretty artistic, just too damn insatiable. She also had no desire for oral satisfaction from a guy, saying it felt like a doctor's examination, which I could not overcome, since it's one of my favorite things to do. Her sister read Tarot cards and told me my life would be quite interesting, and Alice wasn't going to be part of that.

The most philosophical Alice could get was wondering if I would crash the car if I had an orgasm while she gave me oral sex while driving down the highway. Of course, I didn't. She was shocked to hear me continue conversing with her after I achieved satisfaction, claiming most other guys would just ignore her at this point, or do what Elton did, turn up his music loud and drive on with a big smile on his face, speechlessly satisfied.

Her method of inviting some sexual contact was by simply stating: "So, are you gonna boff my noodle?" Her libido was pretty much directly to the point. Alice eventually told me we weren't right for each other, and I agreed, and felt no regrets never hearing from her again. The whole relationship lasted only a few weeks. A few years later, Elton told me she called him, asking him why he and I were posing as police and bothering her, which of course we weren't, and I thought that was pretty funny, in an over paranoid sort of way, which I don't remember her being.

Sex for me was always a question of how to satisfy my woman, and not to worry about getting my own satisfaction, which could be achieved easily or by literally hanging around. Nothing is more satisfying or exciting to me than watching my woman get satisfaction and writhe in ecstasy from the personalized use of my tongue. I know most women don't always achieve orgasm, and actually fake it to satisfy the ego of the man, which is unacceptable to me. No girl I was ever with was not satisfied, or failed to achieve an orgasm, and if they did fail, they wouldn't be with me for long, like Alice. I know none faked with me, simply by asking, which I do constantly, but who can tell?

Men are easy to please, and there is no faking possible, which I always thought was a little unfair, along with the fact that men can become physically worn much quicker, women have no concerns about keeping any part of them hard enough to continue and they can continue indefinitely it seems. The best possible scenario I can think of is my favorite position, the sixty-nine. Reaching a peak simultaneously is my idea of true sexual satisfaction, both ways.

Another interesting observation I made was that most of my girlfriends requested that I get a shower first, to rid them of my odor, which seems common for women, but I think for most men it makes no difference how clean a woman is, whether they took a shower five minutes ago or five days ago is irrelevant, unless it's truly intolerable or disgusting.

Alice was the only girl I knew that it didn't matter how clean I was, I guess being a nymphomaniac has its advantages. The only fetish I could share about sexual contact that I have besides water would be the removal of all pubic hair, my girlfriends and my own, to enhance the feeling, and promote cleanliness. No need for electronic devices, pocket pussies, remote control electronic portable clitoral stimulators, or anything our bodies weren't born with.

I could never figure how some girls and guys like only some things, and didn't like others. Once you actually love or think you love someone, all inhibitions should wash away like the tide, allowing your true passion and pleasure to surface and mature, and it saddened me to think that most women cannot get the fulfillment they need.

I also believe most of us guys have no concern for that issue, having seen it for myself, which really defies logic. I knew one guy who claimed he would kick his girl friend out as soon as he reached orgasm, couldn't stand to even look at her after that. I doubt he gave any thought about his girl friend's needs, which I thought was extremely shallow. Why any woman would want him, I couldn't even guess. He was a fellow prisoner when I met him, which may explain much.

So I continued to hang around Shelly, Bethanie, Jake, Elton and go to school at night with Beth, where we had some great fun with the learning process. I remember one acid trip there, where I understood more about the quadratic equation that night than I ever did for the rest of the year. It finally made sense, too bad the sense wore off as the trip did and the knowledge dissipated. I still understood it, just didn't see the possibilities surrounding the use of it as I did that day. That I thought was interesting.

We were strait in class most of the time, just not every time, and we studied together all the time, made sense and mockery of all assignments and projects. I dropped that school when a Jamaican teacher failed a test of mine in computer Basic, because I didn't close the little flow-chart boxes around the symbol, I just put the symbol next to the command correctly. This, apparently, wasn't good enough for him, so I said kiss my ass and left.

Now I'll present some poetry I wrote, just for fun, three different ones, just try to separate them however you like. "I feel sincere in what I say, the strength in knowing I'll live through the day, I sense the presence of my friends, the people I love see me through the ends, of my plight through this life, they make it worthwhile, overcome my foes, they clear my mind, and make me smile, each one I hear at certain times, the words they speak without the rhymes, words I trust as nothing but fact, the grains of life's' salt are all they lack, for is it not much better in the end, to ward off enemies, and accept a friend? Tis those ones I'd rather be made a fool of, because I know it's more out of love, a foe could only mean you harm, no matter how much fact, or how much charm, why should people show anger or hate, when pain and suffering is what they cannot relate? All mankind will know of our mission, all things will fit into place slowly, as destiny will assist to point out our position, my facts are strait, my blood is drawn, who knows what pain is felt between dusk and dawn, to idly sit by and watch the space grow, when words alone could end the low, or words of trust can easily be dealt, but it's just a guess at what is actually felt, I ask not of change, or mere acceptance, since I would not myself, ride upon that fence, where you lean so far, and to no avail, if it's games you seek, I'd be better off in jail, the love I hold will suffer much, until I'm released by the ultimate touch, where my very soul you will unveil, and I become whole, the truly human tale, we all suffer loss of those we hold near, once destiny states their time has ceased, but we hope for the best simply out of fear, that we know one can't replace loved ones, our pain seems endlessly increased, we see no clearly totally happy finish or end, to any relationship that we encounter, a memory, a fleeting glimpse over the counter, why don't they end as easily as they start? If we could answer that question it would set us apart, from the rest of nature which just comes and goes, we are the only creatures who's lives depend on how much one grows, or how quickly one learns, or even how much one owes, to themselves, someone else, or even possibly how much one earns, so let's search our lives path for a hint of a sign, that I will find you one day, so that I can be yours, and you can be mine, together forever, caged within time, a fate such as that would, for me, assure true inner peace of mind".

Around this time Jake and I were playing with a BB gun that we bought in Pennsylvania while we were there visiting Wilma. One day, while going to Elton's in the Jeep we honked the horn in front of Elton's house. Jake got up in the driver's seat and aimed the gun at Elton's front doorbell. Cosmo, Elton's little brother, came out, and Jake made a hole in the house's siding a few inches away from where Cosmo's head was when he opened the door.

He was aiming at the doorbell, but missed. Cosmo was not happy, and never forgot the day Jake shot at him. The BB gun didn't last long, we shot it mostly in Jake's basement or in the woods, but I gave it away eventually. Amazingly, we never broke a single window, hurt a single person, or used this gun destructively under any circumstances, besides that one time at Elton's, and we always used it on unextrodinary targets.

Jake and I had an idea once for a comic called "trip strips". Totally Realistic/Ridiculous Insights People Share is what it was supposed to stand for. The rest could of stood for: To Reduce Individual Personal Suffering, but we couldn't decide on a format, my only thought was a comic about two geeks who cruise the universe in the lady, which would be a space ship now, solving galactic problems with humorous consequences.

That thought never made it anywhere unfortunately, but I still liked contemplating it sometimes. The theory was to have us find the path needed to help effectively anyone in distress. Path would stand for; "Positive Advances Towards Humanity", or "Perpetual Actions Terrifying Humanity", but we could never decide which it should be, just that it affected and ended with "Humanity".

So Elton, Jake and I were all addicted to cocaine around this time, and all we did was work and party, party and work. Beth connected us to most of our connections in Newark, Guido was his name, and we took it from there, so that part of my personal history is quite foggy, the events were clouded more so than with use of any other substance, and I would not recommend the use of this drug any more than once in a life time, just to discover how nasty it can be coming down from it.

It helped me understand Sigmund Freud's downfall into that world. I was slightly shocked to read about Sigmund's experience with coke in one of my textbooks, but realized that in his time this substance would be viewed differently than it is now. It almost killed Elton, Jake, Beth and me, along with wasting a lot of money. Jake and I would shoot pool in his basement all night, or play video games, while indulging in the substance and discussing trip strips. We both hated the dead, empty feeling your left with after the good effect wears off, making you only desire more to offset the down.

Alcohol helped, sedating the senses enough to actually go to sleep eventually, but it took a lot.

Elton had found his own connections in Elizabeth, in the very bad seaport section. I think he met them through a different girl he was dating and living with, Helen was her name. They lived in the same apartment complex that Jake and Frieda did later on, but not till years after Jake moved there. Jake and I went with him one night, and since we're all over six foot tall we weren't too worried about the danger.

Elton went into a bar alone, claiming his "dude" didn't like new faces, and he had to go alone. Jake and I waited, hanging out smoking and waiting for Elton's appearance. Then Elton came out with two guys, short Puerto Rican guys who looked much too suspicious and concerned that Jake and I were hanging out at Elton's car. We tried to be friendly, just fellow partiers looking for fun, but one of the guys started squaring off towards me, like he was ready to fight, babbling in some foreign language I couldn't understand. I started laughing out loud, not taking the scene too seriously, and Jake was also amused.

As I poised myself back towards the guy, ready for anything and still smiling, Elton went to the guy and was talking low to him, while Jake and I just stood around obnoxiously, and made fun of the challenge. Elton said to us we shouldn't antagonize these guys, like they were so dangerous or something, so we just got in the car and waited some more for Elton to come out again, since he went back inside to talk the guys into calming down.

Jake and I mused for a while, knowing what a non-fighter Elton was, how he was going to solve these idiots dilemma without getting hurt or needing us to rescue him. He did somehow, though, and we went home to partake in our bounty, which wasn't all that great anyway. Elton said he'd never take us anywhere again, which made us both laugh and was fine in our minds. Not worth the effort.

We both couldn't believe how addicted and cloak and daggerish Elton became, wasn't like him at all. I half believed my thought that his pay back for getting me to smoke was this addiction, which made me laugh for a while, since it took so long and was so very unforeseen and unplanned. Shelly nad her boyfriend and his brothers were heavily into the stuff.

So now I was working with Jake on odd carpentry jobs and hanging out at a place in Linden called Boss Tweeds, the true eighties disco you hear about. That's where we always went at night from my house, Jake looking endlessly for 'hot' women to fool around with, believing a disco would be a major place for meeting women, which was true in that day and age.

Everyone was dressed in polyester, and Jake loved to dance, but I wouldn't. I recall that most of the people there made fun of the fact that I wouldn't dance, and I was just some strange wallflower that wouldn't have a chance with any girl, but that didn't matter.

Watching the drunken idiots go through their mating rituals like some species of birds flaunting their plumage was entertaining enough for me as usual. That, plus I was a good conversationalist for the girls who were tired and wanted to sit for a while, as long as they weren't as empty-headed as they appeared to be while dancing around. Too bad most of them were, along with usually being so drunk they couldn't remember having talked to me at all.

Jake met his wife there, Frieda, and Elton and I held the ladder against her bedroom window for him to climb and propose to her. I was the best man at their wedding, which pissed Elton off since he knew Jake many years longer than I, but Elton got to be head usher, and we all had much fun there at Snuffy's in Scotch Plains.

My speech was "I just want to say I've never known a more natural or beautiful couple in my life, so here's to you, brother!" and Jake would echo brother as we all toasted their happiness. Frieda said she didn't know I had it in me, though I felt that I had understated the moment anyway. Before that, at the church, after the ceremony Elton and I threw some firecrackers, and the priest came screaming out of the church about how he was calling the police and this was an outrage and stuff. He even cursed, which I never heard a priest do. Everyone felt he over reacted a lot, fortunately.

I sucked at giving bachelor parties; all I did was take Jake and Elton to bars, got wasted, shot pool and just had fun. He never told me he expected anything more and it was fine, but I still felt bad for doing nothing special in the end. I had no idea what else I could have done so I did what we always did anyway, seemed appropriate.

During this disco barrage, I was sort of seeing one of Frieda's friends, Rosanne. We cruised around and made out some, nothing more, but she wasn't too into the scenes Jake and I were and had no philosophical insight at all. She wound up married to Danny Lucas, who was the son of the owner of Woodbridge Oldsmobile, who became Jake's best friend after a while.

That made sense since Frieda and Rosanne were best friends, and Frieda never really liked me much, never understanding my way of looking at things, only thinking that I was bad company for Jake, and enough nagging from her convinced Jake eventually to believe it too for a while. I even recall her threats to Jake about our friendship ending, or their sex life, his choice. Easy choice for Jake, but that turned out to be an empty threat anyway. Jake would give up sex for no person, just like Fred or Elton.

I remember going to a club in New York with Jake and Frieda once, and this place wouldn't let me in the first time I went because my boots weren't shiny enough. So we had to leave that night. Then we went back again, after I got my boots polished, and we got in this time. It was a place just like the Tweeds, but much fancier and more expensive, and it was opened till six in the morning.

This place had lines of coke in the bathroom for free, just so patrons could dance all night long and consume lots of liquor. It was called the Roof Top. So we all indulged in that all night, and I remember leaving when the sun came up, which made me think about how this day coming was going to be wasted, because all we could do with the time left in it was sleep.

I also met Frieda's cousin Lilly, who was quite nice and attractive, yet she appeared to be in need of a pedestal for someone to put her upon, and didn't see me as a candidate capable of that I believe. She was sociable enough though, and we laughed some at things. Jake and I went one night with two cars down to Lilly's house down at the shore, Lilly and I in one car, Frieda and Jake in another.

As we were going down the Jersey Parkway shortly after the Cheese Quake rest area around two AM, we saw a white VW Rabbit parked across the first two lanes, apparently wrecked. Jake pulled over and we pulled over behind him, a short distance after the car. Jake wanted to help move the car off the highway. So we went over to the car, the guy inside was unconscious, and we started pushing the car off the road. I was pushing from the closest point to the third lane, and as I started, I heard the squeal of brakes behind me, and then a crash.

When I turned around, there was another car that was in the process of slowly trying to pass the one we were pushing, and another car that was in the third lane still going very fast slamming into the car trying to get around us, not even two feet from where I was standing. Then I looked back up the highway and saw yet another car, all dark with fluids leaking all over the road from it, sitting sideways in the second lane, it had been hit by the same car that wound up smashed into the back of the other car next to me.

So now four cars were wrecked, and finally a state trooper came to the scene that we were standing in the middle of. The car behind us leaking fluid was still running, so I ran up to it while Jake, the state trooper and another bystander who stopped to help pushed the original car off the road.

I had to smash in the window to turn off the ignition, since this guy was only semi-conscious and not responding to my request to turn the car off. All the drivers of the wrecked cars were completely drunk, and the driver of the car I turned the ignition off for got out of his car and start arguing with the other driver about who did what.

Jake and I went to the police car and told the officer we'd set up the flares on the highway to try and make the traffic slow down, which we did. Walking up a dark road where cars going sixty to eighty miles an hour are coming at you is not exactly my idea of entertainment, but it was different. Then, as the arguing began to peak, Jake and I just got back into the cars with Frieda and Lilly, who never left the cars, and continued down the road.

No one got our name or any information about us, and that's the way we wanted it, totally anonymous. So now when Jake and I discuss the white rabbit in the middle of the road, were not referring to common Jersey rabbits that end up as road kill, or Bugs Bunny either.

After that, we went to a party with some of Lilly's friends, a bunch of jerk offs who only laughed mockingly while they videotaped us all hanging out in the kitchen, making Jake, Frieda and Lilly very uncomfortable in the crowd who all seemed to be living some sort of joke, based on anyone who didn't fit in their little click.

They were all very trimmed, proper, boring, drunk, and Jake and I appeared like we just came back from the swamp, sweaty and disheveled from our adventure. I couldn't have cared less, and thought the whole party was a waste of time. Lilly reminded me of Cheyanne a lot, small, with dark hair, and she never showed any interest in me, and I didn't really have any interest in her either, but she was fun to party with and basically a nice person.

Around this time I was re-introduced to one of Shelly's friends, Dude Allen, he was possibly one of the more secluded and private people I knew. Dude had a very good view on things I thought, and was mellow and low-key as if trying to avoid being observed constantly. He also wasn't into victimization or abuse.

He was into the drugging and drinking type of entertainment, as I've been known to be minus the drinking till recently. He was also into guns, which I wasn't, even though I was an expert marksman at all my summer camps. For some reason, I recall knowing him for much longer, I just don't remember exactly when we met, but I'm sure it was before this time period.

He had a girlfriend named Thelma Sakenslut, who I also recall being Theo's girlfriend for a while at some point before being Dude's. She became Shelly's friend, and we went to a hotel room party together, Shelly and Donald, Charlie, Thelma and me. Dude had broken up with her some time before this party, calling her the biggest bitch he ever met and the only woman he seriously considered hitting, but he never did.

So she was available at the time and showed interest in my direction while we were partying, which is odd that I picked up on, since I usually don't. She wasn't that attractive, large thick glasses, no rear, thin, and she was kind of pale. But she was very deep into trying to communicate openly in her own way, which I respected and liked. I discovered later that she enjoyed doing massive lines of cocaine while talking and fondling genitals, an effect that for me was just great, like sex, communication and philosophy all rolled up into one action.

She claimed that the experience we shared so suddenly was not her usual way, since we wound up having sex after Charlie left, with Shelly and Donald also indulging in the other bed at the same time. She said she usually liked to wait awhile before doing what we did, and was no slut. She was a housekeeper and nanny, for a rich Bernardsville couple named Trainer.

Her father was a police chief, and they were German so she always called me her little vutz, or pig. She was the only girl who I was involved with that was older than me, but only by about two years. Of course, I don't know how old those hookers were, I'm sure they were older than I was, but they don't count as examples of relationships in my opinion.

I became part of the little girl's family that she watched, went to company picnics with them, where I hit a grand slam in the softball game, sending the ball into the cornfields around the edge of the park, much to the surprise of all the spectators. I went to the kid's birthday parties and events that were always lavish since her parents were quite well off.

I think the little girl's name was Crystal. They were very nice people, who were repaid for their kindness by having Thelma steal jewelry from them, and getting me to sell it to get our coke. Though I wasn't sure of where the jewelry came from, her saying it was hers, or her mom's or something, I suspected that this wasn't entirely true but didn't act on it or allow myself to believe she was lying.

Frieda Blue's house is where we went to meet our coke supplier, and we spend many days there at Frieda's house hanging out with that crowd, which included Beth, of course. I remember being there once and hearing a girl screaming at the top of her lungs like she was dying, only to discover later that Frieda was just having sex upstairs with some guy, and she made some incredible noises while doing so. This was very funny to anyone in attendance, except Beth, who found out later that the guy upstairs with Frieda was Roland. I always thought she was better off without him, I guess she was beginning to think so too now and much consoling was needed.

Thelma and I would leave and go to the Kings Inn in Green Brook every weekend and get the room with a round, king size waterbed in it, room number nineteen I think, and just talk and have massive sex and coke all night. That was how we spent most of our time together, and we even were able to use her employers house when they went away, pretending it was ours and living well in their million dollar home. The only difference being that there was no waterbed here.

She was pretty flaky and unstable, and when she wasn't doing drugs she was very paranoid and insecure, which grew tiresome after a while and made her into a real bitch, even according to Dude. But naturally that would not faze me, I always saw past that type of defense, and she was no exception.

One day my parents went out for the night, and Thelma told me she had never done acid before, and I convinced her to try it at my house that night while Shelly and Bethanie were there. She had her own horror story about it; a friend of hers had a bad trip once, so she was pretty scared and reluctant.

During the forty-minute wait for the effect to begin, she became totally paranoid and thought I was trying to kill her, and she locked herself in one of the bathrooms of my house. I couldn't talk her out, and neither could Shelly or Beth, so I took the hinges off the door and went in to find her sitting in a ball crying in the bathtub. She was screaming: "don't hurt me, please, don't hurt me!" and I told her to stop listening to herself for one minute and hear me, as I guided her back to the living room where Beth and Shelly were. I had Dark Side on, and I told her to sit and listen to it, and relax.

She was good at discussion, very open and willing to debate anything usually, and I attempted to point out the fact that no one was doing anything to her, we were just listening to Floyd. I told her that the first effect she felt was not going to last long, and to clear her mind if she could. The music and peaceful atmosphere finally took effect and relaxed her, and then she couldn't understand why she was so upset at first.

We all ended up laughing about it for hours, while drinking, Floyding and tripping the hours away. During the trip, she claimed this was the most intense and interesting thing she ever felt, but then for some reason, after the trip she said she never wanted to do that again, but coke was OK to do and she wanted some now. That was odd, I thought, and so did Beth and Shelly.

Beth and I always had the idea to go gamble in Atlantic City, simply because she was the luckiest girl I had ever known. For instance, at carnivals and boardwalks she could pick the winner on the wheels they spin where you have a one in fifty chance at winning. So I thought we'd capitalize on her luck, and Thelma felt no jealousy when Beth and I headed off to get a room and gamble all night together, even though she knew we had to pretend to be husband and wife to get a room.

We both were very wasted, partying along the way and after we got there. We were never shy about each other and got decked out in our dress clothes in the same room, basically getting completely undressed in front of each other. I remember her stating while we dressed that she didn't feel one bit shy or uncomfortable about undressing around me, and I concurred with that, which only solidified my belief about how close we were.

We were always very comfortable together, happy, and having a great time, never getting too hung up about how to act towards each other, knowing we didn't need an act to impress each other, and enjoying life to its fullest. I would admit, when Beth was about to reveal herself to me and be totally naked, I did have to go into the bathroom and pretend to need it, the site of her would have been too much even for me to handle and I may have regretted my actions at that point.

I was also just in my underwear, still very comfortable, but I couldn't bring myself to look upon Beth's body, that may have pushed me over my edge, she was a gorgeous specimen of a woman, thus I adverted my eyes and walked away, it may have been the biggest opportunity to change my path that I missed, but I had a girlfriend who trusted me and that's who I was, a trustworthy fool. The other time I had seen her in the buff Jake was there anyway, this would have been completely different. I never considered myself the greatest lover either, so I didn't want to disappoint her in any way.

So off to the casino we'd go after being dressed, full of all the excitement and anticipation you'd expect going into a casino. I would stand behind her at the black jack table and take her winnings and stuff them into my pocket, which eventually became several hundred dollars. Then we'd go back to the room to party a while, and come back down several times that night.

Beth met two guys there, and she invited them up to our room to party some, which was fun, but I don't trust people quite as easily as she does, so I was leery for a little while. They turned out to be OK, and had some fun with us for a few hours. At about six am, just before the casinos close for a while, Beth became a little greedy and lost most of the money within ten minutes to a very quick-handed dealer. I did manage to hold two or three hundred, and I blamed myself for letting her have the chips back and not preventing the loss.

I spent several months with Thelma, being a roofer for one company then a salesman for Macys immediately after that, because I hurt my neck carrying two bundles of shingles up a ladder with them balanced on my head. That's when I decided I disliked manual labor, but would go on to do more later anyway. While I was roofing, I discovered that one of the three co-workers I worked with decided he didn't like me or my philosophical attitude, and he made the point clear by stating to me: "shut the fuck up, asshole, before I kill you!"

I laughed, of course, and said: "you feel froggy? Jump scumbag, I close my mouth for no one! Come on, punk bitch, try something!" We were working with hot tar, and this guy decided to smack my bare legs, which were always bare in the summer, I wear cut-offs non-stop when I can, with the hot tar mop, causing a good burn sensation like hot wax on my legs. I laughed in his face and asked him: "is that the best you can do faggot? Better try again!"

He became very angry when I continued smiling and talking, and tried to hit me with his fist. Of course, he missed and I swept his legs and made him fall against the tar kettle, spilling it half over his body and all over the roof, while I was still smiling and talking the whole time. He got up with some more anger, began to come towards me, and the owner of the company got between us and told him to leave, knowing I did nothing and he instigated the violence.

The owner was pissed that we wasted all the tar and fired this guy on the spot, while I stood there, picking tar off my legs and laughing. No matter where you go, there's always some idiot who feels the need to confront you for no apparent reason, and I never saw that foolish looser again. Thought I was a kid again, watching a re-run of the assholes actions I observed many years ago. I guess twenty years difference makes no difference. I yelled to this guy as he left: "come on back now, any time you feel like really having fun!" But he never turned back around.

After all that and my job with Haynes, Thelma and I decided that since the people she worked for finally reported their stuff missing to the police, that we should leave the state. She found out because her friend told her the police were looking for her. She thought I knew where the stuff was coming from she claimed, but I had hoped I was wrong.

At this point, I owned a seventy-seven white Ford LTD, which the driver's door broke on and Thelma's brother replaced it for me with a brown one. I don't remember where that car came from; I think it may have been one of my parent's neighbor's cars. It didn't really matter to me, I was with her, good or bad, and this was beginning to sound like another adventure was about to commence.

The big white ford with one brown door is what Thelma and I headed towards California in. But not before getting a map from Bill and Jim's Exxon station in Summit, the place where my parents and I always went to for car service for many years. It was the eighty-four Rand McNally road atlas, and I still have it to this day.

She had cousins in Van Nuys, and even though we had warrants out for us, I was able to get a job as the nighttime security guard at the Van Nuys airport, because her cousin was in charge of personnel there. He was also a traveling hair stylist, who went to people's homes to do their hair, and a cocaine and pot addict and dealer as well. Before we got there, the trip was pretty uninteresting, we had no party material, and so she had her bad attitude on for much of the trip.

I got her hooked on gambling in Reno, which we stopped in and sold some personal belongings at a pawn shop to be able to continue our trip. She had lost the rest of our money an hour after we got there, and became quite violent when I declined to give her more money to "win it all back" with, as she said. That's when I knew we had to leave with what we had left from selling things.

We were also treated to the sulfur-smelling towns of Wyoming, which I remembered from my other trip, but that was about it for the trip, which took route eighty the whole way, and route five down to Los Angeles. I drove the whole way, very quickly and expedient, not wanting to stop too much and get caught up in some town on the way.

I actually got a few paychecks from the airport job, and we lived with Thelma's aunt and uncle the whole time. I finally called my mother, which I always did, and she said the prosecutor claimed that if I came home that I would not go to jail, since it was Thelma who did the stealing and they knew this from prior evidence, and my parole had ended the previous summer anyway.

Good thing, because with parole, if you violate it, you go back for the full sentence, no matter when you violate it, which I would not have been pleased with. Apparently, I was not the first of Thelma's' boyfriends she did this with, just the one who got caught.

My mother wired me six hundred dollars via Western Union, and that day when I dropped Thelma off at the job she got, I filled the Ford with gas, and the attendant happened to be from Scotch Plains New Jersey. After philosophizing with him about this strange coincidence for a while, I bought some good herb for the ride, from the Mexicans hanging out on the street her uncle lived on, and headed back towards New Jersey.

A song by Boston was the last song I heard on the radio before getting out of range of any stations. Just moving along, I think it's called, where it say's "I'm just taking my time, just moving along, you'll forget about me after I've been gone", sort of fit the moment perfectly that day.

Now I was going through Death Valley and the car decided to overheat. I stopped at this tiny gas station just before the sign saying: "Las Vegas two hundred miles", and they told me I needed a new head gasket, whatever that is. Apparently this gasket holds the oil in the engine, and they wanted five hundred to fix it, but I had a thirty-gallon jug of water from my dad's lab in almost every car I owned, so I just refilled the radiator and the jug, and headed towards Vegas.

Had to stop a few times and observe desert life, not entirely by choice, but I enjoyed it anyway. Caught a couple of rattlesnakes, bull snakes and lizards I couldn't identify, I think they were skinks. But I made it to Vegas that night, got a room, and went out on the town for a while. I couldn't get a big win, but I did walk away with a little more than when I started, by a hundred or so. Played for a good four hours, I believe.

It was odd being there, just off on my own, doing nothing but traveling, very surrealistic. When I got up, a gas station attendant in the local Mobile station took a screwdriver and hit something in the engine. Then he said I'd be fine, but it would take longer for the car to heat up, and that all he did was pop the thermostat out. He told me there was no charge, but I gave the guy some California stuff anyway, which made his eyes light up, so he definitely appreciated that, and I was on my way again.

I went home a different route, zigzagging my way through states I had never been to, especially the states missed on the trip I went on with Eric so many years ago. I drove and smoked my way through every state from California to Indiana, north and south, and I stopped at the Indiana College Madeline was going to on my way home. I told her I'd be there one day many years ago, and I was, much to her shock.

It was sort of dramatic, all very amusing regarding how I wound up in the neighborhood. I stayed that night; we didn't do anything with each other except reminisce about a different time. I got to see some artwork of hers, she got to hear some more weird tales, like this one I was on now. But people were waiting on me, so I had to leave to face the music. Never saw her again to this day.

When I got home, I was just given a statement I had to sign of the knowledge I had of the situation of the people Thelma worked for, and that was about it. Probation for a year, some community work at Overlook Hospital, and I was free. I found out the last gold bracelet she stole was worth three thousand, we only got four hundred for it from the jeweler in New Providence.

I will now bore everyone with some philosophical rambling I had written while crossing the country, just to give an idea of the frame of mind I live in basically every day. As far as anyone can tell, the standard for life is family, friends, money, and peace of mind. How we achieve these goals can be as unique as the goals themselves, and most are unable to achieve all combine results in the positive. I observed that these goals of most are at times, even to the achievers, inadequate to one's self. There must be more to the picture, more interest and dreams, although peace is a kind yet unpredictable fate. The ultimate life is one of constant turmoil, and trying to obtain peace can often lead in that direction. Not usually by choice, since ultimately there is no bartering for the past, the course laid is too often followed. Does then change of action solve the need for adventure? Can a person change course so often as to never see the original map? Life can be such an infinite sea of courses, nearly as many as there are present in the world of a golfer, and much like destiny, once you hit the ball, there is no recourse or re-teeing off. The mulligan of life would be your second chance.

So the only real life is the one you believe to be real, and go on living within. Obviously, the ultimate plan of the future is to migrate into the vastness of space. This would truly satisfy most humans' need for change, and the need for exploration. I saw a movie that involved saving our wildlife and plant kingdom by sending giant greenhouses into space, and other than the plot, I foresaw the truth and realism in the concept. Fortunately, during my life span, the Earth will still be large enough to withstand man, and much still needs to be learned right on our own crumb of a planet, hopefully, before we destroy it. Traveling the world and exotic living is still only obtainable to the wealthy class. We adjust our needs to suit the surroundings in which we live. Enjoying things that make us feel happy, even if we're not. Thus the conflict comes, between living and existing. Trying to find the one idea that no one else can, and then putting it to use for everyone, some feel that this is the real challenge, and the question of skill enters the mind. What do we have for skills? Is skill just a word for someone able to do one or more things better than the average person? Then what is an average person? I would have to assume that an average person is one with no true gift or skills, and makes a mere living. I find that thought and faith are the only true tools or skills needed to obtain most things.

By thought I mean that thinking about what you need as the day goes by tends to make someone take steps in obtaining those needs. Faith can be held for nearly anything, yet the faith in one's self is the hardest and most essential thing to achieve. I believe I'm happy, and I can find some good in the reasons that I was created, thus this is my faith. Someone needs to create a sweat less cup, before all hell freezes over! Why not I? Silly things to that effect can change life once again. True insight is usually found at times of inconsequential thought, and thus never explored by the average person to any end. Much like Ralph Kramden, who had strange ideas in that character, although few ever work, it only takes one idea at a time to explore, or be caught in the never ending idea category, in which few are followed fully, or even come close to the ends that were meant to be reached.

A trapped soul within the hearts and minds of those who know you as you are. A pointless path of flight into realms of deep peace, where all is calm and tolerable, and no existing force can inhibit or change the mood. True ignorance of selfless life and all its glory, sorrow, pain, and sheer delight are unobtainable for most and second nature to others. Understanding, though thought to be immeasurable by any standards, can always assume to exist, whether or not it does or is achieved. Never seeing others views and yet not understanding anything but. Application is itself an understanding of the basic method with which to comprehend a point, but only if the result is understandable or applicable. To apply untested knowledge or theory can often resolve uncertainties. I have often wondered what could be held within the vast universe that is known as the mind. For in this world of incredible wonder, the smallest things and the obvious ones elude understanding. I have attributed much of my experiences to that so little known mind of ours and its endless maze of possibilities. Never knowing if a solution to the puzzle would ever surface. So far, this is not the case.

I always felt that pain, anger and fear were completely useless, thus casting aside needless suffering and finding the true meaning of life, unless it turned out to be exactly that. To suffer, hurt, and achieve heartache and torment could be the entire reason for existing, since everyone suffers to some degree in life. Thus, I can expect no more or less from life, and death must be the school of complete understanding. This does not mean suicide could even be considered within the choices we make to endure or adore life, since there is nothing natural about it, we are not lemmings. I would assume an unnatural fate is also related to an unnatural existence after life. Who on this planet would want to live if life after death were more pleasant? Yet never knowing the consequences of any action one can always claim destiny is at fault. As the child who idly watches traffic go by, amused and puzzled by the anonymous nature of those he sees flash before his eyes for mere seconds, and wondering when the path they are on will meet his own one day and why, he may think, what's the rush about? Where do they all go in such a hurry with such driven intent? I see much in the path of time that will change all courses within the galaxy, changes made just by the belief they will occur, and focused belief tends to become fact. Life has more meaning than living and dying, or perpetuating our species. The desire to be remembered by millions could be the sole catalyst for the need to achieve our goals, realistic or not. I need only to know I exist, but occasionally choose not to believe I do.

The ability to transcribe pure thought into words is believed to be my only need and sole gift. Daunted by a bizarre childhood, my only wall, savior and subject. The ability to help others through life was a gift and never coincided with the ability to apply such knowledge to myself. Thus agonizingly true, I could only assume that having the answer made the questions irrelevant to myself. Many times in my life I was able to aid others through kindness and honest forethought, only to see that such ideas in social logic and deep felt searches through the heart became more unreachable to my own sense of personal love for myself. I matter little to myself at times, less than others I love matter to me. I need not love everything about me, but love myself enough to want to live life out, and see the entire destiny that awaits me with utter cold fact. Can't I just like things within me, yet love all that surrounds me?

Though unable to express feelings in the standard context, I must share the unique methods by which I have learned enormous lessons in life, love, pain and sorrow, that by expressing them to your eyes, you may see and make your verdict on whether or not my story is worth knowing. Gifted in the term incorrigible, which was also cast upon my person by whatever force decides these things from the time we are conceived, I abide life with all its amazing twists and turns, ups and downs, looking for the reasoning and most pleasant path to follow. My dreams will not go unnoticed, and most have been experienced in the realistic mode of thought, known as consciousness. I know no one who has had more dreams come true, good and bad, but not out of some telepathic realm of science fiction, instead, just knowing this to be destiny, controllable or not. My mission is clear.

So now back the reality of my life, this is when I began hanging around with Beth again, after my return from California. It wasn't too soon after that she and Crystal were working together at Hubbard Cupboard for a while. Crystal was the manager, and all they did was lots of coke in the back room during slow times.

I discovered later from them they liked to throw stuff around the store, and do whippets, which is performed by draining all the gas out of the Redi-whip whipped cream can into your lungs. I've tried this, not recommended for anyone, can drop someone fast, as in kill you. Not that anything can't, this is just too stupid a way for anyone to go, killed by a whipped cream can.

But we were having fun, I was having the usual relationship with Wilma again, and had her becoming addicted to things too, at the time her personal favorites were acid and speed. Sex was fun while doing speed, acid made it pointless to even try. Just as I overcame my addictions eventually, so I hope she did as well. Although she still believed she and I would just be one forever, a different type of addiction for her, I knew in my heart this was not going to be somehow. I also was hanging around Beth, Shelly and Crystal again, wondering if any of them might be the path to my future, as time had gone by so quick, I hoped that some attitudes or feelings changed as well.

Ultimately I was sentenced to volunteer work for the stolen stuff from the Trainer's house, community service at Overlook hospital, where I met and worked for Mrs. Brown. This person was so well known there that every door I encountered was opened simply because I stated her name.

That was interesting, and I learned a lot about hospital procedure from that experience, though I wouldn't pursue it as a career. I didn't really like being around the sick all the time, it was far too depressing. I also could not get a day job because of this, so I looked to the midnight shift type of work.

At this point, my parents began to show some confidence in me, as I became interested in the duties of a hotel night auditor, and knew I could do the job well. I had to lie about the record I had, which worked, and I've really never taken anything that didn't belong to me again, at that point being twenty-five years of age. The criminal tendencies or urges to steal or destroy became things of the past and no longer part of my personality.

My parents bought me their friend's seventy-three Plymouth fury, and I worked for Holiday Inn of Springfield as my first hotel related job. Just a note on all my jobs, I always went on interviews with the attitude that I already work there, and instead of debating if I should work there, I point the conversation to when I can start working and how much I intend to contribute to the interviewers business. Yes, that almost never failed.

So now I decided to visit the Hubbard, to tell someone friends of my new career, knowing Beth and maybe Crystal were there, although now since Crystal got in trouble from patrons telling on her, she wasn't so pleasing to be around in the store.

Someone else was working there this day, and though at the moment I didn't know it, this other girl told to Beth she knew she would marry me one day, as soon as I walked out the door.

Her name was Marie Theresa Harbinger. I thought she was gorgeous, she was tall, about five ten, and she had a perfect face with light brown hair she dyed blonde, but I never approach good-looking women or make eye contact, expecting the worst to come of it. I usually ignore pretty women, just peaking at them when I think they're not looking, hoping to not get caught, marveling at their natural beauty.

That was until Beth told me what the girl thought about me some time later, and I just couldn't believe someone that pretty liked me at all. I'm sure it wasn't Beth's intention to be the matchmaker, but we discussed things so openly that any topic became part of our normal conversation. I knew when I met Marie that something about her was different; she was not like anybody I knew when compared to the diversity of people I was close to.

It was odd at first, because while I went to the store and saw Marie, I also saw her current boyfriend, Bif Pots, and Marie appeared as though she had interest in no one else while Bif was around or not, she looked taken. I worked with Bif for a while at Quaalco; he even hung out at Blue Star back in the day so I knew him for a long time. A fact I did not remember at first.

I was still seeing Wilma and I was still me, not really interested in competition of ego with fellow men or getting involved with more than one girl at a time, too much drama, as I learned before. Marie wasn't sure at this point that I had any interest in her, since

I never show much of myself in that way, but Beth told her this is how I am, and she knew me well enough to know, I assumed she told Marie to just be patient.

I began going to find Marie more often, going to the beauty parlor she worked at across the street from Hubbard's, called The House of Styles. She worked there for many years, and I would just go to see what she was doing and if she was available to hang out with me, or Beth and me, or even with Wilma, Beth and me, at that point just another female friend who I enjoyed being around. We would hang out and bullshit a while, getting closer and more open with each other, discussing all of life as I had done so many times with my friends, getting together more and more often as time went by.

Thus, having found myself in the beginning of my life's greatest diversion, I must end this portion of my life's saga, since destiny has provided a new life and path through the result of all the events I have written about, and the next series of events are no longer solely mine. They are shared with Marie, and this whole document is a tribute to my quest, faith and belief that I would find her one day, regardless of what the future holds for us or the fact that I had no idea what she was going to mean to my life at that point. I cannot think of a better reason than my love for her as my inspiration to write how I got to where I am now, as unlikely as it seemed while I grew up, leading to such a possibly normal life.

These stories I have written are completely true, and are testimony to the unusual path I have followed, which is a much happier and satisfying path than I could have ever imagined so far. It proves that no matter what occurs in life, very little is permanently set in stone, and you can always improve any situation by having enough faith in yourself to believe you can, having an open mind, and never compromising that who you are is who you are.

I'm sure the next book will overlap this novel some, but that doesn't matter, since I feel the best is yet to come, which I believe to be true for everyday of my life. Now I can finally say my life is an open book and mean it. It is also a testament for the ones who gave me up, hoping life would be better for me yet never knowing if this would be so, a gamble that they may never know the results of, unless they read my story someday, about the person known simply as Greenie.

The names have been changed to protect the innocent, indifferent, and to irritate the guilty. I know many things will be missed in the end, since total recall of all things would likely be a novel of unrealistic proportions and each sentence could be expanded a thousand fold, each paragraph a novel within its self. It would not be worth the time to read, and would take another lifetime to write, but I think and hope I made someone somewhere believe that no matter what it is they have done or not done, accomplished or failed at, experienced negatively or positively, that their life is worth living, for every single amazing second of it, regardless of how they entered this world or how they will leave it.

I would like to give thanks to the two people I never knew, who found enough love for long enough to be able to conceive me; you made the right decision to give me life, where ever and whoever you are. I can forever ponder who may exist in this world that is part of my blood, sisters or nieces I never knew, brothers or nephews I never played with, relatives who are more of a mystery than substance, and maybe one day I will know them too, if my path has that course in its future. Thanks to all the characters that made my life what it was, and shared or influenced my path, bad or good, positively or negatively, with their own personal input that made who I am now possible, whether you knew me as Greenie or not. But the biggest and greatest thanks goes to my parents, who are the best one's any child could dream of, and I am thankful that they picked me, loved me, and never gave up on me. Truly the most outstanding people I knew or ever will know throughout my life. I'll see you all on the dark side of the moon, if that's where you believe you'll find me. The beginning.